Erich Mendelsohn's buildings, erected throughout Germany between 1920 and 1932, epitomized architectural modernity for his compatriots. In this study, Kathleen James examines Mendelsohn's department stores, office buildings, and cinemas, the downtown counterparts to the famous housing projects built during the same years in Frankfurt and Berlin. Demonstrating the degree to which these buildings' dynamic presence stemmed from Mendelsohn's attention to their consumer-oriented functions, James shows Mendelsohn to be more than an Expressionist, as he is usually characterized. James recounts how his architecture closely reflected the controversies over modernity, including relativity, consumerism, and urban planning, that raged during the years of the Weimar Republic. She also illustrates how much Mendelsohn's thriving practice depended on the patronage of his fellow German Jews, many of whom shared his commitment to creating alternatives to the nationalistic historicism of the late Wilhelmine period.

ERICH MENDELSOHN AND THE ARCHITECTURE OF GERMAN MODERNISM

MODERN ARCHITECTURE AND CULTURAL IDENTITY

Modern Architecture and Cultural Identity will comprise monographic studies of important movements and buildings by European and American architects created roughly between 1850 and 1950. Unlike the first histories of modernism, which stressed the international aspects of modern architecture, recent scholarship has attempted to clarify the delicate balance achieved by architects working in a modernist idiom who maintained, nonetheless, a strong allegiance to their cultural roots. This series has been developed in response to this trend and will explore the complex interplay between modern identity and local, regional, national, and related cultural traditions.

ERICH MENDELSOHN AND THE ARCHITECTURE OF GERMAN MODERNISM

KATHLEEN JAMES
University of California, Berkeley

PUBLISHED BY THE PRESS SYNDICATE OF THE UNIVERSITY OF CAMBRIDGE
The Pitt Building, Trumpington Street, Cambridge CB2 1RP, United Kingdom

CAMBRIDGE UNIVERSITY PRESS
The Edinburgh Building, Cambridge CB2 2RU, United Kingdom
40 West 20th Street, New York, NY 10011-4211, USA
10 Stamford Road, Oakleigh, Melbourne 3166, Australia

First published 1997

Printed in the United States of America

Typeset in Sabon and Futura

Library of Congress Cataloging-in-Publication Data

James, Kathleen, 1960–
Erich Mendelsohn and the architecture of German modernism /
Kathleen James.
p. cm. – (Modern architecture and cultural identity)
Includes bibliographical references and index.
ISBN 0-521-57168-5
1. Mendelsohn, Erich, 1887–1953 – Criticism and interpretation.
2. Expressionism (Architecture) – Germany. 3. Functionalism
(Architecture) – Germany. I. Title. II. Series.
NA1088.M57J36 1997
720'.92 – dc20 96-38999

*A catalog record for this book is available from
the British Library*

ISBN 0 521 57168 5 hardback

To

JULIA BRUCE DOBBIN

and

to the memory of

KATHLEEN BRUCE

and

MARK DALLAS BUTLER

CONTENTS

ILLUSTRATIONS

ACKNOWLEDGMENTS

FROM the picnic during which Robert Wolterstorff suggested that I write my dissertation on Erich Mendelsohn through the final illustration collected by Greg Castillo, this book has been a collective effort in which I benefited from the ideas and assistance of a great many people. First among those I wish to thank are David Brownlee and Barbara Miller Lane. In addition to supervising my dissertation, they have guided me through the often complicated process of transforming it into this book. Their enthusiasm, knowledge, and patience have been as invaluable as the standards they set for me in their own work. I have also been challenged and inspired by the teaching of Renata Holod, William Jordy, Vincent Scully, and Irene Winter.

With my graduation from the University of Pennsylvania I acquired an amazingly talented collection of colleagues and students at the University of Minnesota and the University of California, Berkeley. I have learned an enormous amount from them, but I remain most indebted to those friends whose own passionate engagement with art, architecture, and German modernism had already prepared me for these extraordinary communities. The conversations – almost all stretching across more than a decade – in which Al Acres, James Buckley, Samuel Goodfellow, Elizabeth Grossman, Friedegund Holzmann, Sally James, Nina James-Fowler, Jennifer Jardine, Michael Lewis, Darielle Mason, Thomas Newlin, Steve Perry, Santosh Philip, Oliver Radford, Peter Reed, Erika Salloch, Jonathan Schwartz, Susan Solomon, Marc Vincent, Robert Wojtowicz, and Rebecca Zurier demanded that I defend my inchoate ideas against their far clearer thinking comprised the foundation of my life as a scholar. Furthermore, the encouragement, and in many cases the hospitality, of these individuals sustained me as I researched and wrote.

A wide variety of people whose lives intersected with that of Mendelsohn and with his built work proved invaluable. Esther Mendelsohn Joseph, Julius Posener, Gabriel Epstein, H. J. Katzenstein, and Dionne Niedermann Neutra recounted their memories of Mendelsohn for me, and Mrs. Neutra allowed me to read unpublished papers. At the Einstein Tower, Potsdam, the Kameleon Store in Wroclaw, and the businesses housed in the Weichmann Silk Store in Gliwice and the Steinberg, Hermann factory in Luckenwalde, people took time out of their workdays to show me proudly around the buildings of which they have taken such good care.

Fellow scholars were also generous. Thomas Hines and John Stachel helped me locate information in the papers of Richard Neutra and Albert Einstein. Maud Lavin and Fritz Neumeyer shared with me their provocative ideas about Weimar-era art and architecture. Sigrid Achenbach gave me access to the Mendelsohn archive. Ita Heinze-Greenberg kindly provided me with copies of Mendelsohn's letters to his wife. Hans Morganthaler, whose invaluable bibliography provided the foundation for this study, facilitated my research with a number of helpful insights. Miles David Samson made the unpublished results of his research on Mendelsohn's first trip to America available to me.

The staffs of the archives in which I worked – the Schocken Library, Jerusalem; Nederlands Documentatiecentrum voor de Bouwkunst, Amsterdam; Kunstbibliothek, Staatliche Museen Preußischer Kulturbesitz, Berlin; Akademie der Wissenschaft der Deutschen Demokratischen Republik, Berlin; Special Collections, University of California, Los Angeles; and the Getty Center for the Visual Arts and the Humanities, Santa Monica – went out of their way to locate material for me and graciously provided me with pleasant environments in which to study. So did Alan Morrison and the staff of the Fine Arts Library of the University of Pennsylvania, Joon Mornes of the Architecture Library at the University of Minnesota, and Elizabeth Byrne and Kathryn Wayne and the staff of the Environmental Design Library at Berkeley.

As a graduate student, I was supported by a Jacob Javits Fellowship from the U.S. Department of Education. Later, a Faculty Summer Research Fellowship paid for a return trip to Germany, and a Humanities Research Fellowship from the University of California, Berkeley, released me from a semester of teaching. The illustrations, and the money to hire Greg Castillo to gather them, were generously provided by a Hellman Family Fund Award.

An earlier version of Chapter One was published as an article in the *Journal of the Society of Architectural Historians* (December 1994).

Finally, I am grateful to Christian Otto, Beatrice Rehl, my anonymous readers, and, above all, Richard Etlin for their careful readings of my manuscript and for their tutelage throughout the final stages of its completion.

INTRODUCTION

IN December 1919 an extraordinary exhibit of architectural drawings entitled *Erich Mendelsohn, Architecture in Steel and Reinforced Concrete* opened at the Paul Cassirer Gallery in Berlin.[1] The work of an entirely unknown thirty-two year old, the drawings were enlarged versions of the tiny sketches for imaginary buildings, mostly factories, which Mendelsohn had been making since early 1914 (Fig. 1).[2] Many dated to the time he had spent in 1917 and 1918 as an army engineer on the eastern front during the First World War. Although executed with little attention to plan, program, construction, or context, these deftly drawn perspectives offered a bold new vision of an unornamented, frankly modern architecture. Their considerable vitality sprang less from any ostensible function than from the compelling shapes into which Mendelsohn proposed molding monolithic reinforced concrete, shapes whose solid masses were relieved only by equally dazzling open-work grids of steel and glass. Here, in images which remain among the best-known designs from the war-torn 1910s, the architect accorded factories, as well as an airport, and, less surprisingly, a train station, an overblown scale and monumental presence worthy of a medieval cathedral or of the vast institutions of the nineteenth-century nation-state.

The authors of the reviews of the exhibit that appeared in several major art magazines paid only brief attention to Mendelsohn's debut, however, which they interpreted as an unpromising attempt to revive the Art Nouveau (better known in German as Jugendstil, or "youthful style") architecture popular for a short time two decades earlier.[3] For them, the small Mendelsohn exhibit was overshadowed by the larger and far more controversial *Exhibit of Unknown Architects*, sponsored earlier in 1919 by the Arbeitsrat für Kunst. The Arbeitsrat,

FIGURE 1

Erich Mendelsohn, project for an AEG factory, 1914. (Source: *Erich Mendelsohn: Das Gesamtschaffen des Architekten,* Berlin, 1930.)

a group of artists and architects whose leaders included Walter Gropius and Bruno Taut, had been formed in part to lobby the new Social Democratic government to support innovative art and architecture. On the other hand, three young visitors to the Mendelsohn exhibit, Oskar Beyer, Henricus Theodorus Wijdeveld, and Hermann George Scheffauer, were sufficiently impressed to write and publish articles which quickly brought Mendelsohn an international reputation.[4] From as far away as Oklahoma City and Los Angeles, architecture students soon came under his spell.[5]

After it closed in Berlin, the Mendelsohn exhibit traveled to Hanover, Hamburg, Breslau, Chemnitz, Stuttgart, and Cologne.[6] During the next fourteen years, Mendelsohn would build in four of these six cities. This was only one of the many ways the exhibit was prescient of his career in Germany (he emigrated in March 1933, less than two months after Hitler became chancellor). The emphasis in the Mendelsohn exhibit on the individual designer rather than on the larger community as in the Arbeitsrat's earlier effort was characteristic. Although Mendelsohn would become one of the Weimar Republic's most successful architects, he would always remain slightly outside the inner core of architects dominated by Taut, Gropius, Ludwig Mies van der Rohe, and Ernst May with which he is most closely associated. Foreigners, however, continued to see him as more representative of modern German architecture than did his own compatriots. Nor did the central tenet of Mendelsohn's approach to design vary much from that which was displayed in the exhibit. Even though only one of his buildings, the Einstein Tower, resembled, albeit remotely, the drawings at the Paul Cassirer Gallery, Mendelsohn developed the germ of each in perspectives drawn in the same freehand style and with the same predilection for curvilinear forms. Most important, for as long as he remained in Germany Mendelsohn continued to maintain a precarious balance between matter-of-fact representation of modern industry and technology and an expression of the vitality he believed to be inherent in these aspects of modern life as well as in the modern materials of which his buildings were constructed. This balance, and its relationship to other aspects of Weimar culture, is the subject of this study.

This approach, which I have chosen to call dynamic functionalism, integrates stylistic experimentation, constructional innovation, and disparate influences from the surrounding culture.[7] Mendelsohn was slow to articulate fully his theoretical position, but the exhibit at the Cassirer Gallery already displayed his talent for resolving the expression of often conflicting modernisms – in this case, Expressionist painting, reinforced concrete construction, and industrial imagery – into forms that were often complexly asymmetrical, but always visually unified. Unlike today's deconstructivists, Mendelsohn sought to transcend rather than to expose the contradictions which destabilized the modernity he prized. During the twenties, he expanded the elements of this synthesis to include a wider range of building materials and sources from the visual arts. Scientific theory (relativity), urbanization (especially increased automobile traffic), economic integration (department stores), and new forms of entertainment (movies) also triggered his invention of lively new architectural forms. Dynamic functionalism encompassed economical construction, efficient spaces, and the latest mechanical systems, but whereas other architects focused on industrial imagery and standardized construction, Mendelsohn excelled at making industry's effect upon life far from the factory floor thrilling rather than threatening.

"Is not mass consumption, rather than mass production, the definitive drive of modernity?" asks Terry Smith in *Making the Modern*. Later, he answers his own question, "The true move to modernity, then, was the move to consumerism. The true site was not the factory, but the creation and circulation of market imagery."[8] Today, Smith's view is shared by most historians of Weimar culture, but its implications for architectural history remain largely unexplored.[9] While the work of many of his colleagues in the modern movement, above all that of Gropius and Mies van der Rohe, often appear to be stepping stones on the path to the architecture of the 1940s, 1950s, and beyond, Mendelsohn's attention to contemporary life resulted in buildings which fell out of fashion exactly because of their distance from the more abstract aesthetics and theories that informed the seemingly timeless buildings of his colleagues. Furthermore, having created a modern architecture of mass consumption, which celebrated rather than disguised its origin in mass production, Mendelsohn found his contribution devalued when the spectacles he had excelled at staging became tainted during the thirties by the effective use that Albert Speer made of similar strategies at National Socialist (Nazi) Party rallies.[10]

Today, many people are profoundly uncomfortable with the environment within which Mendelsohn developed dynamic functionalism into some of the most exciting urban architecture of this century, preferring, instead, the obvious social benefits if more banal forms of the workers' housing constructed during the same years. At the time, however, the two projects were more closely related than they now seem. Although the modernization of distribution systems and mechanization of entertainment which Mendelsohn celebrated in his department stores and cinema were certainly part of the expansion of an often dehumanizing capitalism, most of those who condemned these phenomena during the 1920s were either Marxists or right-wing nationalists. Like many of his socialist and centrist contemporaries, Mendelsohn believed that mass production offered the best hope of a more democratic society, and he equated industrial imagery with a utopianism just as passionate as that expressed in Taut's dreams of crystalline community centers or the realization of thousands of apartments.[11] And as was the case for many of his fellow Jewish Germans, the attacks upon modernization made by Nazis and other anti-Semites buttressed Mendelsohn's belief in an economic system whose unalloyed identification with Enlightenment rationalism as a humanist project he might otherwise have questioned.

Dynamic functionalism has too often been confused with Expressionism. This is not to say that Mendelsohn was not an Expressionist, especially during the 1910s and early 1920s, but that Expressionism alone does not adequately define his distinctive position in the larger story of German architecture during the Weimar Republic. What now seems to be Mendelsohn's distortion of the Platonic forms proposed by contemporaries like Mies van der Rohe was more than the result of an individual's artistic temperament. It was usually closely related to the function – and to the importance of a thrilling image of modernity to that function – of Mendelsohn's commissions. The number and range of his buildings remained unmatched throughout the decade among the adherents of the Neues Bauen (New Building), the term that was most commonly employed in Germany during the 1920s.

The split between organic architecture and the International Style, first posited by Bruno Zevi in the 1950s, like the later separation of Expressionism from the New Building, ignored the ideological continuities that often knit together what at first appear to be stylistic fault lines.[12] Mendelsohn's Expressionism was never identical with Taut's, nor was his romanticization of industry a reflection of Gropius's, but, as his contemporaries at home and abroad were well aware, Mendelsohn was no less central than Gropius and Taut to the architecture of his own day. Hans Hildebrant, for instance, who is best remembered today for translating Le Corbusier's *Vers une architecture* into German, believed that Mendelsohn's work was at once highly personal and entirely typical of contemporary architecture, "based," Hildebrant added, "on objective grounds, not generated by a raving drive and external formalism. The language is modern, because it is spoken by a man who is modern by nature, and because tasks which our period poses in this manner for the first time, can also only be solved in a new manner."[13]

Others echoed Hildebrant, while pointing to the components of Mendelsohn's success – fantasy and fashion – that were later seen as more problematic. Erwin Redslob praised Mendelsohn's substitution of "construction laws dictated by the materials, dynamics, fulfillment of function, logic, and the inexorability of reason" for outmoded materials and ornament and noted:

> Just as the many architectural fantasies drawn by him are also germ cells for functional buildings, so are his functional buildings at the same time very bold fantasies that independently of their functional fulfillment tower before us like monuments of a new will. This flow from the sphere of the real into the metaphysical, and from the metaphysical into the real, is a trait in which one can recognize the artistry of Erich Mendelsohn.[14]

Another influential German critic, Karl Scheffler, dwelt on the extent to which Mendelsohn, and by extension all contemporary architects, was more an engineer than an artist and described how Mendelsohn had recast curvilinear form in a fashion influenced by industry. Scheffler continued in a more critical vein, "Mendelsohn's buildings are robust, but they lack strong nerve; therefore their effect is most powerful on first viewing after which they lose some of that effect. Nevertheless, the final result is that Mendelsohn manages to interest the whole world in his buildings so that people do not shy away from long walks in order to look at them."[15] The experience of a young Italian architect bore him out. Remembering the way he had marveled at Mendelsohn's "dazzling" Herpich store – "fully opened with glass, with large clear panes that hugged the sinuous body" – when he came upon it under construction in 1924, Carlo Belli continued, "The sense of magic that emanated from the windows radiant with electric brilliance made me ecstatic."[16]

Such praise demonstrates the degree to which architects and architectural critics identified Mendelsohn with modernism; even more compelling was the recognition accorded him by the popular illustrated press, whose representations of contemporary culture in visual terms included photographs of his architecture. The Ullstein press's *Berliner illustrirte [sic] Zeitung*, the German forerunner of Life magazine, published photographs of a number of his buildings; so did Ullstein's rival, the Mosse publishing firm, whose Berlin headquarters Mendelsohn renovated and expanded.[17] Nor was the suitability of such images entirely coincidental; Mendelsohn himself commissioned the photographs of his buildings by Arthur Köster, which were frequently reproduced in Germany's many art and architecture magazines.[18] He also wrote three books, all published by Mosse, only one of which was a conventional monograph devoted to his career. The other two chronicled Mendelsohn's travels to the United States and the Soviet Union; the first look in particular, illustrated in part with his own photographs, reached an audience stretching far beyond his profession.

Mendelsohn's anomalous position in architecture as a wildly successful yet always slightly peripheral figure was also partly attributable to his religion. Jewish at a time of revived anti-Semitism in Germany, Mendelsohn could not hope for unquestioning acceptance from either the architectural community or the general public.[19] Mendelsohn's talent for overturning Alfred Messel's specifically patriotic precedents would be the source both of his fame and of controversy as, especially after 1924, Mendelsohn set the tone for the rapid expansion of downtowns during the Weimar Republic, designing department stores, office buildings, and a single, but extremely influential, cinema. Mendelsohn's career in Germany depended almost entirely upon the support of Jewish patrons, many of whom hired him in part because they shared his Zionist politics; at the same time, he was easily tarred with the Nazi brush that condemned all Jewish involvement in German culture and society, from Albert Einstein's theories of relativity to Hans Lachmann-Mosse's newspaper empire and Salman Schocken's department stores.

The purpose of this study is to reconstruct rather than deconstruct dynamic functionalism's original context, to identify the ways in which Mendelsohn's vivid forms emerged, for both their creator and his contemporaries, out of the conditions of modern (especially urban) life, out of its problems and its passions. Mendelsohn's buildings offer apparently sensible and pragmatic responses to many of modernity's problems without draining its corresponding passion from either individual cities or the culture as a whole. Finally, my subject is Mendelsohn's approach to the representation of modernity; I have not chosen to write a biography or to consider all aspects of his career. I have focused on those writings and especially those buildings that were most central to the creation and expression of dynamic functionalism. In particular, I concentrate on buildings rather than on projects and on those commissions in which economic viability most likely would have been an issue. Those facets of Mendelsohn's architecture which are not a part of my story, particularly his domestic commissions around Berlin; religious buildings in East Prussia; commissioned, but unrealized, schemes for sites in Europe and in what was then the British Mandate of Palestine; and the lively sketches he continued to make of entirely imaginary projects remain for others to explore.

The dual function of the Einstein Tower as a monument to and laboratory for research into relativity is the subject of Chapter 1, which also examines the impact of relativity upon Mendelsohn's thinking about architecture. Mendelsohn's proud association with a theory attacked by anti-Semitic nationalists as irrational established the pro-modern stance from which he would never waver. Following this initial exploration of dynamic functionalism, Chapter 2 looks at Mendelsohn's architectural theory in relation to his travels to the Netherlands, the United States, and the Soviet Union. While the first destination was of importance primarily to architects, the latter two countries were crucial to the broader debate in Germany during the 1920s about the appropriate relationship between industry, politics, and culture. Mendelsohn's writings helped shape that debate even as his firsthand experience of these places enhanced his stature with his colleagues and patrons. Because of his ability to express himself in the language of the popular press, his exposé of the gap between architectural image and technological fact in both American historicist and Soviet constructivist architecture reached the same broad audience as his buildings.

Although it was the Einstein Tower, far more than the exhibit at the Paul Cassirer Gallery, that established Mendelsohn as one of Germany's leading architects, the gap between his purpose in designing the extremely unusual looking Tower and the way others understood it, as well as difficulty constructing it, led Mendelsohn in new directions. The stylistic aspects of his search, conducted against the backdrop of Germany's deepening economic crisis, are the subject of Chapter 3, which focuses upon the Steinberg, Hermann hat factory in Luckenwalde; the renovation and expansion of Mossehaus, an office building in Berlin; and the Mendelsohn office's first store, the Weichmann Silk Building in Gleiwitz (now Gliwice, Poland). These three works, all designed and built between 1921 and 1923, demonstrate the range of Mendelsohn's experimentation with new, formal expressions of dynamic functionalism, as well as the complex workings of his office, in which he shared credit with talented collaborators, above all Richard Neutra.

In 1924, the same year as Mendelsohn's trip to America, the infusion of dollars under the Dawes Plan temporarily stabilized the German economy, ushering in a building boom that, although it lasted only five years, transformed German downtowns. Often overlooked in accounts of the period, which have paid far more attention to housing, this boom offered Mendelsohn his greatest opportunities to build new and to renovate and expand old commercial buildings, as well as to insert housing into increasingly dense urban cores. It enabled him to create an abstract, industrial face for exactly those same consumer-oriented building types that in other countries would continue to be dressed up with the most ornament.[20] By substituting lettering and lighting for allusions to the past, Mendelsohn invented a more democratic, but equally seductive architecture, one animated by sleek details and bold cantilevers, which replaced the Wilhelmine emphasis on taming, even disguising, the new world of consumerism.

Chapter 4 focuses on Mendelsohn's role in urban planning debates in Berlin, in which the architect sought to give order to the almost chaotic vitality of the modern metropolis without rejecting modernity itself. Throwing a light harness over the inevitable results of rapid urbanization and real estate speculation, he respected traditional street lines and mixed-use development while delighting in traffic, height, and new building types. The chapter opens with the controversy over the C. A. Herpich store, a furrier on the Leipzigerstraße, Berlin's most famous shopping street, in which Mendelsohn substituted horizontals, inspired in part by speeding automobiles, for the more stable verticality of Messel's commercial architecture. Analyses of Mendelsohn's WOGA development on Berlin's Kurfürstendamm and his involvement in the redevelopment of Potsdamerplatz in the same city – the site of his high-rise office building Columbushaus – illustrate Mendelsohn's approach to more comprehensive urban design projects. In all three cases, radically simplified, and often taller, buildings seem poised to respond to the energies of the city whirling around them, appear almost ready to spin into motion themselves.

The other two most effective magic wands in Mendelsohn's toolbox of dynamic effects were electric light and transparency. Originally developed just before the war in Bruno Taut's Steel and Glass Pavilions as well as, in the case of transparency, in the factories designed by Peter Behrens and Walter Gropius, by the early twenties both were indivisible from utopian Expressionism. Mendelsohn commercialized their use without rejecting their visionary connotations. In his hands, they became effective advertisements for a new generation of elegant stores and – following in the footsteps of Hans Poelzig – cinemas. Focusing on Herpich Furriers, the Petersdorff store, and the Universum Cinema, Chapter 5 examines Mendelsohn's role in this invention of a new immaterial and abstract image of modern luxury.

No architect works in a vacuum. Chapter 6 considers the more overtly functional aspects of Mendelsohn's department stores in relation to his most extraordinary patron, Salmann Schocken for whom Mendelsohn built stores in Nuremberg, Stuttgart, and Chemnitz. In place of the elegant details of the Herpich and Petersdorff stores, Schocken favored an explicit correlation of the sites of production and consumption: the factory and the department store. This emphasis upon mass production as a substitute for earlier Expressionist utopias is also the subject of Chapter 7, which demonstrates Mendelsohn's continuing exploration of functionalist imagery and his allegiance to architectural forms under attack by right-wing nationalists. The competitive spirit that kept him abreast of the latest designs by rival architects, including most notably Mies and Gropius, is also treated in this chapter in the coupling of the Schocken store in Chemnitz with the Mosse pavilion at the Press Exhibition in Cologne, with Mendelsohn's own Berlin house, and with Columbushaus. All were designed in 1928, the year after the controversial Weissenhof exhibit in Stuttgart. The book concludes with a brief appraisal of dynamic functionalism during Mendelsohn's career in exile in London, Jerusalem, New York, and San Francisco.

10

ERICH MENDELSOHN AND THE ARCHITECTURE OF GERMAN MODERNISM

Weimar Germany was the crucible in which a new approach to architecture was forged, one whose influence would eventually stretch around the world. Erich Mendelsohn was far more important to the original formulation of that architecture than he was to the approach that would later triumph abroad. Examining Mendelsohn's contribution in the context of its creation enables us to recover the complexity that existed within the New Building from its inception and remember the reasons for the initial popularity of its aesthetic.

1

A CONCRETE MONUMENT TO RELATIVITY

IN September 1921 readers of the *Berliner illustrirte Zeitung*, a tabloid with the largest circulation of any European periodical, found splashed across the cover of their paper a photograph of one of the most unusual looking buildings ever seen (Fig. 2).[1] Only a few may have recognized it as the built version of the drawings on display at the Paul Cassirer Gallery less than two years earlier or may have heard of its architect, Erich Mendelsohn. Most readers probably regarded it as yet another example of the breakdown of established Wilhelmine society and, above all, as a building as eccentric as the scientific concepts with which it was associated: Albert Einstein's controversial theories of relativity. Indeed, it became known almost immediately as the Einstein Tower.[2] Constructed on the grounds of the Astrophysical Observatory in Potsdam, the Tower represented Mendelsohn's sole attempt to realize in an actual building the dynamic functionalism he had espoused in his sketches.[3] Mendelsohn intended the Tower to be a monument to Einstein's theories as well as a laboratory in which they could be studied. From the beginning, however, astonishment at the Tower's dynamic form obscured public understanding of the way that its form related to its functions or of the degree to which Mendelsohn's own understanding of dynamism was the product of his exposure to relativity.[4] In fact, Mendelsohn's awareness of the startling new theory can scarcely be separated from the evolution of his architectural ideas during the war, although the actual commission dated only to 1918.[5]

The Tower established Mendelsohn's position in the many debates over new ideas and artistic forms that characterized the divisively politicized cultural life of the Weimar Republic and came to encompass passionate arguments for and against his architecture. Relativity

FIGURE 2

Erich Mendelsohn, Einstein Tower, Potsdam, Germany, 1920–21. (Source: Staatliche Museen zu Berlin, Kunstbibliothek.)

became the first of many battlegrounds on which Mendelsohn proudly fought for the modernist side. He sought to create in his design of the Tower an architecture in which new forms and building materials would produce valid symbols for the postwar era. The Tower's monumentality was intended to support the new cultural conditions of the Republic. Yet it remained part of the lingering fascination prewar German architects had with architectural permanence, an issue whose importance would quickly wane.

The Einstein Tower became the most important built symbol of German architecture immediately after the First World War and quickly brought its architect enormous fame. But Mendelsohn never counted the Tower among his finest works. Instead, he learned from its construction that his original understanding of the character of the reinforced concrete used in building it had been flawed. Furthermore, its reception (most critics interpreted the Tower as an example of antirational mysticism) taught him that it was easier to attract the public's attention than to send it a message. Mendelsohn's interest in motion and in light, which had been fueled by his engagement with relativity, would, however, continue to be a key component of his dynamic functionalism.

THE COMMISSION

The formulation of relativity was contemporary with the birth of Expressionist art, whose path it was to cross in the Einstein Tower. The relationship was not entirely the result of chance. In the early decades of the twentieth century, proponents of artistic reform, Mendelsohn among them, frequently defended stylistic changes in the arts as the logical outgrowth of scientific and technological discoveries and innovations.[6] Mendelsohn's acquaintance with relativity was almost accidental; the relationship between his rejection of accepted scientific ideas and artistic styles was not. Relativity encouraged Mendelsohn to think about the relationship between mass and motion and gave him the opportunity to create a building whose modernity was as much the product of its function as of its form.

In 1905 a twenty-six-year-old physicist named Albert Einstein began to publish papers outlining new relationships between light, space, and time. According to Einstein's special theory of relativity, the speed of light is constant while measures of duration and distance depend on whether the observer is at rest or in motion. Einstein's work united seemingly contradictory observations from mechanics and electrodynamics, two different branches of physics. In the first of these articles Einstein included his famous formula, which states that energy equals mass squared, or that mass and energy are different manifestations of the same physical forces.[7] In 1907 and 1908 Einstein expanded his analysis of light, claiming, in his first step toward his general theory, that light could be bent by gravity.[8] In a 1911 article he suggested that this idea could be tested during an eclipse by measuring the degree to which the sun's gravity deflected the light of stars beyond it.[9]

This suggestion brought Einstein, by this time a professor at the German University in Prague, into contact with astronomers, including Erwin Finlay Freundlich, who in 1910 had become the youngest assistant at the observatory in Babelsberg just outside Berlin.[10] Although the quality of his scientific work was questionable, Freundlich was an enormously talented organizer and did much to establish Einstein's fame and to publicize relativity.[11] The two men quickly became friends. Freundlich, excited by relativity's prospects for revolutionizing his own field, proposed to lead an expedition in August 1914 to the Crimea, where he hoped to observe a solar eclipse and make the measurements that might validate the general theory. The outbreak of World War I resulted in his team being deported from Russia without conducting the experiment. Disappointed, Freundlich returned to Berlin, where he kept in close touch with Einstein, who had moved to the German capital in 1913.[12]

Perhaps as early as 1913, Freundlich introduced Mendelsohn whom he had met through Mendelsohn's fiancée, Luise Maas, to Einstein's general theory, even before the physicist had completed its formulation and well before awareness of its implications spread beyond a small community of physicists and other scientists. By 1916 this new theory about gravity and its relationship to space had replaced Newton's.[13] The tone of Freundlich's explanation can be reconstructed from a book that he published in 1916. The first book devoted to the subject, Freundlich's *The Foundations of Einstein's Theory of Gravitation* included a preface by Einstein, to whom the manuscript had been submitted for approval.[14] Freundlich's was a low-key and somewhat mathematical account of the way in which general relativity altered classical mechanics, specifically Newtonian concepts of gravity and inertia. Freundlich explained that the theory upset the traditional understanding of time and space, but he did not illustrate this change with the apparently irrational examples that would characterize many later popular accounts. Similarly, he mentioned time as the fourth dimension in mathematical equations but did not make the later common error of trying to visualize it.

For the rest of the war, Freundlich sought facilities where he could mount a second attempt to prove relativity through astronomical observation. He hoped by comparing the spectra of artificial light and sunlight to find that sunlight was the redder of the two, evidence of a gravitationally caused shift in its mass. In 1915 he published an article outlining this potential experiment, and Einstein assisted him in an attempt to gain access to the equipment of the Babelsberg Observatory.[15] Its director, Hermann Struve, refused their request, however, in an argument quickly buttressed by an attack made upon the proposal by Hugo Ritter von Seeliger, the director of the Munich Observatory.[16] By July 1918 Freundlich had decided to build his own institute. Encouraged by an offer from Gustav Müller, who was the director of the Astrophysical Observatory in Potsdam, of a site on his observatory's grounds, Freundlich sent a detailed description of his proposed building's program, complete with sketches of a possible elevation and ground plan, to Mendelsohn, then stationed on the French front.[17]

Mendelsohn had time to make only a few preliminary sketches before the events which led to the end of the war intervened.[18] Once he was back Berlin, however, any hope that his discussions with Freundlich would soon lead to an actual commission were quickly dashed. Only after November 6, 1919, when the Royal Society and the Royal Astronomical Society met in London to hear that the experiment Freundlich had hoped to perform in the Crimea in 1914 had been completed by two British expeditions, producing proof of Einstein's theory of general relativity, did the Tower again seem buildable. The once esoteric theory almost instantly became the stuff of popular science, and Einstein became the first celebrity of Germany's recently founded Weimar Republic, effortlessly attaining a fame he had done nothing to court. The difficulty of the theory was no obstacle to its popularity, which depended more on the pride that a defeated nation could take in such a high level of intellectual achievement than on the theory's scientific details. Thus Einstein's trips abroad in the early twenties, especially those he made to France, where other German scientists remained unwelcome, were widely reported in the German press.[19]

Celebrated as much for political reasons as for scientific ones, Einstein, a Jewish pacifist with a Swiss passport, was vulnerable to criticism on these grounds. One indication of the weakness of the Republic, which had been brought to power by the November revolution and legitimized the following year by the Weimar constitution, was the opposition voiced by right-wing nationalists, none of whom was expert in theoretical physics, to Einstein's seemingly objective theory. The nationalists labeled the theory irrational and thus un-German. Advocates and opponents of relativity carried the debate outside the normal channels of scientific discussion. By August 1920 Einstein's unprecedented public response to an equally unprecedented public airing of opposition to his work – an antirelativity meeting held in Berlin's Philharmonic Hall – was front-page news in the *Berliner Tageblatt*, the city's leading liberal newspaper.[20] The arguments offered against relativity were tinged with anti-Semitism and based more on politics than on strictly scientific speculation. They set a precedent for the reactionary German critics who attacked every Weimar-era contribution to artistic experimentation and other forms of modernity. With science first and foremost among the victims of this anti-intellectual nationalism there would be plenty of venom left for more subjective artistic targets.[21]

Meanwhile, the initial enthusiasm for relativity that followed the British announcement spurred Freundlich to organize in Einstein's name a foundation which could fund the construction of his observatory. Freundlich worked quickly. Only a month after Einstein and his theory became world famous, Freundlich issued a public appeal for half a million marks to be applied to German research which would be undertaken by the newly founded Einstein Foundation on the General Theory of Relativity. He secured the signatures of eight of the country's leading scientists, including Max Planck and the directors of Potsdam's two observatories. The call, couched in nationalistic terms, pleaded for money to support just one site where German research could be given a chance to compete with research being conducted in England, France, and America, the countries that had defeated Germany only a year earlier. Freundlich also lobbied the Prussian state government for an appropriation of one hundred fifty thousand marks to purchase a spectrograph, the proposed observatory's most important and expensive instrument. By May 1920, when Mendelsohn began full-time work on the Tower's design, Freundlich had raised two hundred thousand marks.[22]

PRELUDE: EARLY DRAWINGS

The story of the Tower's design process is inextricable from that of the drawings, many of them exhibited in 1919 at the Paul Cassirer Gallery, that Mendelsohn had been sketching since 1914. If, over the next six years, an extraordinary number of ideas from the visual arts served as the weft of his architectural vision, relativity was the warp around which Mendelsohn threaded these largely – but by no means exclusively Expressionist – artistic elements.

Expressionism as an artistic movement was founded by painters and dramatists during the first decade of the new century. Expressionist painters working in a number of German cities, most notably Munich, Dresden, and Berlin, and deeply influenced by the writings of the philosopher Friedrich Nietzsche, sought to create a vital art that would stem the supposed decline of German and Western culture.[23] For Mendelsohn, the strands of Expressionist theater and painting that flourished in Munich, rather than the painting and poetry of the Berlin circles that influenced his fellow Expressionist architects such as Bruno Taut, were most important.[24] The result was Mendelsohn's strong commitment to curvilinear form, complemented by his nascent awareness of unusual lighting effects and sense of abstract art and gesture as vehicles for influencing the general public.

Mendelsohn was born in 1887 in the East Prussian city of Allenstein (today Olysztyn, Poland). He first came to Munich in 1907 to study law.[25] His return to Munich in 1910 after two years as an architecture student in Berlin was probably prompted by a desire to study with Theodor Fischer, the most influential German architecture professor of his generation.[26] Mendelsohn graduated in 1912 and opened his own office, but he received no architectural commissions to place beside the funerary chapel for the Jewish cemetery in his hometown that he had completed while still a student.[27] For two years he busied himself designing posters, concert programs, shop window displays, furniture, theater costumes, and stage sets.[28]

In his letters to Luise Maas, whom he married in 1915, Mendelsohn noted his interest in Wassily Kandinsky's Blue Rider circle and the other painters, such as Pablo Picasso, whose works they occasionally imported to exhibit beside their own, but it was theater that drew Mendelsohn into active participation with Expressionists.[29] Mendelsohn probably met Max Reinhardt, Germany's leading director of Expressionist theater, in 1912 when the architect decorated the hall for the Presse carnival ball, which Reinhardt had returned to Munich to stage.[30] While in residence from 1909 to 1911 at Munich' Künstlertheater, Reinhardt had borrowed from vaudeville and traditional pageantry to transform literary classics into highly popular spectacles. The director had also come to increasingly rely upon the communicative powers of gesture rather than the spoken word, and had used innovative sets and dramatic lighting effects to further supplement the efforts of the actors.[31]

In the spring of 1914, Mendelsohn and Hugo Ball, at that time the dramaturgist at the Kammerspiele and later a founder of Dada in Zurich, led an attempt to regain Expressionist control of the Künstlertheater, which had been rented out to actors from Düsseldorf. They hoped to mount new productions of ancient and modern classics as well as to introduce audiences to Japanese drama and to Kandinsky's highly experimental theatrical compositions *The Yellow Sound* and *Violet*.[32] Proof of Mendelsohn's involvement with the Blue Rider at this point comes from Ball's notes for a planned but never realized second edition of the group's *Almanach*. These show that Mendelsohn was to contribute an article on stage design.[33] As the struggle for control of the Künstlertheater demonstrates, Reinhardt's activities complemented those of the Blue Rider and had, by 1914, attracted the attention of Kandinsky, who was looking for a venue for *The Yellow Sound* and *Violet*. It is unlikely that, had they been staged, Kandinsky's works would have attracted the enormous audiences that often flocked to Reinhardt's productions, but Kandinsky planned to use similar popular sources of spectacle, preferring,

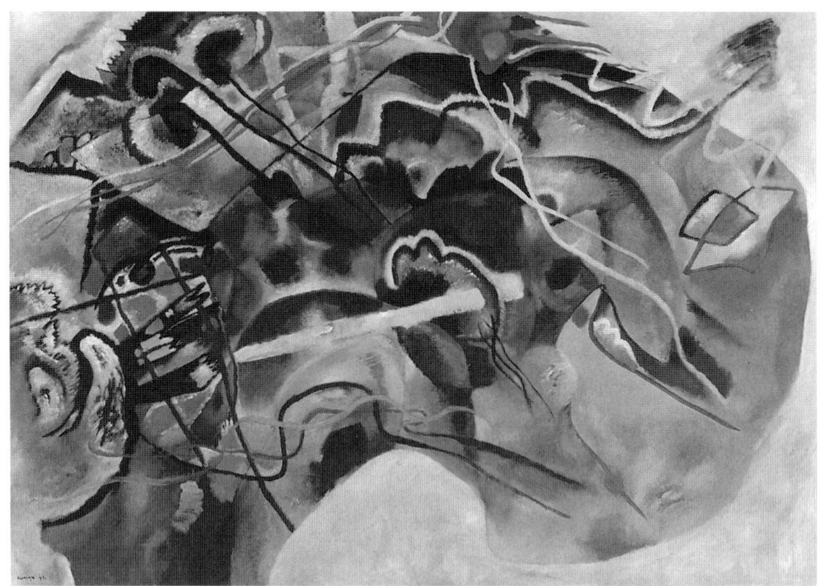

FIGURE 3

Wassily Kandinsky, *Painting with White Border*, 1913. Solomon R. Guggenheim Museum, New York, Gift Solomon R. Guggenheim (Source: Carmelo Guadagno, © Solomon R. Guggenheim Museum, New York.)

he wrote, "vaudeville, circus, cabaret and film" to "museum-forms." Kandinsky believed he could express "spiritual values" through the invention of radical new art forms; above all, he relied on the emotional effects of color. Although his plays contain some dialogue, gesture and lighting dominate his attempts to imagine an abstract yet populist approach to theater.[34]

Munich's Expressionist painters focused on themes of spiritual renewal.[35] Kandinsky joined apocalyptic imagery with vivid brushwork poised on the brink of abstraction. As he experimented with the solid areas of color such as were commonly found in Bavarian folk paintings on glass, he realized that color could be just as expressive as representation (Fig. 3). In his short but enormously influential book *Concerning the Spiritual in Art*, Kandinsky explained color's role in evoking universal empathetic responses and argued that abstraction was an appropriate vehicle for a spiritual art uncontaminated by the materialism of literal representation.[36]

For Mendelsohn, the forms, as much as the message, of Expressionist painting were crucial. Kandinsky's painting led Mendelsohn to appreciate the Jugendstil in which motifs taken from nature had replaced historically derived ornament. An art that deployed increasingly abstract forms according to familiar conventions of ornamental placement, this style had flourished across Europe at the turn of the century. Most importantly for Mendelsohn, Hermann Obrist, the Jugendstil's major advocate in Munich, continued to think in terms of "dynamism," a word that Mendelsohn would adopt as his own.[37]

FIGURE 4

Hermann Obrist, embroidery for a silk blouse, circa 1898. (Source: *Dekorative Kunst*, 1898.)

Kandinsky provided an important precedent for the young architect's interest in Obrist from whom the painter had absorbed his own taste for curvilinear forms.[38] In November 1914 Mendelsohn wrote that he found in Obrist "a preparation for and an indication of the correctness of my own formal expression."[39]

Although by 1914 a somewhat peripheral figure in the artistic life of the city, in 1896 Obrist had exhibited embroideries introducing the Jugendstil to Munich (Fig. 4). By stylizing windswept plant forms, he drew attention both to nature and to his own artistry. His interest in dynamism eventually triumphed, however, over references to nature. As Obrist and his students searched for appropriately modern decorative vocabularies, they progressed to an entirely nonrepresentational art that anticipated Kandinsky's paintings.[40] Obrist was also keenly aware of the architectural implications of the Jugendstil. He claimed that the style's transformation of the decorative arts could be extended to architecture through the use of new building materials, methods of construction, spatial arrangements, and decorative vocabularies. Although Obrist himself had no training as an architect, in his designs for tombs and fountains, for the most part unbuilt, he edged toward that profession.

Reinforced concrete seemed to Mendelsohn to be the material best suited to approximate the forms found in Kandinsky's paintings. For

FIGURE 5

Max Berg, Centennial Hall, Breslau, Germany (now Wroclaw, Poland), 1913. (Source: Gustav Platz, *Die Baukunst der neuesten Zeit,* Berlin, 1927.)

instance, in the Garrison Church in Ulm, built between 1906 and 1911, while Mendelsohn was his student, Theodor Fischer achieved generous spatial effects at little cost by leaving the church's arching concrete ribs exposed in the interior.[41] But nowhere did the use of reinforced concrete achieve effects more closely ressembling those of Kandinsky's paintings than in the almost biomorphic character of many of the interior details of the Centennial Hall in Breslau (today Wroclaw, Poland), dedicated in 1913 (Fig. 5). Designed by Max Berg, the city architect, this building united abstract form with an unparalleled feat of engineering. Its dome, for a time the world's largest enclosed space uninterrupted by supports, concluded a brief but extremely imaginative phase of concrete construction in Breslau.[42] Although basically a frame construction, the ribbed span was supported in part by four enormous arches, whose splayed curves, along with the angled supports of the gallery behind them, moved toward a monolithic approach to using concrete. These aspects of the building also provided Mendelsohn with a dramatic example of the way in which physical forces could find architectural expression through revealed construction. Mendelsohn's only criticism was that a restrained exterior cloaked the drama within.[43]

In March 1914 Mendelsohn made a statement that hinted at the impetus for the far more radical drawings he may already have been making in drawings in which he turned buildings like the Garrison Church and Centennial Hall inside out. Here, for the first time, as he would throughout his career, Mendelsohn equated dynamism with structure:

> Every building material, like every substance, has certain conditions governing the demands that can be made on it. . . . Steel in combination with concrete, reinforced concrete, is the building material for the new formal expression, for the new style. . . . The relation between support and load, this apparently eternal law, will also have to alter its image, for things support themselves which formerly had to be supported. Walls are kept in place without the weight of the roof pressing on them and holding them together. Ceilings over our heads and vaults reach out without any intermediate supports being necessary. Towers mount and grow out of themselves with their own power and spirit and soul.[44]

This approach characterizes what are perhaps Mendelsohn's earliest factory sketches, a set of designs for an imaginary machine factory for the AEG, the electrical firm that had commissioned Behrens's Turbine Hall, a building Mendelsohn greatly admired.[45] The final version of Mendelsohn's scheme shows three enormous concrete towers supporting a concrete shell that is punctuated by vast grids of steel and glass (Fig. 1).[46]

This design represented an enormous creative breakthrough. In place of the recognizably historicist, if abstract, imagery of his earlier designs, Mendelsohn now employed a far more fluid manipulation of complex forms in which both the towering cantilevers and the smoothly curved ground floor corners show his fascination with curvilinear form. No hint of ornament mars the carefully conceived graphic power of the contrast of black ink against white paper. The square openings in the projecting pylons, for instance, provide an effective foil for the steel grid of the glazed sections between and behind them. Through his engagement with industrial architecture, Mendelsohn shifted the locus of the Expressionist goal of reforging a community divided by modernization from the institutions of the state, including such public sponsorship of the arts as theater and museums, to the very center of the process that had caused the fragmentation in the first place – the factory itself.

The distance Mendelsohn had quickly traveled and the individual nature of the result can be measured in part by comparing the imaginary factory in his sketch with the Fagus Shoe Last Factory in Alfeld designed by Walter Gropius and Adolf Meyer (Fig. 6). [47] Although the materials – and thus the appearance – of the two factories were distinctly different, the three architects shared a faith in industrial

FIGURE 6

Walter Gropius and Adolf Meyer, Fagus factory, Alfeld-an-der-Lahn, Germany, 1911–25. (Source: Bauhaus Archiv, Berlin, Neg. 5939/21.)

buildings as the model for a new approach to architecture. In this new architectural style, aestheticized references to construction and function would replace historical ornament, and "true" monumentality would be derived from the technological requirements of production rather than from, as had been the case with "falsely" grandiose public buildings, the tired rhetoric of Wilhelmine politics. The degree of artistry that remained in this new style is particularly obvious in Mendelsohn's reliance upon Kandinsky for inspiration and in the highly stylized glazed corner and canted piers of Gropius and Meyer's administration block.

The differences between these two factories presaged the different directions Mendelsohn and Gropius would take after the war. Mendelsohn's sculpted concrete pylons and Gropius's tautly linear surfaces reflected their respective apprenticeships with Fischer and Behrens. Mendelsohn's preference for concrete and Gropius's for steel frames only increased this formal distance. Throughout Gropius's career his buildings often served as didactic illustrations of his architectural theory and teaching philosophy. In contrast, Mendelsohn trusted much more in pure form, which he used to communicate an emotional rather than an intellectual message. He directed this message not only at other architects but also at anyone who might walk past his buildings or see them illustrated in a weekly newspaper.

This new focus upon the factory as the locus of architectural reform coincided with and was encouraged by the activities of the German Werkbund. Founded in 1907 by a coalition of architects, designers, critics, and industrialists, the Werkbund (of which Fischer was the first president) sought to reconcile industrialization with the preservation of what the group saw as national craft-based artistic

FIGURE 7

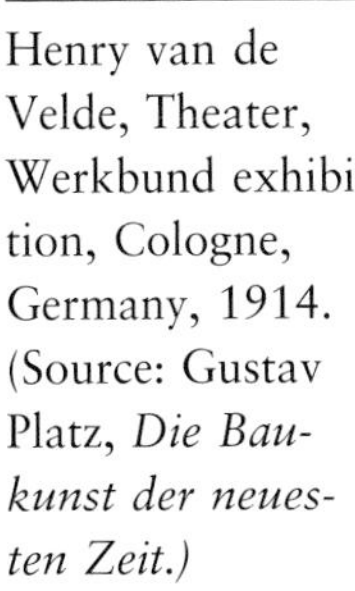

Henry van de Velde, Theater, Werkbund exhibition, Cologne, Germany, 1914. (Source: Gustav Platz, *Die Baukunst der neuesten Zeit.)*

traditions.[48] The Werkbund's activities included the publication of a yearbook and, in the summer of 1914, the mounting of a large exhibition in Cologne. Mendelsohn paid close attention to press reports of the exhibit's architecture as well as to the controversy over the future direction of the Werkbund. Mendelsohn, who was more interested in the Jugendstil than in the restrained historicism that characterized most Werkbund-approved products and buildings, singled out Henry van de Velde's concrete theater for praise, crediting its architect with "really searching for a form" (Fig. 7).[49] He also sympathized with van de Velde's theoretical position when, in a debate that nearly split the Werkbund in two, van de Velde opposed Hermann Muthesius's call for standardization with a spirited defense of artistic individuality.[50]

The tension between these two positions continued throughout Mendelsohn's career. Although by the midtwenties Muthesius's was the more popular view, Mendelsohn always adhered to van de Velde and Kandinsky's defense of artistic creativity. He was fascinated by mechanization's importance for architecture but believed ultimately in the artist's role in shaping form. He wrote in 1915:

> The work of every artist has only one aim – to achieve complete unity between functional form and artistic form. That is what is called style. . . . The machine, as the point of departure for the new culture, already has within it the fulfillment of this law. The age of mechanization will subject every manifestation to it, both our senses and our ideas. Everything apart from it seems to me worthless.[51]

Relativity also played an increasingly important role in Mendelsohn's thinking. Mendelsohn and Freundlich spent many evenings together in 1915, both before and during the architect's army training.[52] The two men shared interests in art, music, and science. Freundlich, who was married to a van de Velde student, greatly admired the sculptor Auguste Rodin and was, like Luise Maas Mendelsohn, a cellist.[53] Accompanying Freundlich on a trip to Babelsberg, Mendelsohn met Max Planck, a Freundlich supporter and as the father of quantum theory one of Germany's most distinguished scientists.[54] Spurred by the precedents of the AEG and Fagus factories and by the Werkbund's stance that art and industry are compatible, Mendelsohn believed that the possible commission for an observatory – a type of specialized scientific building not previously associated with architectural innovation – offered him an outstanding opportunity to display his emerging Expressionist style.

From May 1917 until at least May 1918 Mendelsohn was stationed on the Russian front.[55] Although hostilities did not officially cease until the signing of the Treaty of Brest-Litovsk in 1918, this front became relatively quiet after the outbreak of the March 1917 revolution in Petrograd (today St. Petersburg). Despite his guard duties, Mendelsohn was able to correspond regularly with his wife and with Freundlich, to attend concerts, and to sketch. In response to letters from Freundlich, he made at least ten studies for an astronomical observatory.[56]

These drawings and the letters that accompanied them offer insight into the connections Mendelsohn was beginning to draw between relativity and Expressionism. In several of the sketches, the hierarchical arrangement of the masses culminates in a centralized dome, which stabilizes the composition, creating a feeling of balanced movement rather than total calm (Fig. 8, *top*). In other sketches, however, this stability has vanished (Fig. 8, *bottom*). The crest of the dome appears to be propelled forward on the wavelike profile of the platform. This sense of motion in Mendelsohn's sketches appears to have had a dual origin in Kandinsky's paintings and Einstein's theory. In a letter to his wife in which he enclosed several of the drawings, Mendelsohn describes his interest in the depiction of motion. His language recalls relativity:

> The balance of movement – in mass and light – mass needs light, light moves mass – is reciprocal, parallel, complementary. The mass is clearly constructed, if the light balances the mass. Returning in conclusion to the contour! The light is properly distributed, when it equalizes the moving mass. Returning in conclusion to the representation! This is the general law of the art of expression.[57]

While it is not a coherent philosophical statement, relativity did not appear to be rational. A sleight of hand, or at least of words,

FIGURE 8

Erich Mendelsohn, sketches for an observatory project, 1917. (Source: Staatliche Museen zu Berlin, Kunstbibliothek.)

was in order. Throughout his career Mendelsohn would attempt an expressive use of curves to invoke the energy he saw as latent in architectural mass, substituting this implied movement for the impossibility of converting the material fact of the building into energy.

POSTWAR BERLIN

Despite Mendelsohn's emphasis on the individual, it was his defense of mechanization that separated him from his fellow Expressionists upon his return to Berlin on November 7, 1918.[58] He arrived just in time to witness a revolution that he welcomed. As early as August 1, 1914, when almost all of Germany was swept up in a patriotic frenzy, Mendelsohn had recognized "that we cannot win, but can only lose everything."[59] During the next several years, he frequently stated his opinion that Germany would lose the war and that its cataclysmic defeat would so discredit the monarchy and the military that their nationalistic politics and academic art would be replaced by a belief in the common humanity of all peoples and the espousal of a new artistic style. In his final wartime letters to his wife, written from the French front where he was frequently under fire, Mendelsohn at times expressed cynical doubts about what even a relatively liberal German politician such as Walter Rathenau could achieve and wondered whether the Allied leaders were really any better than the German generals and admirals they were defeating.[60]

Although he had lived in Berlin intermittently since 1914, Mendelsohn began to make contact with fellow architects in the city only after the November Revolution spurred the establishment, in late 1918, of groups of prorevolutionary artists and architects. He was a founding member of the Novembergruppe, which was initially dominated by painters, but was a latecomer to the more architecturally oriented Arbeitsrat für Kunst, whose leadership included Taut and Gropius.[61] Mendelsohn did not participate in the Arbeitsrat's *Exhibit of Unknown Architects* in April 1919, which focused on the mystical philosophy, crystalline forms, and new uses of glass favored by Taut and his followers, or in a third group, the Crystal Chain, whose members circulated letters and drawings in which they advocated a variety of fantastical antiurban utopias.[62] However, his new friendships with Hans Scharoun, Wassili Luckhardt, and Hermann Finsterlin kept Mendelsohn abreast of the Expressionist mainstream.[63]

Berlin offered Mendelsohn other opportunities to present his point of view. In the spring of 1919 he gave a series of eight lectures in Molly Philippson's parlor.[64] Better remembered is "The Problem of a New Architecture," the speech that he delivered at the opening of his exhibit at the Paul Cassirer Gallery and then repeated early in 1920 for the Arbeitsrat.[65] This text offers evidence of his resistance to the ideas and fantasies of his peers. Most distinctively, while other Expressionist architects believed that technology had been discredited by the emergence of so many new killing machines during the war, Mendelsohn retained an optimistic view of industry and its products.[66] Between the lecture's introduction and its conclusion, whose utopian language was obviously indebted to Taut, Mendelsohn voiced perhaps the most complete faith in forms derived from new materials heard in Berlin in 1919. In contrast to Taut, Mendelsohn combined visionary language not with fantastic drawings of cathedrals located high in the Alps or even on stars, but with illustrations of factories and of grain silos that he borrowed from the Werkbund's *Jahrbuch*.[67]

FIGURE 9

Erich Mendelsohn, project for an optical instruments factory, 1917. (Source: *Erich Mendelsohn: Das Gesamtschaffen des Architekten.*)

And what would this new architecture look like? The free forms allowed by reinforced concrete in particular were anticipated, Mendelsohn said, by van de Velde and Joseph Marie Olbrich. Both of these architects transformed the shape of entire buildings rather than focus on ornament, a mistake Mendelsohn believed Otto Wagner had made in his Schönbrunn station. Mendelsohn also used as an illustration two structures in Buffalo, New York, in which he saw the unification of form and structure. In the Washburn-Crosby grain silos and in Frank Lloyd Wright's Larkin Building, he argued, architectural space had broken free from the straightjacket of the classical grid. Mendelsohn was more critical of Behrens's AEG turbine factory, whose design he found to be too detached from the static realities of its materials. He concluded with his own design for an optical instruments factory, the most completely realized of the projects on display at the Cassirer Gallery (Fig. 9).[68] Of it, he said, in words that captured the purpose of his work to that point:

> Here is an attempt towards architectural independence and legitimacy in a self-sufficient expression of the formal realization of the functional requirements.
>
> The wall masses finally lose their outdated character as sides of a quadrangular box that have to be divided up somehow from the center of their plane: form itself has become function. . . .
>
> Whereas in the classical principle of support and load a quietness of massing is declared as the highest goal, here the building's massing itself has overcome gravity and inertia and has compressed all energy together into the center of its own spatial being.
>
> The undeveloped quality of these experiments may seem awkward now.

> The determination of their form appears as forced birth.
> Their plainness appears as a lack of sensuality.
> However, as this is the way towards a new architecture, their expression cannot be strong enough, the force of their countenance cannot be reckless enough.
> The cult of construction seems to be the only expression of determined honesty, its strictness merely introspection, its force expressing the will to create monuments.[69]

Although Mendelsohn's wartime drawings are usually interpreted as examples of visionary Expressionism, he believed them to be buildable.[70] Not yet having tested his designs against this standard, Mendelsohn had little sense of their limitations. Other German architects made their compromises with utopian visions only later, when they realized that they would have to turn to other forms to realize more limited social change, but Mendelsohn was already yearning to build. This early restraint, in which artistic effects were apparently inseparable from the actual demands of modern construction, and which would soon be harnessed to an explicit functionalism not yet visible in the drawings on display at the Cassirer Gallery, quickly reaped enormous rewards.

DESIGN AND CONSTRUCTION

In the spring of 1920 Mendelsohn began to work full-time on the design of the Einstein Tower. The path from the proposals Freundlich had made two years earlier to actual completion of the building was littered with obstacles. Many were the result of the economic collapse and political turmoil that had followed Germany's defeat in the war. Also not inconsequential was the daring nature of Mendelsohn's design. Accompanying the design's evolution, in which Mendelsohn was influenced by specific technical requirements, was the architect's increasingly sophisticated understanding of the limitations of experimental architectural representation. The task of converting the dynamism of his drawings into built form proved far more difficult than he had originally anticipated.

For nearly two months beginning in early May 1920, and aided by the staff of his small office, especially by a man named Kaprowski, Mendelsohn produced a steady stream of sketches, models, and working drawings for the Einstein Tower.[71] This intense burst of activity was initially sparked by a trip Mendelsohn and Freundlich made to meet with the staff of Carl Zeiss, the optical instruments firm in Jena that would manufacture most of the lenses and other scientific apparatus for the building.[72] Mendelsohn was responsible only for designing an appropriate shell for the Einstein Tower's technical equipment. Freundlich left to engineers, including two from Zeiss, the task of determining the detailed requirements which this equipment would impose upon the building's architecture.[73] The engineers and Freundlich, not the architect, were responsible for making such basic decisions as the height and width of the cupola housing the observatory, of the interior tower, and of the underground laboratory, as well as for details of the construction of this tower and the laboratory. This arrangement was typical of the agreements in which Germany's most talented prewar architects, individuals who often had little expertise in the details of industrial and scientific equipment, turned factories and other industrial structures into the most elegant and influential new buildings in all of Europe.[74]

Freundlich's original letter to his architect, written in 1918, revealed the influence upon his thinking of a series of solar telescopes built at the Mount Wilson Solar Observatory near Pasadena, California, under the supervision of George Ellery Hale. For two decades Hale, a pioneering astrophysicist, had experimented with new scientific equipment and the structures necessary to house it adequately. Before beginning work at Mount Wilson, he had commissioned and participated in the design of the Yerkes Observatory in Wisconsin for the University of Chicago. There he had been troubled by the way in which the mounting of the extremely powerful telescope precluded experimentation with rigidly mounted spectrographic instruments. He attempted to rectify this situation in the Snow telescope at Mount Wilson, completed in 1905. Here a coelostat (a pair of rotating mirrors) reflected light directly through the fixed telescope into a horizontal spectographic chamber. Difficulties with regulating temperature and controlling wind led to further experiments with increasingly tall towers and with the adjacent laboratory spaces. In 1908 Hale completed a sixty-foot tower directly adjacent to the Snow telescope, and for the first time he raised the coelostat high above the spectographic chamber, which he now located underground.

The drawings that Freundlich incorporated into his letter were apparently based on a photograph, which Hale published in 1907 (Fig. 10), of the Snow telescope's long shingled laboratory and this tower. Freundlich was also influenced by details of a second, taller, tower, completed in 1912, but already published in 1910. Here as in Freundlich's sketch, an open latticework of steel obviously supported the actual cupola, now completely enclosed so that the coelostat, too, could be kept at a constant temperature while light from the coelostat

FIGURE 10

Vertical coelostat and horizontal laboratory, Snow telescope, Mount Wilson, Pasadena, California, 1907. (Source: *Annual Report of the Director*, Mount Wilson Solar Observatory of the Carnegie Institute, 1907.)

reached the laboratory through a separate free-standing light well at the center. This one-hundred-fifty-foot tower telescope sat above a slightly larger underground chamber, lined in concrete, and still oriented vertically. Freundlich's major contribution was to place a *horizontally* oriented chamber under the tower. This combination would produce far more generous work and circulation spaces than existed at Mount Wilson.[75]

Whereas Freundlich's letter of 1918 was the basis for Mendelsohn's placement of the exterior and internal towers upon the bulk of the underground laboratory, it offered few clues about the arrangement of the underground spaces.[76] After returning from Jena, Mendelsohn experimented with a scheme in which the building resembled a tethered animal straining at its leash.[77] The form depicted and the manner of the depiction added to the excitement the drawing aroused. Reproached by an acquaintance of his wife who maintained that a new architecture was impossible because architects were tied to conventional representations of their buildings, Mendelsohn cited the Blue Rider painter Franz Marc as an appropriate model for a more dynamic approach to drafting.[78]

As Mendelsohn moved beyond this design, he began to pay more attention to mass instead of to line, which had initially bewitched him. He turned to using models to work out the details of the building, commissioning at least three in the first three weeks of June alone.[79] Only now did he begin to consider seriously what materials he would use for the tower's construction. He first expressed the hope, in May, that he might build the entire structure out of concrete.[80] A month later, Mendelsohn was still not sure that this would be possible, although he was enthusiastic about the sense of energy the use of concrete could bring to the building.[81] Growing out of his frustration with the paper architecture of his contemporaries, his new concentration on mass and construction culminated in his statement that "line must die, [it] must become the contour of the mass. . . . Architecture is domination of the mass."[82]

Among the solutions tried and quickly discarded in favor of the final design that emerged from two long days of experiments was a drawing in which the tower shaft was clearly articulated into four vertebrae, each with a shallow concavity in front (Fig. 11).[83] The energy of this drawing was evident more in the dynamic lines below and to the right of the tower than in the design for the building itself, where Mendelsohn definitively moved the office block to the rear.[84] The tower shaft had now become rectangular – a more economical solution – and its location between the entrance and the workrooms solved the problem of the building's terminus at the rear of the site. Mendelsohn wrote to his vacationing wife of his pride in the tension he had achieved between the two active forms, the entrance and workroom.[85] He also experimented with stabilizing the tower through the addition of tiered semicircular projections (Fig. 12). In the final design, he grafted a new tower onto the body of a much earlier scheme.[86] Besides being thicker, this tower differed from its immediate predecessors in the unarticulated rise of its front and rear elevations. In front, a concave apron separated two parallel stacks of four small side windows. The architect admitted that he liked the play of the shaft's inset corner windows against the "membrane" of the building's skin.[87] By the end of June only the task of developing new ground plans, and from them working drawings, remained.[88]

Throughout June, as he shifted his attention from the design itself to the completion of construction documents, Mendelsohn became increasingly frustrated at the difficulty of converting his visions into actual architecture.[89] This frustration was compounded by the difficulty of getting the design approved. Freundlich, whose enthusiasm seems never to have ebbed for an instant, was able to convince his board (of which Einstein was a member) to support Mendelsohn's design, but problems occurred with building inspectors.[90] Eventually, Freundlich had to appeal to the minister of education to gain consent for a preliminary version of the design.[91] The tactic was particularly risky, since at one point it appeared that the ministry might replace Mendelsohn with a government architect, and officials did not like the design even after they had been persuaded not to forbid it. It was

FIGURE 11

Erich Mendelsohn, Einstein Tower, perspective sketch, 1920. (Source: Staatliche Museen zu Berlin, Kunstbibliothek.)

FIGURE 12

Einstein Tower, perspective sketch, 1920. (Source: Staatliche Museen zu Berlin, Kunstbibliothek.)

also at this time that Mendelsohn was forced to raise even his most optimistic estimate of the building's cost to three hundred fifty thousand marks, a figure which assumed that most materials would be donated at cost.[92]

Construction of the Einstein Tower began in the summer of 1920, soon after Mendelsohn completed the necessary drawings.[93] The contractors were A. F. Bolle and Dyckerhoff-Widmann.[94] The exterior structure of the building was completed by October of the following year. The process was not without incident. Years later, Luise Mendelsohn recalled her nightmares that the building would slide down the hill.[95] In his description of his design her husband stated, "The architectural form meets the inner needs and adheres to the formal conditions of reinforced concrete."[96] Shaped by an aesthetic sense of the possibilities of monolithic reinforced concrete construction rather than a truly technological understanding of the material, the deliberately sculpted profiles of the Tower proved extremely difficult to build because of the complexity of the necessary formwork.[97] The situation was perhaps complicated by a postwar shortage of concrete, which Freundlich had hoped could be obtained largely through donations.[98] By the end of October 1920 economic considerations forced Mendelsohn to compromise.[99]

Reluctantly, Mendelsohn substituted stucco-covered brick for poured-on-site reinforced concrete for all the aboveground portions of the building except the entrance (which, with the basement laboratory, had already been successfully constructed out of concrete) and the cupola. He took care to achieve a uniform surface treatment between the two materials. But by this stage it was too late to alter the design to conform to the more mundane choice of material. Instead, the most important change Mendelsohn made to the design at this point was the addition of windows to the first floor workroom.[100] He was enormously disappointed. At the end of his life he wrote that he had mistakenly emphasized form over structure.[101] That he would build nothing else that remotely resembled the Einstein Tower can be attributed above all to the disillusionment produced by his new firsthand experience with on-site poured-concrete construction. Having already struggled with a variety of authorities while "giving birth" (his expression) to the building's design, Mendelsohn now found himself unable to redesign the tower shaft midway through construction to reflect the actual materials of which it was being built.[102]

Hyperinflation in postwar Germany raised the building's final cost from the 181,207 marks set for construction in a contract of July 6, 1920, to 850,000 marks, a figure that included Mendelsohn's fee of 65,000 marks.[103] Inflation also prevented the Carl Zeiss Company from installing until 1924 the equipment that the firm had donated at cost. The company began its work in the spring of that year and completed it in time for the December 6 dedication ceremony.[104]

Work on the interiors began in December 1921 and was completed by the following July.[105] Mendelsohn wrapped the walls of the ground floor workroom in a mixture of shelving and desks which, except for the taller bookcases inserted on either side of the rearmost window, included a continuous table-high work surface (Fig. 13). In

FIGURE 13

Einstein Tower, workroom, 1921–22. (Source: Staatliche Museen zu Berlin, Kunstbibliothek.)

the center of the room were a table and armchairs. Chairs of the same design sat in front of the desks.[106] All of the furniture was made of wood. Chair and table legs came to sharp points, and table and desk surfaces were also angled. Very simple to construct, these designs reflected the widespread influence upon German Expressionism of crystalline and Cubist forms.

Although the story of the Tower's design process necessarily chronicles the translation of unbuildably energetic drawings into more sedate construction documents, the degree to which the completed building conveyed the animation of his drawings remains one of Mendelsohn's greatest accomplishments. Like the buildings in the drawings, the Einstein Tower as built appeared almost able to stride across its site. Compared to the Tower, none of the largely paper schemes of the first years of the Weimar Republic came so close to the technological boundaries of construction or converted into the three dimensions of architecture so much of the dynamism which had become commonplace in the flat surfaces of Expressionist paintings.

A FUNCTIONING LABORATORY AND OBSERVATORY

On the most obvious level, the sophisticated requirements for housing the delicately calibrated instruments in the observatory and laboratory determined the Tower's general elevation and ground plan and exerted an important functional check on Mendelsohn's otherwise dynamic design.[107] Freundlich's disposition of the scientifically most significant parts of the building was, of course, determined by the nature of the experiments he planned to conduct within. In his theory of relativity Einstein calculated that as light travels it loses mass, a loss which can be measured through the increasing reddening of its rays when they are broken by a prism into a spectrum of colors. Proof of the redshift in the color of light would be proof of this hypothetical equivalency between mass and energy that lay at the core of relativity. In the Tower, Freundlich would be able to measure and compare the spectra of starlight and sunlight with that of two earthly light sources, an oven and an arc lamp.[108]

The building's first programmatic requirement was thus for an astronomical observatory through which sunlight and starlight could be captured. The revolving cupola could be positioned to face in any direction. Light fell through its opening onto the coelostat. The coelostat's two enormous mirrors could also each be positioned in a variety of ways. They directed light from the reflector downwards through lenses that were set parallel to the observatory's floor. The coelostat had to sit absolutely level on a stand impervious to any disorienting motion. A separate interior tower built of two independently constructed wooden lattices supported this extremely heavy piece of sensitive equipment. This tower rested in turn upon four concrete corner pillars connected by arched vaults. These pillars (*A*) were located in the underground laboratory immediately below the perimeter of the exterior tower (Figs. 14 and 15). The interior walls of this tower, like those of the observatory, were originally painted yellow.[109]

Light from the coelostat fell at the bottom of the tower into the underground laboratory where a mirror, which stood on an independently grounded pillar (*B*), deflected it perpendicularly into the spectographic chamber (*C*). This chamber – fifteen meters long, two meters high, and two meters wide – was thermally constant. All of its walls save the one connecting it to the laboratory were isolated by a one-meter gap (*D*) from the building's exterior walls. The chamber itself was wrapped in Torfoleum, an insulating substance. Three more pieces of spectographic equipment rested on freestanding concrete pillars (*E*, *F*, and *G*). The first, set into the wall between the laboratory and the spectographic chamber, held the aperture through which light passed into the chamber (*E*). The aperture was arranged

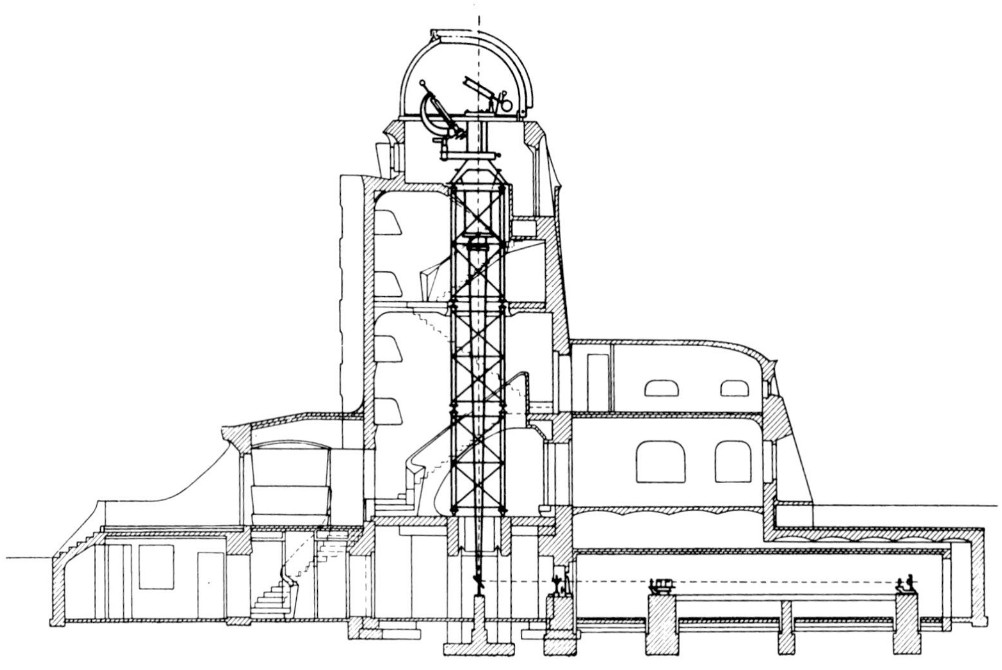

FIGURE 14

Einstein Tower, cross section. (Source: *Erich Mendelsohn: Das Gesamtschaffen des Architekten.*)

with the aid of prisms so that up to three light sources could pass through it simultaneously. Below this were additional apertures holding photographic emulsions onto which fell light that had been reflected back from the camera lenses of two pieces of equipment located within the chamber: the prism spectograph (*F*) three meters away and a gridded spectograph twelve meters away (*G*). The prism broke the light into spectra, allowing Freundlich to analyze the proportions of different colors within the light from different sources. The gridded spectograph enabled these fine distinctions to be measured.[110]

The two earthly light sources – the arc lamp (*H*) and the spectral oven (*I*) – were located in the laboratory just outside the spectographic chamber, one on each side of the mirror used to direct cosmic light sources into the chamber. This laboratory lay under and to the left and right of the tower shaft; the spectographic chamber began under the workroom and stretched back beyond the building's aboveground structure. The arc lamp was an especially complicated piece

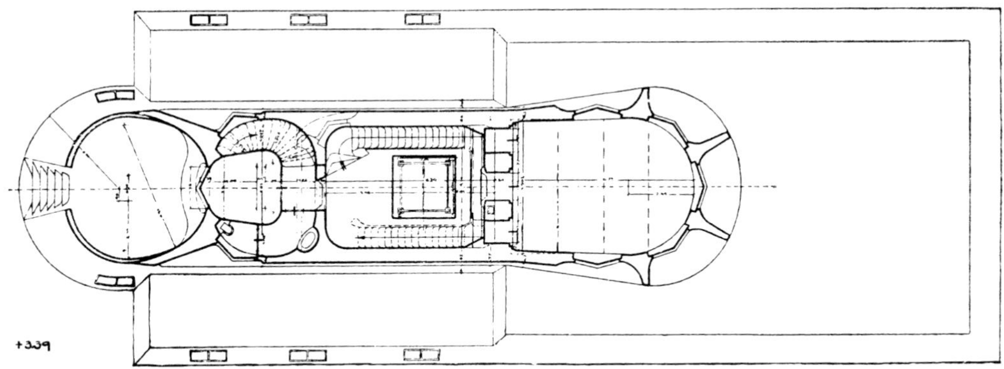

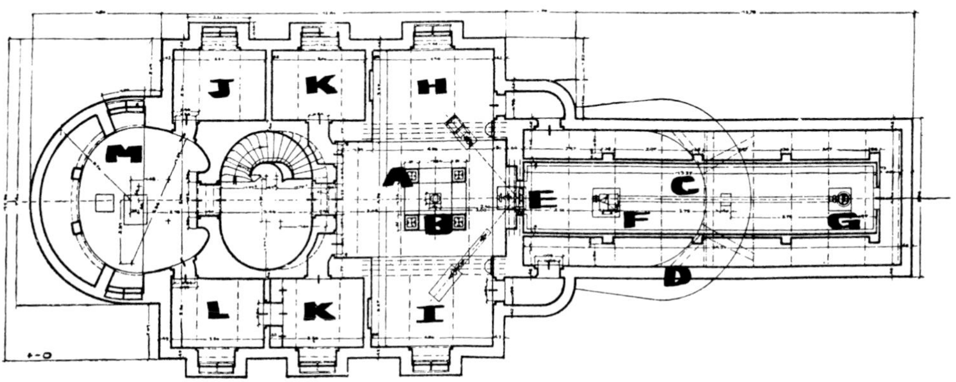

FIGURE 15

Einstein Tower, ground and basement floor plans. (Source: *Erich Mendelsohn: Das Gesamtschaffen des Architekten.*)

of equipment because it ran on a second type of electrical current. This current and the huge wattage required by the spectral oven were both supplied by generators located elsewhere on the grounds of the observatory, although a side room in the front of the Tower (*J*) did hold a high-voltage battery. Freundlich believed that the spectral oven, with a temperature of 3,000 degrees Celsius, produced light in conditions that reproduced those of the coldest stars. Despite these high temperatures a layer of cold, flowing water kept the exterior of the oven cool enough to touch.[111]

Other underground rooms included two equipment rooms flanking the staircase (*K*) and a darkroom in front, opposite the battery room (*L*). Under the Tower's entrance was the microphotometer room (*M*). This piece of machinery could enlarge the images of the spectra to the point where comparisons between them could be made. This room and each of the eight side chambers (the laboratory encompassed the rear chambers on each side) were lit by hooded windows. The rear six were cut into the building's turf-covered platform; the front two emerged directly from the concrete sides of the open porch. These interiors were painted red and black.[112]

Mendelsohn tightly bound the building's complex technical requirements to his vision of energetic form. Concrete buttresses gave the building much of its character. The depth of these buttresses created deep niches shading the angled windows of the workroom and the overnight room above it (Fig. 16). By pushing the two front corner supports for the tower shaft forward of its main body, Mendelsohn created lively corner windows. The curve between the two piers extended the internal buttress that separated the vestibule from the rest of the ground floor. Outcroppings on both sides of the building, one pair just below the roof of the vestibule and the second below that of the overnight room, served as drainspouts. For Mendelsohn, these forms corresponded as well to his personal understanding of a theory he believed was emblematic of what was best about the new German republic.

COMMEMORATING RELATIVITY

If Mendelsohn's stylistic predilections were one reason for the Einstein Tower's unusual appearance, another was his desire to mark relativity as an appropriate subject for a new kind of monument, one that would replace the commemoration of militarism and nationalism that had proliferated in Germany during the reign of Wilhelm II. By championing relativity in these terms Mendelsohn also indicated his support for a rational political democracy that could win international respect through scientific achievement. Although the building's association with Einstein's controversial theories drew widespread public attention to his design, Mendelsohn proved no more successful in communicating his complex allusions to the theories' workings than he had been in erecting it entirely out of reinforced concrete. Relativity appeared to many among its lay audience, admirers and detractors alike, to be irrational and thus in keeping with the growing appreciation of Expressionism, whose literature, theater, cinema, and art were now enjoyed by a far larger public than the Berlin and Munich café coteries engaged in their production before the war. Einstein, however, continued to insist that relativity had been a prod-

FIGURE 16

Einstein Tower, rear view. (Source: Staatliche Museen zu Berlin, Kunstbibliothek.)

uct of careful deductive reasoning, although not all of his fellow scientists viewed it in this way.[113] This debate encouraged Mendelsohn to maintain his tenuous position between the utopian speculation characteristic of many of his fellow Expressionists and Einstein's unwavering loyalty to scientific method.

For Mendelsohn this antirationalism never extended, as it did for so many of his contemporaries, to a *völkisch* political outlook in which racial ties were to transcend democratic political institutions. In June 1919 Mendelsohn spent a day in Potsdam discussing relativity with Freundlich and a Professor Rosenstein. Out of these conversations sprang a characteristic declaration of the relationship between matter and energy:

> Dispute between the three of us about unsuspected connections and congruences of energy and matter, which according to Einstein are not separate notions but the same source of life, however under different labels, from which can be inferred the congruence of the spiritual and the animalistic in contrast to the traditional separation of these notions. From this follows the probability of the freeing of energy through external factors – i.e., through experience – and not morphologically through hereditary and the autocracy of the power of blood.[114]

This passage is also important for the political implications of its pseudoscientific philosophy. The dichotomy between the spiritual and the animalistic was an Expressionist cliché. The need that Mendelsohn and his friends felt to establish grounds for removing the debate from the arena of Social Darwinist discussions of racial characteristics popularized by right-wing nationalist thinkers like Oswald Spengler was great enough to inspire the tenuous logic of the argument just outlined. The three men obviously hoped that recent events, especially the November Revolution, would produce real social as well as political change.

In the final decade before the outbreak of the First World War, German architects became increasingly interested in monumentality and in primeval form. In this spirit, Mendelsohn attempted in the Einstein Tower to create a mythic architectural symbol for the postwar era, replacing literal references to the historical past with organic evocations of a timeless harmony between art, science, and nature. The prewar turn toward monumentality had taken a variety of directions. Some architects, such as Behrens, revived the stark Paestum-style classicism introduced to Germany more than a century earlier by Friedrich Gilly.[115] Others, such as Fischer's former assistant Paul Bonatz, designed unornamented buildings inspired by even more archaic architecture, the buildings of ancient Egypt and Mesopotamia.[116] Mendelsohn carried his early interest in monumentality over into his design for the Einstein Tower where, however, he substituted a Jugendstil-inspired organicism for references to ancient architecture.

No one served this prewar taste for monumentality more successfully than did Bruno Schmitz, who built a succession of state-sponsored behemoths. In 1913 the last and largest of these piles of reinforced concrete and roughhewn stone – the Battle of the Nations Monument in Leipzig (Fig. 17) – was finally dedicated. In this, the most pretentious of all Wilhelmine structures, Schmitz applied a shallow Assyrian-inspired style of carving to the heavily rusticated masonry popularized by the American architect Henry Hobson Richardson.[117] For the boldly simple geometries favored by Richardson, however, Schmitz substituted a far more complex manipulation of site and mass, one which made his building appear to spring from deep within the earth.

Although Mendelsohn deplored all that the Battle of the Nations Monument stood for, he recognized the effectiveness of many of Schmitz's formal decisions. Schmitz's siting was especially masterful. The building was deeply rooted in, yet rose triumphantly out of, the surrounding landscape. The architect carved its forecourt deep into

FIGURE 17

Bruno Schmitz, Battle of the Nations Monument, Leipzig, Germany, 1898–1913. (Source: *Deutsche Bauzeitung*, 1913.)

the earth and prominently defined the resulting space by flanking it with tall grass-covered bunkers. These extended beyond the rear of the monument to form a meadow raised far above grade, from which in turn sprung the side and rear facades of the tower itself. Mendelsohn adapted some of the same strategies for the Tower. Although it was not sunken, his entrance conveyed a strong sense of enclosure that captured the flavor of Schmitz's forecourt, and the concrete-framed windows of the underground laboratory peeked out of a raised grass-covered platform that – as did the one in Leipzig – almost literally anchored the building in the surrounding landscape. Because this platform sheltered the laboratory, it, too, stretched beyond the rear of the aboveground workroom to the limits of the extruded underground space.

At the same time, Mendelsohn's desire to represent relativity architecturally as well as to celebrate it led him to Futurism. Throughout the design process he attempted to animate the Tower, giving it the appearance of a body moving through space. This was easier to achieve in perspective sketches than in an actual building, but the completed Tower nonetheless succeeded in conveying the appearance of movement. Most importantly, its windswept shape gave the sense

FIGURE 18

Umberto Boccioni, *Unique Forms of Continuity in Space*, 1913. Bronze (cast 1931), 43⅞ × 15¾". The Museum of Modern Art, New York. Acquired through the Lilie P. Bliss Bequest. (Source: © The Museum of Modern Art, New York.)

of a body in motion shedding mass. This effect was strongest in the profiles of the four pairs of side windows cut into the tower shaft, which sloped down and back as if carved by wind or water. To achieve the illusion of motion, Mendelsohn seems to have turned to Futurist works such as Umberto Boccioni's *Unique Forms of Continuity in Space*, an exploration of the human figure moving through time and space sculpted in 1913 (Fig. 18).[118] For Mendelsohn, the "dynamic" (a word Boccioni himself frequently used) quality of the curved, and apparently windswept, figure must have recalled Obrist and Kandinsky. And, although Boccioni based the work on a study of time and space rather than of nuclear physics, its form was also suited for communicating Mendelsohn's message that the energy needed to propel motion comes from the loss of mass.[119]

This dynamism was for Mendelsohn indivisible from an organic interpretation of technology influenced by his understanding of relativity. In a 1923 lecture in which he described the Einstein Tower as "a clear architectural organism," Mendelsohn also stated:

> Ever since science has come to realize that the two concepts matter and energy, formerly kept rigidly apart, are merely different states of the same primary element, that in the order of the world nothing takes place without relativity to the cosmos without relationship to the whole, the engineer has abandoned the mechanical theory of dead matter and has reaffirmed his allegiance to nature. . . . The machine, till now the pliable tool of lifeless exploitation, has become the constructive element of a new, living organism.[120]

These views led Mendelsohn to make the Tower's design in part an analogy between a particular industrial technology – reinforced concrete – and the human body.[121] The form of the tower shaft resembled human vertebrae, and the imagery worked on several levels. First, it represented the truth of reinforced concrete construction in which a steel frame or skeleton supported and stiffened the concrete flesh. Second, Mendelsohn was able to depict the stresses shaping the form that he had chosen (in this case, the compression and tension of both reinforced concrete and the human body). For him, this process was not an arbitrary decorative strategy, but was instead indivisible from the actual demands made upon the building by its construction. Third, the intricate curved pieces of the human spine corresponded to Mendelsohn's aesthetic taste and to Jugendstil precedent. Finally, the design gave the building a human presence that could arouse the empathy of viewers.

RECEPTION AND REPUTATION

In 1921 the Einstein Tower was the most startling new building in Germany. Because of its association with relativity and its unusual appearance it quickly became one of the most famous buildings of its day. Like everything connected with Einstein in the early 1920s it attracted enormous publicity.[122] This publicity, which may have been sought by Freundlich but apparently not by Mendelsohn, provided many with their first glimpse of a new style of architecture, a style that was as astonishingly antitraditional as any political, scientific, or artistic development of the day of which they were aware.

Familiar to the German public at large and in architectural circles abroad, the Tower served, throughout the 1920s, as a lightning rod in discussions about what contemporary architecture should look like and, in particular, about what balance should be struck between individual expression and functional form. While many had faith in the Tower's modernity, others – including to some degree its own architect – came to believe that the Tower embodied the hopes of only the immediate postwar years, and they prepared to turn toward a less obviously allegorical architecture.

Einstein himself flattered Mendelsohn when, in a one-word review of the Tower, he labeled it "organic."[123] A magazine article of 1926 described the modernity of Mendelsohn's design to a lay public as a new form made out of new materials.[124] The reception of the building among architects and architectural critics was much more varied than this easy acceptance of Mendelsohn's aims. A photograph of the Tower was first published in the Dutch architecture magazine *Wendingen* in October 1920, just after construction began.[125] During the next decade it was featured in many of Europe's leading architecture magazines and included in surveys of modern architecture published on both sides of the Atlantic.[126] Discussion centered on the issue of whether the Tower was indeed new and, if it was, if this was what the new architecture should look like. Despite Mendelsohn's failure to construct the entire Tower out of concrete, it was also included in surveys devoted to that material. In this context, the architect won high praise for his convincingly monolithic approach to the material.[127]

Mendelsohn's Jugendstil sources were recognized by a number of commentators.[128] Others associated its unusual form with the popular occultlike view of science characteristic of many projects by members of the Crystal Chain rather than with the spirit of scientific inquiry of the experiments conducted within it. Hermann Scheffauer, for example, wrote:

> The building, mysterious even in its outward aspects, attains to something of an esoteric scientific uncanniness within. We are in the brilliant crypt of the modern alchemists and sorcerers, in an arcanum of subtle discovery, one of the radiant poles where the ultimate mysteries of the cosmos, of time, of space, and of the eternal forces are being weighed, analyzed, and interpreted.[129]

Although in his 1919 lecture Mendelsohn had attempted through frequent references to modern machinery and technology to distance himself from this mystical attitude toward science, throughout the

1920s both champions and detractors of the Einstein Tower saw the observatory as characteristic of this immediate postwar preference for individual expression at the expense of function.[130] Behrens, who was now experimenting with neo-Gothic forms, commented along these lines in a lecture delivered in 1924 in which he labeled the Tower romantic and fantastical.[131] Five years later, Karl Weidle published a book entitled *Goethehaus und Einsteinturm* in which he described the Tower as the epitome of architectural individuality.[132] In 1930 Paul Schmidt, citing this element of architectural fantasy, called the Tower "a final tribute to the emotional and chaotic time of the revolution, a direct transfer of the dynamic principle to crystalline structure, without the intermediary architectural methods."[133]

The building was lauded by some who were uncomfortable with the more overtly industrial architecture adopted during the midtwenties for striking the proper balance between individuality and function. These admirers praised the Tower as the embodiment of modernity. Arthur Segal expressed his appreciation of it in a 1924 letter to Mendelsohn in which he also attacked more extreme forms of functionalism.[134] Walter Müller-Wulkow, in his photographic surveys of German architecture published in the twenties, noted the Tower's "organic simplicity" and its combination of functionalism and powerfully felt sensualism.[135] And in commentary written from the same aesthetic position, Fritz Hellwag in 1926 equated the modernity of the Einstein Tower with relativity itself.[136]

As the decade progressed, the building was, however, increasingly criticized by proponents of the more sober, or *sachlich*, architecture which began to replace the most visionary aspects of Expressionism. These critics generally based their attacks upon photographs that offered little insight into the Tower's use and were concerned almost exclusively with the building's apparently irrational design. The first and most bitter of these attacks was written in 1923 by Paul Westheim, the editor of *Das Kunstblatt* and one of Germany's most radical and perceptive art critics. Westheim, an opponent of Expressionism, condemned the Tower for its monumentality and grouped it with with the reactionary imperial-era architecture of the Battle of the Nations Monument and the Berlin Cathedral. He dismissed Mendelsohn's attempts at symbolism as pure advertising – advertising, he wrote, not for the observatory, but for Mendelsohn himself.[137]

The criticism of the Tower as an extreme building detached from considerations of program and construction wounded its architect, who thought of himself at the time he designed it to be more interested in exactly these issues than were most of his colleagues. However, just two years after the building was completed and one year before it was dedicated, Mendelsohn admitted that it was not a purely functional design.[138] He must have been disappointed that although the critics recognized the Tower's monumentality and were willing to equate its form with Einstein's equally unsettling ideas, no one had noticed the degree to which he had attempted to represent that theory. Moreover, the Tower's style, which had proven less responsive to the capabilities of reinforced concrete construction than Mendelsohn had hoped, quickly appeared dated. The Tower, through which its architect had intended to express modern science and technology, became identified instead merely with Expressionism. The liberation from traditional architecture that Taut and his circle had provided Mendelsohn had in the end constrained his message. Just as Expressionist architecture vanished into history without realizing its vision of a reformed society, Mendelsohn had been encouraged to unleash a form whose novelty came to triumph over its meaning. The Einstein Tower thus has endured as an exemplar of an innovative but often irrational style rather than as the embodiment of the theory it was intended to serve.

Mendelsohn's innovative responses through dynamic functionalism to motion, light, and space – the architectural issues that he believed were affected by relativity – kept him, however, in the forefront of modern architecture throughout the years of the Weimar Republic. Never after the Tower did his forms appear fantastic; indeed, he became one of the first architects to employ industrial imagery to signify the functionalist approach that few had recognized in the Tower. Ultimately, dynamic functionalism proved uniquely suited to the expression of capitalism's mix of efficient production and glamorous consumption. The Tower's inventive silhouette was tied to specifications established by engineers, who controlled the dimensions of its tower and planned the basement laboratory. So, too, did Mendelsohn's own understanding of monumentality and relativity produce in these commercial settings lively forms inseparable from very different functions: shopwindows, night lighting, and staircases.

Mendelsohn's success in this arena arose from his ability not only to fulfill a commercial patron's program but also to represent it metaphorically, a synthesis he first achieved in the Einstein Tower. The functional details of the Einstein Tower limited its architect's formal choices and established tight boundaries around what has too often been seen as merely eccentric architecture. In particular, his understanding of relativity encouraged him to believe that the same unstable plastic forms that proved commercially popular arose directly from scientific principles. At a time when many of his colleagues were moving toward austerity as a metaphor for rationalism, dynamic functionalism enabled Mendelsohn instead to celebrate modernity through the complex individuality of his commissions.

2

"RHYTHMS OF MOTORS AND SPEED OF LIFE"

THE APPEAL OF FOREIGN MODERNISMS

THE Einstein Tower was an unmistakably German building. The confluence of artistic, technological, scientific, and political forces that shaped Mendelsohn's first major commission could have occurred in no other country. Furthermore, Expressionist architecture was an almost entirely German phenomenon. However, as citizens of a nation widely viewed as an international pariah, many Expressionists sought to ally themselves with other Europeans who were inventing architectural forms inspired by nonrepresentational painting and by machine-age technology and imagery. At the same time, the German public became fascinated by the alternate models of modernity offered by the United States and the new Union of Soviet Socialist Republics. Indeed, Germans often viewed the very process of modernization as, for better or worse, one of internationalization.

Mendelsohn anticipated these developments. He traveled widely during the twenties. Initially he seems to have been searching for the sense of security and community that eluded him at home. Uncertain during the early years of the decade about economic and political conditions in Germany, he considered emigrating either to the British Mandate of Palestine (now Israel) or to the United States.[1] With the exception of the American Frank Lloyd Wright, Mendelsohn felt closest to those foreign architects who were also Jewish: Henricus Wijdeveld and Michel de Klerk in the Netherlands, Ely Jacques Kahn in the United States, and El Lissitzky in the Soviet Union. This must have helped Mendelsohn compensate for his failure to establish similar ties with the other leading German architects of his generation. In the absence of such ties, the key to his continued professional success lay in his ability to shape the German public's image of foreign modernity through his writing and buildings.

Palestine, which Mendelsohn visited in 1923, almost certainly had the most profound personal effect upon him, and his other destinations included cities as varied as London and Paris, Copenhagen and Cairo, Athens and Saint Moritz. But it was Mendelsohn's experiences in the Netherlands, the United States, and the Soviet Union that had the greatest impact upon his architecture. The architecture of these three countries most closely dovetailed with the popular images of modernity he would manipulate so deftly.[2] Mendelsohn lectured in the Netherlands in 1921 and 1923, at a time when recent Dutch architecture had considerable influence in Germany (the Dutch had been neutral during the war, and construction had continued in the Netherlands throughout the 1910s). In 1924 Mendelsohn sailed to the United States. He was among the first in a long line of German architects and critics after the armistice to report back on what many viewed as a look at their not entirely welcome future. In the Netherlands Mendelsohn had focused on stylistic differences between two rival groups of modern Dutch architects; in the United States he faced, for the first time, the conflicts between the competing aesthetics of modern production and modern consumption. The following year, Mendelsohn embarked upon the first of his three visits to the Soviet Union, having received the first significant Soviet commission bestowed upon a foreigner. In the United States Mendelsohn had been troubled by the persistence of historicism; he found, in the Soviet Union, the existence of a modern style divorced from economic reality just as unsatisfying.

During the 1920s, all of Mendelsohn's most important statements about architecture were either delivered abroad or prompted by his encounters with foreign modernity. The lecture he gave in the Netherlands in 1923 is the single most significant statement of his theoretical position, and his books, inspired by his travels to America and the Soviet Union, established him as an expert on issues – especially on the diverse architectural images of modernity – that were as important to potential clients as they were to his fellow architects. A survey of Mendelsohn's experiences in the Netherlands, the United States, and the Soviet Union and of the writings that resulted from these experiences is therefore essential for understanding the impact of these countries upon his built work.

The tensions between the dynamic and the functional aspects of modern life and of the architecture which claimed to mirror that life

FIGURE 19

Michel de Klerk, Eigen Haard housing and community post office, Amsterdam, the Netherlands, 1917–20. (Source: J. G. Wattjes, *Niew Nederlandsche Bouwkunst.*)

were as obvious in a German metropolis like Berlin as they were anywhere else in the world. Nevertheless, Mendelsohn's attempts to come to terms with modernism's inherent contradictions were directly inspired by his encounters with foreign cities and their architecture. Of course, he was also influenced by his situation in Germany. But Mendelsohn set forth his theoretical position in written texts that either were prepared for foreign audiences or described what he had seen abroad. Mendelsohn almost always began by condemning extreme examples of the direction in which he himself would soon be moving. His rhetoric varied as much as did his architectural style, which was always in flux as its creator adjusted to his changing perception of the world around him.

AMONG FRIENDS: LECTURE TOURS IN THE NETHERLANDS

The closest international equivalent to German Expressionist architecture could be found in the Netherlands, especially in the work of the Amsterdam School. Grouped around Michel de Klerk, these architects integrated Dutch vernacular references and craft techniques into designs for enormous model apartment buildings for the working class (Fig. 19).[3] At the same time, other Dutch artists and architects were among the first to explore the implications for architecture of rigidly rectilinear abstract painting and thus prepare the path many German architects of Mendelsohn's generation would take when they began to move beyond Expressionism (Fig. 20).[4] By 1923 Mendelsohn, who had been initially sympathetic to the Amsterdam School, also became intrigued by the group's De Stijl counterpart.

FIGURE 20

J. J. P. Oud, factory project for Purmerend, the Netherlands, 1919. (Source: Wattjes, *Niew Nederlandsche Bouwkunst.*)

The Dutch debate was largely over an appropriate formal language, but for Mendelsohn it also served as a vehicle for his own struggle to define the way in which industrialization should be represented architecturally.

Mendelsohn first came to the attention of the Dutch in 1919, when Henricus Wijdeveld, the editor of *Wendingen*, a lavishly produced journal closely identified with the Amsterdam School, visited and was impressed by his exhibition at the Paul Cassirer Gallery in Berlin. The next year Mendelsohn was the subject of an entire issue, which included an article by J. F. Staal, another one of the school's most prominent adherents.[5] It would be four more years before Mendelsohn would attract comparable attention at home. In the meantime, Wijdeveld invited him to lecture in the Netherlands on the problem of a new architecture. In March 1921 Mendelsohn delivered in Rotterdam the talk he had first given in 1919 at the opening of his Cassirer Gallery exhibition. He also visited Amsterdam.[6]

Because his wife accompanied him and Mendelsohn had no need to describe the trip in letters home to her, his first reactions to the Netherlands remain unrecorded. But in a letter to Wijdeveld the following summer Mendelsohn made clear his affection for that architect, his admiration for de Klerk, and the importance to him of the Amsterdam School.[7] He also complained about the pretentiousness of architectural circles in Berlin, where he felt he was not understood. Admitting that the war and revolution had had a positive effect on his art and on architecture in general, Mendelsohn nonetheless expressed reservations about more recent developments. He was, however, glad to have so much work (he listed four projects, including the Steinberg, Hermann factory). And, equally importantly, he believed that in Amsterdam he had finally found congenial colleagues who grasped what it was he was doing. In Amsterdam, he wrote, architects understood the proper relationship between reality and art and the struggle to create form.

By 1923 those German architects who had espoused Expressionism immediately after the war were beginning to embrace more pragmatic approaches, ones in which utopian aims remained but were subordinated to an acceptance – indeed, a celebration – of modernity. In conjunction with the stabilization of the German economy in 1924, this shift created a situation in which the issues dividing the architectural community became not whether their work should represent modernity but how. While previously Mendelsohn had been more interested in function than many of his colleagues, now it was his dynamism that distinguished him from their often more rational approaches to a society whose most prominent characteristic appeared to be mass production. Slow to embrace the implications of this reading of modernity, Mendelsohn remained dedicated to finding ways in which new materials and construction techniques could be used to represent the dynamism of contemporary life.

The Einstein Tower and the buildings that followed had by 1923 made Mendelsohn one of Germany's foremost modern architects. In comparison, Taut's star had faded, and Gropius was just beginning to emerge from his temporary postwar eclipse. Poelzig and Behrens, although respected as architects, were also older than Mendelsohn and more conservative. Despite his prominence, Mendelsohn felt threatened by the new interest in industrialization. At first he saw it not as stimulating the creation of bold expressions of dynamic functionalism – although he would eventually use it in this way – but as an unwelcome return to a kind of formalism in which the influence of painting triumphed over that of construction, whereas he believed construction should be the primary focus of architects. His concern was awakened by his visit to Weimar in August 1923 for the opening of the Bauhaus exhibition *Art and Technology – The New Unity*, and he expressed it in a lecture he delivered in Amsterdam that fall entitled "The International Conformity of the New Architectural Thought, or Dynamic and Function." This lecture contains Mendelsohn's most complete statement of dynamic functionalism, which he advocated as an expression of modern life to be rooted directly in the client's program and the means of construction.[8]

The 1923 exhibition of work produced at the Bauhaus since its founding in 1919 was accompanied by a smaller exhibit of international architecture and by speeches and statements in which members of the faculty, led by Gropius, enunciated their vision of the school and of the direction that the arts should take in an industrialized society. Mendelsohn was particularly disturbed by Gropius's call, in an attempt to make architecture responsive to the conditions of industrial production, for standardized building units, which Mendelsohn interpreted as a return to the controversial position espoused by Muthesius at the 1914 meeting of the Werkbund in Cologne.[9] There Mendelsohn had sided with van de Velde, as had Gropius. Nine years later, Gropius had changed his mind; Mendelsohn had not.

One cannot exaggerate the impact that the increasing rationalization of mass production had upon Germany's cultural life by the mid-1920s, especially as the country's industry rebounded from conditions at the end of the war. Henry Ford's assembly line methods were introduced into German factories, often accompanied by infusions of American capital. Taylorization – the redesign to maximize efficiency of movements made by factory workers – captured the imagination not just of industrialists but of all Germans interested in achieving a rational society and reviving the country's depressed economy. As slogans for a new economic order, efficiency and rationalism became heard far beyond factory walls to justify all types of cultural modernism as well as business monopolies and their activities. Mendelsohn soon shared Gropius's enthusiasm for these pervasive images of modernity, although he would always prefer to stress their dynamic implications over their rational implementation. In 1923, however, Mendelsohn was particularly distressed to hear the call for standardization in association with what he condemned explorations of pure form.

Gropius's exhibition of international architecture attempted to prove, by gathering together apparently similar buildings and projects from all over Europe, the existence of formal prototypes for a new mass-produced architecture. Although he included Mendelsohn, he focused on Le Corbusier and the Dutch architects associated with De Stijl, who saw architecture largely as the extension into three dimensions of explorations into the nature of space that had been initiated in abstract painting and studied by Bauhaus students in their preliminary course.[10] Mendelsohn, suspicious by 1919 of the validity of any architecture derived from painting, despite his own ties to the Blue Rider group, insisted that function must grow out of the demands of program and construction rather than painting or mass production.[11] He must have been particularly disturbed by the rejection of the curvilinear plastic forms so easily realized in his favorite building material, reinforced concrete, in favor of an apparently more "rational" rectilinearity inspired by a view of industry that did not attempt to represent its dynamism.

Mendelsohn's contradictory attitude toward the new direction of the Bauhaus crystallized during a lecture he attended in Weimar by the Dutch architect Johannes Jacobus Peter Oud.[12] Oud, who had been invited to speak because his architectural style appeared to correspond with the formal unity sought by Gropius, delivered an overview of contemporary architecture in the Netherlands in which he must have contrasted the Rotterdam-based De Stijl architects, whom he led, with the Amsterdam School. Although Mendelsohn disagreed with Gropius, he had been impressed by Oud's buildings. He realized that he had as much in common with Oud as he did with his friends in Amsterdam. Yet Oud's extreme theoretical position clearly exasperated him. In working out in his own mind his place within this debate, Mendelsohn arrived at an important statement of his own beliefs as they related to those of both his Dutch and German colleagues.

Oud had probably attended Mendelsohn's 1921 lecture in Rotterdam, and he had worked for three months for Theodor Fischer. But no evidence of any contact between the two architects can be found until their meeting at the Bauhaus exhibition in Weimar. In 1916 Oud, who was three years younger than Mendelsohn, had met Theo van Doesburg, who included him the next year among the founding members of De Stijl, a circle of Dutch artists and architects grouped loosely around a journal of the same name edited by van Doesburg.[13] Although by the time of his Weimar lecture he had broken with van Doesburg, Oud remained De Stijl's leading architect. Furthermore, as city architect of Rotterdam Oud had ample opportunity to put his ideas into practice.

Oud's lecture prompted the most famous remarks of Mendelsohn's entire career. In an analysis of the Dutch architectural scene and his response to it, Mendelsohn wrote his wife:

> Amsterdam is betraying the faith; it abandons the new discoveries in favor of overdrawn, emotional, romantic irrelevancies and loses itself in variegated modern trifles. Only what is simple can be understood collectively: what is individualistic remains, in the last analysis, meaningless. Here is where I seem to detect an understandable tactical error on the part of Oud. Oud is, to borrow Gropius' language, functional. Amsterdam is dynamic.
>
> A union of both concepts is conceivable, but cannot be discerned in Holland. The first puts reason foremost – perception through analysis. The second, unreason – perception through vi-

> sion. Analytic Rotterdam rejects vision. Visionary Amsterdam does not understand analytic objectivity.
>
> Certainly the primary element in architecture is function, but function without sensual contributions remains mere construction.
>
> More than ever do I stand by my program of reconciliation. Both are necessary. Both must find one another.
>
> If Amsterdam goes a step further towards ratio, and Rotterdam does not freeze up, they may still unite. Otherwise both will be destroyed, Rotterdam by the deadly chill in its veins, Amsterdam by the fire of its own dynamism.[14]

Refraining from an outright attack on Gropius, Mendelsohn found it easier to take a middle position in a debate between his old friends in Amsterdam and Oud, whom he greatly admired, than to participate directly in its German counterpart.

Within a week after hearing the Dutch architect's lecture Mendelsohn began to correspond with Oud. In his first letter, Mendelsohn repeated verbatim parts of the earlier letter to his wife. In it he toned down the disagreement between the Amsterdam architects and Oud, whose architecture he recognized as more up-to-date than de Klerk's. He pointed out that Oud, visiting a Germany torn by political conflict, must have found honest people espousing the causes of both sides. Similarly he himself could, he claimed, as a German, look dispassionately at the struggle between Dutch architectural factions and spot the appeal of an intermediate position between the two extremes.[15] In a second letter, Mendelsohn drew subtle distinctions between Oud's condemnation of Expressionism, with which he agreed, and his own continued faith that the representation of movement was not a contradiction of function but an architectural expression of "the revolutionary play of the forces of tension and compression in steel."[16]

Although Oud remained unconvinced, this letter contains the seeds of a lecture that Mendelsohn delivered in Amsterdam, the Hague, and Rotterdam in November 1923. This tour was directly inspired by his desire to see Oud again and to visit his buildings. No doubt Mendelsohn's existing connections in Amsterdam also played a role in its organization. That December, excerpts from Mendelsohn's lecture were published by the *Berliner Tageblatt* in conjunction with the completion of Mossehaus, giving Mendelsohn a German audience for his remarks.[17] In his lecture, Mendelsohn criticized the formalism featured in Gropius's exhibit. Although he acknowledged that geometry was the wellspring of all architectural creation, he did not believe that it alone offered a sufficient basis for architecture. He took aim at the designs by Le Corbusier, Ludwig Mies van der Rohe, Farkas Molnar, and Karl Lönberg-Holm favored by Gropius. He offered instead Gropius's own Chicago Tribune Tower entry, de Klerk's Vrijheidslaan housing, Wijdeveld's Volkstheater project, Vladimir Tatlin's Monument to the Third International, and his own Mossehaus and Weichmann Silk Store as examples that he believed exhibited organic rather than analytic forms and captured the dynamism of modern life. In a second alternative to Gropius's position, Mendelsohn espoused dynamic compositions created out of industrially produced materials as the means by which industrial processes should be integrated into modern architecture. Characteristically, he proposed that the properties of steel and reinforced concrete rather than the assembly line should determine the forms of the new architecture. Through the transformation of engineering to produce organic forms in harmony with the natural laws of physics, architecture, Mendelsohn claimed, could achieve the spiritual fulfillment that remained Gropius's ultimate goal.[18]

Mendelsohn sought not only to reconcile dynamics and function but also to cast the machine in a positive light. "The machine," he wrote, "previously the obedient handyman of deadly exploitation, becomes a constructive element of a new living organism." At the same time, he believed that the chaotic forces unleashed by industrialization could be contained. He declared that the task of a restructured postwar Europe was "to sustain the multiple correlations between a growing population and increased production, between industrialization and rising consumption, to regulate these correlations and to master their effects."[19] His conclusion balanced reason and vision:

> It is our task to respond to turmoil with prudence, to exaggeration with simplicity, to insecurity with clear rules, to rediscover the elements of energy in destruction and to form out of them a new whole. Seize, construct, and convert the earth! Form the world that is waiting for you! Form the functions of its reality with the dynamics of your blood – raise its functions to dynamic transcendency. Make it as simple and secure as the machines, as clear and bold as the construction. Create art out of valid assumptions and intangible space out of mass and light. But do not forget that individual creation is to be understood only within the context of the phenomenon of time. Creativity is bound within the relativity of time as the present and future are bound within the relativity of history.[20]

Mendelsohn's lecture revealed the continuity in his architectural theory from the 1910s into his stylistic experimentation of the early 1920s. His interpretation of relativity and faith in the expression of the statics of materials accorded with positions he had outlined in the teens, as did his conviction that the aesthetics of painting had little place in architecture. Architecture, Mendelsohn believed, should translate technical conditions into spatial creations and infuse geometric relationships with emotion. As had his lecture in 1919, his 1923 speech again signaled his independence from the mainstream of architectural innovation, but although his new viewpoint remained at odds with that of many of his modernist colleagues, two important voices quickly echoed key aspects of it. In 1925 and 1926 respectively, the architect Hugo Häring and the critic Adolf Behne published theoretical statements in defense of an organic, curvilinear approach to architecture. This approach to form was predicated on functionalism rather than on industrialized construction methods and thus different from the more Platonic approach generated by Gropius's interest in standardization.[21]

COLORED LIGHTS AND CHAOS: AMERICA

Architects and lay audiences, avant-garde and establishment, French and Germans, all were united during the 1920s by their fascination with America. Photographs of New York City skyscrapers filled the European popular press. Jazz wafted out of cabarets. Charlie Chaplin smiled, tripped, and danced across movie theater screens. New York's towers, like the Ford motor car, which was another popular symbol of America, epitomized the American technological prowess that all Europeans recognized had been a key component of the Allied victory in 1918. Jazz, that strange, syncopated music, evoked a world shorn of tired European precedents.[22]

In Germany as elsewhere in Europe, *Amerikanismus* also had an economic component. After the war, the direct economic impact of American aid fostered German interest in the rational organization of business and industry and in the possible cultural applications of industrial models of production. By 1924 the German economy was tightly bound to its American counterpart through the Dawes Plan.[23] Providing Germany with a measure of economic stability, this infusion of dollars spurred a five-year building boom. The emerging German mass culture, centered on radio broadcasting and cinema, also had ties to its American counterparts. Pro-American liberals in

Germany saw American technology, coupled with the high wages paid automobile workers by Henry Ford, as a blueprint for a new social order in which a general improvement in living conditions would decrease class tensions. For almost every German the United States seemed the prototype of modern civilization, and debates about the inevitable modernization of Germany often centered on the appropriateness of American models.[24]

Itself a young nation, Germany had been interested in America long before the war and that captivation had extended to architecture. Mark Twain compared Chicago to Berlin, two centers of industry and commerce that grew rapidly during the last third of the nineteenth century, and a number of designs by Henry Hobson Richardson and his imitators had been published in the *Deutsche Bauzeitung*, where they were often praised for their rational planning.[25] On the eve of the war, the Wasmuth publishing house issued its two famous editions of Frank Lloyd Wright's work, and Gropius contributed a sheaf of photographs to the Werkbund *Jahrbuch* of American grain silos and factories constructed out of reinforced concrete.[26] Prewar German fascination with American architecture was often the extension of a more general German interest in cultural origins, the primeval, and the primitive. Here the New World was interpreted as the modern equivalent of a mythic Egypt or Sumeria.[27]

The interest of prewar German architects in American technology and architectural style was reawakened following the armistice. The architects were particularly curious about the American metropolis, to which they looked for solutions to issues of urban development in the age of the automobile, and in rationalized American building methods. Wright's buildings were widely regarded as prototypes for a more sedate post-Expressionist architecture, and like the public at large, German architects held skyscrapers in awe.[28] Mendelsohn shared in this general enthusiasm, and his lectures included several stereotypical images of America: Wright's Larkin Building, grain silos in Buffalo, a Ford factory, and a view of Lower Manhattan. But as Mendelsohn was to discover, America's architectural culture was not limited to such easily appreciable images; it also included the bright lights of Times Square and the Woolworth Building's Gothic details. Modern consumerism played a far larger role than did architects such as Wright in shaping American cities. Whether the mask was modern or historicist, its ornamental overlay effectively disguised the industrial origins of its products. While German enthusiasm for America often conflated mass production with its effects upon popular culture,

Mendelsohn's tour of the United States made him acutely aware of the distinction between the two.

Mendelsohn's conclusions reached a large audience whose understanding of their often similar experiences they helped shape. His letters home were adapted for two articles published in the *Berliner Tageblatt* and then revised and expanded in 1925 for his book *Amerika: Bilderbuch eines Architekten* (America: Picturebook of an Architect), published in early 1926, and in a second, expanded edition in 1928.[29] Funded in 1924 by the prosperous Mosse publishing house, Mendelsohn could travel while correspondents for smaller journals and other private individuals were still recovering from the devastating inflation of the previous year.[30] The American trip became as obligatory as earlier study tours to Italy. Most of the editors of Germany's numerous architectural magazines quickly followed Mendelsohn's example, and all published extensive articles on the subject of American architecture; in 1927 and 1928, the Union of German Architects led tours of the United States.[31] Mendelsohn's comments also set the tone for a generation of German intellectuals (many of whom later found themselves in exile in the United States) and for those Americans who were beginning to see their own country through the eyes of European modernists.

Mendelsohn's impressions during his westbound shipboard experience presaged his attitude toward the supposed front of the modernity to which he was committed. He admired the machinery of the ocean liner, but its interior decoration appalled him. (His antipathy toward purely decorative columns was aroused repeatedly on the trip; likewise, he preferred rear alley facades to the ornamental veneers that screened the street facades of the steel frames of most tall buildings.)[32] Mendelsohn's shipboard letters dwelt not on architectural matters, however, but on the amusement and pleasure he derived from traveling with Fritz Lang, the German film director, whose *Metropolis* is partly based upon his reactions to New York City. Although Mendelsohn made constant fun of Lang's pretentious monocle, which he rather hoped would "accidentally" fall overboard, he found the director himself "a thoughtful, active, and certainly a daring man."[33] Fittingly, Mendelsohn's first recorded impression of America describes a glimpse of the Woolworth Building, then the world's tallest building, seen through the clouds of an October sunset. Later, against the full moon, the ship sailed past the Statue of Liberty. Although Mendelsohn dismissed the statue as sentimental "nonart," he admitted that it was a "sign of freedom for thousands, nay hundred of thousands of new citizens." As an admirer of American democracy, he could not help but be moved. In the distance, he spotted the red beacon atop the Woolworth Building.[34]

Mendelsohn's American tour awakened in him feelings of both awe and disillusionment. In the United States, as in the Netherlands, he was hesitant about, even critical of, developments that would later be prominent in his own designs. American wealth and technology far exceeded his expectations but did not produce the benefits he expected. The country's much-vaunted industrial efficiency was marred by its irrational progeny: frenzied real estate speculation, chaotic development, and slums. Initially, Mendelsohn found this chaos to be more frightening than exciting. Over the next month, Mendelsohn visited New York, Buffalo, Pittsburgh, Detroit, and Chicago. He also traveled to the University of Michigan in Ann Arbor and to Frank Lloyd Wright's home and school, Taliesin, in Wisconsin. He had hoped to go to California but found soon after his arrival in New York that the distance was too great. In Pittsburgh and Ann Arbor he delivered lectures. In each city, he met with local architects and visited important buildings. As his choice of photographs for his book demonstrated, Mendelsohn was far more interested in – if not always pleased by – the anonymous American cityscape than he was in prominent architects and their work. The cities he visited had taller buildings and were more crowded and more modern in their construction and illumination than anything he could have seen in Europe. To a German eye accustomed to the understated, clearly ordered buildings of Alfred Messel, Peter Behrens, and Hans Poelzig American downtowns, with the exception of those parts of Chicago built a generation earlier, had failed to tame the chaotic forces unleashed by rapid urbanization and the new consumer culture.

During his whirlwind tour of New York, Mendelsohn arranged the details of his midwestern itinerary and photographed the avenues and sidestreets around Wall Street and in midtown Manhattan. The city's scale, speeding traffic, illuminated advertisements, and – at times – its organization, thrilled him. But he found its uncontrolled growth and tawdry billboards horrifying, and the prevalence of traditional symbols of wealth appalled him.[35] A champion of American technology, he was, however, profoundly uncomfortable with the country's wealth. It had been a decade since he had savored the prosperity of prewar Munich; he had not yet visited London or Paris, the less modern but equally splendid capitals of the other two major Allied victors. For a man whose wife had struggled to feed their

FIGURE 21

Fritz Lang, photograph of Times Square. (Source: Erich Mendelsohn, *Amerika: Bilderbuch eines Architekten*, Berlin, 1926.)

infant daughter during the war, who still lived in a tiny apartment, and who only the year before had had to cope with out-of-control inflation, the riches of New York could border on the obscene.[36] He found it tragic that Americans could not celebrate their political freedom and modern technology without resorting to "Cathedral of Commerce" – style metaphors, which he believed were emblematic of spiritual poverty.

Mendelsohn was not immune, however, to New York's futuristic qualities. He particularly appreciated the excitement of Times Square at night, although he found its advertising disturbing in daylight (Fig. 21). He discovered no recipes in the city for a modern style, but he was intrigued by the details of urban organization he found in the efficiency of Arthur Loomis Harmon's brand new Shelton Hotel and the elevated automobile streets wrapped around Grand Central Station. On the other hand, he described the development of Park Avenue, with its rows of palacelike apartment buildings and its meager greenery, as symptomatic of the evils of uncontrolled growth, as was its proximity to the slums that lined the East River. And, although moved by the contrast between Trinity Church and the more modern financial district that surrounded it, he was repelled by the cacophony of historical styles along Fifth Avenue.[37]

Only in Buffalo, where Mendelsohn spent three days, did he begin to visit buildings whose modernity he was trained to see and could appreciate. There he toured reinforced concrete grain silos and Frank Lloyd Wright's Larkin Building. Neither disappointed him. Once again he was dismayed by the city's disorganized development, which shook his faith in capitalist efficiency. But in Wright's work, including his Martin House, and in the almost pure geometry of the grain silos, Mendelsohn found the promise of a new and democratic world.[38]

In Pittsburgh, buoyed by a friendly reception, Mendelsohn relaxed for the first time, enjoying the sensation of imagining what America was capable of becoming. Listening to the "terrific syncopation" of the noontime clanging of the bells of the city's many downtown churches, he wrote that he heard:

> Percussion rhythm whipped "with cream. . . ."
>
> Rhythm of the motors and "speed of life," of which they partake without understanding, that they understand without being able to analyze, analyze without being able to pull it together.

And, he continued:

> Fire under the soles; into the hands, wrecking capitals, columned bases of the skyscrapers.
>
> Do you want beautiful skins pumped up with air or do you want first to build scaffolding out of steel, visible, preferably naked and powerful rather than draped with pearl necklaces, a dollar apiece [a reference to the inexpensive necklaces worn by Larkin Company secretaries, which he had admired earlier in the letter]?[39]

Mendelsohn took the train from Pittsburgh through Cleveland to Detroit. The center of the American automobile industry, this city was growing even more quickly than New York or Chicago. It provided the strongest example of what was for him the typical American contrast between the productive organization of industry and the confusion resulting from unbridled real estate speculation. In neighboring Ann Arbor, where he lectured at the University of Michigan, Mendelsohn was able to compare his own observations with those of two recent émigrés, the Finnish architect Eliel Saarinen and Karl Lönberg-Holm, a young Dane whose Chicago Tribune entry Oud had admired. Mendelsohn also met Albert Kahn, the architect of the Ford factories already famous in Germany before the war. Kahn's enormous office provided, he thought, an architectural equivalent to Ford's mass production of automobiles.[40]

Mendelsohn believed that the industrial technology he saw in Detroit overwhelmed the accomplishments of the European avant-garde (Fig. 22). Commenting upon a tour with Lönberg-Holm of a power station, he wrote, "Fantastic Piranesi scenes in tubes, out of which purely technical details suddenly emerge, like new births of the future, leaving behind the whole of constructivism as a little transitional ornament."[41] It would be left to Europeans, however, to use this technology as the basis for a new architecture. Lönberg-Holm wrote to Oud after Mendelsohn's Ann Arbor lecture: "The poor students. They ought to become absolutely confused. Vignola or Mendelsohn? Make your choice. Take a chance."[42]

The climax of Mendelsohn's trip was the more than two weeks he spent in Chicago, with a side trip to Taliesin, where he was a weekend guest of Wright's. Barry Byrne, a former Wright employee who had visited Mendelsohn in Berlin, helped show him around the city.[43] Together they toured Oak Park, the Coonley House, and Midway Gardens. Byrne probably also introduced his German colleague to the history of the tall office buildings in the Loop. Mendelsohn's snapshots of the Reliance, Monadnock, and Schiller buildings – the work of, respectively, Daniel Burnham, John Root, and Louis Sullivan – would soon reintroduce them to a European audience. He also photographed Raymond Hood's winning Chicago Tribune entry, still under construction, and more grain elevators, and he purchased a copy of Sullivan's just-published *Autobiography of an Idea*.[44]

At Taliesin, Mendelsohn was welcomed by Wright, who particularly enjoyed the homage the young European paid him at a time when his reputation at home had been seriously eroded.[45] For Wright, the visit represented one of the first tangible proofs that his European admirers could play a part in returning him to the center stage he coveted. Mendelsohn discussed with Wright Wijdeveld's upcoming book on the American architect in which the younger generation of Europeans, including Mendelsohn, would record their

FIGURE 22

Charles Sheeler, 1927 photograph of Albert Kahn Associates, powerhouse and coke ovens, Ford River Rouge complex, Dearborn, Michigan, built 1922. (Source: Erich Mendelsohn, *Rußland-Europa-Amerika*, Berlin, 1929.)

praise of him.[46] Mendelsohn's former employee, the Austrian architect Richard Neutra, who was then working for Wright, played translator, toning down the criticism each made about the other to the amusement of Neutra's wife, of the visiting Swiss architect Werner Moser, and of Moser's wife.[47] The result was a highly congenial weekend, which encouraged both men's belief that they were following the right architectural path.

Mendelsohn's interest in the history of American architecture grew when he reached the Midwest. In New York he had met Lewis Mumford, the author of *Sticks and Stones*, a history of American architecture published earlier in 1924.[48] The book overlapped in two ways with Mendelsohn's view of America. Mumford condemned America's history of real estate speculation, and he praised the work of the same figures admired by Dutch and German architects, Richardson, Sullivan, and Wright. Although Mendelsohn was disposed to notice this issue and these architects for himself, Mumford's attitude reinforced Mendelsohn's statements on these subjects and contributed to the lifelong friendship that sprung up between the two men. While Mumford enhanced Mendelsohn's view of America, Mendelsohn was instrumental in creating Mumford's European reputation. He offered to translate *Sticks and Stones*, which was published in Germany in 1926.[49] He also called Mumford to the attention of Wijdeveld, and he wrote a letter of introduction to Mumford for Gropius.[50] Mumford became the only American besides Wright to have a significant voice inside German architectural circles during the twenties. When he wrote *Sticks and Stones*, Mumford had not yet been to Chicago, and he downplayed that city's importance in the book. Spurred no doubt in part by Mendelsohn's *America*, of which he received an author's copy, Mumford traveled to the Midwest in 1927. This trip inspired Mumford's second major study of America's architectural and cultural history, *The Brown Decades*, published in 1931.[51] Because Byrne showed both men around the city on their separate visits, it is not surprising that Mendelsohn's *America* prefigured Mumford's equally influential book.[52]

Mendelsohn's interest in going beyond what was already valued by either the American or the German public distinguished his book about his trip to America from the most significant of its contemporary competitors, Werner Hegemann's *Amerikanische Architektur und Stadtbaukunst* (American Architecture and Urban Planning), published in 1925.[53] Hegemann had spent ten of the years between 1904 and 1922 in the United States before becoming editor of *Wasmuths Monatshefte für Baukunst*, Germany's most splendid architecture magazine. Unlike Mendelsohn, Hegemann was firmly aligned with the American status quo. He relegated Sullivan and the Chicago School to the closing pages of his book, while turning center stage over to the City Beautiful movement's Beaux Arts schemes for the civic center. Construction and technology played a minor role in Hegemann's account.

Most of the remaining difference between the two volumes came from Mendelsohn's increasing involvement with mass culture, which separated many aspects of his book from its more conventional counterpart. Rather than an academic presentation of the subject, *America* reads and looks almost like the kind of *sachlich* advertisement pop-

FIGURE 23

Karl Lönberg-Holm, photograph of Cass Gilbert, Woolworth Building, New York, built 1913. (Source: Erich Mendelsohn, *Amerika: Bilderbuch eines Architekten.*)

ular in Germany during the twenties. The crisp, choppy prose of the book, which the architect also employed in a number of his public statements during the twenties, echoed the language of marketing slogans. Mendelsohn wrote of the Woolworth Building (Fig. 23), for instance:

> Early period of skyscrapers, 45 stories. Height of the Ulm Cathedral. Great technical achievement. All decorations of sheet copper, but the upkeep on this copper Gothic eats up $200,000 per year. This romantic combination is splendid and grotesque at the same time. The tragic expression of America today.[54]

The emphasis in most advertising on visual imagery over brief text was reflected in the layout of Mendelsohn's eye-catching book in which only a few lines of almost telegraphic writing were placed opposite every full-page plate; in contrast, Hegemann's far more substantive text was illustrated by a number of smaller photographs. Finally, in a typical example of the economic integration characteristic of mass culture, the editors of the *Berliner Tageblatt*, the leading organ of the Mosse advertising and publishing empire, drew attention to Mendelsohn's book and its author through a campaign that blurred the boundary between news and advertising. In addition to printing Mendelsohn's essays on his trip, the newspaper published favorable reviews of the book, photographs excerpted from the book, and frequent advertisements trumpeting the book's success.[55]

Mendelsohn's illustrations also accounted for much of the book's appeal. Whereas Hegemann's photographs were entirely conventional, often reproduced from the pages of American architecture magazines, Mendelsohn selected photographs taken by himself and other architects that were in themselves dynamically charged views of the American scene. Indeed, *America's* photographs were almost certainly a more important contribution than its text in shaping the image that the European avant-garde and general public had of the United States. Largely taken by Lang (Fig. 21), Lönberg-Holm (Fig. 23), Mendelsohn himself (Fig. 24), and Mendelsohn's assistant Erich Karweik, the photographs are, for the most part, amateurish in technique, yet their striking compositions and iconic subject matter made them a notable contribution to the history of photography.[56] In the nineteenth century, architect's travel sketches had been featured in the new architectural magazines and in exhibitions. Mendelsohn's decision to use photographs in place of the more personal sketch represents his championship of an industrialized order. He noted: "Nothing appeals more to modern man than pictures. He wants to understand, but quickly, clearly, without a lot of furrowing of brows and mysticism."[57] The oblique angle of Lönberg-Holm's photograph of the Woolworth Building and the streaks of light speeding through the night captured on Lang's negative for his Times Square photograph reflect the dynamism of the modern metropolis, while Mendelsohn's own photographs convey the scale and texture of the American cityscape.[58]

The European audience for Mendelsohn's book was fascinated by its depiction of a world few had seen for themselves. The German playwright Bertolt Brecht read it in 1926 and found it to be one of the best books of the year. It was an important source for the image of America in his early plays.[59] In the Soviet Union, El Lissitzky was interested as much in the freshness of Mendelsohn's photographic technique as in the book's content. In a letter to its author, he praised the lively, cinematic effect of the book's images.[60] He added, in a review:

> This "Architect's Album" which has just come out in Berlin is of course immeasurably more interesting than those photographs and

FIGURE 24

Erich Mendelsohn, photograph of Broad Street, New York. (Source: Erich Mendelsohn, *Amerika: Bilderbuch eines Architekten.*)

postcards by which we have known America up to now. A first leafing through its pages thrills us like a dramatic film. Before our eyes move pictures that are absolutely unique. In order to understand some of the photographs you must lift the book over your head and rotate it.[61]

Mendelsohn's book also exposed Americans to the current European view of the United States and to the aesthetic that accompanied it, in turn encouraging the development of an American equivalent.[62] For instance, Hermann Scheffauer, who had introduced Mendelsohn

FIGURE 25

Norman Bel Geddes, model of a diesel-powered yacht, 1934. (Source: *Pencil Points*, 1937.)

to readers of the American avant-garde journal *The Dial* in 1921, wrote an article for the *New York Times Magazine* on Mendelsohn's critique of American skyscrapers.[63] Although Mendelsohn also influenced the work of artists and fellow architects, he had his greatest impact upon the image of American modernity in industrial design. In his initial visit to New York and, again, just before he sailed back to Germany, he met Norman Bel Geddes.[64] The two shared a talent for dramatizing industry. Six years Mendelsohn's junior, Bel Geddes had attracted attention on both sides of the Atlantic for his set designs. In 1927 he launched a career as one of America's first industrial designers.[65] His streamlined product designs were loosely based on the aerodynamics of a body in motion, but, above all, they were sleek packages that disguised rather than exposed modern machinery.[66] Although Le Corbusier was also fascinated by ovoid forms, Bel Geddes's largest debt was undoubtedly to Mendelsohn. In 1923, for example, Mendelsohn had described the way a ship is designed to move efficiently through water, while noting, however, the limited applicability of this effect to buildings, which stay in place (Fig. 25).[67] Bel Geddes apparently translated the curved forms seen in Mendelsohn's wartime drawings as well as in the architect's more recent designs into the curved and polished surfaces of his own prototypes for a variety of machines including this diesel yacht, the character of speeding motorcars or diesel locomotives. The excitement Bel Geddes's designs communicated about new mass-produced products quickly became a staple of American popular culture.[68]

At the end of his introduction to *America*, Mendelsohn concluded, "This country [has] everything; the worst strata of Europe, abortions of civilization, but also hopes for a new world."[69] From his American travels he had learned that neither technology nor a lack of history could produce the architectural answers for which he was searching. Both conditions, however, could be combined with the energy of the nocturnal American streetscape into an architecture in which the architect maintained control over the built environment. This balance of discipline and vitality would lead to an engagement with industrial imagery entirely dissimilar from what Gropius had advocated in 1923.

"STUCK FAST IN THE SUBURBS OF KÖNIGSBERG": THE SOVIET UNION

The United States was not the only nation to offer a vision of the future to Weimar-era Germans. The Soviet Union, the product of the first successful Communist revolution, fascinated Germans as well as frightened them. Following the signing of the Treaty of Rapallo in 1922, Germany and the Soviet Union restored diplomatic and economic relations. This action supplemented the cultural ties that had bound circles of artists in the two nations since the revolutions of 1917 and 1918. The German popular press was full of photographs of Soviet political demonstrations and of the agitational art that accompanied them. Soviet artists visited Berlin frequently, and the Russian director Sergey Eisenstein's films, in particular, enjoyed large audiences in that city. Especially on the left, Germans appear to have been more interested in Soviet dreams of a reformed society and in the country's new art than they were in the reality of a still largely rural Soviet economy. And during the brief period of relative prosperity in Germany at the end of the twenties, many Germans were more excited about imitating Constructivist art than Communist politics, although the Soviet Union's Five Year Plan announced in 1928 did inspire hope that economic planning offered a fruitful alternative to capitalism.[70] Surprisingly, Soviet enthusiasm for American technology, coupled with this emphasis on rational planning, meant that many Germans viewed the Soviet Union and the United States as complementary models for their own development. This view was enhanced by Henry Ford's emphasis, in his autobiography (a best-seller in Germany after its publication there in 1923), on the opportunities America afforded its workers, who had to be well paid in order to spur economic development by buying consumer products.[71] German architects in particular were likely to have dual loyalties.

In his book *Rußland – Amerika – Europa: ein architektonischer Querschnitt* (Russia – America – Europe: An Architectural Cross Section), Mendelsohn took issue with the extent to which either the United States or the Soviet Union offered a prototype for the incorporation of technology into modern architecture. He focused on the gap between the modernity that Germans so admired and the architecture and society that he found during his three trips to the Soviet Union.[72] He used the book to express again his ideas about the direction architecture should take – that it should encompass planning based upon organic patterns of social and urban development and a mystical creativity emanating from the soul. Not surprisingly, his own work soon revealed a debt to Soviet architects even as in his commercial architecture he transposed their propagandistic strategies, developed in the service of a revolutionary state, into capitalist advertising.

During the twenties, Soviet architects created a new architecture, whose startling abstract form charged with their enthusiasm for technological imagery they saw as paralleling the political changes spurred by the Revolution of 1917. Constructivist architecture grew out of the abstract explorations of form and space made by painters and sculptors, especially the Supermatist Kasimir Malevich, in combination with enthusiasm for functional planning and a politically conscious understanding of social institutions. Rationalists, however, espoused a more purely formal approach to architecture. Both movements produced many more competition entries and designs for imaginary projects than they did actual buildings.[73] The Constructivists, in particular, enjoyed an international reputation by the mid-twenties, but aside from his admiration for El Lissitzky, whom he met in 1923, Mendelsohn had kept his distance from the Soviets.[74] The slight degree to which these architects were involved in real construction immediately aroused his suspicion. Although Mendelsohn had admired Tatlin's Monument to the Third International, he was uncomfortable with the Constructivist's formalism. At the same time, he did not need the Soviet example in order to experiment with modern engineering; steel and concrete – the "new" materials championed by the Rationalists – were already familiar to him.

Mendelsohn was, however, the first foreign architect to whom the Soviet government turned. In August 1925 a Soviet delegation visited him in Berlin to discuss the possibility of his designing a knitwear and hosiery factory in Leningrad.[75] They were interested in him because the complex included three dyeworks, and they wanted to duplicate the innovative ventilation he had developed for such buildings. Although Mendelsohn eventually became so contemptuous of Soviet standards of construction and of the liberties taken with his

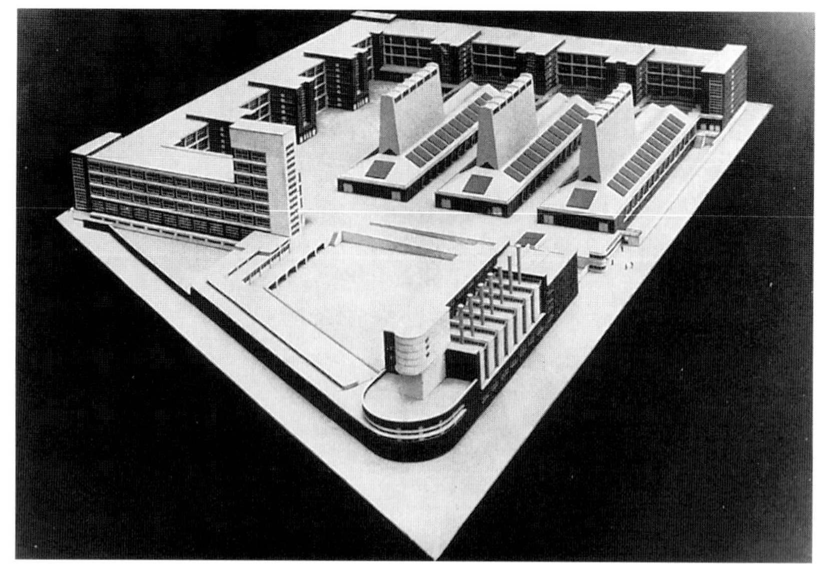

FIGURE 26

Erich Mendelsohn in collaboration with Laaser and Salomonson, Red Flag textile factory, model, Leningrad, Soviet Union (now St. Petersburg, Russia), 1925. (Source: Staatliche Museen zu Berlin, Kunstbibliothek.)

design that he disavowed any connection with the Red Flag (Krasnoje Snemja) textile factory after it was built, he frequently published photographs of the model (Fig. 26).[76]

Mendelsohn visited the Soviet Union for the first time in connection with this project in the fall of 1925, and he returned twice in 1926.[77] His May 1926 trip, in which he visited Moscow, was enough of an event to be reported in the city's newspaper *Izvestia*.[78] A final trip followed in late July and early August.[79] During his travels, Mendelsohn resumed his friendship with Lissitzky; met the Vesnin brothers, Konstantin Melnikov, and Alexei Shchusev (all except Shchusev were leading Soviet modernist architects); and studied the integration of propaganda and abstract form that characterized Soviet architecture.[80] Yet clearly what most captivated Mendelsohn about the country was its past and its exoticism. During his third trip he started planning a book.[81] He began to take photographs, concentrating on historical architecture rather than on the few revolutionary projects that had actually been built. When he sat down to write in July 1927, the manuscript quickly grew into a comparison of his American and Soviet experiences, offering a blueprint for the way in which technology should be integrated into European society and architecture.[82] Although rational organization of industrial production in the United States and of economic planning in the Soviet Union offered apparently similar models of modernity, Mendelsohn used the very different architectural pasts and presents of the two nations to represent them as opposing visions of a new world. For him, the American model was marred by a romantic historicism, while the preindustrial character of Soviet society undermined the Soviet emphasis on planning.

Mendelsohn tested his argument in a lecture he gave in Berlin in February 1928,[83] and Mosse published the new book in early 1929. Because in this book Mendelsohn quoted less from letters to his wife who accompanied him on one trip, the text lacked *America's* freshness. The book's visual impact was also more diffuse, as the illustrations came from a motley variety of sources and included many that lacked the aesthetic impact of the *America* images.[84] The book's purpose, he wrote his wife, was to present "a credo of our age, of the future, as a product of mechanization and divine mystery."[85] In it Mendelsohn grappled with the gap between the contribution that he, like almost all Germans of his generation, assumed was made by the spirit of the times to a society's art and architecture and the reality of his American and Soviet experiences. He also defended the continued importance of the emotional and spiritual at a point when an extreme antihumanist position, identified most closely with Hannes Meyer, had become popular among younger German architects.[86] Mendelsohn found that his colleagues in both the United States and the Soviet Union used architecture to mask cultural deficiencies. He faulted Americans for hiding their technological accomplishments behind a nostalgic screen and the Soviets for betraying their country's innate mysticism in favor of an unattainable industrialized utopia. However, by combining American technology and Russian spiritualism Europeans, he wrote, could create an architecture which through plan and materials would master the machine and transform it into an instrument for social unity.[87]

Mendelsohn's emphasis upon Russian spirituality was an outgrowth of his perception of the country as an Oriental one whose fundamental nature presented a contrast to European rationalism. As a Jewish East Prussian who occasionally described himself as an "Oriental," he was attracted by this otherness.[88] For the first time since his student days he was drawn in the Soviet Union to the architecture of the past. In an opening section devoted to historical Russian architecture, he identified the medieval edifices he visited in and around Moscow as Oriental (Fig. 27). Even when he visited buildings designed by émigré Italian architects he saw in them traces of Islamic and Byzantine rather than Renaissance traditions.[89]

Spiritual rebirth had been a recurrent theme in Expressionist art, and many Expressionists, Taut among them, had sought inspiration in Eastern religion and art.[90] German architects who emerged from

FIGURE 27

Erich Mendelsohn, photograph of Ascension Church, Kolomenskoe, Russia, built circa 1532. (Source: Erich Mendelsohn, *Rußland-Europa-Amerika.*)

this movement continued throughout the twenties to believe that the architecture they were creating was rooted in semimystical truths that transcended mere form and function.[91] Mendelsohn, a disciple of this creed since his Munich days, was appalled to witness the development of an opposing doctrine. Led by Hannes Meyer, from 1928 to 1930 the director of the Bauhaus, many young architects came to regard architecture as a method of production rather than as a creative process. They focused on plan and program, completely denying an architectural role for metaphor or emotion.[92] Mendelsohn, accustomed to seeing himself as a pragmatist, used his new book as a platform for his criticism. He repeatedly defended the importance of the creative spirit. His analysis of the Soviets made clear, however, that spiritual beliefs alone could not be the basis for modern architecture but must be tempered by the rationalism he recognized in American construction methods and zoning.

Mendelsohn doubted, for instance, that the Soviet Communists could create a rational society. He also questioned the capacity of the Russian people, whom he saw through the lens of Orientalism, to participate in such a society. Finally, his experiences in Moscow and Leningrad made him distrust the government. More than an abstract political critique, his abhorrence of the Soviet system was based on its inability to better the lives of its citizens. He reserved his strongest criticism for his letters, keeping the book's commentary abstract. He wrote his wife in 1926 from Moscow, "Russia, the former colossus with clay feet, lives today from its heart after chopping off its feet for, rather than continuing to vegetate, it preferred to cripple itself." The country was too busy, he continued, keeping alive the flame of revolution through dictatorship and too little concerned with freedom for its people.[93]

At different points in the book Mendelsohn blamed the technological emphasis of Soviet architecture for betraying the legacy of Russian spiritualism and paradoxically characterized this as yet another example of an unrealistic Russian utopian vision.[94] His arguments were based entirely on practical rather than aesthetic grounds. They were shaped both by his own frustrations with building in the Soviet Union and by the preference for practice over theory that could be found since 1919 in all of his pronouncements about architecture. Struggling with the Leningrad authorities over the construction of his textile factory, he commented dryly, "They look to America but are stuck fast in the suburbs of Königsberg," a city then on Germany's East Prussian border.[95] Soviet construction was labor intensive and largely unmechanized, a situation that he believed called for pragmatic designs which responded to these realities.[96]

Mendelsohn included a cross section of contemporary Soviet design from both the Constructivist and Rationalist camps in his book, illustrating the work of Shchusev, the Vesnin brothers, Malevich, Lissitzky, and Ivan Leonidov, among others. He was particularly critical, as usual, of paper architecture. For example, although Malevich's Suprematist juxtaposition of rectilinear parts in architectural drawings and sculptures, which were an important source for the formal language used by the Constructivists, paralleled his own Wright-inspired work of 1922–23, Mendelsohn complained that Malevich avoided reality by working on abstract designs rather than on solutions appropriate to the limited constructional technology available to him.[97] Mendelsohn voiced similar reservations about Leonidov's 1927 competition scheme for the Sovkino film production complex (Fig. 28):

> Painterly, constructivist graphics instead of . . . sober construction:

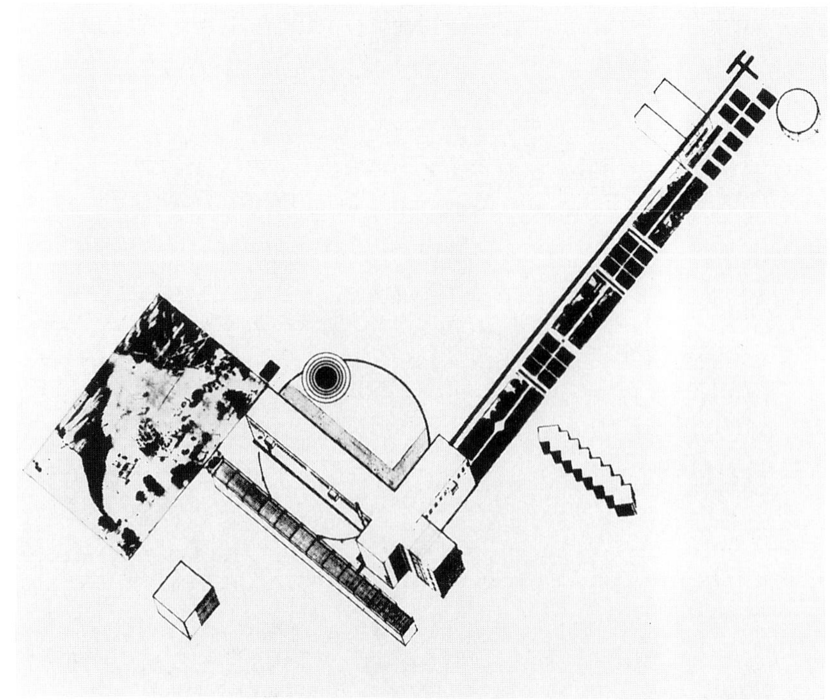

FIGURE 28

Ivan Leonidov, competition entry for Sovkino film production facility, 1927. (Source: Erich Mendelsohn, *Rußland-Europa-Amerika*.)

> Design representation through axionometry, landscape replaced with film reels. The design is the means of communication for everyone, and not just a crossword puzzle for the initiated.
>
> But this kind of rendering only means unnecessary dimming of the design's clarity, is but a graphic cliché.
>
> It is *l'art pour l'art*, individualistic and anti-technological.[98]

Mendelsohn's tone, however, remained largely enthusiastic, inspirational rather than confrontational. Soviet buildings adhered more closely to structural truths than one would have expected from architects' drawings. American construction techniques and zoning continued to offer hope that the New World might provide models for European development. Europe could mediate between the two and sustain its own traditions of intellectual achievement. He singled out the work of his Dutch friends Oud and Wilhelm Dudok for special praise, offering them, along with his own design for the Leningrad factory, as examples of the direction Europeans should take.[99]

In his three best-known polemical statements from the twenties, each responding to his encounter with a different foreign culture and its architecture, Mendelsohn sought to define the direction modern architecture, rooted in the realities of the industrial revolution, should take in Germany and across Europe. Throughout the decade, he remained skeptical about the usefulness of purely theoretical models, but he was also dissatisfied with the reality of the unrestrained development he saw in America. In the book based on his Russian experiences, for instance, he frequently praised rational planning, an issue he did not mentioned in his Dutch lecture of 1923. Studying the solutions foreign architects had developed out of their encounters with modernity stimulated Mendelsohn to improve upon their faults and integrate their successes into his own work. As he moved beyond the Einstein Tower, the Dutch, American, and Soviet buildings he had seen firsthand would replace their prewar German counterparts as his most important sources of inspiration. In particular, he would move beyond the almost purely formal concerns that had characterized his discussions of Dutch architecture to address the themes of mass culture, communication, and consumption whose impact upon American and Soviet design had both excited and appalled him. Dynamic functionalism became a tool with which he could adapt the images of foreign architectural modernity that filled every popular newspaper to the specific conditions of individual German cities, patrons, and building types. It was a tool flexible enough to dramatize the often disparate, even conflicting, aspects of contemporary modernism without falling prey to their threat of chaos.

3

THE DOCKING OF THE *MAURETANIA* AND OTHER EXPERIMENTS IN "STYLE MENDELSOHN"

MENDELSOHN'S trips abroad, particularly those he took between 1923 and 1926 to the Netherlands, the United States, and the Soviet Union, encouraged him to think and write about the appropriate balance between the rationalizing and dynamic forces of industrialization and the modernity it had spawned. He was also interested in the role that function should play in shaping an architecture that could express this dynamism. Since 1921, Mendelsohn had been experimenting with formulations of dynamism that took him far away from what he saw as the flawed assumptions embodied in the Einstein Tower. At the same time, he gained experience with a wide variety of building types, including the high-rise office building and the elegant shop, his command of which would lead to many commissions. This chapter explores three quite different buildings designed in the Mendelsohn office between 1921 and 1923: the Steinberg, Hermann hat factory in Luckenwalde; the renovations and an addition to Mossehaus, the Berlin headquarters of a large publishing firm; and the Weichmann Silk Store in Gleiwitz. They were less sculptural than the Einstein Tower and had little of the industrial imagery found in many of Mendelsohn's later work, but the modernism of these buildings was evident in their complicated massing, their lack of ornament, and the varied textures of their materials. They also reflect the influence of Mendelsohn's talented assistant, Richard Neutra. No other German architect of Mendelsohn's modernist generation received comparable opportunities to build during this period, a situation which made him, briefly, the most prominent young architect in the country. Finally, these commissions demonstrated Mendelsohn's command of those issues – urban siting, advertising, and industry – which would continue to be crucial in his later German work.

The five years separating the November Revolution and the hyperinflation of 1923 were difficult for all Germans. The period was studded with attempts by both the left and the right to supplant the shaky republican government and was fraught with economic uncertainty. Nonetheless, between 1921 and 1923 Mendelsohn was occupied with three projects in Haifa (a port city in what was then the British Mandate of Palestine and is today Israel) and, in Germany, two villas and the renovation of a factory in addition to the Steinberg, Hermann factory, Mossehaus, and the Weichmann Silk Store.[1] The use of a historical forms and concrete construction were the only constants in Mendelsohn's search for individualized solutions to the problems of industrial, residential, and commercial architecture posed by these commissions. In the earliest of these commissions, the Steinberg, Hermann hat factory, Mendelsohn placed a functionalist harness over the faceted forms favored by Taut, considerably simplifying them in the process. He added sleek bands of ceramic tile and aluminum to his repertory when he participated in the renovation of Mossehaus. Finally, in the Weichmann Silk Store, he experimented with an abstract version of the dynamic tension between masses characteristic of Frank Lloyd Wright.

These commissions also reinforced the affiliation, apparent in the Einstein Tower, between Mendelsohn's buildings and the larger culture of modernism. His factories furthered the prewar Werkbund's aestheticization of industry, Mossehaus allied him with the liberal Jewish press and advertising, and the Weichmann store – his first commercial commission – enhanced his awareness of the connections between marketing and architecture. His strong sense of architecture as image, even as he experimented with the style of the image, remained an important factor in his designs.

THE STEINBERG, HERMANN HAT FACTORY

Mendelsohn's first revision of dynamic functionalism determined the design of only a single commission, but the work that resulted – the hat factory for Friedrich Steinberg, Hermann and Company in Luckenwalde – was unquestionably the most important product of the five-year period that separated the completion of blueprints for the Einstein Tower and the first drawings for the Schocken store in Stuttgart (Fig. 29). Designed and built between 1921 and 1923, the Stein-

FIGURE 29

Erich Mendelsohn, Steinberg, Hermann Company hat factory, Lukenwalde, Germany, 1921–23. (Source: Foto Marburg/Art Resource NY, Neg. 1.150.172.)

berg, Hermann factory was the most widely published industrial structure erected in Germany since the Werkbund exhibition of 1914, a masterfully crafted object which fulfilled but did not represent its industrial purpose. It also won praise throughout the twenties and into the thirties as an outstanding example of functional design. Its ventilation system, a significant technical innovation which alleviated the dangers toxic fumes posed to workers laboring in dyeing sheds, demonstrated the practical advantages of architectural experimentation. Mendelsohn also studied recent concrete factory halls to ground himself, after the problems that had complicated construction of the Einstein Tower, in the conventions for building with his favorite material. Despite the general resemblance of its interior to these factories, the Steinberg, Hermann factory was an intellectual position paper in which Mendelsohn allied himself with older architects, although the work of none of these individuals completely forecast his own use of austere profiles and rich textures. And, although the factory had a symmetrical plan, the dramatically cropped and angled views of it which Mendelsohn chose to publish hinted at the dynamically charged asymmetry to which he would soon turn.

The Steinberg, Hermann factory was a key building in the transition from Expressionism, with its air of utopian longing, to the reawakened interest in industry characteristic of the architecture which followed the return of financial stability to Germany in 1924.

Although Mendelsohn's fellow Expressionists were also beginning in the early twenties to turn away from visionary schemes, and although Mendelsohn himself certainly made use of their earlier drawings in his design for the factory, in the eyes of his contemporaries the finished complex transcended all other architectural designs of the inflationary years.[2] In the factory's bold composition the architect had synthesized many of the most respected aspects of pre- and postwar architecture to create a set of forms that made almost everything – including his own sources – appear obsolete to those who regarded the design as an important step in architecture's relentless march toward greater abstraction. The degree to which Taut's faceted forms inspired Mendelsohn's austere geometries helped to point toward industry as the locus of a new utopia, one which was potentially far more real than the dreams of crystalline community halls which it replaced.

The Einstein Tower has dominated all accounts of Mendelsohn's architectural activity between 1919 and 1921, but it was only one of several projects in the young architect's busy office. Gustav Hermann, a hat manufacturer in Luckenwalde, a small city south of Berlin, was his principal patron during these years. In 1919 and 1920 Mendelsohn built for Hermann workers' housing, a garden pavilion, and an extension to a hat factory.[3] All were in Luckenwalde. Mendelsohn's career was marked by his ability to please patrons, and Hermann was the first of three men who would again and again present him with the opportunity to build. Although far less is known about Hermann than about the other two – Hans Lachmann-Mosse, the heir with his wife to the Mosse family publishing and advertising empire, and Salman Schocken, the owner of a chain of department stores – only an adept businessman could have commissioned such a string of projects, albeit small ones, in 1919 and 1920.[4] Even before 1922, when the hat factory operated by the Hermann brothers since 1883 officially merged with its local rival, Friedrich Steinberg, which had been making hats in the city since 1885, the two firms had jointly planned the construction of a new factory.[5] Not surprisingly in light of his previous work for Hermann, Mendelsohn was entrusted with the commission. He designed the factory in 1921 and 1922, and construction was completed in 1923.[6]

Four skylit manufacturing sheds (Fig. 30 shows the spinning hall) lay at the heart of the factory complex. Here Mendelsohn substituted for his earlier monolithic approach to concrete a more conventional, if still sculptural, skeletal frame. Hinged concrete piers that braced

FIGURE 30

Steinberg, Hermann hat factory, spinning room interior. (Source: Staatliche Museen zu Berlin, Kunstbibliothek.)

FIGURE 31

Allgemein Hochbau Gesellschaft, Fritz Cohen Company textile factory, Mönchen-Gladbach, Germany, 1923. (Source: *Deutsche Bauzeitung*, 1923.)

as well as supported the roof structure separated the sheds from each other. Mendelsohn elegantly tapered these piers at the peak of the roof and where they met the floor, two points where less stiffness was required.[7] In 1924, discussing the spinning hall photograph shown as Figure 30, he pointed out "the running of the power transmission-shafts in the factory-lofts through the lower part of the girder, which also serves as a support for the main belt and pulley system."[8] Technically only this detail, which subtly emphasized the tensile strength of the piers by creating a void exactly where the load would be centered in masonry construction, distinguished the spinning hall from factory halls being built all across the country (Fig. 31).[9] The handsome profile of Mendelsohn's girders, and of the hall itself, offered eloquent proof, however, that technical competence alone did not satisfy their architect.

This was true even though Mendelsohn's new ventilation system proved as newsworthy as the factory's design. The dyeworks stood in front of the first manufacturing shed. The steep profile of its roof might seem merely an exuberant Expressionist gesture, but in fact it was the key to its use as an exhaust stack. In the past, fumes from dyeworks had damaged workers' respiratory tracts. Mendelsohn inserted vents along the sides of the roof of the dyeworks that drew off some of the noxious odors. A second grill, built into the highest point of the ceiling, led to a funnel-shaped chimney surmounting the entire shed and itself crowned by a third vent. The height of the chimney, aided by the ventilators, created an upward flow of air that drew off the remaining fumes. Mendelsohn supplemented his system with two pneumatic ventilators designed to completely change the air in the shed every half hour.[10]

Ultimately, however, concerns about function complemented rather than replaced the aesthetic issues involved in the creation of a dynamic architecture. As with the Einstein Tower, Mendelsohn turned to the recent past for inspiration, but in this instance his sources were almost entirely different: the work of Olbrich, de Klerk, and Poelzig. Their boldly formed and darkly colored buildings were admired in the early twenties by many German architects, who often transposed them into more literally historicist terms. Mendelsohn did just the opposite, making them more abstract. Furthermore, he moved beyond his 1919 lecture "The Problem of a New Architecture" to draw upon the faceted forms used by Taut and the Czech Cubists, which, in 1921, were still the postwar era's most obvious signifiers of architectural modernism. These buildings also proved far easier to construct than the biomorphic curves of the Einstein Tower. Mendelsohn's synthesis of the plastic forms of the architects he most admired with the most buildable aspects of Expressionism resulted in his designing buildings in which historicist references were abstracted to the point where they could hint at future utopian communities while fulfilling the needs of the industrial present.

This synthesis can be seen in the paired gatehouses that completed the Steinberg, Hermann factory project. Designed in June 1922, they were the subject of one of the most delicate and realistic of all Mendelsohn's drawings (Fig. 32).[11] In it Mendelsohn reinterpreted Olbrich's entrance for *A Document of German Art,* an exhibition held in Darmstadt in 1901 (Fig. 33). Mendelsohn's jagged geometry distinguished his gatehouses from their more plastic model, whose pi-

FIGURE 32

Erich Mendelsohn, Steinberg, Hermann hat factory, sketch of gatehouses, 1922. (Source: Staatliche Museen zu Berlin, Kunstbibliothek.)

oneering wrap-around window bands they clearly echoed. As built, Mendelsohn's gatehouses were closer together than they appeared in the drawings, and their triangular overhangs were slightly smaller. Like much of the complex, they were constructed of concrete.

Brick, however, was an equally important material in the factory as a whole and helped establish the distinctive texture of the complex. Here the architect was inspired by another Olbrich building in Darmstadt, the Wedding Tower of 1908. After seeing it for the first time in June 1922, Mendelsohn wrote, "A single flash of genius up there . . . The Wedding Tower is wholly *built*. A strong impression and encouragement."[12] Along the walls of the dyeworks and manufacturing sheds, Mendelsohn tiered stepped bands of projecting brick. Although they lacked Olbrich's decorative gilding, entirely inappropriate for the factory district of a small but smoky city, these bands seem to have been inspired by the crest of the Wedding Tower. Out of them Mendelsohn made a projecting ledge that supported the power station's concrete superstructure; similar ledges supported the roofs of the dyeworks and manufacturing sheds. The combination of materials was especially effective in the dyeworks. There, as in the

FIGURE 33

Joseph M. Olbrich, gatehouse, *A Document of German Art* exhibition, Darmstadt, Germany, 1901. (Source: *Joseph M. Olbrich, 1867–1906: Das Werk des Architektens*, Darmstadt, 1967.)

manufacturing sheds, a plain brick wall reached to the sill of the low windows. Above this level, every other course jutted slightly further forward, producing an increasingly rougher texture. This emphatic horizontal note created a deft counterpoint to the vertical crevices between the roof planks.

Although far less idiosyncratic in the Steinberg, Hermann factory, Mendelsohn's juxtaposition of textures and of emphatic horizontals and verticals was also indebted to the example of the housing projects being built in Amsterdam by Michel de Klerk and his followers. When he traveled to Amsterdam in 1921 Mendelsohn may have seen, for instance, de Klerk's recently completed third block on the Spaarndammer Plantsoen (Fig. 19). This block of workers' housing was the last of three that the Dutch architect completed for Eigen Haard. On its facades, de Klerk matched brick, laid both horizontally and vertically, with wooden window frames, painted white, and orange roof tiles. The hat factory is directed and purposeful in comparison to de

FIGURE 34

Hans Poelzig, Milch and Company superphosphate chemical factory, Luban, Germany (now Lubon, Poland), 1911–12. (Source: Walter Müller-Wulkow, *Bauten der Arbeit und des Verkehrs*, Königstein im Taunus and Leipzig, 1929.)

Klerk's whimsical composition and imaginative flourishes. Mendelsohn probably admired de Klerk not so much for his craftsmanship, but because the Dutchman took so little of the tradition he manipulated for granted. Mendelsohn also approved of de Klerk's commitment to the actual construction of architecture at a time when many seemed to prefer to talk and write about it.

Although influenced by Olbrich and de Klerk, Mendelsohn's design for the Steinberg, Hermann factory grew more directly out of prewar German factory architecture, a Werkbund-influenced tradition that included factories by Behrens, Gropius, and Poelzig. When the Werkbund had begun its reform of industrial architecture by imposing formal order on industrial function, the group's goal was as much to turn industry – the most vibrant sector of the German economy – into an important architectural patron as it was to revitalize architecture through the use of an industrial aesthetic. This approach is particularly characteristic of the industrial architecture of Hans Poelzig. Poelzig was a key figure in both the pre- and postwar Werkbund and became president of the organization in 1919. In the early twenties, his Milch and Company chemical factory of 1911–12 in Luban (today Lubon, Poland), near Posen (now Poznan), was the prewar factory that commanded the most respect among the Expressionists (Fig. 34).[13] Indeed, after the war Poelzig eclipsed Behrens as Germany's most admired architect, one of the few figures appreciated by young and old alike.[14]

The Steinberg, Hermann factory was far more closely related to Poelzig's chemical factory, clad in faintly medieval dark brick but completely ahistorical in form and detail, than to Gropius and Meyer's prewar Fagus factory, the most important precursor of the Bauhaus. Yet Mendelsohn's responsiveness to technological imagery and changes in factory organization surpassed that not only of Poelzig's but also of Gropius and Meyer's work to date. His spare lines made the stepped composition and often small windows of the Luban factory seem fussy and arcane, and his single-story sheds were more efficient than the out-of-date multistoried American daylight factories imitated by Gropius and Meyer. In particular, the simplicity of the exposed concrete of the Steinberg, Hermann factory's power station, its expansive windows and almost square shape, signaled the arrival of a new era. Although the industrial sector of the economy expanded in 1920 and 1921 and the pages of the *Deutsche Bauzeitung* were full of new factories, Mendelsohn was the only German architect to push the design of factory exteriors beyond prewar solutions.[15]

Mendelsohn's factory was described by one contemporary as a swiftly springing tiger seizing the functionalist position ignored since Gropius and Meyer's prewar factories.[16] The hat factory was widely hailed as the epitome of functionalism by critics ready to turn away from the Expressionist visions that were fashionable immediately after the war.[17] Ironically, during the twenties, for all the attention that Germany's leading architects gave to imposing solutions derived from industrial architecture upon other building types – particularly upon worker's housing – they spent very little time actually designing factories. Only at the end of the decade, and more often abroad than in Germany, did the progeny of the Fagus factory begin to outnumber those of the Luban chemical works.

Mendelsohn, however, quickly embarked on new stylistic experiments. He applied the technical solutions realized in the Steinberg, Hermann factory to the Red Flag factory in Leningrad and continued to construct concrete frames infilled with brick, but he never attempted to duplicate the Luckenwalde factory's success through the repetition of any of its motifs. In the Steinberg, Hermann factory Mendelsohn stepped back from his youthful dreams of monolithic concrete construction. Concentrating on what had already been proven possible, he built a concrete skeleton inlaid with brick and wood. Setting aside his earlier fascination with biomorphic imagery, he turned to the task of converting more fashionable, yet still dynamic, angular forms into agents of practical industrial purposes. By balancing dynamism and function, he solved programmatic problems pragmatically, without ever claiming in his later discussions of the factory that its function had determined his aesthetic goals.

MOSSEHAUS

Mendelsohn's renovation of Mossehaus, the Berlin headquarters of the Rudolf Mosse Publishing Company, best known as the first international advertising agency in Germany and for its flagship newspaper, the *Berliner Tageblatt* was an exact contemporary of the Steinberg, Hermann factory, yet about all that the two buildings had in common was the use of concrete frames (Fig. 35). Mendelsohn designed Mossehaus in collaboration with his assistant Richard Neutra and with Rudolf Paul Henning, a sculptor who worked in ceramics, and he always credited both of these men for their contributions.[18] Their communal effort stimulated Mendelsohn's interest in Wright, for whom Neutra hoped soon to work in America, but it also highlighted his unease at working with talented associates rather than loyal subordinates. In Mossehaus, Mendelsohn addressed for the first time the relationship between modern architecture and traffic, and he returned to the problem of representing motion architecturally. The sweeping, horizontally banded arc between and above the two prewar facades of the existing building by Cremer and Wolffenstein was the first built example of a new kind of dynamism, the horizontally directed rounded forms that enlivened most of Mendelsohn's later German buildings. And it was on the Mossehaus exterior that Mendelsohn's office first employed the metal detailing that was to become an important component of machine-age imagery. Finally, the prominence of the patron and of the building's site in downtown Berlin added enormously to Mendelsohn's reputation and strengthened his identification with Jewish support for the Weimar Republic.[19]

The mixture of modernity and publicity that characterized Mossehaus and, for that matter, Mendelsohn's career throughout the decade was in keeping with the history of the Rudolf Mosse Advertising Agency and Publishing Company. On January 1, 1867, Rudolf Mosse announced the opening of an international advertising agency that would place advertisements from at home and abroad in the German press. The agency was an enormous success. The new revenues it brought to German newspapers, previously dependent mainly on subscribers for their income, helped to lower newspaper prices, making them available for the first time to a broad public.[20]

FIGURE 35

Erich Mendelsohn, Richard Neutra, and Rudolf Paul Henning, Mossehaus renovation and addition, Berlin, Germany, 1922–23. (Source: Staatliche Museen zu Berlin, Kunstbibliothek.)

In 1871 Mosse founded the the *Berliner Tageblatt*, the first of a chain of newspapers that would grow to include the *Berliner Morgen-Zeitung*, founded in 1889, and the *Berliner Volks-Zeitung*, bought in 1904. The *Tageblatt* was a left-liberal paper with extensive coverage of culture and politics; the *Morgen-Zeitung* and the *Volks-Zeitung*, which were directed at the middle and working classes, also advocated representative government. By 1916 the combined circulation of the three newspapers stood at nearly half a million. Their editorial stance, although not opposed to the war once it broke out, was otherwise distinctly antimilitaristic.

Rudolf Mosse's liberal politics and his economic success, which made him one of Berlin's wealthiest men, were paradigmatic of the contributions the first generations of emancipated Jews made to the development of a modern Germany. This group also pioneered the development of the country's department stores, electronic industry, and financial markets. While most successful capitalists in Germany and abroad allied themselves with the traditional prewar elites, Jewish entrepreneurs like Mosse could be critical of them, in part because of discrimination against them in such imperially controlled institutions as the army and the university system.[21] Many well-to-do Jews also patronized new styles of art, although Mosse himself did not. After the war, these Jews usually supported the Weimar Republic, one of whose leaders until his assassination in 1922 – Walter Rathenau, son of the founder of the AEG – was one of their own.[22] Mendelsohn was more an advocate of architectural reform than of economic revolution. He built his career upon commissions from this caste after coming to their attention through the publication of the Einstein Tower, named for the community's most prominent member. These alliances with patrons and purposes associated with distinctly modern enterprises reaffirmed Mendelsohn's interest in and talent for creating a radically new architecture and insured that the modernity of his work would be widely recognized.

In 1874 the entire Mosse business moved to Jerusalemerstraße in the heart of Berlin's newspaper district.[23] Between 1901 and 1903 the architectural firm of Cremer and Wolffenstein replaced the old Mosse building with a sandstone-fronted six-story iron-and-brick-framed headquarters large enough to house the advertising agency and the growing newspaper chain.[24] In January 1919 the Sparticist revolt against the republican government was centered in this part of the city, and the elaborate corner entrance of the publishing house was badly damaged in the attacks on the revolutionaries, who were using the building as their headquarters to the dismay of the ailing Mosse.[25]

That was not the only time that Mossehaus had been the site of important political events. The German Democratic Party, founded in support of the new republic and later described as "the natural political home of German Jews," was born on November 10, 1918, in a Mossehaus conference room.[26] Theodor Wolff, Mosse's nephew and the editor of the *Tageblatt*, organized the initial meeting, and Friedrich Naumann, earlier one of the founders of the Werkbund, became the party's first chairman.[27] The party captured a significant share of the popular vote only once, in the first elections held under the republican regime, and its generally poor performance at the polls

FIGURE 36

Erich Mendelsohn, competition entry for the design of a high-rise office building on Kemperplatz, Berlin, 1922. (Source: Erich Mendelsohn, *Skizzen und Entwurfe*, Berlin, 1924.)

highlighted the tenuousness of the new form of government. At the same time, however, Wolff's background as a playwright whose work had been produced by Reinhardt and Naumann's involvement in the Werkbund were indicative of the wide-ranging union between commerce, politics, and culture that drew many Jewish Germans into the orbit of Mendelsohn's architecture.

After Mosse's death, his place as the head of the firm was taken by Hans Lachmann-Mosse, the husband of his adopted daughter Felicia. Lachmann-Mosse was only two years older than Mendelsohn. Cut out of the editorial process (Mosse's will stipulated that Wolff continue to edit the *Tageblatt*), Lachmann-Mosse increasingly devoted himself to real estate, beginning with the rebuilding of the firm's headquarters.[28] Probably inspired by the *Tageblatt's* coverage of the Einstein Tower late in the summer of 1921, he hired Mendelsohn to renovate and enlarge the damaged structure after surveying his employees about their opinion of the Tower.[29] It is also likely that he knew the colorful Hausleben Insurance Company facade nearby, which Mendelsohn had built in 1920 just off Friedrichstraße and which the company used in its advertisements.[30] In true Werkbund tradition, Lachmann-Mosse chose architecture as the means to create a more modern image for the company he headed.

The existing curved entrance determined Mendelsohn's conception of the building from the beginning.[31] It was the only aspect of his initial concept to survive as part of the final design. In the end, bold horizontals united the entire new construction, as Mendelsohn created yet another formulation of dynamic architecture. The architect's interest in the impact of such powerful horizontal bands was first apparent in his competition entry of 1921 for a high-rise office building on Berlin's Kemperplatz (Fig. 36).[32] Upon a base that repeated

FIGURE 37

Hans Poelzig, office building on Junkernstraβe, Breslau, 1911. (Source: Foto Marburg/Art Resource NY, Neg. Z.14.378.)

the angled window recessions of the Steinberg, Hermann factory sheds – here less completely glazed—Mendelsohn, on the Kemperplatz design, alternated projecting dark bands of concrete and the recessed light-colored bands that contained the windows. He used these bands to modernize Mossehaus, giving the lower part of its central bay smooth horizontal lines, which stood firmly counterpoised against Cremer and Wolffenstein's vertically organized composition. For Mossehaus, Mendelsohn increased the amount of glazing within each window band of the Kemperplatz entry, wrapping them in eye-catching unbroken curves that went around the corner of the building. The most striking of these was the projecting cornice, which Mendelsohn now dropped from the level of the roof to a position just above the doorway. Above the existing structure, Mendelsohn repeated the bay system established by Cremer and Wolffenstein, although the progressive recession of these additional two stories added to the building's overwhelmingly horizontal character.

Mendelsohn believed that horizontal compositions best expressed the character of reinforced concrete slab construction and overthrew a dependence upon columns and piers that dated back to ancient Greece. He found support for this position in Hans Poelzig's office building of 1911 in Breslau, the most important source for his Kemperplatz and Mossehaus designs (Fig. 37).[33] Like Berg's Centennial Hall in the same city, Poelzig's office building was one of Germany's most important prewar concrete buildings. Mendelsohn probably saw it during his visit to Breslau in 1913. Certainly Poelzig's postwar fame again brought it to his attention. Poelzig's innovative use of concrete, which he dared to leave completely exposed a dozen years before Mendelsohn would cautiously clad Mossehaus with stucco and tile, and the almost complete absence of ornament made Poelzig's building in some ways more radical than Mossehaus. In comparison to its successor, however, it was an aesthetically crude effort, squat and heavy, while the new stories added to the publishing firm's headquarters appear almost weightless.[34]

This lightness imitated the uninterrupted exposed ends of the Breslau office building's floor slabs. Poelzig's example offered Mendelsohn an innovative alternative to the emphasis in most prewar architecture, including the original Mossehaus, on vertical piers. Thus Mendelsohn accented the continuous sweep of the horizontal sills in the central bay of Mossehaus rather than the divided verticals whose impact in the upper stories was further diminished by their recession. He believed in the dynamic possibilities inherent in the concrete floor slab, which, like the pier it replaced, was the direct product of construction. The concrete slab opened up vistas of an architecture whose blurring of verticals and extending of horizontals reflected the way automobile passengers traveling at high speed perceived the buildings they drove past.[35] Claiming in 1923 that modern architecture should be an expression of such speed, Mendelsohn buttressed his argument with political, economic, and religious analogies. For instance, he declared that horizontal organization corresponded to the way that small nations after the war had replaced the vertical organization of the old empires. He similarly condemned the vertical hierarchies of economic trusts and orthodox religion.[36] Mendelsohn added that horizontal movement alleviated the stress of modern life:

> Medieval man, amidst the horizontal tranquility of his contemplative working day, needed the verticals of the cathedrals in order to find his God high above. Modern man, amidst the excited flurry of his fast-moving life, can find equilibrium only in the tension-free horizontal. Only by means of his will to reality can he become master of his unrest, only by moving at maximum speed will he overcome his haste. For the rotating earth stands still![37]

Mendelsohn's formula for transposing into architecture the velocity of the machinery of modern transportation became a staple of his work after 1924. Mendelsohn's staff jokingly declared that the addition to Mossehaus represented "the docking of the *Mauretania* in Berlin."[38] Their reference to one of the most famous ocean liners of the day captured the intrusiveness – despite the subtle scaling of details – of the building's huge size, its hint of machine-generated speed, and the mechanistic connotations of its aluminum mullions, banding, and lettering. The architect himself resorted to images of the surrounding traffic to describe the effect he had sought:

> An attempt has been made here to express the fact that the building is not an indifferent spectator of the careening motorcars and the tides of traffic in the streets, but that . . . it strives to be a living, cooperating factor of the movement. Just as it visibly expresses the swift tempo of the street, and takes up the accelerated tendency to speed at the corners, so at the same time it subdues the nervousness of the street and of the passers-by by the balance of its power.[39]

The design of the first three floors of the entrance bay, on which Mendelsohn collaborated with Henning and Neutra, gave the team the most trouble. Lachmann-Mosse was not always sympathetic to their goals. In April Neutra's fiancée Dione Niedermann wrote her mother:

> Mosse throws his hands over his head concerning Mendelsohn's designs and proposes for instance the following: Mosse: "Mr. Mendelsohn, the entrance portal *must* be in style." Mendelsohn: "Naturally." Mosse: "*Real* style, not style Mendelsohn. I have to travel to Italy and could bring back a portal in the classical style."[40]

In June 1922, while Henning was vacationing in Switzerland, Mendelsohn partially redesigned the canopy Henning had presented two months earlier in a one-twentieth scale model of the central bay.[41] The issue was not resolved until August, however, this time with the assistance of both Henning and Neutra and after discussions with the newspaper's architectural critic, Fritz Stahl. The main problem was the depth of the canopy, which exceeded the permitted limit. Mendelsohn had to appeal to a committee of architects and to the city government to build it according to his wishes. It was crucial, he believed, to his conception for the building. "The canopy must be carried through," he commented, using imagery that reflected his passion for Bach, "otherwise the fugue will lack its bass notes."[42]

There is no reason to attribute to Henning the force of the great curve that dominated the Mossehaus facade or the mechanical detailing in smooth aluminum and ceramic that reiterated the sleekness of this curve. Instead, it would appear that Mendelsohn, seeking such an effect, hired Henning, whose expertise in ceramics could help him achieve it. The Mendelsohns had known Henning since at least 1918.

A year older than the architect, Henning had contributed architectural ornament to several prewar buildings in Berlin and during the war had been in Zurich with Mendelsohn's friend Hugo Ball, one of the founders of Dada. Henning was now ready to develop an abstract rather than figural approach to the architectural use of his favorite material.[43]

Henning's views about the use of ceramic tile in architecture were neatly positioned, like Mossehaus itself, between Expressionism and a more pragmatic approach to architecture as construction. He praised the economical, versatile, and colorful material for the contribution it could make to the "matter-of-fact," or *sachlich*, buildings that he believed were replacing the excesses of Expressionism, and he claimed for ceramics a larger role than mere decorative effect, whether historical or exotic in flavor. He thought that cladding walls in ceramic tile created the best transition between large areas of glass and either the concrete or steel-pier systems that were taking the place of load-bearing walls.[44]

By the summer, Mendelsohn began to feel the strain of the collaboration, which took its toll on his patience. He wrote in June:

> As my solutions can only be of a functional nature, it is stupid to bring in a sculptor, and particularly someone who, with his sense of his "artistic freedom" is not wholly to be trusted.
>
> In architecture everyone fails who is not a firm character in all things.
>
> In particular it seems to me impossible to find someone who can make additions to my own distinctive vision of proportion.
>
> Every centimeter is sacred to me, it chokes me if it does not receive its due.[45]

Although Mendelsohn was referring specifically to Henning, his remarks were colored as well by his reservations about Neutra.

As the size of Mendelsohn's office grew rapidly in the early twenties, he came increasingly to depend on his assistant, whom he hired in October 1921. The relationship was not easy for either man. Mendelsohn worried that Neutra would set up his own practice and woo clients away. Neutra, only five years younger than his employer, longed for independence and recognition. Both men profited, however, from their two-year association. Mendelsohn learned much from Neutra's enthusiasm for Frank Lloyd Wright, while Neutra had the opportunity to observe the operation of a large and successful office. In June 1920, when he was designing the Einstein Tower, the Hermann factory, and the Hausleben facade, Mendelsohn employed only three other architects.[46] By the fall of 1921 he had plenty of work for talented help. Neutra joined five other assistants.[47] Throughout the next year the size of the staff grew to nine. At one point in the twenties it numbered forty, making it reputedly the largest of any private architectural office in Germany.[48]

Neutra had graduated from Vienna's Technische Hochschule with an architecture degree after serving as a cavalry officer in World War I. Perhaps most importantly for his architectural career, he was a friend of the city's most radical architectural theorist, Adolf Loos. From Loos's enthusiasm for the United States, where he had spent three poverty-stricken years, Neutra developed a fascination with that country. His friend Rudolf Schindler emigrated from Vienna in 1914 and worked for Wright first in Chicago and later in Los Angeles. Neutra dreamed of following him to California and of meeting Wright, whom he admired above all others. The war, Neutra's position as an enemy officer, and restrictions placed upon American immigration in 1921 all interfered with fulfilling this desire.[49]

From March to November 1921 Neutra worked as the Luckenwalde city architect. There he saw Mendelsohn's exciting plans for the Steinberg, Hermann factory. Spotting a notice in a Berlin newspaper for a position as chief draftsman in Mendelsohn's office, he applied and was offered work, even though he had not brought any drawings along.[50] Neutra was initially enthusiastic about working for Mendelsohn, who, he wrote, "is considered here *the* new man, who even tops Poelzig," although Neutra admitted to advocating a different style of architecture.[51] Mendelsohn was the only one of the radical architects, Neutra noted, who had enough commissions to give him the experience he needed in practical construction. That his fiancée Dione Niedermann and Luise Mendelsohn were both cellists was also a fortunate coincidence. Luise Mendelsohn was able to recommend that Niedermann travel from Switzerland to Berlin to study with Hugo Becker, her own teacher, a proposal which, of course, accorded with the young couple's wishes.[52] The new assistant worked on the exterior details of the Mossehaus design from its inception, and eventually Mendelsohn entrusted him with its most important interior, Lachmann-Mosse's office. Because Mendelsohn had no experience in the field, Neutra also designed the landscaping for the Einstein Tower.[53]

By April 1922 Neutra was expressing the reservations of any skilled, opinionated assistant subjected to the somewhat different aesthetic of a more successful contemporary.[54] Meanwhile, Mendelsohn, while admitting he could not run the office without him, also understood that Neutra was more committed to his own career than to his employer. The two men spent August 1922 negotiating Neutra's place in the firm. Neutra sought a partnership agreement, which would have enabled him to support a wife. Mendelsohn, anxious to secure a place in the firm for his trusted friend Charles Du Vinage, whom he rightly sensed was more likely to remain with the firm and to subordinate his ego to Mendelsohn's, refused to agree. Instead, he recognized Neutra's contribution through a complicated contract that protected his assistant from the ravages of inflation but forbade him to work independently in Berlin for three years. Neutra was not entirely satisfied but realized that he could do no better.[55]

Despite the lack of respect that sometimes infected his dealings with Mendelsohn, whom the impoverished Neutra had every reason to envy, the young assistant fully recognized his employer's talents. His descriptions of Mendelsohn, however, failed to include references to the design details of individual buildings or to Mendelsohn's general architectural style. The young assistant, confident of his own taste, admired Mendelsohn mostly for being able to run a successful office:

> He is an artist who thinks only of his art and this permeates his personality. As far as form is concerned, his behavior towards me could not be more correct or, according to his character, hardly ever less open and without ulterior motives. Sometimes he is exhausting but hardly ever acutely inconsiderate. In financial matters, he is much my superior, not so much because I lack intelligence, but because of his incessant, imperturbable interest in it. Whoever takes a bet regarding his career is on the right track as far as he is concerned, and his success so far is much greater than any of you can evaluate.[56]

Neutra brought to Mendelsohn's office not only the skills of a superbly talented draftsman but also the imagination of an architect who later in the decade would become celebrated in his own right. The impact upon Mendelsohn of Neutra's friendship with Loos remained subtle; not so the impact of Neutra's interest in Wright, which affected the Mossehaus design only slightly but characterized the work of Mendelsohn's office for the rest of 1922 and throughout 1923. Equally importantly, Neutra's presence challenged Mendelsohn to remain innovative rather than be satisfied with either the Steinberg, Hermann factory or Mossehaus. In the design of the upper floors of Mossehaus, the two men turned toward the efforts that other Expressionists were making to find a middle ground between visionary dreams and actual construction. Mendelsohn and Neutra joined Bruno Taut's brother Max and his collaborator Franz Hoffmann in following the example of Czech Cubism, creating faceted forms that were reminiscent of the crystalline imagery of the immediate postwar years yet were completely buildable.[57] This aspect of Mossehaus, foreshadowed in both the Hausleben building and the Steinberg, Hermann factory, would, however, turn out to be a dead end. For a brief moment though, this kind of architecture represented the most compelling path toward an urbanism that was shaped more by the demand for office space than by the concerns about advertising that contributed so powerfully to Mendelsohn's later commercial architecture.

In his drawings for Mossehaus, Neutra fixed many of the building's exterior details and had total responsibility for the design of Lachmann-Mosse's office. He also oversaw the building's construction and participated in meetings with the authorities whose permission was required to build the unusual design.[58] On the facade he concentrated on the two floors added above the bulk of the existing building. This section of the building was covered with a layer of stucco, and its window frames and mullions were built of steel.[59] After much experimentation with more complicated forms reminiscent of the Hausleben facade, Neutra designed for each window a hood that jutted forward from the top and one side of the wall plane. The windows themselves were deeply recessed in two stages and separated by a thin mullion about a quarter of the distance from the sill to which they ran parallel. This detail reinforced the horizontal flow of the composition, overriding the vertical divisions of the panes. Finally, the accumulated stories had a stepped profile and were terminated by bands of moulding, each projecting out above the one below. This contrast between projection and recession was typical of the entire composition and added subtly to the generally sweeping effect of the whole.

Although largely responsible for detailing the Mossehaus window surrounds in Mendelsohn's manner, Neutra personally preferred the paintings of two fellow Viennese Expressionists, Egon Schiele and Oskar Kokoshka, whose drawing style he imitated, to the faceted forms favored by the Czech Cubists and Berlin Expressionists. Neutra's distance from the Berlin group was apparent in his design of Lachmann-Mosse's office (Fig. 38).[60] The room, located in one of the upper stories of the building's central bay, featured two angled interior walls lined with bookcases, which hid the curved profile of the original building. Neutra's many studies for the general arrangement

FIGURE 38

Richard Neutra, Mossehaus, office of Hans Lachmann-Mosse. (Source: Staatliche Museen zu Berlin, Kunstbibliothek.)

of the room and its made-to-order furniture chart his shift toward Wrightian planar surfaces and the substitution of Wright's delicately balanced cantilevers for Loos's sense of fixed mass. The office's chairs and tables were models of caution compared to their counterparts in the Einstein Tower. Unlike these predecessors, Neutra's furniture was fashioned from rectilinear members that met the floor firmly. The textures and colors of their plain wood surfaces and fabrics remained warmer, however, than the metal finishes popular by the end of the decade and already foreshadowed on the Mossehaus facade.

Neutra's introduction of Wright into the work of the Mendelsohn office set the stage for Mendelsohn's lifelong admiration for the American, who quickly supplanted Olbrich and van de Velde's privileged position in his pantheon of architectural deities. Wright's Robie House was an archetype for the European understanding of the American. Its interlocking forms interrupted by a minimum of ornamental detail offered a vision of a new architecture dependent upon structure rather than history.[61] During the teens, Wright's work was studied by almost all of the European architects who would rise to prominence in the next decade, but, as was also the case in the early stages of Expressionist architecture, only the Dutch were immediately able to build a substantial body of work in the Wrightian manner. For instance, Mendelsohn referred admiringly to the American as early as 1917, but he began to design in a Wrightian idiom only after he had hired Neutra.[62] Mendelsohn's taste for Wright was undoubtedly also enhanced by his 1921 visit to the Netherlands. In his wartime drawings, Mendelsohn conceived of buildings as single, plastic volumes rather than as the compilations of separate parts that fascinated Neutra.[63] The subtle, yet still dynamic, balancing of cantilevers and insets seen, for example, in the light fixture designed by Neutra, which hung over Lachmann-Mosse's desk, became, however, yet another of Mendelsohn's formulas for the architectural representation of motion.[64]

Inflation and the shortage of foreign exchange twice threatened to curtail severely the scope of Mossehaus before construction could begin in the fall of 1922.[65] During the winter Mendelsohn once again learned that concrete had limitations he had not dreamed of while a soldier sketching in odd moments at the front during World War I. He had specified concrete slab construction for the new stories added atop the existing structure. One cold day in January 1923 a construction worker, acting independently of the architect's office, piled up sand on the crowning slab until it was as tall as a man. The slab, which had not yet set (perhaps because of the cold), collapsed, crashing into the existing building where the newspaper's staff had continued to work throughout the construction process, and fell all the way to the basement. Fourteen people were killed and a number of others injured.[66]

Despite this disaster, construction continued. An unusual technological experiment reflected the postwar economic crisis, then reaching its peak as the inflation rate soared daily. The Mossehaus roof was covered with a type of poured concrete called "Nonplus," whose ingredients included gravel and slag. It was meant as a replacement for tile and brick whose manufacture required expensive amounts of coal. For Lachmann-Mosse, the use of this material typified the economic benefits that could be realized through the patronage of a modern architecture shorn of the "petty" details popular a generation earlier.[67]

Nine stories tall at its center, the completed building was briefly, except for church towers, the most prominent feature on the Berlin skyline. Together, Mendelsohn, Neutra, and Henning reaped the benefits of dramatic size, while mediating less obtrusively between old and new scales. Although the details of the addition made Cremer and Wolffenstein's ornament appear fussy, only the corner windows and the canopy were actually dramatic gestures. In the rest of the new exterior the team broke details, such as the scale of the windows and their panes, down into small parts that did not overwhelm the older facades. Similarly, the tile banding directly above the canopy and on each side of the lower pair of wrap-around corner windows fragmented this area of the facade into pieces only a fraction the height of the original six stories. This juxtaposition of old and new was further complicated by differences in texture, color, and form between the lower tile-sheathed part of the addition and the stuccoed upper stories. The contrast between the lingering Expressionism of the side facades and the machine-age aesthetic of the tile-and-aluminum section fragmented the enormous scale of the addition. The new stories floated high above the street atop a dark pool of glossy tile.

Mossehaus's astonishing appearance, prominent location, and publicity-minded patron ensured the building's fame. Beginning with an article published by Fritz Stahl in the *Tageblatt* itself, Mossehaus was included in guidebooks to Berlin and in a number of German as well as foreign surveys of contemporary architecture.[68] Writers noted the effectiveness of the new style when seen in its crowded setting surrounded by the conditions that had generated it.[69] One Communist critic, however, dissented from the general praise. "The more forms and possibilities result from the constructive consequences of materials in keeping with the times," he stated, "the more the building loses its constructive organization, decorative eyewash takes its place, and its purposeful lines are kitschified."[70] The building had been designed to attract attention, and Mossehaus's publicity value extended beyond notices in the architectural press. The building's image was featured prominently in the publishing company's promotional material, appearing almost as a trademark in advertisements for the company's publications and in such extras as calendars.[71] On the building itself aluminum lettering affixed over the doors and above the side windows identified the firm and listed its activities.

For Mendelsohn, Mossehaus was an incomplete effort, limited by the participation of collaborators, however talented, and by vestiges of classicism in its old facades and Expressionism in the new ones. Successful on its own terms, it did not offer a formula for the future. However, with Mossehaus, for the first time, Mendelsohn built horizontal curves and supervised experiments with Wrightian juxtapositions of rectilinear planes. Equally importantly, Mossehaus demonstrated to Berliners, and to all who kept up with events in the city's downtown, the dynamic contribution that new architecture could make to the life of the modern metropolis. This dramatic demonstration was to win many clients for Mendelsohn and other German architects as they began after the collapse of inflation at the end of 1923 to contribute new facades and, less frequently, entirely new buildings to urban centers across the country. Expanding upon

FIGURE 39

Erich Mendelsohn, Weichmann Silk Store, Gleiwitz, Germany (now Gliwice, Poland), 1922. (Source: *Erich Mendelsohn: Das Gesamtschaffen des Architekten.*)

the exploitation of economical building materials and the advertising power of architecture that Mendelsohn pioneered in Mossehaus, their designs would produce a marriage of convenience between modern architects on the one hand and tightfisted store owners and real estate developers on the other.

WEICHMANN SILK STORE

By 1922 Wright had become for Mendelsohn the most important architect of the previous generation. In a series of projects from 1922 and 1923, interlocking rectilinear forms covered in stucco replaced the irregular sculpture of the Steinberg, Hermann hat factory and the unifying sweep of Mossehaus in Mendelsohn's architecture. It is likely that Mendelsohn's talented assistant was largely responsible for this shift.[72] Neutra was one of the employees delegated to work on the Weichmann Silk Store in Gleiwitz, a small commission that in 1922 marked Mendelsohn's entry into the field of store design (Fig. 39). Here the lessons of Lachmann-Mosse's office interior appear for the first time on the exterior of a Mendelsohn building.[73]

In a March 1922 letter written to Lilly Müller Niedermann, his future mother-in-law, Neutra provided a glimpse of the project's earliest moments. Anxious to prove to Niedermann that he was a respected figure in Mendelsohn's office, Neutra recounted:

> Today the client from Silesia came again. I was in my element, spoke like a waterfall. For the time being, the client thinks I am his man. He trembles that Mendelsohn might change my design sketches. This, however, he has no intention of doing. On the contrary, he is radiant.[74]

Mendelsohn's letters show that he was preoccupied with Mossehaus and delegated the details of the Weichmann store to at least three different employees, of whom Neutra was the most important. The first mention of the project in his surviving correspondence came in June, when he wrote his wife that Arthur Korn "broods over Gleiwitz."[75] Two months later, he mentioned that Neutra and Erich Karweik had taken over the job. Mendelsohn traveled to Silesia to arrange the construction contract, but the letters reveal only one detail of his thinking about the design, that it must be "racy."[76]

Gleiwitz was a small provincial city in a heavily industrialized part of Silesia close to the Polish border. Wilhelmstraße, the main street leading from the railroad station to the old center of town, was lined with plain yellow-and-brown-brick boxes encrusted with stone ornament, a breath of Wilhelmine neo-Baroque giving life to the ghost of Schinkel. Erwin Weichmann hired Mendelsohn in part as an exercise in civic pride; he wanted to commission a design that would outshine larger, more famous stores in bigger cities. His company's lawyer wrote in a laudatory description included in a Chamber of Commerce–type publication that the store functioned "not only [as] a prominent landmark of the city of Gleiwitz and even of the province of Upper Silesia, but it embodies the healthy, straightforward, and clear-sighted business spirit which understands the great economic connections that pervade this building."[77]

Weichmann could not afford a large or heavily ornamented building. Instead, he sought to make an impression through excellence in design. The site was a mere sliver along Wilhemstraße, although a small promenade next to it gave the building extra prominence by leaving the side facade exposed. Three stories tall in front and four in the rear, it was smaller than most of its neighbors. Neutra recorded how his business sense had helped win the commission, claiming, "I developed the idea to form a corporation, produced all sorts of proofs to show what income my scheme would produce, and behaved like a wise, gray bearded expert of finance and a real estate broker."[78] It may have been his idea to place two bachelor apartments atop the

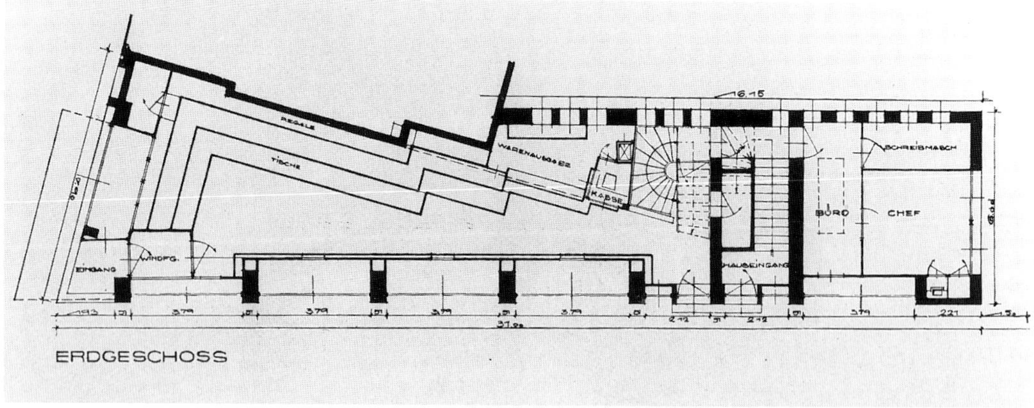

FIGURE 40

Weichmann Silk Store, plan of ground floor. (Source: Staatliche Museen zu Berlin, Kunstbibliothek.)

two floors of commercial space, although such an arrangement hardly seems unusual.

The only surviving hints of Expressionism were the acute angles of the store's facade and interior cabinetry (Fig. 40). Mendelsohn and his assistants enlivened the narrow rectangle through the way in which they eroded and displaced corners. The joint between the two featured facades was deeply inset at street level where plate glass display windows further reduced its solidity. Three levels of notched entablatures extended out even beyond its cantilevered mass. Sandwiched between them, the windows of the second-story salesroom were set back at the corner. On the other end of the promenade, the entablature ran beyond the main mass of the building, and on the upper stories, a staircase tower provided a counterweight to the missing corner area. The placement of windows at the intersection of the two main facades created similar tension.

Mendelsohn's aesthetics meshed effortlessly with Weichmann's Werkbund-tinged philosophy. The patron recognized in the building's style the same clarity, purity, and reliability that he valued as the economic principles upon which he based his new business.[79] The concrete bands, simpler than the aluminum-plated Mossehaus version and painted in a darker color than the stucco facade, provided the only touch of ornament; cantilevered and towered massing effectively substituted for more expensive effects. Nor did the architects diguise the location of the steel piers running just behind the thin layer of exterior stucco.

The architectural style that Mendelsohn's office fashioned for this commission and continued to use as long as Neutra worked there was stripped of all but a hint of Expressionist detail. As in most of

FIGURE 41

Wilhelm Dudok, Dr. Bavink School, Hilversum, the Netherlands, 1921. (Source: Wattjes, *Niew Nederlandsche Bouwkunst.*)

Mendelsohn's work, volume played a more important role than surface treatment. Only in Mossehaus, where the shape and size of the container were largely dictated by the original building, did he stray from this emphasis. The way in which the Mendelsohn office crafted the composition of rectilinear volumes in the Weichmann store for maximum functional purpose and aesthetic drama was new, however. This commission was also the first in which the office experimented with asymmetry; concrete mouldings wrapped from the long facade around each of the short ends of the building, accenting the joint between the two facades rather than the center of either.

As contemporary critics immediately noted, one could find in the work of Wilhelm Dudok, a Dutch architect three years older than Mendelsohn, ample precedent for the Wrightian aspects of the Weichmann design.[80] After the war, Dudok breathed new life into Wright's style during his long tenure as the city architect of Hilversum. He transformed this small city between Amsterdam and Utrecht into a site of pilgrimage for those interested in progressive design. His Dr. Bavink School of 1921, for instance, illustrates the lessons Mendelsohn would learn from Dudok's interpretation of Wright (Fig. 41). A comparison of the school with the Weichmann store also demonstrates the degree to which Mendelsohn simplified Dutch models.

The Hilversum school was a mature appreciation of Wright rather than a slavish copy of a particular building by the American architect. The same might be said of the relationship of the Weichmann Silk Store to such Dutch precedents. The resemblances were at the level of conception rather than of detail. Dudok built his school of brick and gave it a dramatic corner tower. Revealed constructional piers and interlocking rectangular volumes gave it a Wrightian character. In the Weichmann store, Mendelsohn repeated this type of composition but drastically slashed the number of separate volumes, a reduction that produced a far leaner set of profiles. This and the acute angle at which he joined the two principal Weichmann facades enhanced the dynamism of the store's composition, in itself a contrast to the inherent stability of Dudok's building, which had a monumentality appropriate to public architecture.

In his description of the Weichmann store, Mendelsohn rejected such stability as an architectural goal. Instead, in language that echoed his wartime letters written under the influence of relativity, Mendelsohn described effects of light and movement, now obtained using a completely different formal vocabulary from that of his early industrial sketches:

> The spatial development clearly shows the power and striking force of the structure in its light and shadow.
>
> The narrow front rises at the junction of the neighboring building with a movement which is strongly supported by horizontal beltcourses.
>
> The broad front continues the movement, brings the entrance into relief and graduates the movement up the staircase tower.
>
> Here it takes a steep plunge down to the lowest level in order to make the
>
> View towards the tower, the focal point of the street, free to the eye.[81]

In the Weichmann store, more than in any building since the Einstein Tower, the Mendelsohn office was able to create architectural forms that through the juxtaposition of masses captured the dynamic tension between tensile and load-bearing capacities that Mendelsohn believed was inherent in reinforced concrete. The store was more important as an example of this phase of Mendelsohn's career than it was as an individual commission. Under the influence of Neutra's enthusiasm for Wright and Mendelsohn's continued contact with Dutch architecture, the office changed the way in which it achieved its characteristically dynamic effects, shifting from surface treatment back to volume. At the same time, the design, by moving further than any earlier German commercial building toward the radical simplicity of the decade's avant-garde architecture and by fulfilling its patron's desire for inexpensive functionalism, anticipated Mendelsohn's position later in the decade as Europe's leading department store architect. The links between the Weichmann store and other prominent modern buildings were recognized by French critic Jean Badovici, for instance, who in 1926 noted the store's similarity to contemporary buildings by Wright, Robert Mallet-Stevens, and Tony Garnier, as well as Dudok.[82]

Neutra left for America in October 1923, having resigned his job in Mendelsohn's office that July. After his departure, rectilinear volumes became an undercurrent in Mendelsohn's work, supplemented by the stream of ideas flowing from the Steinberg, Hermann factory and from Mossehaus. Mendelsohn's enthusiasm for Wright remained, however. For the rest of Mendelsohn's life, Wright was the architect that he most admired. Nevertheless Mendelsohn's stylistic references to the elder architect's work never grew any more specific than they were in the buildings and projects designed while Neutra was working for him. And Wright reciprocated. In the forties, when a number of former Wright disciples, including most notably Gropius and Mies van der Rohe, had gathered in America safe from the Nazi condemnation of the Bauhaus, Mendelsohn was the only European to enjoy an unstrained relationship with the aging but still productive master.[83]

In the two years following the publication of the Einstein Tower, Mendelsohn refused to capitalize on his new fame by repeating himself. Instead, he experimented with a variety of styles, searching for forms that more completely realized his wartime goals of using light and shadow, the appearance of motion, and reinforced concrete to create a dynamic yet functional architecture. The range of sources upon which he drew – Olbrich, Poelzig, de Klerk, Wright, and Dudok – should not obscure his own accomplishments. His persistent interest in the machine prepared the way in Germany for the technological imagery of the second half of the decade. In Mossehaus he laid the foundation for streamlining, one of the most popular aspects of architecture and industrial design, for the remainder of the interwar period, especially in America. By finding patrons in Berlin and the provinces willing to build this new architecture, Mendelsohn demonstrated to his compatriots that what appeared to be a radical aberration from architectural standards in fact offered the most practical and most economic method of design and construction available to them.

4 AN ARCHITECTURE FOR THE METROPOLIS

THE sketches Mendelsohn exhibited at the Paul Cassirer Gallery in 1919 all showed designs for individual buildings floating in space. No hint of context was given. Such perspectives continued to be crucial to the architect's design process, but as more of his commissions were for downtown sites, he began to pay increasing attention to the buildings' place in the city. For Mendelsohn, the city was never an abstract plane upon which to inscribe a rational new order. He found in its speeding automobiles and bustling crowds, its flashing lights and soaring heights, an experience whose intense modernity equaled that of the factory floor.[1] Even more than for the locus of production, he believed it necessary to shape this site of consumption in ways that expressed its vitality but tamed its tendency toward the chaos that had appalled him in America. Charged with integrating large buildings into contexts built on a more modest scale, Mendelsohn fused a bold architectural vocabulary with plans and massing that respectfully clarified the urban order.

Like his consistent praise for the machine, Mendelsohn's enthusiasm for the metropolis – especially for the downtown that was its pulsing heart – separated him from Expressionist critiques of the "City," as Germans called their downtowns.[2] Since the turn of the century, German critics, most notably the sociologist Georg Simmel, had noted and lamented the substitution in the modern metropolis of a money-based economy and nerve-wracking clock-driven life for an "organic" preindustrial culture that supposedly emphasized spirituality and community.[3] Even before the Expressionist attempt led by Bruno Taut to regain this "utopia," German architects of the previous generation – above all Adolf Messel and Peter Behrens –

struggled to create a rational architecture whose vigorously shaped and sparsely ornamented forms, accompanied by references to the historical past, imposed continuity and order on the unstable modern urban environment. Mendelsohn, however, openly welcomed many of the developments that made Simmel uncomfortable, objecting only to the cacophonous historicism that Wilhelmine buildings too often shared with their American cousins. Furthermore, Mendelsohn interpreted Messel and Behrens's adaptations of the regular rhythms of neoclassical columns and Gothic piers to stabilize and solidify new skeletal construction in steel and concrete as betraying the spirit of the age, itself the product of speeding traffic and the only slightly slower bustle of pedestrians.[4]

A decade later Mendelsohn would have agreed with Karl Scheffler's 1913 description of the range of conditions that any new metropolitan architecture must address. "Each prerequisite for a higher architectural culture," Scheffler wrote, "is at times fully raised in the tremendous, but also violent development of the democratic freedom of individualism, of industrialization, of capitalism, of world travel and urbanization, in all the din of economic and social transformation, in all the terrific confusion of the changes."[5] Mendelsohn responded with an architecture of almost equal complexity and flexibility – multiuse buildings and developments whose bold horizontally oriented street walls channeled and contained the urban energies they dramatized.

The city proved an appropriate arena for Mendelsohn's dynamic effects. "Cut[ting] off," as one enthusiastic Berliner, the writer Franz Hessel, described it, "the rascal's head with the clear, simple lines of a new facade, and remov[ing] all the curly-cues," Mendelsohn and his many imitators severely reduced the amount of visual information the city dweller or awestruck visitor from the provinces needed to process.[6] At the same time, inspired above all by the roar of traffic and by what he continued to see as the dynamic qualities of steel-and-concrete-frame construction, Mendelsohn tailored his sleek facades to participate in rather than dam the frenetic movement that surrounded them. Poised on the verge of kineticism, his buildings seemed almost ready to step down into the rushing avenues they framed.

Although famous as a paper architect, Mendelsohn was never – unlike Le Corbusier or, back in Germany, Ludwig Hilberseimer – a paper urbanist.[7] Instead, his urban schemes, even when they remained unbuilt, were crafted in response to particular places and (at least potential) patrons. There was no room within dynamic functional separation of living and work that characterized Le Corbusier and Hilberseimer's attempts to integrate city and country. Like Martin Wagner, whom he helped install as Berlin's city architect, Mendelsohn preferred the more picturesque lessons he had learned through his teacher Theodor Fischer's admiration for Camillo Sitte. These he resolutely reworked to harmonize with the modern metropolis, above all, Berlin.[8]

In 1920, after annexing its almost equally urban neighbors, Berlin, with a population of four million, was the largest city on the European continent.[9] The capital of a united Germany only since 1871, the city had during the nineteenth century become the center of German transportation, industry, government, and culture. Retaining only vestiges of its eighteenth-century past, Berlin was a preeminent emblem of German modernity. By 1924, when an infusion of American capital generated across Germany a small building boom and a far larger number of renovations and additions to existing downtown structures, Berlin became the most important battleground in the struggle over the direction that German urban architecture and planning should take. The debates, like the urban development that triggered them, centered on the appearance of the downtown just west of the old royal and imperial seat of power and – slightly further west – the Kurfürstendamm, the broad boulevard that led towards the city's most elegant suburbs.

Here, too, were Mendelsohn's most prominent commissions. C. A. Herpich Sons, Furriers, on Leipzigerplatz, established – over the objections of city building authorities – the direction that commercial architecture would take until the end of the Weimar Republic. Working more harmoniously with Martin Wagner, Mendelsohn also built the WOGA complex on the Kurfürstendamm and contributed Columbushaus to Potsdamerplatz, a hub of train, automobile, and subway traffic.[10] Far more than the somewhat eccentric circumstances surrounding the Einstein Tower, this activity brought Mendelsohn into contact and agreement with the other leaders of the New Building, whose support he received in his struggles with Berlin's building authorities. Although others took the lead in building thousands of units of low-cost housing on the urban fringes, Mendelsohn's staging ground remained the "City." In Germany's downtowns, unthreatened by the blurring of urban edges into parkland, the contest was between the cacophony of Wilhelmine commercialism, encrusted (like the Battle of the Nations Monument or the older stories of Mossehaus) with outmoded ornament, and a new, almost animate architecture that had slipped its moorings in the past to sail proudly upon a sea of automobiles into the present.

HORIZONTALITY AND THE BATTLE OVER C. A. HERPICH SONS, FURRIERS

Mendelsohn's unusual designs were not popular with local authorities, to whom the approval process gave the power to criticize on aesthetic as well as on constructional grounds. It required powerful and politically adept clients to shepherd the Einstein Tower and Mossehaus past often reluctant inspectors. In 1924, Mendelsohn used the commission he received to renovate and add onto C. A. Herpich Sons – located on Berlin's most prominent shopping street – to challenge the precedents established by Messel's nearby Wertheim Department Store (Fig. 42). The Wertheim store, perhaps the city's most admired building designed since the death of Schinkel in 1841, was the model for almost every major store built in Germany for over two decades (Fig. 43). Mendelsohn's lack of respect for Messel's prototype triggered the opposition, once again, of city building officials. In the ensuing furor, the most important architectural battle to take place in Berlin during the Weimar Republic, proponents of change gradually marshalled their forces to both challenge the authority of the city's official architect Ludwig Hoffmann and create a climate in which the New Building could flourish as long as there was enough money for construction.

Germany's most luxurious, and eventually Europe's largest, department store, the Wertheim store was built in five stages. Messel designed three of these, of which the Leipzigerplatz addition, completed in 1904, was the most influential.[11] Eschewing the complicated detail of most contemporary architecture, Messel represented the vertical members of his steel-frame building rationally, turning to a loosely Gothic style as much for its structural connotations as for its historical and cultural associations with the merchant society of late-medieval northern Europe. Messel also replaced the most obvious market-oriented features of department store architecture with an emphasis on understated monumentality. For instance, he located the display windows behind an arcade that presented a resolutely civic face to the downtown's prime public space.[12] In the Leipzigerplatz facades, Messel demonstrated that modern commercialism could be tamed through an artful integration of historicism and rationalism.

Two decades later, Mendelsohn proposed to replace this whaleboned corset with something far less fussy. In place of the Wertheim

FIGURE 42

Erich Mendelsohn, C. A. Herpich Sons, Furriers, Berlin, 1924–28. (Source: Staatliche Museen zu Berlin, Kunstbibliothek.)

store's somewhat ponderous arcade, Mendelsohn offered a curtain of travertine and bronze, suspended from a steel frame above an almost fully glazed ground story. Lightweight and light-filled, Mendelsohn's solution was further energized by tautly attenuated hori-

FIGURE 43

Alfred Messel, Wertheim Department Store, Leipzigerplatz facade, Berlin, 1897–1904. (Source: Deutsche Fotothek Dresden, Neg. FD.192.785.)

zontals, which sent its energy shooting in either direction down Leipzigerstraße, redefining the street as a narrow, tightly bounded stream of cars and people. Led by Hoffmann, who remained in his post as city architect until April 1, 1924, but who, in the absence of a successor, continued after his retirement to influence the approval process, opponents of the Herpich store design focused on Mendelsohn's bold rejection of Messel's model. Mendelsohn had carefully considered the urban context of his site; he saw it, however, as a locus of traffic and salesmanship unsuited to the gracefully ornamented detailing of its older neighbors. The ensuing battle over permission to renovate the Herpich store was one of the most important fought during the 1920s between the pre- and postwar generations of German architectural reformers. For a year and a half, city officials, including the mayor, although they did not reject Mendelsohn's proposed design outright, threw up one obstacle after another against it. Twice Mendelsohn was forced to file official complaints and rally support for his design in order to win approval to build. The controversy drew attention to the entire approval process and to its manipulation by politicians opposed to architectural innovation.

Mendelsohn recognized that Hoffmann was his major adversary. One of his Herpich drawings is emblazoned, "Trotz Hoffmann!" or "Despite Hoffmann!"[13] Hoffmann was Berlin's city architect for nearly thirty years, heading an office that supervised the city's building inspectors in addition to its responsibility for designing schools, hospitals, and other civic buildings. Appointed to the post in 1896, Hoffmann had once been regarded, like Messel and Behrens, as an architect who wished to reform the ornamental excesses of late-nineteenth-century architecture. Buildings like his Rudolf-Virchow Hospital of 1898–1906, although incorporating a variety of historical styles, were rationally planned and were decorated with restrained ornament.[14] In the postwar years, however, Hoffmann was thoroughly opposed to more far-reaching attempts at stylistic change. His objections were ostensibly focused on the building's height in Mendelsohn's proposal and on the horizontality of the Herpich facade, but in fact they were part of a larger clash over architectural reform.

The first Herpich dispute, which occurred in the spring of 1924, centered on the scale of Mendelsohn's proposal. Mendelsohn met with Hoffmann in April to request permission to add two stories to Herpich's five-story building.[15] Although Hoffmann was simultaneously serving as a consulting architect to a far larger final building phase of the Wertheim store, the municipal council, certainly acting upon his advice, deferred its recommendation on Mendelsohn's Herpich application on the grounds that it could only be considered after new regulations concerning building heights were completed.[16] Because it already had been twice approved by the expert committee, Mendelsohn filed a complaint with the minister of social welfare.[17] The Union of German Architects lodged its own complaint, which, without mentioning Herpich or Mendelsohn, criticized the arbitrary and irregular way that the city handled building applications.[18] Behrens was sympathetic, and Poelzig, whose Capitol Cinema had also aroused Hoffmann's ire, led the general protest.[19] Among the critics who supported the Herpich design was Paul Westheim, otherwise one of Mendelsohn's most vigorous opponents.[20] Mendelsohn finally obtained permission to build the extra stories. In January 1925 he gave out contracts for the building; workers began erecting the scaffolding that February.[21]

Permission to add extra floors did not extend to the alteration of the existing facades, the focus of the 1925 dispute.[22] The new con-

would introduce to a street dominated by the Wertheim store and its imitators.[23] In August 1925 the district mayor finally announced that he had rejected Mendelsohn's permit application, which he labeled "a coarse butchery of outlines and masses."[24] Again Mendelsohn won approval for his design only after he filed a complaint and a second protest was organized. Freundlich hosted a tea at the Einstein Tower for Edwin Redslob, Adolf Behne, Werner Hegemann, and others whom he hoped would defend Mendelsohn's design. Twenty-two of the twenty-three specialists who were asked to sign a petition saying that "a vertical arrangement [of the Herpich facade] cannot be recommended" agreed to do so. Only Hegemann refused.[25] In a final bitter comment on the eighteen-month-long ordeal, Mendelsohn in 1929 made a diagram showing the bureaucratic process he had faced (Fig. 44). Ironically, Hegemann later published it as an example of the obstacles to urban planning reform in the city.[26]

Mendelsohn's battles with Hoffmann were an important factor in the founding of the Ring in April 1924 and in the replacement of bureaucratic obstacles with a climate in which the New Building could flourish. The Ring, whose original members included Behrens, Otto Bartning, Gropius, Häring, Mendelsohn, Mies, Poelzig, and Bruno and Max Taut, became the single most effective group supporting the New Building. Established to inject into the debate over Hoffmann and the choice of his successor a more radical position than that espoused by the Union of German Architects, the Ring went on to play an equally important role in the debate over housing. Pressure from the Ring aided in the appointment of Martin Wagner (who approved the final stage of the Herpich design without incident) as city architect in 1926.[27]

The controversy over the Herpich store indicated the widespread support for the New Building among two generations of architects and their patrons. It also left Mendelsohn free to concentrate on achieving urban drama through tight street boundaries accentuated by bulging balconies and towers, an architecture that participated in rather than resisted the forces shaping the modern city: traffic, trade, and entertainment.

BREAKING OPEN THE BLOCK: THE WOGA COMPLEX

Between 1925 and 1931 Mendelsohn laid out a deep, block-long site on Berlin's Kurfürstendamm, the elegant boulevard that ran from the

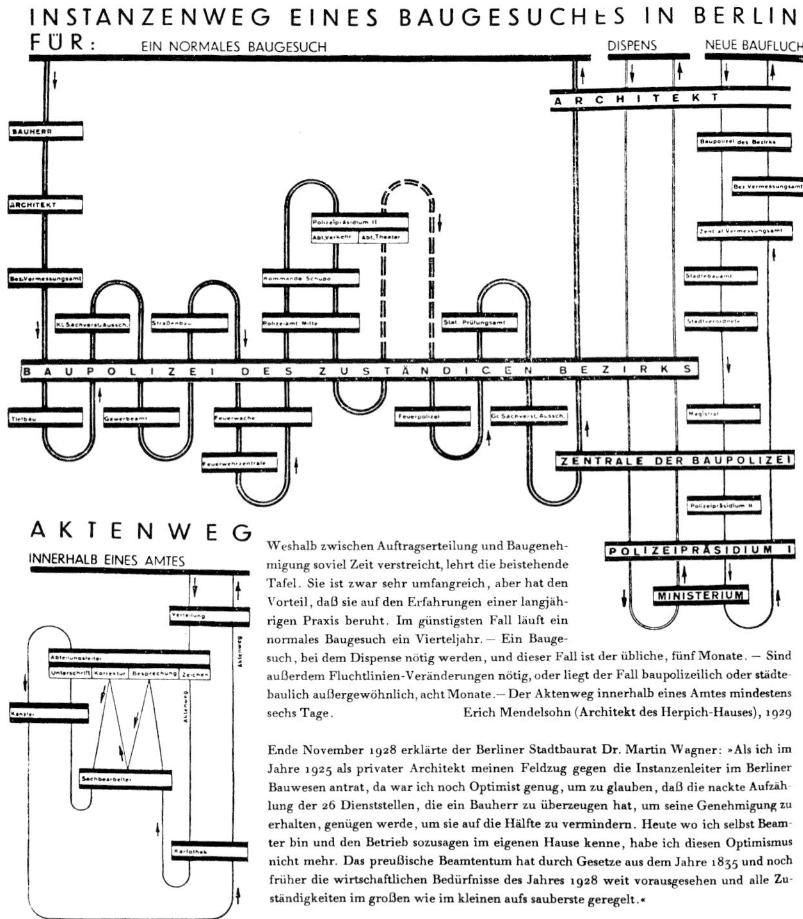

FIGURE 44

Erich Mendelsohn, diagram of process of getting a building permit in Berlin (*top*), and the paper path within each office (*bottom*), 1929. From Werner Hegemann, *Das steinere Berlin*, Berlin, 1930. (Source: Staatliche Museen zu Berlin, Kunstbibliothek.)

city's commercial heart to its wealthy western suburbs. Known as the WOGA complex after Wohnhausgrundstücksverwertungs A. G., the name of the development company, the block included the Universum Cinema, the Komiker Cabaret, and a shopping street – all by Mendelsohn – and apartments by Mendelsohn and a second architect, Jürgen Bachmann. Mendelsohn arranged this disparate collection of functions with one eye on their profitability and the other on the opportunities that the huge site offered for creating an orderly yet exciting alternative to the boulevard's existing apartment blocks. Besides demonstrating his continued championship of a mix of residential and commercial uses, the complex was most interesting for Mendelsohn's decision to build relatively expensive housing in the same style as the tiny apartments for workers that were being erected in the suburbs during the same years.

Not all of the activities that made Rudolf Mosse one of the richest men in imperial Berlin were directly related to the businesses eventually housed in Mossehaus. Mosse had, for instance, also speculated in real estate, buying an enormous block on the Kurfürstendamm. By the midtwenties, this was the last open land on the boulevard.[28] The scale of the site and its prominent location made it the most important area for private development in Berlin during the years of the Republic. Mosse had owned the Kurfürstendamm land, a deep block bounded as well by Cicero, Paulsborner, and Albrecht-Achilles streets and facing Lehninerplatz, since at least 1904. The parcel was located on the western end of the boulevard, on the Wilmersdorf side of the dividing line between that suburb and Charlottenburg, both of which were incorporated into the city proper in 1920, the same year in which Felicia Lachmann-Mosse inherited it. Mosse had rented it out first as a fairground and then, beginning in 1908, to the "Neue-West-Eisbahn," which used it for tennis courts in summer and as an ice-skating rink in winter.[29]

The Kurfürstendamm was the major axis of imperial Berlin's westward expansion. Laid out between 1882 and 1887, it ran from the Landwehr Canal in the east, past the Zoological Gardens and the Emperor William Memorial Church to the western suburbs. It was lined with elegant apartment buildings as well as with the Berlin Secession's exhibition buildings and many cafés, including Café des Westens, a gathering place for Expressionist writers. As the site of an alternative culture to the academies, museums, and opera houses found in the core of the old city, the boulevard was also the natural location for some of the city's first major cinemas.[30] After World War I, the boulevard became the centerpiece of Berlin's consumer culture. Cafés, cabarets, cinemas, restaurants, shops, hotels, and dance halls – among them the city's most elegant – lined the ground stories of the affluent blocks west of the Memorial Church. Prewar facades were refaced in new architectural styles, and bold *Lichtreklame*, or illuminated advertisements, added to old and new buildings alike. Associated in the minds of its right-wing critics with Jewish capital, the boulevard was indeed the antithesis of Knobelsdorff's and Schinkel's preindustrial court-centered city. It was a place where the exotic and the new thrived, where Josephine Baker danced and the artists Otto Dix, Georg Grosz, and John Heartfield gathered.[31]

Mendelsohn's WOGA buildings represented the most coherent attempt made in Berlin during the twenties to rethink the architectural typology of the boulevard and, by extension, the fabric of the Wilhelmine city. Here Mendelsohn demonstrated the ways in which light

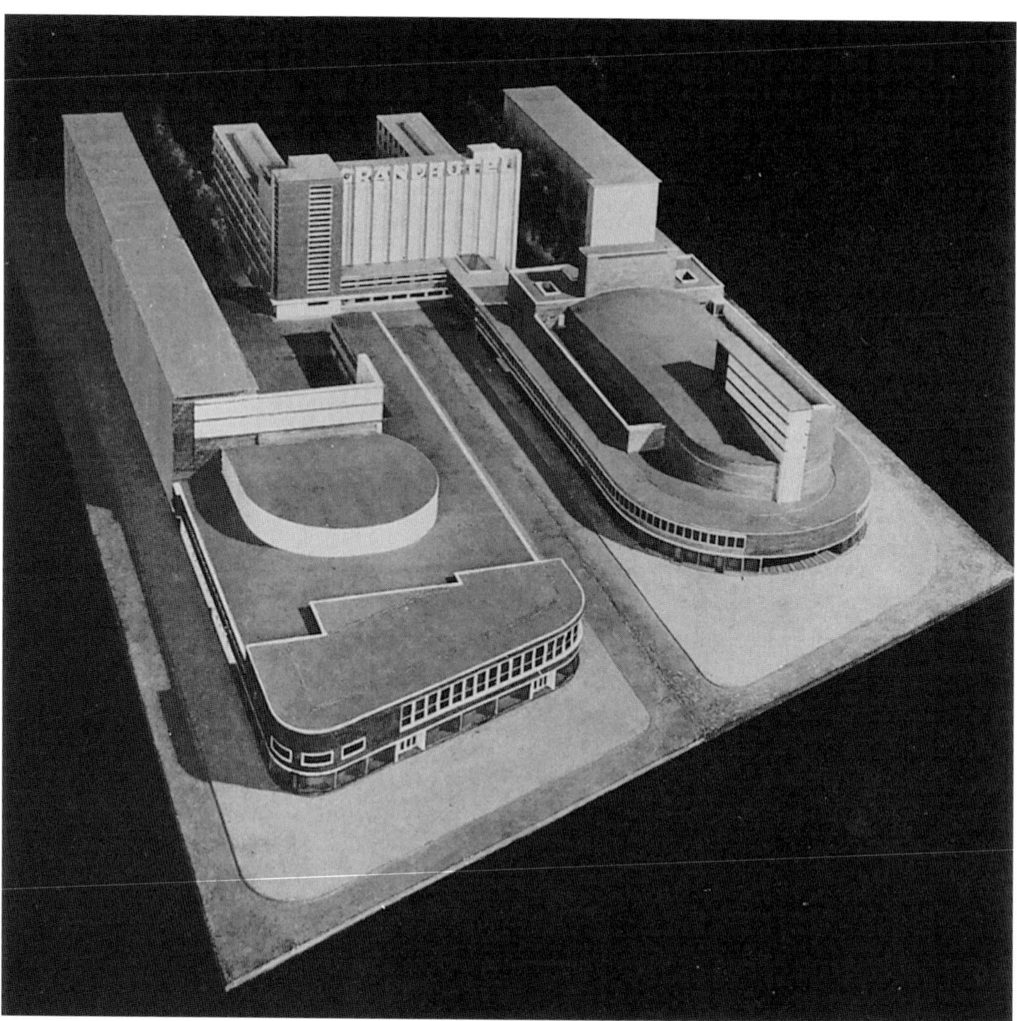

FIGURE 45

Erich Mendelsohn, WOGA complex, model, Berlin, 1928. (Source: Bruno Zevi, *Erich Mendelsohn: Opera Completa*, Milan, 1970.)

and air could be achieved in the housing for all classes through increased commercial activity rather than the separation of residential and retail functions advocated by Le Corbusier and widely adopted after the Second World War, as well as enlivened by new forms of entertainment (Fig. 45). From the time he began work on the design in 1925 until its completion in 1931, Mendelsohn labored to create not merely facades, but a spatial disposition of the various parts. He sought to bring the most light and air into the middle of the block in the liveliest possible manner and to infuse the elements facing the boulevard itself – the cinema and the cabaret – with the necessary drama to compete with the riot of lights and jazz spilling out of

to the east.

Hans Lachmann-Mosse, whose wife owned the property, did not initially consider Mendelsohn for the project. Lachmann-Mosse later admitted that he had not considered it important enough to interest Mendelsohn. Instead, Lachmann-Mosse's real estate developer, a man named Heinicke, hired the less distinguished Jürgen Bachmann. Either Lachmann-Mosse was not satisfied with Bachmann's designs or Mendelsohn got wind of the project and determined to make it his own, since by late June 1925, Mendelsohn was drawing up his own plans for the site.[32] Mendelsohn believed that Lachmann-Mosse had hesitated to turn to him because he wanted "a practical, frugal store building," not one of the "luxury" buildings with which the potential patron had associated the architect.[33] The head of the publishing empire was not yet aware of the functional ethos that characterized the new, ahistorical architecture. Mendelsohn countered with a lesson intended to demonstrate his suitability for the task and the advantages that his design skills would bring to it:

> I reprimanded him, that it is not the function, but the possibility which lies within the function, that is alone decisive, that fertilizes, stimulates, and electrifies. Architecture on an urban scale is always functional, as is every project, and its possibilities dictate the proper projects for our time.[34]

Mendelsohn's campaign to secure the commission was complicated by Bachmann's claim upon the project. The Lachmann-Mosses eventually selected Mendelsohn for the Kurfürstendamm and Cicerostraße sides of the site and awarded Bachmann the commission for the housing on Albrecht-Achilles and Paulsborner streets.[35] A year later construction of the buildings had not yet begun.[36] This delay allowed Mendelsohn to revise his initial design repeatedly. In all, he completed five successive site plans. Only in the first did he deal with the entire plot, although the second (Fig. 46, plan 1a) would have required Bachmann's cooperation, as its coherence depended upon Mendelsohn's ability to determine the footprint of the housing on Albrecht-Achillesstraße.

When Mendelsohn began to design the WOGA commission, he had already worked as an urban planner in two unbuilt projects for the city of Haifa in the British Mandate of Palestine.[37] Certain that the WOGA's new urban scale required the same spatial principles as his purely architectural designs, Mendelsohn was excited by the

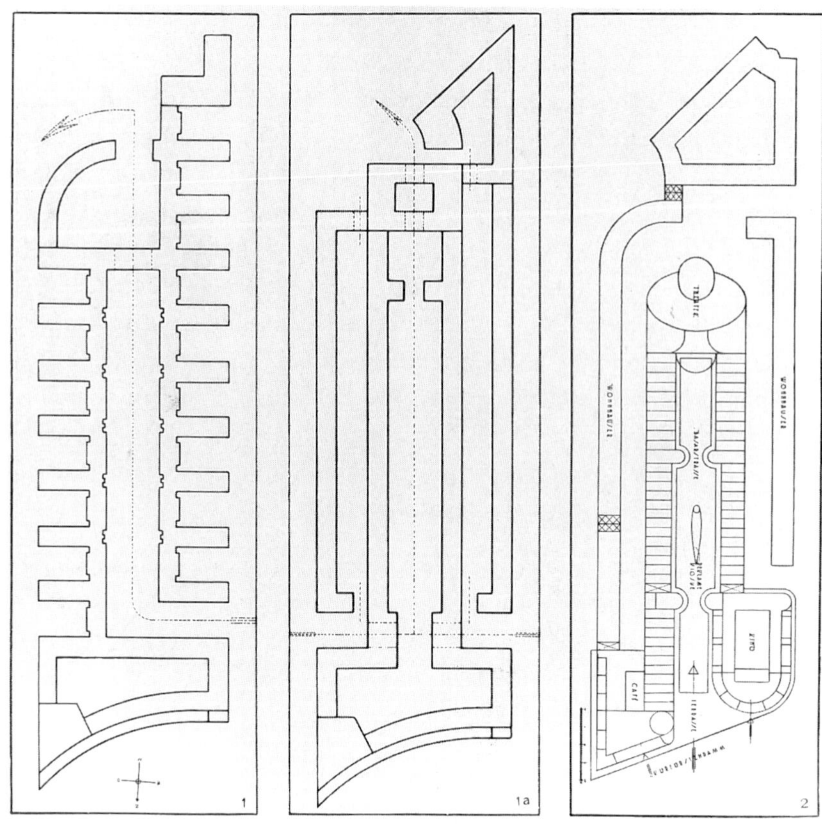

FIGURE 46

WOGA complex, three preliminary site plans, 1925–26. (Source: Staatliche Museen zu Berlin, Kunstbibliothek.)

opportunity to make of the complex more than a mere financial transaction.[38] At the same time, the variety of income-producing properties included in his proposals show his sensitivity to this side of the project. Mendelsohn's initial plan included office buildings, a large garage, a sports hall, and entertainment spaces, all disposed along an internal street approached from Cicerostraße. To face the Kurfürstendamm, he envisaged a traditional block of housing arranged around a courtyard and curved to match the swing of the street (Fig. 46, plan 1). From the beginning, the scheme also included the prominent vertical ventilation flue, which eventually dominated the exterior of the Universum Cinema (not yet a part of the program).[39] This feature would become a cliché of interwar architecture as far away as the United States.

Mendelsohn's goal of designing the most effective and profitable mix of housing and commercial development sparked additional experiments with both forms and uses. To the housing, garage, and shopping street he had initially proposed, Mendelsohn next added restaurants, a cinema, and a theater for revues. He also envisaged a sports hall with six tennis courts for international competitions, which would have replaced Bachmann's triangular apartment block. By now responsible for the entire site plan, Mendelsohn drew up a third scheme in November 1926 in which he broke open the block facing the Kurfürstendamm, providing direct access to a shopping street that led from an entrance framed by the café and cinema to a theater at its terminus (Fig. 46, plan 2).[40] In the penultimate version, for which the drawings – except for the apartment hotel – were completed by April 1927, Mendelsohn abandoned the single giant structure, which had been the goal of the previous schemes, in favor of three free-floating blocks, one of which was attached to Bachmann's unrevised apartments. He also tucked a cabaret behind the café-restaurant facing the Kurfürstendamm.[41] Finally, in the winter of 1927–28, Mendelsohn replaced the revue theater at the end of the shopping street with an apartment hotel, shortened to leave room for tennis courts behind it.[42] This plan had the additional advantage of providing locations for fire exits on all four sides of the cinemas.[43]

All of Mendelsohn's designs show to various degrees the influence upon him of Fischer's admiration for Sitte. In his book *City Planning According to Its Artistic Principles*, published in 1889, Sitte advocated small, irregular plazas in which major buildings were attached to their lesser neighbors as focal points within an organic whole – an alternative to the monumental buildings set in huge open spaces favored by the creators of Vienna's Ringstraße.[44] In projects such as his design for the development of Munich's Kohleninsel (1899–1902), Fischer used Sitte's principles and a slightly abstracted late-medieval style to create a picturesque but orderly series of spaces and vistas (Fig. 47).[45] Mendelsohn's initial three schemes were more regular than Fischer's design, but his interest in an internal street was undeniably inspired by Sitte. Mendelsohn later reversed course, however, loosening Fischer's tightly knit ensemble of parts to focus on the individual drama of his most visible components: the cinema and the hotel. Yet not even the cinema floated free of its neighbors. Bound to the hotel at the rear and reading from Cicerostraße as an extension of the apartment block, it was incorporated according to Sitte's principles into a dynamic whole. The quiet curves of the low café-restaurant and cabaret block set off the taller hotel and cinema to maximum advantage.

Mendelsohn's plan created an exciting disruption of the well-established typology of the Kurfürstendamm, which had been developed almost exclusively as a succession of highly ornate courtyard-oriented apartment blocks with ground floor commercial

FIGURE 47

Theodor Fischer, project for the development of Kohleninsel, Munich, 1899–1902. (Source: Architekturmuseum, Technische Universität, Munich.)

spaces for shops, cafés, and restaurants facing the boulevard.[46] In his review of the complex, Adolf Dornath referred to the Universum Cinema as "an island in the 'water' of the Kurfürstendamm."[47] The architect chose to interrupt this continuity not merely for the dramatic effect that he undoubtedly achieved but also, because he and his contemporaries regarded such blocks and the ornament in which they were invariably encased as the discredited architectural products of imperial Berlin. Furthermore, the boulevard's apartment blocks were only a more spacious reworking of the dreaded *Mietskaserne* (rental barracks) in which the city's workers lived in a density and squalor unparalleled in western Europe.[48]

In the outer suburbs, where land was less expensive, Martin Wagner and Bruno Taut were among those architects who, during the same years in which the WOGA complex was being planned and built, designed the huge settlements of workers' housing constructed by the city government and by trade union–affiliated building societies to replace the *Mietskaserne*.[49] Also admirers of Sitte, Wagner and Taut did not completely reject the traditional city, but created housing blocks that occupied an intermediate typology between rental barracks and

FIGURE 48

Martin Wagner, apartment row at 4–6 Stavenhagenerstraβe, Britz Siedlung, Berlin, 1925–26. (Source: Akademie der Künste, Berlin, Neg. G5/96A.)

FIGURE 49

Erich Mendelsohn, WOGA complex, Ciceroštraβe apartments, garden facade, Berlin, 1926–28. (Source: Staatliche Museen zu Berlin, Kunstbibliothek.)

suburban villas (Fig. 48).[50] With much larger areas of land at their disposal and without the WOGA complex's commercial focus, their site plans inevitably took different forms. What was remarkable was the continuity between the blocks of housing developed for workers and those planned for the solidly middle-class tenants of Mendelsohn's Cicerostraße apartment block (Fig. 49). Mendelsohn's use of this work-

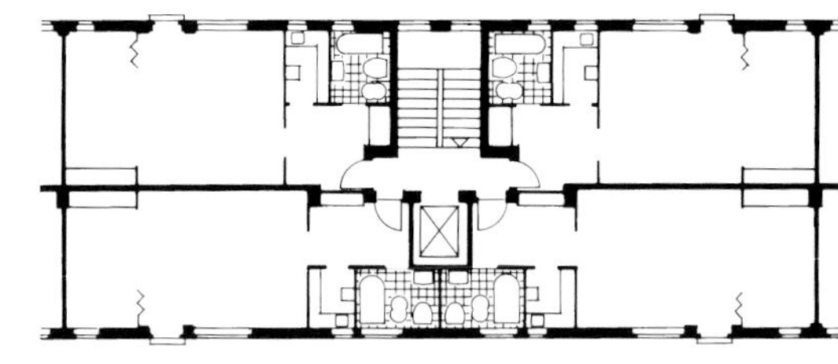

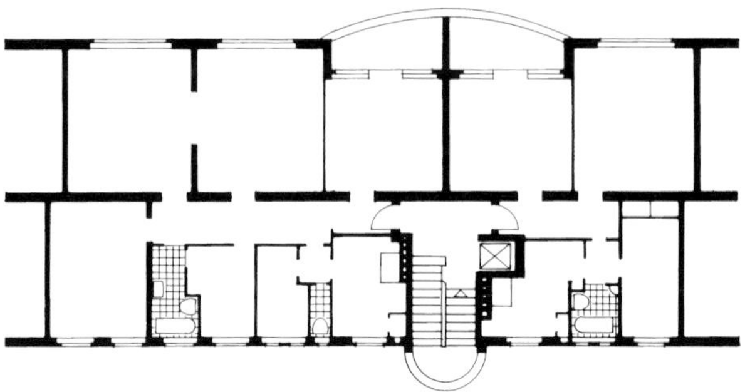

FIGURE 50

Erich Mendelsohn, WOGA complex, floor plans of apartment hotel (top) and Cicerostraβe apartments (bottom), Berlin, 1926–28. (Drawing by Sibel Zandi-Sayak after *Berlin und Seine Bauten*, vol. 4, part II, Berlin, 1974.)

ers' housing typology accorded with his admiration for Wagner and Taut's work and with his belief that similarly strict planning principles should be applied to the Kurfürstendamm. In a manuscript from the early twenties, Mendelsohn wrote that the boulevard was the symptom of the best and the worst in postwar Berlin.[51] Several years later, he specifically praised Taut and Wagner's Britz neighborhood and the Siemensstadt settlement laid out by Gropius as examples of rational urban planning made possible by the new political climate after the November Revolution.[52]

This Cicerostraße housing was almost indistinguishable in exterior appearance from Mendelsohn's favorite examples of workers' housing. No extra richness of exterior details hinted that the apartments within had far more generous plans (Fig. 50). The two-and-a-half- and four-room layouts boasted respectively 76 and 135 square meters of floorspace. Each of the 131 single-room units of the seven-story apartment-hotel – provided with vestibule, bath, and kitchen – was the size of one of Wagner's Stavenhagenerstraße apartments in the Britz. The larger units even featured a guest toilet, while two small chambers, not included in the room count, could be used for storage or for a maid's room.[53] Although only the relatively well to do could afford these spacious apartments and the luxury of an elevator in each of the six entryways, the building was arranged in exactly the same way as Wagner and Taut's workers' housing, with separate entryways for each column of apartments, and it shared the same points of architectural elaboration – the stairwell and the balcony.[54]

The interior street of Mendelsohn's WOGA complex was completed in 1929, shortly before the crash of the New York stock market brought an end to the American loans that had launched and kept afloat the German building boom. Thus it had no immediate successors. Although the pedestrian street had enabled the architect to bring unusual amounts of light and air into the apartment blocks framing three sides of the site, this imitation of the housing typology of the new workers' settlements failed to produce viable commercial space in the core of the block. The stores at the rear of the shopping arcade proved difficult to rent, with only the tenants of the apartment-hotel as captive customers.[55] Only if the Lachmann-Mosses had been successful in establishing a rival to the famous Hotel Kempinski – as they apparently once contemplated – could these stores have flourished.[56]

Far more successful were the complex's two major tenants. Facing the Kurfürstendamm and wrapping around to the shopping street of which it composed one side, stood the commercial building whose most notable tenant was the Komiker Cabaret. In addition to this circular 830-seat balconied dinner theater, the building contained the two-story Café Astor. Mendelsohn published the floor plans of the building as his own work, but he was not responsible for the furnishings of any of the interiors.[57] Across the pedestrian street stood the Universum Cinema, the linchpin of the entire complex. Sited to attract the attention of those traveling from the old heart of the city to its east, it represented the culmination of nearly a decade of innovative German theater and cinema architecture and is discussed in the following chapter.

Mendelsohn's WOGA complex was the most significant private attempt made during the Weimar Republic to integrate the planning aesthetic of the new workers' housing settlements into the existing urban fabric, here for a decidedly bourgeois constituency. Correcting the unsanitary and crowded conditions that threatened the viability of urban life for even the middle classes, Mendelsohn also invented a new architectural vocabulary which superseded the largely classical ornament common in this, the most Parisian, part of Berlin. The result was not identical with either the far more economic workers' housing or the throbbing centers of New York and Chicago, but it did express the centrality of the city in the theory and practice of those who sought during the 1920s to create an architecture responsive to the conditions of modern life. As we shall see, in Columbushaus Mendelsohn would tackle the issues of height that are so crucial to the image of the modern city but had been left unaddressed in the WOGA complex.

EDGING THE PLAZA: COLUMBUSHAUS

The successful completion of the WOGA complex was aided immeasurably by the unusual circumstance of the Lachmann-Mosses' ownership of a large and prominent piece of real estate. Expensive and often unworkable public appropriation was usually required in the urban redevelopment schemes for Berlin's downtown. By the turn of the century, commercial uses had almost completely replaced residences in the downtown with office buildings and stores. Under Martin Wagner's leadership, during the late 1920s, the city government attempted two downtown redevelopment projects: renewal of the somewhat seedy Alexanderplatz at the eastern heart of the downtown and of Potsdamerplatz. The semipublic Berlin Traffic Authority (Berlin Verkehrs A. G.) also sought to build an office complex on a centrally located site bounded by Friedrichstraße, the Friedrichstraße train station, and the Spree River. Mendelsohn helped judge schemes for Alexanderplatz, contributed to the redesign of Potsdamerplatz, and designed one of the winning entries for the Friedrichstraße site. The primary goal of all three schemes was to redistribute and thus alleviate the growing burden of rail, streetcar, subway, and vehicular traffic entering the increasingly congested area. At the same time, new high-rise office buildings – approved by Wagner's office on an individual basis – were transforming the scale and density of the surrounding blocks. Only fragments of this series of ambitious schemes were actually completed: Peter Behrens's two office buildings on the Alexanderplatz and Mendelsohn's Columbushaus on Potsdamerplatz, which opened in 1932 on the tongue of land separating Bellevue and Friedrich-Ebert streets (Fig. 51). The last major building finished in Berlin during the Weimar years and the city's most prominently sited high-rise, the ten-story-tall Columbushaus dominated its surroundings.

The divergent approaches to Großstadt architecture within the modernist camp were most apparent in the Alexanderplatz competition. In 1929 Wagner invited six architects to submit plans for the redesign of the area and called upon entrants to respond to new conditions that made the flow of traffic more important than the

FIGURE 51

Erich Mendelsohn, Columbushaus, Berlin, 1931–32. (Source: Staatliche Museen zu Berlin, Kunstbibliothek.)

buildings framing the Platz. He also stressed the organic relationship between the various elements of urban plazas or squares and declared "color, form, and light (advertising) [to be] the three primary building elements" of such spaces.[58] Mendelsohn, who would have agreed, was a member of the jury that chose the design by the Luckhardt brothers and their partner, Alfons Anker (Fig. 52). The prominent banding of their scheme recalled Mendelsohn's own Kemperplatz competition entry of 1923. Its strong boundary wall contrasted greatly with the absence of closure in Mies's competing entry, a series of slabs set back irregularly from the circular Platz (Fig. 53).[59]

The gap between these two schools of thought was only slightly narrower in the Friedrichstraße competition of 1929, which Mies once again lost, this time to an entry by Mendelsohn and to one by Paul Mebes and Paul Emmerich (Fig. 54). The massing of Mendelsohn's design for the triangular site, arrived at after experiments with a series of models, was a typical example of the architect's sensitivity toward the urban environment. He placed an eighteen-story tower along the banks of the Spree and wrapped a substantially lower office

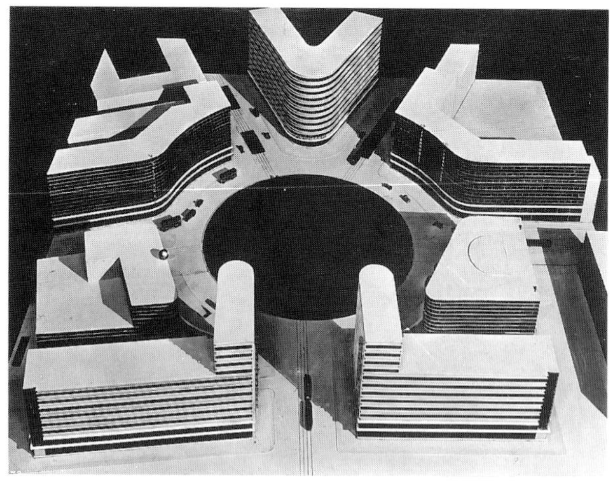

FIGURE 52

Hans and Wassily Luckhardt and Alfons Anker, competition entry for the redesign of Alexanderplatz, Berlin, 1929. (Source: Akademie der Künste, Berlin, Neg. 15.-1.2-2.1.)

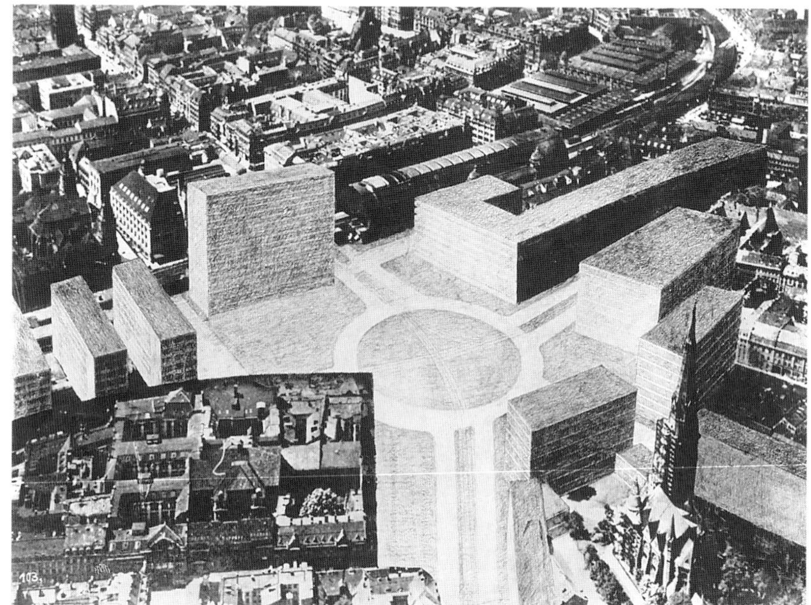

FIGURE 53

Ludwig Mies van der Rohe, competition entry for the redesign of Alexanderplatz, 1929. (Source: Akademie der Künste, Berlin, Neg. StB 5/103.)

block along Friedrichstraße itself. The tower also established a wall strong enough to withstand the necessary break allowing access to the existing train station, which formed the third leg of the triangle. This nuanced articulation of the parts found more favor with the judges than Mies's three gently curving detached slabs of equal height. In each case Mies, following the example of both Le Corbusier and of Hilberseimer, proposed opening up the traditionally dense network of urban streets, producing new, airier configurations.[60] Mendelsohn, the Luckhardts and Anker, Wagner, and the

FIGURE 54

Erich Mendelsohn, competition for an office building on Friedrichstraβe, Berlin, 1929. (Source: Staatliche Museen zu Berlin, Kunstbibliothek.)

other judges of the two competitions favored a less radical approach in which street patterns were not only maintained, but enhanced.

The story of Columbushaus illuminates the different agendas of public officials and private investors. Both parties agreed on the issue of style, but the city's desire to renovate and expand a hub of train, street car, and subway transportation required private capital that would finance urban improvements yet rebuild the area on a scale that would not overload the upgraded transportation system. Once the issue of height was resolved, the project was delayed by the global economic crisis that followed the crash of the American stock market in October 1929. It was completed only as the aspirations of the Weimar Republic for the rational order symbolized by the building were yielding to street battles between Nazis and Communists and to the collapse of the Republic itself.

The importance of Potsdamerplatz on the expanding western edge of Berlin's central business district was enhanced by its proximity to two of the city's major train stations, Anhalter Bahnhof, just down Königrätzerstraße, and Potsdamer Bahnhof, set back only slightly from the square. The plaza was the hub of interwar Berlin and had some of the city's densest traffic. It was an irregular plot of land located just outside what had once been the city limits; its focus was a pair of columned customs gates designed by Schinkel in 1823.[61] These guarded the entrance to Leipzigerplatz, an octagonal space just inside the old city, through which Leipzigerstraße ran towards the city's medieval heart. Potsdamerplatz's traffic patterns, which included a number of criss-crossing trolley tracks, were particularly confusing and consequently were at the center of all plans for reform.

FIGURE 55

Martin Wagner, project for the renovation of Potsdamer- and Leipzigerplatz, Berlin, 1928–29. (Source: Akademie der Künste, Berlin, Neg. StB 4/94.)

In 1924, a small traffic light tower modeled on those used in New York, was installed on an island in the middle of the square.[62]

After Wagner became city architect, his office began work on a plan to enlarge the irregular traffic area into a perfect circle, at the center of which, at ground level, would be a major station for the city's streetcar network and, below ground, a new subway stop (Fig. 55). The previous division between Potsdamerplatz and Leipzigerplatz was to be erased by the removal of Schinkel's temple-fronted pavilions, so that the new circle would serve as the focus of both spaces. The plan required that the city acquire the buildings around the fringes of the original open space. The cost of these sites was to be paid back to the municipal government through the sale of land for new, taller buildings sited further back around the edges of the proposed circle. New buildings would also close the gap where the Potsdamer Bahnhof was set back from the rest of the square.[63]

The project was part of a larger scheme for the reorganization of the city's train traffic. Wagner hoped to tear down both the Potsdamer and Anhalter Bahnhofs and build a tunnel channeling traffic from the Potsdamer Bahnhof site to Lehrter Bahnhof, three kilometers to the north. As in London and Paris, Berlin's major train lines came to an abrupt end on the edge of downtown. Wagner's ambition to create north–south and east–west links between them to reduce the additional burden this traffic placed on the central city was the motivating force behind his plans for Potsdamerplatz and

FIGURE 56

Potsdamerplatz, Berlin, looking northwest with the Hotel Bellevue, Ludwig Heim, 1887–88, left. (Source: Landesbildstelle Berlin, Neg. LBBII 4193.)

for the rest of Berlin's downtown. In the case of Potsdamerplatz, the elimination of the Potsdamer Bahnhof would have permitted the reorganization of an area whose shape had been distorted by the station's need for adequate access to vehicular traffic.[64] One of the buildings slated for demolition in Wagner's plan was the Grand Hotel Bellevue, which faced the Platz and fronted two of the avenues, Bellevue and Friedrich-Ebert streets, that led into it (Fig. 56). Built in 1887–88 by Ludwig Heim, the hotel was a vaguely Second Empire structure with a mansard roof and a plethora of classical details, the epitome of the early imperial or *Gründerzeit* style, which by the mid-1920s was in complete disfavor.[65] The hotel's plan – a triangle with a truncated apex – projected into the space where Wagner wished to place his circle. In exchange for ceding land on the plaza to Wagner's new transportation hub, the site's developers hoped to be granted permission to build adjacent to one of Europe's busiest intersections a branch of the French department store chain Galeries Lafayette.[66] They selected Mendelsohn to be the architect for the skyscraperlike store.

From the beginning, the scheme was plagued by complications stemming from local opposition to this international cast of characters. The store was not to be owned by the French chain but only managed by it for the owners of shares issued at a capitalization of fifteen million marks on the German market. The original organizers were all Germans; the banks to which they turned were German,

Dutch, and French. The city council had debated the propriety of foreign investment, especially regarding the earlier sale of the site by the city to the Canadian Land Company, and the Galeries Lafayette investors stressed the German ownership of eighty percent of the shares.[67]

Mendelsohn assured a newspaper reporter that the building would be built according to the most modern architectural principles, but he was unwilling to provide details until his design had been presented to the municipal authorities for approval. The important issue of the site had not yet been fully resolved. The developers owned Friedrich-Ebertstraße 11–12; and the snack bar, cigarette shop, and two other stores on the site were already empty. In June they bid against Wertheim for an adjacent piece of land. Wertheim offered twice as much for the parcel, leaving the Galeries Lafayette developers with a site whose relatively small size, once at least five hundred square meters were relinquished for the widening of the adjacent plaza, demanded that they be able to build a structure considerably taller than the six-story Hotel Bellevue.[68]

The question of allowing tall buildings in Berlin was one of the chief city planning issues in Germany during the late twenties. While no one argued for towers on the scale of American skyscrapers, the shift from the five-story height of most prewar office blocks to the eight-to-fourteen-story emblems of Berlin's modernity that began to proliferate in the late twenties meant that Wagner, whose office considered each proposed tower individually, took even comparatively small differences in height very seriously (Fig. 57). Berlin's receptivity to high-rise office buildings was in keeping with the general interest in the *Weltstadt* status of the capital, which was enhanced through frequent comparisons in the city's illustrated press of all aspects of metropolitan life with their counterparts in New York, London, and Paris.[69] Until the thirties, ten stories was still an extraordinary building height in London, where most buildings were only half that height; Paris retained its 1902 restrictions that limited building height to – depending on the width of the street and the level of the cornice – just over thirty meters until after the Second World War.[70] Yet already in 1921 Berliners had been fascinated by the entries in a contest for a real skyscraper on Friedrichstraße.[71] In 1903 Mossehaus had been Berlin's first six-story office block; Mendelsohn's renovation made it, at a total height of nine stories, briefly the city's tallest office building.[72] Meanwhile other German cities took the lead. The tower of Jakob Köfer's Hansa office building of 1924–25 in Cologne was an astonishing eighteen stories high but still did not rival the far taller

FIGURE 57

Emil Fahrenkamp, Shellhaus, Berlin, 1930–31. (Source: Foto Marburg/Art Resource NY, Neg. KBB 7950.)

nineteenth-century spires of the local cathedral. The nine eight-to-fourteen-story buildings completed in Berlin between 1928 and 1932 were as a group an achievement unrivaled outside the United States and a focus of civic pride even as the economy began to collapse, leaving much of the newly created office space unrentable.[73]

The key to the design on Potsdamerplatz was the building's context, in which Mendelsohn emphasized the firm edges of the tall prominent corner, but also tempered the structure's intrusiveness by lowering the extreme ends of its facades. He initially envisioned a prominent corner block, which would serve as a hinge between the two facades, and a strongly horizontal arrangement of the long facade facing Friedrich-Ebertstraße. Scarcely discernable in the final presentation drawing were the lower stair tower, which on Bellevuestraße acted as a transition between the bulk of the building and its lower neighbors, and the curve of the Friedrich-Ebertstraße facade where the building stepped down to a mere eight stories for the same

FIGURE 58

Erich Mendelsohn, project for the Galeries Lafayette department store, Berlin, 1928. (Source: Staatliche Museen zu Berlin, Kunstbibliothek.)

reason (Fig. 58). Mendelsohn later wrote that the purpose of this curve was to provide a right angle for the meeting of the two main facades, which he believed would provide the strongest image for the building. At ground level the Friedrich Ebertstraße facade was also enlivened by the curve with which the display windows spun out from behind the corner of the building. In place of display windows, the Bellevuestraße facade sheltered the entrance to a new subway station.[74]

When at the end of 1928 approval seemed likely, the old Grand Hotel Bellevue was demolished. In its place Mendelsohn erected an extraordinary construction fence that sheltered income-producing shops and boldly advertised, among others, the coming store and a brand of soap (Fig. 59).[75] Twenty meters high, the fence wrapped around the site of the old hotel, rather than following the recessed lines of the proposed building.[76] In addition to its obvious advertising value, it raised money for the landowner and kept the project in the public eye.

Meanwhile, Mendelsohn produced two designs of his own for the reconfiguration of Potsdamerplatz and Leipzigerplatz (Fig. 60). In the first, dated "1928," he integrated the two spaces visually into a single octagonal Platz, demolishing Schinkel's pavilions and the two enclosing arms of Leipzigerplatz. New construction, including the Galeries Lafayette, extended the long arms of Leipzigerplatz and created tall defining walls for the Potsdamerplatz edges of the unified space.

FIGURE 59

Erich Mendelsohn, Galeries Lafayette construction fence, 1928. (Source: Staatliche Museen zu Berlin, Kunstbibliothek.)

This scheme, however, did not address the traffic issues that were Wagner's principal concern. In the later drawing, Mendelsohn adapted Wagner's circular reconfiguration of Potsdamerplatz, leaving Leipzigerplatz unaltered. Mendelsohn also revised his design for the central building on Potsdamerplatz, giving it a dramatically double-curved facade. Both drawings can be seen as bids, not for a major role in the city planning office, but for further architectural commissions for the new construction that was to surround the Platz.[77]

There was some support within the city government for the Galeries Lafayette, but in February 1929 Mendelsohn's by then fifteen-story-tall design was rejected by both Wagner and the city traffic authorities who feared that its scale would only increase the area's already endemic traffic congestion. They agreed to allow only a nine-story structure.[78] This decision was ratified in June when it was announced that construction would begin in September or October.[79] Instead, in August, the Galeries Lafayette investors announced that they would build their store in the western part of the city, although they were soon forced to abandon these plans in the wake of the crash of the American stock market.[80]

It took nearly two years for the project's investors to regroup under the name of the Bellevue-Immobilien A. G. In May 1931 the new company announced plans for Columbushaus, a ten-story office building with an optimistically American name.[81] In the meantime, the eco-

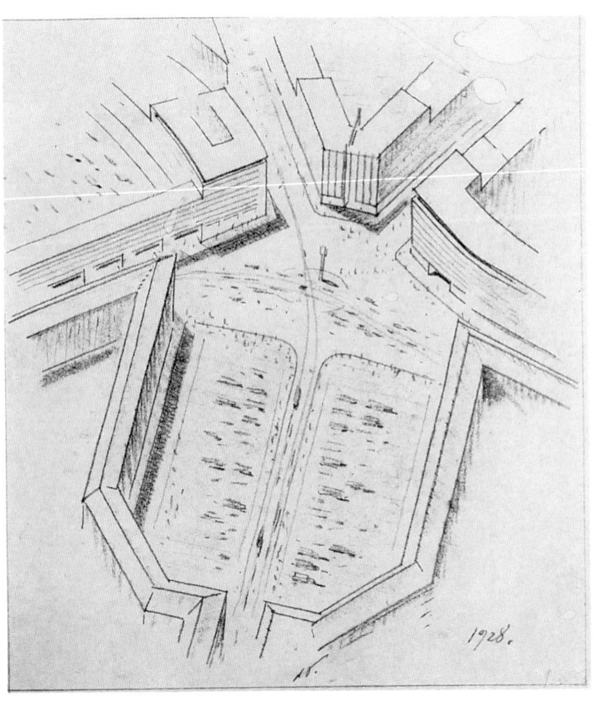

FIGURE 60

Erich Mendelsohn, project for the redesign of Potsdamerplatz, 1931. (Source: Staatliche Museen zu Berlin, Kunstbibliothek.)

nomic crisis had brought to a rapid halt the influx of dollars that had funded the brief and tentative boom in the German economy. Germany was hit as hard by the depression that followed as the United States was; retail sales, for instance, plummeted forty percent between 1930 and 1934.[82] But even this economic disaster, which severely curtailed the ability of Berlin's city government to undertake great urban renewal schemes, failed to dampen the enthusiasm of the city's architects and developers for rebuilding Potsdamerplatz.

In 1931 the Luckhardt brothers and their partner Alfons Anker published a design on which they had been working since 1929 for buildings to surround Wagner's projected streetcar station (Fig. 61). Centered on a cylindrical high-rise, which they titled "Haus Berlin," their design gave architectural character to Wagner's traffic circle. Their fourteen-story tower would have been cheaper to build than the vaguely similar, but much taller, focal point of Wagner's model. This building was to be flanked by Columbushaus and an identical twin of Mendelsohn's building. Three separate versions of the scheme are known, suggesting that work on it may have begun as early as 1930. "Haus Berlin" was intended by its architects and Wagner to attract developers to this key site on which mortgage payments were costing the city three hundred thousand marks a year. Even though it was never built, this evidence of continued interest in the site may

FIGURE 61

Hans and Wassily Luckhardt and Alfons Anker, project for the redesign of Potsdamerplatz, 1931. (Source: Akademie der Künste, Berlin, Neg. 21.-2.-2.5.1.a.)

have encouraged the Columbushaus developers to believe that the area would indeed be a locus of future construction and that Mendelsohn's original Galeries Lafayette design was going to help shape the direction that development would take.[83] The shift in focus from the Galeries Lafayette site to the center of the square, a site on the axis with Leipzigerstraße that Berlin's architects had coveted at least since Schinkel's day, meant that Columbushaus – unlike the Galeries Lafayette – was to be a background building. As such, it lacked the prominent crowning signage now reserved for "Haus Berlin." Although the design of the building changed very little, Mendelsohn and Wagner no longer envisioned it as an individual monument. Instead, it became the prototype for a projected pair of subordinate structures.[84]

In the series of tightly composed views that accompanied Mendelsohn's 1932 article on Columbushaus's, the building's metal frame and gleaming white surfaces were juxtaposed with the wintry silhouette of leafless trees clustered around Schinkel's two pavilions (Fig. 62).[85] These photographs also played down the intrusiveness of the building's scale by showing only portions of it and by exaggerating the height of the few foreground structures. Even as a fragment of a never-to-be-realized whole, Columbushaus served its busy surroundings well. The curve of the Friedrich-Ebertstraße facade, which Men-

FIGURE 62

Erich Mendelsohn, Columbushaus, Berlin, 1931–32. (Source: *The Architectural Review*, 1933.)

delsohn aligned with Wagner's proposed redirected flow of traffic, provided, even without the reorganization of the surrounding plaza, a refinement that, like its setback, tempered the building's otherwise hierarchical quality. Without the planned traffic circle, a mere 2.4-meter wide strip of the extra space was turned over to a new streetcar line on Friedrich-Ebertstraße. The remaining area in front of this facade became a small plaza, a buffer against the worst of the surrounding traffic and a potential site for a future subway entrance.[86]

In comparison with Mies's entry in the Alexanderplatz competition of 1929, Mendelsohn designed Columbushaus to participate in, rather than be set apart from, the life of the city that surrounded it. He reaffirmed his belief that the modern city's need for light, air, larger roadways, and taller buildings demanded a flexible but unified relationship between new construction and the street. As he had done in the WOGA complex, to whose squat brick masses the sleek office building otherwise bears little resemblance, Mendelsohn manipulated the functional aspects of individual commissions in ways that expressed and enhanced rather than undercut urban vitality. Although both fashion and function, continued to change, his approach to the city varied little. From Mossehaus through Columbushaus, Mendelsohn deployed a dynamism as inseparable from the functions of the businesses it served as from modern urban life itself.

5 ADVERTISING, TRANSPARENCY, AND LIGHT

"NO ROCOCO PALACE FOR BUSTER KEATON"

THE role of advertising in Germany expanded enormously during the second half of the twenties. Many equated advertising directly with modernity. Advertising was especially with the shift from the highly charged personal emotiveness of Expressionism to the more disciplined and distant voice of Neue Sachlichkeit art and literature, tinged as this new sobriety was with the drama of American industry and urbanism.[1] American advertising techniques, which emphasized psychological manipulation rather than artistic adventurousness, were little imitated in a society in which Werkbund members were among those consciously working to integrate avant-garde and commercial culture.[2] Mendelsohn's own American experiences forced him to confront the need to bring advertising and architecture together in new ways rather than simply apply one to the other. In his account of New York, for instance, he contrasted day and night views of Times Square. By day, the area "loses the mysteriousness, intoxication, its glitter of the night." At night in Times Square, however, he began to discover the dynamism with which he wanted to imbue his architecture, "the flame-like writings, the rocket fire of the moving illuminated ads, emerging and submerging, disappearing and breaking out again over the thousands of autos and the maelstrom of pleasure-seeking people."[3]

Mendelsohn's fusion of structure and advertising, in which he exploited skeletal-steel-frame construction to enlarge and literally to electrify the displays of the goods for sale and the building itself, was also inseparable from his own highly personal experience of Expressionism. Through this fusion he achieved the mass audiences longed for by Kandinsky. If he failed to literally respiritualize public life, certainly he also did not betray the hopes the Blue Rider had placed in the communicative power of nonrepresentational art. Mendelsohn exploited immaterial effects of transparency and light, seemingly defying gravity, while the immateriality of industrialized entertainment – the movies – challenged him to create almost equally immaterial architecture, which maintained the spell that flickering images cast over their audience.

"BILL-DING BOARD": THE HERPICH STOREFRONT

At the same time that Mendelsohn completely overthrew the specific stylistic premise of the Wertheim store, he was also intrigued by the prewar alliance between German commerce and the visual arts.[4] The Herpich store epitomized the Werkbund's postwar search for an aesthetically compelling and economically profitable relationship between architecture and marketing, one no longer reflecting even as enlightened a historicism as Messel's. Instead of serving history, advertising now emerged as a source of artistic effects that were realized almost exclusively through technology. While Hannes Meyer, for instance, found in industrial imagery an escape from the whims of the marketplace, Mendelsohn believed the two to be inseparable aspects of modernity.[5] Dynamism doubled as functionalism in Mendelsohn's designs for scaffolding, display windows, night lighting, and lettering. He embraced modern construction and modern marketing with equal excitement, integrating rather than juxtaposing these two sources of his new commercial architecture. Architectural imagery could even be featured in print campaigns; newspaper advertisements for the new C.A. Herpich Sons, Furriers, store featured a photograph showing the corner bay at a jaunty oblique angle.[6]

In 1875 the descendents of Carl August Herpich moved the family business he had founded in 1835 to Leipzigerstraße, then beginning its transformation from a street of fashionable townhouses into the city's foremost shopping street.[7] As soon after the First World War as the stabilization of the German currency allowed, the company, which by then also sold clothes and luxury carpets, decided to renovate its adjacent buildings, themselves expansions of the street's original individual townhouses, into a single, even larger store.[8] Berlin merchants, especially department store owners, had vied with each other for the two decades preceding the war, to hire the city's best architects to design the most fashionable buildings on and around Leipzigerstraße. Julius Herpich continued that patronage, becoming the first merchant after the war to build a new *Kaufhaus*, or "store building" (as opposed to a shop within an existing building); he was also the first to hire an architect committed to the New Building.[9] No information survives about the choice of an architect, although Herpich undoubtedly knew the Hausleben building and Mossehaus, each only a few blocks away. The program for the Herpich store called for two additional stories and an entirely new facade. These were to be applied to the firm's two adjacent renovated townhouses and a third unaltered building which it had recently purchased.[10] Only the first two-thirds of the building were constructed during the 1925–27 building campaign.[11] Work began on the final segment – completed in 1928 – after the business, which had remained open to the public, moved from the third townhouse into the new building.[12]

The scaffolding Mendelsohn built in 1925 for the first stage of the Herpich construction set the tone for the advertising content of the building being erected behind it, while meeting the special circumstances of adding additional stories to an existing building, the lowest levels of which projected out beyond the original facade (Fig. 63).[13] This required a system of supports that came to the ground well in front of the existing shop windows. To maximize the interest of passing pedestrians in the Herpich business and to diminish inconvenience to them, Mendelsohn created a covered arcade supported on three angled piers. The shape of these piers and of the slanted advertising panels he inserted between them were his final use of faceted Expressionist forms. They were especially appropriate to the advertising function of the startling scaffolding, which was emblazoned on the front and sides with the Herpich name, as they followed the example of several Expressionist kiosks erected in the city in 1922.[14]

In his Herpich store design Mendelsohn became one of the first postwar German architects to exploit the lightness and transparency of the steel frame (Fig. 42). The pure white surfaces, metal detailing, and expansive windows of the Herpich store pioneered a new commercial vocabulary that quickly eclipsed Messel's timeworn model. Cladding the frame in travertine and accenting its openings with broad bronze sills, Mendelsohn did not quite attain the almost ephemeral enclosure of space he would soon achieve in the Petersdorff store, but he was able to flood the interior with natural light and minimize the boundary between the store's merchandise and its potential customers.[15] At night, new lighting techniques integrated into the architecture rather than applied to it accentuated the sense of the facade as a screen – at times and in places opaque but always

FIGURE 63

Erich Mendelsohn, C. A. Herpich Sons, Furriers, construction photograph, 1925. (Source: Staatliche Museen zu Berlin, Kunstbibliothek.)

an insubstantial barrier sheltering without masking the commerce it glamorized.

After initially experimenting with a facade that wrapped around the projecting bays of the existing buildings, Mendelsohn decided to hang the new facade forward of the existing projections and suspend corner pavilions over the store's ground floor display windows.[16] Although not quite completely glazed, the non-load-bearing facade was now for all practical purposes a curtain wall. With these changes Mendelsohn achieved a new combination of austerity and dynamism. While the Weichmann store had depended upon the juxtaposition of rectilinear volumes, here Mendelsohn returned to the sweeping curved forms of his wartime drawings and the constructional principles he had stressed in his lectures. These he now detached from a dependence upon reinforced concrete construction. Mendelsohn located in the shift to steel his opportunity to express the pace of modern city life; the frame's potential for dramatic quantities of glazing equaled in importance the plastic form that had dominated his thinking about concrete.

Through a careful choice of details, Mendelsohn also emphasized that the facade was but a taut skin, rather than a solid structure. He held the entire composition together at ground level with a single plane of glass that was broken only by the thinnest of mullions and two inset entrances. Spelling out the Herpich name, lettering stretching across a travertine band situated just above these windows provided an additional unifying note.

Mendelsohn cantilevered the end pavilions of the next four stories over the ground floor. Thick and thin mullions interrupted the ribbon windows of the upper stories in a rhythm that emphasized the width of the building over its height. In the center section, the sills projected farther forward than the lintels, a situation reversed in the end pavilions. Such nuances combined with the detailing of the setbacks produced the tension that enlivened the building, sending its horizontals shooting down Leipzigerstraße in either direction.

The Herpich store facade reached beyond the dominant model of the Wertheim store to recall the first phase of German department store architecture. Perhaps aware of merchants' critiques of the uninterrupted glazing of Bernhard Sehring's facade for the Hermann Tietz store at 46–49 Leipzigerstraße, built between 1899 and 1900, which rendered the spaces against the window wall unusable, and certainly curtailed by changes in building codes spurred by higher standards for fireproof construction, Mendelsohn inserted travertine bands, framed by bronze hoods and sills, between each story instead of recreating the full extent of the earlier store's window area (Fig. 64).[17] Mendelsohn's revival of such construction, now shorn of its rich, figurative ornament, points to the cultural obsession Weimar Germans had with cleanliness and openness, which they associated with purity and with social and political progress.

It would be difficult to overestimate the influence upon Weimar culture of German fascination with natural light and fresh air or the degree to which this fascination was seen as complementing rather than contradicting the increasing popularity of an industrial aesthetic. Transcending political divisions between left and right and easily transposed into gleaming white, window-filled surfaces, this obsession had a variety of sources. One was the prewar youth movement,

FIGURE 64

Bernhard Sehring, Hermann Tietz Department Store, Berlin, 1899–1900. (Source: Foto Marburg/Art Resource NY, Neg. 1.115.660.)

whose emphasis on outdoor exercise found an ever-wider audience after the war. Improved standards of hygiene also contributed to the vogue. Influenced by newly accessible technology and scientific discoveries, by the expanded availability of indoor plumbing and by a new understanding of germs, dark, heavily ornamented building surfaces, once esteemed as displays of wealth, were rendered suspect as hatching grounds for microbes. Furthermore, transparency had a political component, as Meyer made clear when he described his League of Nations competition entry as having "no political reception rooms for weary monarchs but hygienic workrooms for the busy representatives of their people[;] no back corridors for backstairs diplomacy but open glazed rooms for the public negotiations of honest men."[18] The new aesthetic was by no means confined to utilitarian buildings and objects, but also shaped contemporary standards of luxury.[19]

Mendelsohn paid especially close attention to the display windows of the Herpich store (Fig. 65). Because he suspended the facade from the upper stories, he was able to set the ground-story pillars behind these windows, attaining at the ground level a pure curtain wall. In

FIGURE 65

C. A. Herpich Sons, Furriers, display windows. (Source: Staatliche Museen zu Berlin, Kunstbibliothek.)

1929 Hegemann declared of the Herpich store, "Compared with its concise elegance, the enormous pillars of the Wertheim building appear already out of fashion and exaggerated in scale."[20] The horizontality of the facade, which eliminated the compositional role of the recessed pillars, was the key to the increase in the area and impact of this economically vital place. Only thin bronze mullions divided the glass membrane separating the pedestrians from the carefully arranged exhibits of merchandise. Even the entrance passageways to the interior of the store were lined with windows.

Under the guidance of the Werkbund, German designers and merchants had worked together since early in the century to create attractive shop windows.[21] During the twenties the literature on these displays spilled out from trade journals and from the Werkbund's postwar monthly magazine *Die Form* onto the pages of newspapers, as the group's members began to think of advertising as a "dynamic means of exchange."[22] The union of new artistic form and the expanding German interest in advertising was predicated on the belief – shared by artists, architects, and businesspeople and encouraged by the Werkbund as well as by the newer Bauhaus – that the best advertisement was a straightforward but lively display of available goods, which was tinted with the implication that they were the products of modern, technological production and was aimed at the masses to whom their widespread availability would bring a higher standard of living.[23] By the middle of the decade, the focus on cooperation between art and commerce had shifted from prewar advocacy of the aestheticization of industry and its products, achieved in part through the use of traditional symbolism and predicated upon distrust of their modernity, to forthright celebration of precisely that modernity, now allied with new forms of artistic expression, as a force for social good.[24] Articles in *Die Form*, for instance, advocated signage and lettering – easily reconcilable with the aesthetics of abstract art – as affordable alternatives to traditional ornament.[25]

After 1926 the Werkbund journal published a steady stream of articles devoted to advertising, an issue that was also treated in the late twenties in the pages of *Das neue Frankfurt* and *Das neue Berlin*. The authors of these articles, who included such advocates of the New Building as Adolf Behne, Hugo Häring, Ludwig Hilberseimer, and Ernst May, attempted to make the commercialization of new aspects of daily life palatable through high aesthetic standards, which, they believed, would sell goods more effectively than "badly" designed advertisements, while making an invaluable contribution to visual culture.[26] Behne, for instance, once defended the different forms of advertising adorning Berlin's stores and cinemas as the city's least expensive and most beautiful art exhibition.[27]

Behne was particularly notable for his championing of well-designed advertising in the context of his larger enthusiasm for America.[28] He embraced mass culture as a pragmatic vehicle for introducing to large popular audiences a new aesthetic, stripped of academic artistic conventions with their cults of individual genius and (by implication, although he did not elaborate upon it) of the traditional social order. That this means of dissemination was necessarily commercial seemed initially not to matter to one who was clearly disillusioned by the failure of Expressionism and Constructivism to achieve the utopias of which he had once dreamed. Instead, Behne focused on the distinction between the cacophony of much "artistic" European advertising and the clearer, more rational – and thus more abstract – distribution of graphic information portrayed in Mendelsohn's illustrations of New York and Detroit.[29] For Behne, wariness about the proliferation of such signage was merely evidence of a typically bourgeois desire to see art "as an aesthetic escape wand," rather than to acknowledge the realities of modern life.[30]

The enthusiasm that some German architects and artists had for advertising was also spurred by their lingering interest in converting large public audiences (often by using overtly theatrical techniques) to the social as well as aesthetic principles they still believed to be inherent in their work. Despite his postwar anti-industrialist position,

Taut, for example, continued to show flair in his designs for architectural advertising. As city architect of Magdeburg and editor of the journal *Frühlicht*, he sponsored the design of newspaper kiosks, addressed issues of signage, continued to propose designs for exhibition pavilions, and published the advertising schemes of other architects.[31] At the Bauhaus, Herbert Bayer incorporated up-to-date De Stijl and Constructivist effects into designs for similar kiosks, while in Frankfurt, the office of city architect Ernst May supervised the design of various sorts of signage.[32]

The economic conditions of interwar Germany also encouraged the development of advertising, again often associated with American marketing methods. "There is no sale without advertising," announced Adolf Schmidt-Volker in a trade journal in 1924.[33] Although industrial production grew enormously during the late twenties, consumer buying power barely rose as workers' salaries remained low.[34] This discrepancy fostered enormous competition between retailers, who turned to the example of the American department store for inspiration.[35] Although few American stores were examples of architectural modernity, all were designed to emphasize the display of goods.[36] Furthermore, American department store managers paid a great deal of attention to promotional strategies within the store and to advertising campaigns disseminated through the media and through mailings.

In the Herpich store facade the ribbon windows of the upper stories reinforced the impact of the display windows, as well as facilitating an innovative system of night lighting, one which once again emphasized the building's advertising qualities (Fig. 66). Into their cantilevered window sills Mendelsohn tucked troughs from which he floodlit the facade's travertine bands.[37] This indirect lighting complemented his conception of the building as it should look both during the day and at night. Only the horizontal composition of the Herpich facade matched the importance of this lighting scheme in changing the face of German downtowns. Nothing of this sophistication had yet been seen in Berlin. Not incidentally, the band between the ground floor clerestory and the shop windows cast a steady glow on the large lettering identifying the store's owners.[38]

Already before the war August Endell had described the way that the play of artificial light in the modern metropolis outshone the unspectacular moon and stars, listing "the green- and yellow-white glow of the gas lights, the mild blue of the ordinary arc lamp, the red and orange colors of the brake lights and the new variety of arc lamps, the red and white of the incandescents and the new metal

FIGURE 66

C. A. Herpich Sons, Furriers, night view. (Source: Staatliche Museen zu Berlin, Kunstbibliothek.)

filament lamps [and] the dark red and green of the signal lamps."[39] During the twenties *Lichtreklame*, or "illuminated advertisements," became a German obsession. In the early years of the decade they were known mostly from newspaper and magazine photographs of Times Square at night and were one of the most potent symbols of New York – *the* modern metropolis.[40] By 1928 there were three thousand of them in Berlin alone, the number growing twenty to thirty percent each year at an annual cost of between 1.8 and 2.7 million marks.[41] When they were introduced in Berlin in the middle of the decade, a campaign began to avoid New York's surfeit of signs chaotically placed atop buildings. Instead, critics, usually associated with the Werkbund's long struggle to raise the aesthetic standards of modern industry and commerce, proposed that the signs be incorporated into the composition of entire facades.[42] The Herpich store was the first to fully realize this dream and was frequently presented as a prototype.[43] For example, Ernst May praised cornice lights, pioneered in this building, as "discreet" and having "an excellent artistic effect."[44]

Many aspects of German culture during the twenties encouraged this enthusiasm for *Lichtreklame*, which also flourished for economic reasons often indistinguishable from aesthetic choices. Wilhelm Lotz, the author of a Werkbund guide to lighting, proposed thinking of light as a building material, an idea in keeping with the increasing popularity of abstraction.[45] The photographer Moholy-Nagy's manipulation of light in nonrepresentational photographs was cited by Ernst Reinhardt in his article on *Lichtreklame*. And the machine romanticism of the period encompassed the electric technology that made *Lichtreklame* possible. Ernst Reinhardt, for example, also illustrated a locomotive headlight.[46] Certainly this new way of looking at the city in terms of illuminated commercialism proved very popular. In October 1928 Berlin celebrated a four-day festival in which light shows, balls, theatrical spectacles, and the illumination of whole blocks complemented the discussion of *Lichtreklame*.[47] Of equal importance were more subtle factors. Blackouts had frequently accompanied civil unrest in the first years after the war. The rising number of *Lichtreklame* in Berlin thus advertised political stability as well as individual businesses and products.[48] The importance of light in Expressionist visions of a new world had by the midtwenties also inspired a transformation of German religious architecture, where lighting effects increasingly replaced ornament in the creation of overtly spiritual spaces. Even Berlin's *Lichtreklame* were thus paradoxically infused with this hope of a better, less materialistic world.

In the Herpich store, Mendelsohn fused his patron's demand for well-advertised fashion with indications that he could transcend a narrowly functionalist interpretation of program. In doing so, he expressed contemporary German hopes that modern consumerism could contribute to social and political stability. Over the next several years, Mendelsohn would push the transparency and manipulation of artificial light, the means through which he achieved this fusion, even further.

TRANSPARENCY: THE RUDOLF PETERSDORFF STORE AND BEYOND

One place that Mendelsohn refined this fusion was the Rudolf Petersdorff store, an expensive ladies' dress shop in Breslau (Fig. 67). Here the architect responded to the demand for a sophisticated image by creating an almost completely transparent facade, balancing the resulting drama against the understated elegance of the store's neighbor. This was only one of a series of shopfronts in which Mendelsohn continued to erode the barrier between the sidewalk and the shop

FIGURE 67

Erich Mendelsohn, Rudolf Petersdorff store, Breslau, 1927–28. (Source: Staatliche Museen zu Berlin, Kunstbibliothek.)

interior, between the potential consumer and enticing displays. In 1929 Mendelsohn's former assistant, Arthur Korn, wrote of such buildings, "The outside wall is no longer the first impression one gets of a building. . . . [It] is barely visible, and can only be seen when there are reflected lights, distortions, or mirror effects."[49] The frequency with which other architects imitated these commissions also demonstrated Mendelsohn's command of the marketing needs of store owners.

Although little is known about the history of the Rudolf Petersdorff business, an article about the new store that appeared in a contemporary trade journal suggested Petersdorff's reasons for choosing Mendelsohn. The author pointed to the "propaganda" value of hiring a famous architect. The new store, he wrote, would attract as much attention as if it were in Berlin or Hamburg, rather than in the distinctly provincial Breslau. In Breslau itself, he added, the store provided a resonant symbol of the city's merchant character, the modern equivalent, another critic noted, of the late-medieval city hall located only a few blocks away.[50]

The Petersdorff store's existing one-story building at the corner of Ohlauer and Schuhbrücke streets and the properties that Petersdorff had acquired for the expansion – the adjacent building on Ohlauerstraße, a five-story structure, and two three-story buildings on Schuhbrückestraße – were located in the heart of the city, close to the market square that surrounded city hall.[51] Mendelsohn's task was to provide two new six-story facades for the store and to renovate and expand the buildings behind them. This process, in which Mendelsohn created a chic reinterpretation of Poelzig's somewhat gawky nearby office building (see Fig. 37) as well as of his own recent Schocken Department Store in Stuttgart, was complicated by the simultaneous decision of city authorities to widen Schuhbrückestraße to allow room for a street car stop. The store owners at the site must have welcomed this prospect for an increase in pedestrian traffic.[52]

The street-widening scheme and the unusual depth of the building together with Mendelsohn's choice of a steel skeleton enabled the architect to open up larger areas of glass, which he paired with the crisp bronze window mullions.[53] At the same time that Mendelsohn was exploiting these highly reflective materials, he continued to experiment with sculptural building masses, carving away the ground story in ways that heightened the dynamism of the building's upper reaches. The smoothness of its surfaces and the dominance of the largely glazed cantilever, which projected four and a half meters from the final line of columns, did much to reduce the sense of the store's bulk. About half of the Petersdorff cantilever – Mendelsohn's boldest yet – projected over the ground-story shop windows, creating an overhang that comfortably sheltered people waiting for the street cars and encouraged them to spend their spare minutes studying the goods on display.[54] On Ohlauerstraße, on the other hand, where the old

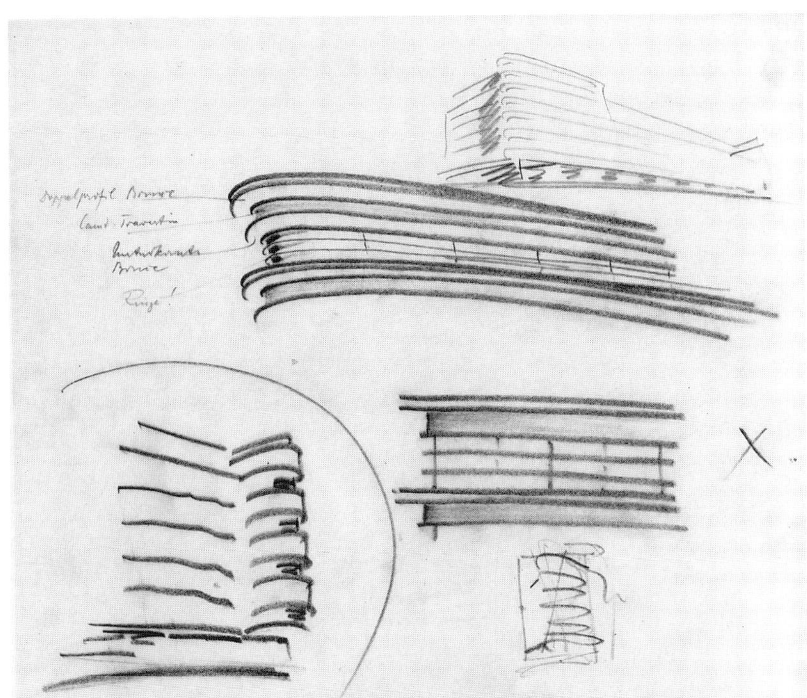

FIGURE 68

Rudolf Petersdorff store, perspective and elevation sketches. (Source: Staatliche Museen zu Berlin, Kunstbibliothek.)

street line remained unchanged, Mendelsohn merely refaced and extended the existing buildings.[55]

In the two facades Mendelsohn quickly arrived at an elegant variation of the solution he had already used in Stuttgart and in an addition of 1926–27 to the Cohen-Epstein store in Duisburg – the rounded cantilever. As in Duisburg and in the early sketches for the Schocken store in Stuttgart, the projection of the Petersdorff store was a marker, rather than a reflection, of the plan. The curving corner of Petersdorff was too narrow to contain stairs. Yet it was not without a function, as it enabled both the store and the streetcar platform beneath the store's Schuhbrückestraße cantilever to be easily spotted at a distance of several blocks. Mendelsohn's sketches for the building included notations about materials and showed him fixing the precise details of the store's bronze windowsill bands and of the entire cantilevered bay (Fig. 68). Mendelsohn also recessed the upper panes of each window (except for the huge ground floor display windows) several inches, further eroding the substantiality of the wall plane. Detail drawings from Mendelsohn's own hand are rare, and their existence here provides additional proof of his concern for the nuances of this facade.

The bronze window frames attracted particular attention. Mendelsohn had already used bronze for the windows of the Herpich store and for some details of the Schocken store in Stuttgart, but here he fully exploited the material to give the Petersdorff facade a machinemade sleekness which surpassed that of even the Herpich store.[56] Featured in advertisements for the industry, the Petersdorff store helped set the standard for European elegance until the outbreak of World War II.[57] Bronze was gaining popularity as a material for external details at the same time that steel was replacing concrete as the material of choice for interior framing. The German Copper Institute encouraged store owners to use copper, brass, and bronze for a variety of purposes but focused on the usefulness of these materials for display windows. Thin metal mullions, institute members claimed, would cast the least amount of shadow on the window displays yet could hold large plates of glass in place, despite wind and changes in temperature.[58]

This use of metal also allowed construction to proceed with unusual speed, adding a new dimension to Mendelsohn's reputation for efficiency. Work on the Petersdorff store began on August 15, 1927; the steel skeleton was finished on September 26; and the completed building opened on March 31, 1928. In two hundred workdays, which included the entire winter, a remarkable 17,400 cubic meters of space were renovated and another 16,300 added.[59]

The Petersdorff store was Mendelsohn's most daring steel skeleton to date, and he clad the result in bronze detailing consistent with the building's metal structure. Conventional signage became almost irrelevant – limited to the two borders of the building – because the entire facade effectively functioned as an advertisement for and attraction to the store. The result was a composition that traditionalists could praise for its historicity, yet one that at the same time responded to the modernist criticism of advertising-laden store facades as "nonarchitecture." Thus the clarity of the building's frame, as echoed in its metal windowsills and mullions, inspired Hegemann to compare its corporeality and reserve to works by Schinkel, whom he revered. At the same time, Hilberseimer's complaint that rather than an "architectural facade," department stores now sported only "a scaffolding for advertising, lettering, and *Lichtreklame*" was answered with an approach in which these often disparate elements achieved a kind of abstract unity instead of simply being separately applied to the existing building.[60]

Despite Hilberseimer's discomfort with *Lichtreklame*, it was the night view of the Petersdorff building, when the broad bronze sills vanished from sight, which garnered the most acclaim. Mendelsohn

FIGURE 69

Rudolf Petersdorff store, night view. (Source: Staatliche Museen zu Berlin, Kunstbibliothek.)

himself noted that the Schuhbrückestraße facade appeared "like a glowing curtain hanging down from the sky" (Fig. 69).[61] He achieved this effect by tucking the lighting into the interior soffits of the window lintels.[62] In a discussion of the store, Wilhelm Lotz praised Mendelsohn for converting light into a building material.[63] The architect himself commented on this balance of structure and transparency, "By the means of glass we are removing the building's sense of enclosure, making it transparent and light where formerly it was massive, enabling it through cantilevered construction to float where formerly it weighed down upon the earth."[64]

In the Cohen-Epstein store and in a Leiser shoe shop of 1930 in Berlin, Mendelsohn established even more complex relationships between the wall plane of the upper stories and recessed display windows (Figs. 70 and 71).[65] In Duisburg, where he had to preserve the exterior columns of the original building, each of these four piers anchored a display area that curved back from the street to meet the deeply recessed plane of the entrance.[66] This arrangement more than doubled the total length of the displays and drew window-shoppers

FIGURE 70

Erich Mendelsohn, Cohen-Epstein store, Duisberg, Germany, 1926–27. (Source: Staatliche Museen zu Berlin, Kunstbibliothek.)

FIGURE 71

Erich Mendelsohn, Leiser Sons shoe store, Berlin, 1930. (Source: Staatliche Museen zu Berlin, Kunstbibliothek.)

into niches in which they were surrounded on three sides by tempting merchandise. By 1930, such spatial complexity had become commonplace in Berlin, but Mendelsohn's shoe store in a residential neighborhood remained noteworthy. Here he doubled the display area by setting the main windows 2.4 meters back from the exterior wall, buttressing the second story with an aluminum-clad column, and wrapping yet more windows around the side of the narrow shop interior.[67] Adequate illumination came through the glazed ceiling. In all three cases, the effect must often have complimented the longing that comes from viewing such displays through one's own reflection.[68]

Sheets of clear glass, sparkling in the sun by day and bathed in artificial light by night, framed in gleaming metal, and inserted between planes of clean travertine – for critics of the day, the facades of Mendelsohn's stores and shops brought the spirit epitomized by the Bauhaus into the heart of German cities.[69] At the same time, however, the advertising dimension of merchandising demanded a far more explicit drama than did most of the commissions awarded to members of the Ring and other advocates of the New Building. For Mendelsohn's store owner patrons, a memorable image was as integral to their buildings' function as an efficient layout and was as modern as the buildings' construction materials. The same was also true for cinemas.

THE UNIVERSUM CINEMA: FANTASY AS FUNCTION

It required only a small step for Mendelsohn to design a cinema, the other building type in which the functional and advertising aspects of light could converge as theatrically as they had in his store designs. Although he was a latecomer to the type, his Universum Cinema quickly won widespread recognition as an exemplar of the technologically generated fantasy for which Weimar-era German cinemas gained an international reputation. German cinema owners, like their counterparts throughout the world, offered a low-priced escape from everyday life. Architecture played an important role in creating for the cinema the sense of an exciting place set apart from the daily routine of increasingly standardized workplaces and living quarters. Through the lavish use of rich and exotic ornament cinemas in America became places where the working and middle classes could enjoy palatial surroundings. In Germany, however, cinemas turned to technological imagery to create the desired atmosphere for their patrons. Germans found using spectacular lighting to be less expensive – and just as effective – as the use of ornamentation by Americans. And because cinemas did their greatest business after dark, their need for impressive exterior lighting exceeded even that of stores.[70]

In Germany, during the twenties, the cinema replaced the grand store as the prime site of popular imaginings. This was especially so in Berlin, an internationally recognized center for the new film industry, whose products were becoming a part of the lives of a large number of its citizens.[71] German films were particularly famous for their technical innovations, such as the use of a completely mobile camera, and for their sophisticated lighting. In addition, the movies' sets were often designed by famous artists and architects.[72] Working within the tight budgets imposed by the economic chaos of the early postwar years, German cinema architects also pioneered a variety of

FIGURE 72

Hans Poelzig, Große Schauspielhaus, lobby with column light fixture designed by Marlene Moeschke, Berlin, 1918–19. (Source: *Hans Poelzig: Bauten und Entwurfe*, Berlin, 1939.)

dramatic effects.[73] Most were inspired by the theatrical experiments of Max Reinhardt, especially Poelzig's remodeled interior of the Große Schauspielhaus in Berlin. This building, which opened in 1919, was, along with the Einstein Tower, the most celebrated example of postwar Expressionist architecture.[74] The building's foyer and lobby demonstrated, even more than did its stalactite-encircled auditorium, what could be accomplished with indirect lighting and with relatively restrained ahistorical ornament (Fig. 72). The almost ethereal light emanating from hidden sources seemed to dissolve the material reality of the columns. In tandem, Poelzig and Reinhardt were able to realize some of the communitarian goals of the younger and more radical Bruno Taut, binding audiences together through emotion-engendering spectacle.

The Große Schauspielhaus provided the point of departure for a decade in which German cinema owners and their architects transformed the building type by substituting ever more pervasive lighting. These cinemas replaced the more conventionally decorative theater-like cinemas of Oskar Kaufmann and the rest of the previous generation. Poelzig's Capitol Cinema of 1925–26, fairly unremarkable on the exterior until its lights were turned on at dusk, also brought

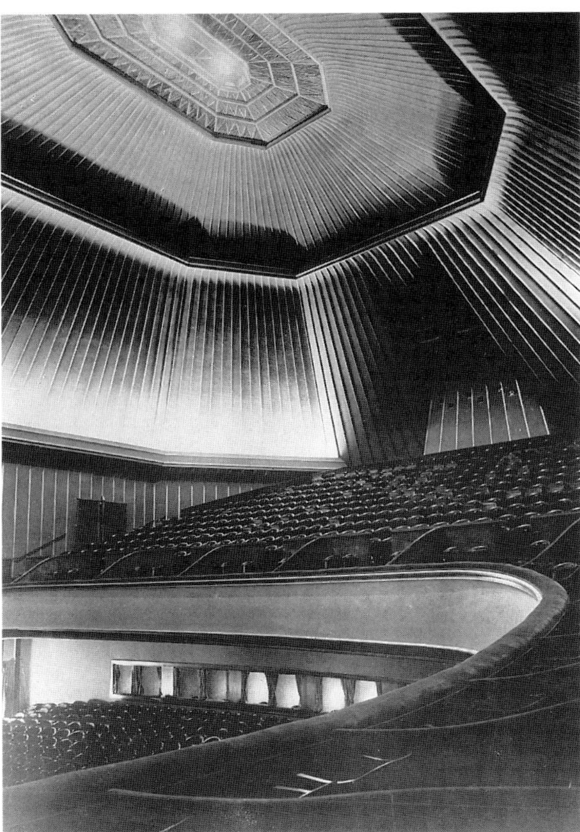

FIGURE 73

Hans Poelzig, Capitol Cinema auditorium, Berlin, 1925–26. (Source: Foto Marburg/Art Resource NY, Neg. 1.168.281.)

a new level of interior drama to the cinema auditorium, achieved by the sophisticated lighting of its high ceiling (Fig. 73).[75] Siegfried Kracauer, who was unusually critical of the new mass culture even while he reveled in its innovations, described the Capitol and its neighbors in the entertainment quarter near the Berlin Zoo as making "day out of the night, in order to scare away the grey of the work day from the night of their visitors." Describing the omnipresent flash of spotlights and neon, he continued:

> The building-high glass columns of light that push colorfully over the bright surfaces of the cinema posters and shove behind mirrors the confusion of tracked tubes, undertake an attack which refracts back the possibility of the emptiness that would like to enter at any price. They roar, they drum, they hammer with the brutality of insanity upon the multitude. An unrestrained sparkle, that in no way serves only as advertising, but which also surpasses its own function. But it swings and circles not only as blissfully as the illuminated advertising in Paris, which finds its satisfaction by forming out of red, yellow, and lilac light its devouring model. It

> is much more a flaming protest against the darkness of our existence, a protest of the greedy life, that flows from itself into the management of amusement as a despairing confession.[76]

Inside, Kracauer found that "their totalizing effects assaults every one of the senses using every possible means." Once again light was crucial:

> Spotlights shower their beams out into the auditorium, sprinkling across festive drapes or rippling through colorful growth-like glass fixtures. The orchestra asserts itself as an independent power, its acoustic production buttressed by the responsory of the lighting. Every emotion is accorded its own acoustic expression, its color value in the spectrum – an optical and acoustic kaleidoscope which provides the setting for the physical activity on stage, pantomime and ballet. Until finally the white surface descends and the events of the three-dimensional stage imperceptibly blend into two-dimensional illusions.[77]

The Titania Palast, built in 1926–27 by the firm of Schöffler, Schloenbach, and Jacobi, and the Capitol provided the two most important precedents for Mendelsohn's Universum. Although the interior of the Titania Palast was less completely oriented toward the screen than was the hall of the Capitol, the illumination of this corner-sited cinema made it one of Berlin's most exciting nighttime sights (Fig. 74). Inside, backlit curvilinear shells framing the screen, ceiling, and side walls competed with a bulging balcony for the spectator's attention. The exterior featured a virtual encyclopedia of available lighting techniques: illuminated letters, strategically placed window openings, floodlit posters, coved cornice lighting, and glowing decorative bands. By day, however, most of this nocturnal sleekness vanished.[78]

The radical nature of the German approach to cinema architecture is highlighted by a comparison with its American counterparts from the same years. During the twenties, American picture palaces offered audiences the opportunity to become actors themselves on splendid – if somewhat superficial – stagesets that offered an illusion of escape easily matching that offered by the films. Richly ornamented facades, often composed of mass-produced terra cotta, distinguished these buildings from their comparatively dowdy workaday companions along neighborhood shopping strips and in the downtowns of countless small cities and towns. Inside, the elaborate foyers of these buildings were based upon such historical sources as the ornate chapel at

FIGURE 74

Schöffler, Schloenbach, and Jacobi; Titania Palast Cinema, Berlin, 1926–27. (Source: Foto Marburg/Art Resource NY, Neg. 7.123.)

Versailles. Although sophisticated lighting techniques were used in the auditoria, most notably in the "atmospheric" theaters designed by John Eberson, their impact remained subordinate to the overwhelming array of decorative motifs inspired by exotic civilizations, including the Mayan and Chinese, as well as by the more usual seventeenth- and eighteenth-century European ones (Fig. 75).[79] It was in this setting that two generations of Americans were inculcated into the new mass culture.[80]

Mendelsohn's Universum Cinema opened on the Kurfürstendamm in 1928 (Fig. 76). Because the auditorium had to be completely dark during film screenings, the building's glazing was limited to the plate glass windows of the shop fronts that the architect wrapped part way round the brick and stucco-sheathed building and to the band of windows that encircled the second story. At night, however, floodlights, signage, and even the very shape of the building attracted attention, while inside, a panoply of colors and lighting effects sustained the magic of the movies being shown. Mendelsohn proclaimed his intentions in a characteristically staccato statement:

FIGURE 75

John Eberson, Majestic Cinema, Houston, Texas, 1923. (Source: R. W. Sexton and B. F. Betts, *American Theaters of Today*, New York, 1927.)

FIGURE 76

Erich Mendelsohn, Universum Cinema, Berlin, 1926–28. (Source: Staatliche Museen zu Berlin, Kunstbibliothek.)

Thus no rococo palace for Buster Keaton.
No stucco pastries for Potemkin . . .
But, also no fear!
No sober reality, no claustrophobia of life-weary brain acrobatics. – Fantasy!
Fantasy – but no lunatic asylum – dominated by space, color, and light.[81]

The Universum, built for the UFA, Germany's national film production company, represented an almost complete rethinking of two key aspects of cinema design – plan and elevation – while simultaneously continuing the emphasis on lighting found in the Capitol and Titania Palast. Its position within the WOGA complex eased the problem of integrating a sufficiently dramatic front, profitable rental space, and the requisite number of escape routes by leaving both side facades accessible. Shifting the shop fronts to the side meant that they did not detract, as they had in the Capitol, from the compositional emphasis on the cinema entrance. And although the curve of the Universum's ground plan was slightly skewed to accommodate the two-story shops, most of which faced the pedestrian street, it did echo the general form of the hall. A critic writing in *Die Form* singled out this unprecedented correlation between exterior form and interior plan for special praise.[82]

As usual, surviving autograph drawings are exclusively perspectives, including three rare interior studies, rather than plans. They show that Mendelsohn considered the cinema's massing in relation to the neighboring buildings before turning to its details.[83] The dominant motif in the final design, a ventilation shaft that doubled as a prominent billboard, evolved from a series of designs for other building types.[84] In the Universum, the tower served a variety of publicity purposes. Its stucco surfaces thrusting up through the red-brown brick mass of the building contained advertising space, which was well lit at night.[85] More important was this tower's function as a marker. Formally, it provided a balance to the fly tower in the rear, drawing attention to the front of the building. Visible from a distance to those traveling up or down the boulevard, it boldly marked the entrance to the cinema.[86] It also echoed the shape of the screen onto which films were projected. Meanwhile, Mendelsohn's elimination of the horizontal mullions in the second-story shop windows left a vertically divided band that Theodor Böll aptly compared to a strip of film.[87] The cinema entrance also was accented with large letters affixed to the roofline, spelling out the theater's name, and with a curv-

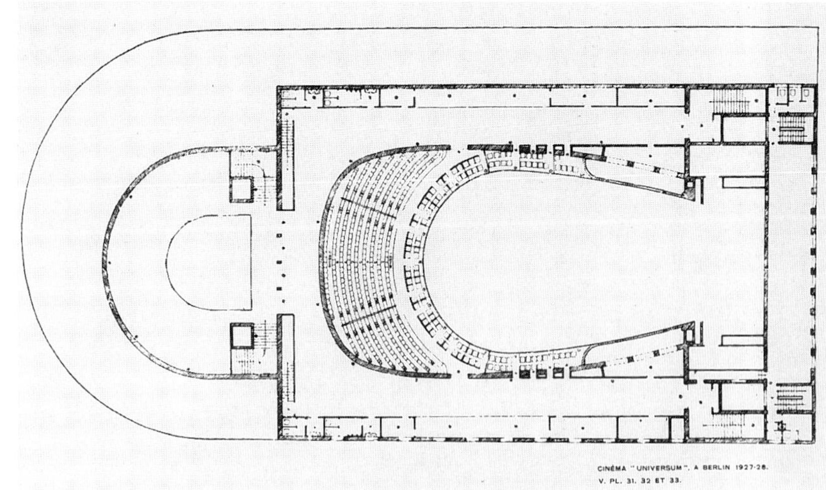

FIGURE 77

Universum Cinema, ground floor plan. (Source: Staatliche Museen zu Berlin, Kunstbibliothek.)

ing billboard for posters announcing the movie currently being shown within.

Descriptions and reviews of the Universum's interior, published at the time of its opening, also took note of its well-organized circulation paths (Fig. 77).[88] A broad covered alcove led into a spacious lobby flanked by staircases to the second-floor balcony and opened onto wide corridors that in turn encircled the orchestra seating. Patrons thus could proceed quickly into the theater and, at the conclusion of the show, leave with equal ease through paired doorways opening onto Cicerostraße or – in an emergency – the shopping street as well. The lobby, a galleried two-story atrium, marked a calm, but carefully lit, moment in the procession from the boulevard into the auditorium (Fig. 78). Here moviegoers paused to buy tickets and shed coats. Yellow stone floors and wainscoting gave way to indirectly lit walls painted in ivory. The underside of the second story was painted a deep blue; the velour carpet leading to the balcony was also blue.[89] The cashier's window, a pavilion of opaque glass and bronze mounted on a stone-faced base, divided the flow of traffic swirling toward the auditorium. Its bow echoed the curve of the balcony and of the horseshoe of glass set into the ceiling above. Bands of light troughs tucked behind matte-finished glass radiated from this central motif outwards over the lobby balcony.[90]

Although already an integral part of German cinema architecture, Mendelsohn's use of indirect and other lighting effects in this room and throughout the Universum interior also had its roots in his earlier work. In a small 1927 shop interior for Herpich at Leipzigerstraße 123a, for instance, a lit ceiling band repeated at a slightly reduced

FIGURE 78

Universum Cinema, lobby. (Source: Staatliche Museen zu Berlin, Kunstbibliothek.)

scale the P-shaped layout of the space, anticipating the role of the great horseshoe crowning the Universum atrium (Fig. 79). There Mendelsohn also tucked cove lights under the cornice, separating the cabinetry from the luminous panels above it to cast a warm glow on the walnut cases. In conjunction with the dark coloration of the Universum lobby's first-floor ceiling, cove lights – now used on a much larger scale – produced a sense of wall planes floating like curtains suspended in open space.[91]

These effects reached their climax in a dazzlingly lit hall, a tight curve whose every detail focused one's attention on the screen (Fig. 80). The curve of the auditorium echoed in Mendelsohn's own mind his fascination with the "moving" quality of movies and responded to the specific sightlines required by film.[92] Older cinemas, following the precedent established by conventional theaters, were often too wide for the new concentration on a single flat surface. The architect compared the effect – enhanced by the striped housing of the organ pipes at either end of the balcony, the great curve of the balcony itself, and the linear panels of ceiling lights – to that of a camera.[93] Because the theater was designed primarily for the new "talkies," the sunken orchestra pit was small and even the organ was of secondary importance.

The Universum auditorium was only slightly more richly decorated than the lobby. Mendelsohn clad the wainscoting with mahogany paneling; all the seats were covered in a corresponding red-brown

FIGURE 79

Erich Mendelsohn, C. A. Herpich Sons shop, Leipzigerstaße 123a, interior, Berlin, 1927. (Source: Foto Marburg/Art Resource NY, Neg. 1.182.688.)

FIGURE 80

Erich Mendelsohn, Universum Cinema, auditorium (Source: Staatliche Museen zu Berlin, Kunstbibliothek.)

velvet. Red velvet curtained the screen, and an inner curtain was the color of old gold. The striped organ pipe casings were brown and grey. Carl Grossberg painted the balcony walls with parallel bands of yellow, blue grey, and soft red.[94] One visitor commented:

> The sensation is of a hall which leaps out from the proscenium and is caught as it were on the rebound and immobilized. The interior shimmers and moves; yet it is static in the sense that the vault is static. One feels that in these forms there is latent a fine adjustment of mechanical forces. It is not inert architecture, in the sense of load and ample support. It is cantilevered, stressed, tense, yet strong in the same way that the wings and stays of an airplane are strong. One might almost say that this is aeroplane architecture.[95]

The Universum amply demonstrated Mendelsohn's ability to rethink typological conventions in ways that enhanced the dynamism of the cityscape without exacerbating its chaotic appearance. Moreover, it was Mendelsohn's celebration in this building and in the Herpich and Petersdorff stores of precisely the programmatic aspects of these commissions, factors which had most troubled architects of the previous generation, that accounted for this success. For Mendelsohn, advertising and the mass culture to which it belonged were forces to be exploited as well as tamed, just as the modern city was to be enjoyed as well as reformed. The spectacles he mounted on his city-scaled stage seemed to star the fur coats and silk dresses in the Herpich and Petersdorff windows, but his use of industrially produced materials and technological effects could also undercut class-based sales tactics and lead to a far more democratic image of luxury than its Wilhelmine predecessor or that which continued to prevail in the United States and much of the rest of Europe.

6

"BANANA WHOLESALERS AND COMBINES THAT RUN DEPARTMENT STORES"

THE opening of the addition and renovation of the Cohen-Epstein store in Duisburg in 1927 was accompanied by an advertisement whose text, located below a Mendelsohn drawing of the new display windows, announced:

> A new type. The new building is simple and clear. Everywhere the unrestrained light flows in the broad space that stretches from street to street. Electric pumps continually ventilate the buildings; autos enter in the cellar and sweep back into the street filled with goods; speedy elevators bring the customers up and down. Everything serves a purpose. Here luxury would be wasteful, an ugly excess. Hand in hand architect and merchant have built this store. Each penny is accounted for. On this spot the accountant's pencil has always ruled in order to achieve the best and not to squander. The organization depends on fifty-eight salespeople competing with one another to serve the customer.[1]

This pragmatism led Mendelsohn, at almost exactly the same time that he was inventing a modern approach to luxury in the Herpich and Petersdorff stores and to fantasy in the Universum Cinema, to pioneer as well a more efficient approach to department store design in which he explicitly equated the store and the factory, banishing the illusions usually so important to the marketing of mass-produced goods.

Mendelsohn's skill at adapting his architectural vocabulary to the needs of his diverse clientele is nowhere more apparent than in the difference between the elegant Herpich and Petersdorff stores and (even more than the relatively minor Cohen-Epstein commission) the three practical department stores he built in Nuremberg, Stuttgart, and Chemnitz for the Schocken chain. In Salman Schocken Mendelsohn found the most munificent and challenging patron of his career, one who was well versed in contemporary architectural theory and who demanded that his architect live up to his own functionalist claims.[2] Alert to the degree to which dynamic effects doubled as advertising, Schocken nonetheless refused to sanction any departure from the strict economy he prized. Although in public Mendelsohn maintained that architects should respect economic limitations imposed by clients, in private he complained that "the client is in all cases a petty grocer, who only respects intelligence when it delivers the goods to him. He is only too glad to declare his respect for art . . . but only in order to get a thousand-pound pig for the price of a piglet."[3] That Schocken was no petty grocer did little to smooth their relationship. Schocken took a far more active role in the design of buildings than did Mendelsohn's other patrons, and the two proud and stubborn men were often at odds. Nonetheless, as a team they created a new type of department store explicitly purged of the appeal to social status previously intrinsic to the marketing of many commodities.

The tenth son of a village shop owner, Schocken was largely self-educated, a key figure in Jewish intellectual circles, and a Zionist.[4] In 1901 he began working for his older brother, who had just opened a department store in the Saxon city of Zwickau. Three years later, he founded his own store in Oelsnitz. The family chain, centered around a Zwickau supply center that the brothers organized in 1907, grew to ten stores by the outbreak of World War I. A second phase of expansion between 1926 and 1931 included at least seven more stores, three of them designed or remodeled by Mendelsohn.[5] Schocken was also active in trade groups and was a leading German proponent of "scientific" management.

Schocken brought timely reforms to the German department store business, which grew rapidly during the first decade of the century. Operating in provincial cities, the Schocken chain concentrated on providing consumers with the best goods at the lowest prices and substituting the single well-made product for the plethora of brands offered by rival stores. All goods, except for groceries, were selected and purchased by the Zwickau office, a procedure that ensured a uniform standard throughout the chain.[6] Such methods anticipated the interest German manufacturers and entrepreneurs would take during the twenties in "Taylorization" and other modern management techniques as they reexamined all aspects of production and distribution and created ever larger and more tightly integrated organizations in the name of American-style efficiency and rationalization.[7]

Although Schocken advocated standardization of manufactured products, he never attempted to impose a prototypical architectural solution on his store buildings. The chain's early stores were local versions of the Messel model or older structures bought from other firms. In a prewar speech, the store owner admitted that it was through architecture that German department stores had surpassed their French and American rivals. He complained, however, that, following the lead of Messel's Wertheim palace, German stores had forsaken the emphasis on inexpensive goods with which they had made their original reputation.[8] Only after the war did Schocken begin to search for an architectural solution that would match his pragmatic approach to store management. His first tentative experiment with new architectural forms, a facade added in 1922–23 to the flagship store in Zwickau, was a vaguely Expressionist billboard.[9]

Mendelsohn first came to Schocken's attention when the dedicated Zionist visited the 1919 exhibition at the Paul Cassirer Gallery of a Palestinian sculptor. There he also saw the young architect's exhibit of wartime drawings and models.[10] Five year later, Mendelsohn's friend, Kurt Blumenfeld, the president of the German Zionist Organization in Berlin, wrote Schocken on Mendelsohn's behalf.[11] Given the opportunity to hire a Zionist architect, it is unlikely that Schocken would have done otherwise. That this Zionist architect was a proponent of inexpensive, functional construction and someone who understood Schocken's needs as a merchant further cemented the bond. Nevertheless, Schocken later admitted that there was no one with whom he had battled as much as he had with Mendelsohn.[12]

Schocken dispensed architectural patronage shrewdly. For his smaller stores, he continued to hire local architects unlikely to hold their own against him in conflicts over design details. The 1926 Cottbus store, close to Mendelsohn's own style, was designed by the firm of Stiefer and Könecke.[13] Although such firms were easier to work with than a nationally known architect with a highly individual style, they could not provide the publicity generated by a landmark building. For highly visible commissions, Schocken consistently turned to Mendelsohn. Mendelsohn renovated the building Schocken had bought in Nuremberg and built entirely new structures in Stuttgart and Chemnitz. He also designed a Berlin office for Schocken.[14]

Schocken was also an intellectual interested in a wide range of challenging modern thought. In 1930 he founded the Research Institute for Jewish Poetry. Shortly afterward his life-long interest in Judaica led him to establish a press in Berlin dedicated to Jewish culture. He began new publishing ventures after moving to Jerusalem.[15] He also corresponded with the poet Else Lasker-Schüler, who was one of the many intellectuals he helped to support.[16] The years between 1940, when he moved to the United States, and his death in 1959 were marked by his involvement with a second Schocken press, which he founded in New York in 1945. In addition to publishing Judaica, both presses specialized in publishing the work of Franz Kafka.[17] This activity demonstrated a commitment to the new which easily transcended the sensitivity to fashion demanded by his profession.

THE DEPARTMENT STORE

Department stores had emerged in the middle of the nineteenth century in London, Paris, and New York. They grew out of the arcades that had already spread across Europe and the eastern United States in the first half of the century. As the urban counterparts to the factories producing many of the goods that they sold, department stores were inextricably intertwined with advances in production and transportation brought about by the Industrial Revolution.[18] Like the arcades before them, their newness as a building type allowed for considerable architectural experimentation, especially with the use of iron. Gustave Eiffel collaborated on the interior atria of the Bon Marché store in Paris in the 1870s; exposed exterior iron framing distinguished several important turn-of-the-century stores in Paris and Brussels, including Frantz Jourdain's Grands Magasins de la Samartaine in Paris and Victor Horta's Grands Magasins de l'Innovation in Brussels. Two important Chicago stores, William Le Barron Jenney's second Leiter store of 1891 and Louis Sullivan's building for what is now Carson, Pirie, Scott, built intermittently between 1899 and 1906 (when it was completed by Daniel Burnham's firm), pioneered the rationalized expression of first iron- and then steel-skeletal-frame construction in an American setting indivisible from parallel innovations in the design of neighboring office buildings.[19]

Signaling the expansion from manufacturing into commerce of economies of scale, the giant stores were emblems of modern economic organization and urban development. The transportation systems that enabled them to draw upon a vast network of suppliers were also crucial, as were the mass-circulation newspapers in which they could advertise their wares, the public transportation that brought shoppers to their doorsteps, and the gas and eventually electric illumination that enabled them to stay open in the evening. Equally modern were the selling methods they pioneered, in which a much larger proportion of available goods was displayed for the perusal of the potential customer, who, once she had decided upon or been coaxed into making a purchase, did not need to bargain with the shop assistant because clearly marked uniform prices had been set by the management in advance. Department stores gathered an enormous assortment of merchandise, ranging from housewares to drygoods, and played a particularly important role in the growth of the ready-made clothing trade.

Nineteenth- and early-twentieth-century department store architecture was never a pure expression, however, of the many sorts of systemization that made the stores possible. Instead, store owners and their architects relied upon sumptuous surroundings to attract customers into buying what were largely, and often most profitably, fashionable luxuries rather than bare essentials. Ornamental embellishment played an important role in the facades of even the Jourdain, Horta, and Sullivan stores, especially on the lower stories, where the customer encountered the building most directly. Inside, atria were as important for creating an imposing atmosphere as for bringing natural light into the core of the building or for announcing to the customer the existence of multiple floor levels, more often actually reached by elevators than by the largely ornamental staircases (Fig. 81). Consumption, rather than labor, became the primary economic function of many middle- and upper-class women in Europe and America over the course of the nineteenth century, and the department store catered to satisfying the reality as well as the fantasy of upward mobility and economic empowerment, often by echoing aristocratic models of both architecture and servility. Furthermore, at least the illusion of participation was available to almost all; unlike small shop owners, who continued to equate entrance into their store with the intention to make a purchase, department store owners made it clear that browsers were welcome.[20]

Because industrialization occurred later in Germany than in its Western neighbors Britain, France, and Belgium, the first flowering of German department stores came only in the final years of the nineteenth century. Eventually, though, the stores came to play a larger role in Germany than anywhere else. Most of the major firms, which included those founded by Rudolf Karstadt, Hermann Tietz, Leonhard Tietz, and A. Wertheim, grew during the imperial era from single shops into chains of enormous and imposing stores scattered

FIGURE 81

Alfred Messel, Wertheim Department Store atrium. (Source: Foto Marburg/Art Resource NY, Neg. 1.034.538.)

widely around the country.[21] For Schocken, however, the enticement of luxury, whether implied or real, held little appeal as a marketing strategy. He believed in a rational world in which the consumer would buy the merchandise that best combined high quality and low price, that if she picked one of these pots out of the pile, weighed it in her hand, and inspected such details as the fastening of the handle, she would be satisfied both by the pot and its cost and make a purchase (Fig. 82). The product required no seductive packaging. That was supplied instead by the architecture of the store itself, whose exterior delivered the dual promise of factorylike American efficiency and enthusiasm for a technological society befitting the mass-produced goods for sale inside.

NUREMBERG

Mendelsohn's first commission from Schocken, a department store in Nuremberg, opened in October 1926 (Fig. 83). Here the architect's task had been to renovate and expand an existing factory. The first Schocken department store was one of its architect's least dynamic designs, conforming instead to its patron's ascetic tastes.[22] This adherence to the wishes of the patron, along with the expansion of the display methods introduced in the Herpich design but unveiled here

FIGURE 82

Albert Renger-Patzsch, photograph of aluminum cooking pots on display at a Schocken department store. (Source: Albert Renger-Patzsch, *Die Welt ist Schön*, Munich, 1928.)

six months before the smaller Berlin store was completed, made the Nuremberg store a landmark in the history of German commercial architecture.[23] The store's stark interiors, which retained their original factory atmosphere, were equally revolutionary. Patron and architect agreed that the new store represented a modern aesthetic in which function triumphed over ornament.

Schocken had first approached Mendelsohn about the project in late 1925.[24] Six months later, in May 1926, the architect completed his design. After the inevitable tussle with the local building authorities, work began in June.[25] Schocken was willing to compromise with the building inspectors and asked Mendelsohn to work in collaboration with a local architect; in the first documented dispute between the two, Mendelsohn refused. Proud of his battles with the Berlin authorities, Mendelsohn had a different perspective than Schocken, whose overriding concern was to get on with construction.[26] The existing complex faced three streets with Mendelsohn responsible for renovating only two of the three facades.[27] As in the Herpich store, the ribbon windows of the upper stories reinforced the emphasis on the shop windows. The Nuremberg windows were much shorter than their Herpich counterparts, as Schocken insisted that they not interfere with the height of the interior cabinetry he placed below them, while their interior ledges were quite deep, enabling Schocken to mount unusually comprehensive displays.[28]

FIGURE 83

Erich Mendelsohn, Schocken Department Store, Nuremberg, Germany, 1925–26. (Source: Staatliche Museen zu Berlin, Kunstbibliothek.)

In comparison with the more elegant Herpich and Petersdorff interiors, the Nuremberg shop floors bluntly preserved the factory atmosphere of the original building (Figs. 84 and 85). The four floors of well-lit sales space (above them in the rear was an additional stockroom floor) were clear and open. Cabinets stretching all the way to the clerestory windows lined the exterior walls. Mendelsohn grouped other displays around structural piers or ran them along long aisles.[29] He strung large globe lights down the middle of each aisle. Although the basic arrangement was the same as in the Herpich and Petersdorff stores, the rich carpeting, mirrored and glazed cabinetry, and expensive woods of those establishments did not suit either Schocken's taste or the plainness of the household goods he was trying to sell. The Herpich and Petersdorff stores marketed a small num-

FIGURE 84

Erich Mendelsohn, C. A. Herpich Sons, Furriers, interior. (Source: Staatliche Museen zu Berlin, Kunstbibliothek.)

FIGURE 85

Erich Mendelsohn, Schocken Department Store, Nuremberg, sales floor. (Source: Staatliche Museen zu Berlin, Kunstbibliothek.)

ber of luxury goods to wealthy customers, upon whom staff waited attentively. Schocken sold a large number of goods to a more diverse group of consumers. He placed many of these wares on open counters, where they could be easily inspected and handled by potential customers with minimal aid from a proportionally smaller sales force.

Both Mendelsohn and Schocken spoke at the October 11, 1926, opening of the store.[30] Schocken's exposition of the economic principles of his firm was studded with implications for his architectural patronage. "Much is being said," he declared, "about standardization and normalization; more said than done."[31] Yet his firm, he claimed, had not recently adopted this now fashionable slogan, but had espoused it for twenty-five years. Only such good production methods, he claimed, could fulfill the retailer's purpose, which he defined as efficiently meeting the needs of the consumer. Schocken added that the merchant must be open to the new. He recognized that his pragmatic economic policies could be allied with a new aesthetic, an aesthetic which he defended. "The art of a master," he declared, "shows itself in the ability for selection and reduction, in the ability to refrain from the inessential, to restrict material, to recognize the supporting columns, to shape what is needed with a few strong lines."[32]

Mendelsohn's speech combined an explanation of the store's simplicity with a call for the more dynamic architecture that characterized both the Herpich store and a second Schocken store in Stuttgart which he had already begun to design. He defended his choice of architectural style, as usual, with the argument that it fit the new spirit of the times, a spirit of "Bare knees and short haircuts/Radio and film/Car and airplane/Banana wholesalers and combines that run department stores."[33] Because the Nuremberg store facade lacked the dynamic imagery of his recent buildings in Berlin, Mendelsohn defended its design in terms of the character of the goods it sold. "Do you want to be deceived by the things that surround you, by your house, the shops you buy from?" he asked. "Are they, then, things that do not belong to you, your electric cooker, your safety razor – so functional, so simple, and so natural?"[34] Mendelsohn concluded with a poetic invocation of the machine in motion as the source of his architecture. These remarks were directed at his patron, whom he hoped would allow him in Stuttgart to weld more dynamic facades onto the frugal interiors he had developed in Nuremberg:

> Only he who has no rhythm in his body – don't think of jazz, be serious! – Fails to understand the metallic rhythm of the machine, the humming of the propeller, the huge vitality which thrills us, overjoys us and makes us creative . . .
> Do not let yourself be hurried, master the age.
> Do not let yourself be duped. You are the master. Be a creator, shape your own age.
> These are your responsibilities.[35]

In Nuremberg, architect and patron achieved an extreme of objective sobriety. Mendelsohn inserted into their next collaboration, a far larger store in Stuttgart, far more of "the metallic rhythm of the machine," using it even more deftly than he had in his more luxurious stores as an economic – and explicitly modern – substitute for what both men believed to be the superfluous clutter and wasted space of Wilhelmine commercial architecture.

STUTTGART

In Stuttgart, Mendelsohn and Schocken continued to replace fantasies centered on social aspirations and achieved through the purchase of luxury goods with faith in the egalitarian potential of efficient economic organization. Although Mendelsohn himself described his design process in musical terms, surviving documents make clear the role that the urban site and the city authorities played in shaping his largest commission to date.[36] He clearly designed from the outside in, experimenting with the building's massing in relation to its urban context long before he turned to the details of its plan. He also combined advertising components familiar from the Herpich store – bands of display windows, night lighting, and prominent lettering – with influences drawn from the architecture of factories and other department stores. This created a clearly identifiable image of efficiency whose democratic as well as urban character was enhanced by Mendelsohn's reorganization of the building type's previously atrium-centered plan. In particular, the displacement of the atrium's metal-and-glass skeleton to the store's corner tower brought the building's most dramatic motif out onto the street.

Schocken and Mendelsohn discussed the new department store as early as January 1926.[37] By July 11, Mendelsohn could write his wife that the initial phase of the design, the basic arrangement of its facades, was nearly complete.[38] The site was an entire city block in the heart of Stuttgart's old city, bounded by Eberhard, Hirsch, Geiß, and Steinstraßen. Eberhardstraße was a major artery, Hirschstraße an important cross street; Geiß and Steinstraße were narrower back streets. The design process, meticulously documented in the files Schocken kept to record each contact between their two offices, notes frequent disagreements but also makes clear the extent to which Mendelsohn, despite his depiction of himself as a master with an intuitive talent, actually responded in detail to the specific conditions of the commission, including both the site and the appropriate image for the building.

As was his custom, Mendelsohn began by drawing perspective and bird's-eye sketches of the building, in this case focusing on the Eberhardstraße facade as seen in perspective from Hirschstraße. He described the process in a letter written the next year:

> I see the site, the surface area, the space above it. Generally the architectural idea already appears spontaneously at this moment. I fix it in the form of a sketch. This means that the knowledge, the exact information about the actual requirements enters one's subconscious; the surface area comes to life as a ground plan, the empty space as a spatial shape, a two-and-three dimensional experience at the same time.
>
> I keep this first sketch. For, as an experience, as a vision, it has concentrated reality, plan, and structure into one architectonic organism. An inspiration, an act of creation.[39]

In the letter Mendelsohn exaggerated his genius, as the surviving drawings for almost all of his buildings demonstrate a great deal of experimentation with their forms. The sketches for the Stuttgart store – in colored chalk and often stacked, one atop another, on a single sheet – show that from a very early stage of his thoughts about the building, Mendelsohn planned to juxtapose two towers situated on opposite ends of the Eberhardstraße facade and possibly pointed in opposite directions (Fig. 86). This can be seen in the middle sketch on this sheet, also the one with the most complex articulation of the tower of the Hirschstraße end of the building (on the left).

Mendelsohn conceived of such dynamic juxtapositions in musical terms, calling them contrapuntal. The architect, a Bach devotee who proudly shared the master's birthday, frequently listened to gramophone records of Bach and other classical composers while he sketched.[40] He also drew during the many public and private concerts he attended, usually accompanied by his wife, a talented cellist. One early sketch for the Stuttgart store is on the back of a program for a Bach Evening sponsored on June 26, 1926, by the art historian Oskar Beyer. That evening Luise Mendelsohn played the Cello Sonata in D Major.[41]

In an article published in 1925, Mendelsohn wrote about architectural composition in musical terms. Here he employed analogies between the design process in architecture and two ways of composing music: harmony and counterpoint. The goal of both art forms, he wrote, was to achieve a composition in which individual parts were locked together into a single, organic whole. Although Mendelsohn had nothing against harmonic composition, he was clearly more attracted to counterpoint, the method Bach had used in writing his fugues. Identifying with their placement in a musical score, Men-

FIGURE 86

Erich Mendelsohn, Schocken Department Store, Stuttgart, perspective sketches, 1926. (Source: Staatliche Museen zu Berlin, Kunstbibliothek.)

delsohn equated melody with horizontal movement in architecture and chords with vertical movement. He used as an example the play in a church building of nave against tower and described the place where the two met as a "solitary interval, the unanticipated change of direction."[42]

The Stuttgart store was a study in contrapuntal composition. Mendelsohn began by placing the tall towers in opposition to the long facades and then turned them against one another. Once he had fixed the basic spatial relationship between the store's masses, he sought to add a new dimension to his fugue, to bring the building to life by imbuing it with more vibrant movement. Having already experimented with stringing letters spelling out the Schocken name across the front of the Eberthardtstraße facade, he now focused upon the form of the two towers (Fig. 87). Rectangular volumes in his first drawings, they now gained curving profiles, accented by ribbon windows. Mendelsohn was now satisfied with the embryonic design. As he had done in letters he wrote while designing the Einstein Tower and in the 1925 article on music, Mendelsohn clearly equated the

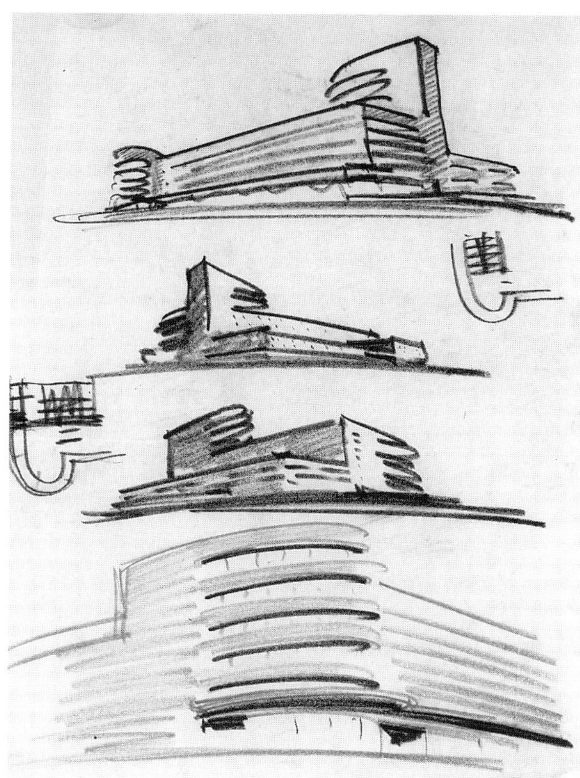

FIGURE 87

Schocken Department Store, Stuttgart, perspective and plan sketches, 1926. (Source: Staatliche Museen zu Berlin, Kunstbibliothek.)

formation of architecture to the creation of living beings. He wrote his wife, "The enclosed sheet shows [the Stuttgart store's] directness as a spatial organism. To alter it, i.e., to eliminate or add anything, will call for new work and a new design. So it will be better to push it through as it is and thus bring it to life."[43]

Mendelsohn planned his buildings in terms of mass seen in perspective, a method that fulfilled his concept of organic unity by transcending the two dimensionality of individual elevation studies and stressed the urban context over the details of interior arrangement. He altered the contour of the towers in order to enliven the building's exterior before finding an internal reason for this change – casing for stairs originally located further from the street – rooted in the building's plan. Although each drawing pictured the building in a void, from the beginning the architect had a sense of the relationship between the various facades and the streets on which they faced, shifting the height and prominence of each facade to match its circumstances. Thus the Eberhardt and Hirschstraßen facades dominated their Geiß and Steinstraßen counterparts, and Mendelsohn made the corner between them the focal point of the entire composition. Dependent upon the image of the building for his initial burst of inspiration, Mendelsohn at first conceived of its plan primarily in terms of four facades grouped around a courtyard; he settled upon its internal details much later in the design process.

Mendelsohn is best known for his drawings, but models played a crucial role in the development of his designs. The model for the Stuttgart store, completed by September 1926, was far more detailed than any surviving drawing from his own hand.[44] Earlier he had balanced the tension between the two towers, their curved contours, and the rectilinear volumes of the rest of the store's masses. Now he added depth and texture. The building's principal facade was composed of alternating bands of windows and wall surfaces which were in turn subdivided into strips of brick and travertine. Mendelsohn placed the brick bands slightly forward of the travertine walls. In the towers he set off attention-grabbing completely glazed steel skeletons against plain brick frames and projected the horizontal steel bands far forward from the glass and the vertical mullions.

The model also allowed Schocken to observe a final device for producing the dynamic contrapuntal effect Mendelsohn sought. The surface and height of each facade treatment wrapped around sections of two different faces of the building (Fig. 88). Thus each individual elevation included at least two different heights, and except for the plain brick Geißstraße facade in the rear, two types of masonry cladding. Furthermore, the architect placed the office tower off center in the midst of the Steinstraße facade, rather than on a corner, a decision that also masked a bend in the street. From any single vantage point, the building was thus obviously incomplete. This encouraged the viewer to turn the corner in search of an elusive fulfillment found only once the building had been circumnavigated and studied. The composition had the added benefit of establishing strong horizontals that held their own against the steep drop the site took between Eberhardt and Geißstraße into which Mendelsohn was able to insert an extra story.

By April 1927 Mendelsohn had proposed an additional story. At a meeting of patron, architect, and their respective staffs on June 13, Mendelsohn sought and won this adjustment to the design proposed in the model. The recessed extra story raised the building's height, excluding the Steinstraße tower, to six floors in front and four in back. At the same time, Mendelsohn also added a story to both towers, increasing their prominence.[45] He intended the increased height of the towers to enhance their dramatic effect. In the rest of the building, the extra story, set back to be nearly invisible from the

FIGURE 88

Schocken Department Store, Stuttgart, 1926–28. (Source: Staatliche Museen zu Berlin, Kunstbibliothek.)

street, met Schocken's demand for more space.[46] This added height was the product of one of the most bitter arguments between patron and architect.

Initially, Mendelsohn found the process of designing the Stuttgart store and seeking the approval of city building authorities unusually peaceful. Beginning in the fall of 1926, however, disputes between architect and patron dominated their correspondence. Schocken began this exchange in September by expressing his eagerness to embark upon construction. He worried that the townspeople would forget about the store or, worse yet, not take seriously any enterprise that was so slow to be built.[47] He prodded Mendelsohn by hiring a contractor and awarding a local company the contract for the steel frame.[48] Schocken also complained that the sight of an empty building site drew the unwanted attention of building inspectors.[49] Then he turned to the issue of construction time, insisting that the store should take only five or six months to build.[50] Overberg,

Mendelsohn's assistant, demurred in a letter written while Mendelsohn was on vacation. The preparation of the foundation and the erection of the steel skeleton alone, Overberg countered, would take four months.[51]

Schocken was accustomed to exerting authority over those who worked for him. Mendelsohn, who exploited the freedom from established constraints that German culture allowed artists much more in his relationships with patrons than in his relatively conventional private life, refused to confer such authority upon Schocken, whom he regarded as an equal rather than as an employer. Schocken had hired Mendelsohn in part because of the architect's reputation for practicality, and he was shocked to find in Mendelsohn the intransigence of an artist willing to place personal creativity above the patron's program. For nearly six months, from the end of December 1926 until mid-June 1927, the two battled over whether Mendelsohn would be able to build the design represented by the model completed in September, a design that did not meet Schocken's demand for a taller building. The two men reached a compromise in the spring of 1927, agreeing to add a single story to the entire building. Schocken attempted to establish that he, not the architect, controlled the project by requiring that on Gießstraße this story be brought forward flush with the facade, a solution which flouted local height restrictions.[52]

The June 13, 1927, meeting of patron and architect was an almost complete victory for Mendelsohn and fixed many details of the project. Schocken finally agreed to Mendelsohn's decision to recess all four facades of the extra story. Now attention could shift to the building's construction. Together, patron and architect chose materials, including bronzed steel for the window frames and a Rheinish iron brick for the cladding. They also decided to use travertine if it were not too expensive; after inquiries into its cost, they hired Adolf Lauster and Company in early July to supply the material.[53] The same week the Stuttgart authorities gave their final approval to the design.[54]

One reason for the building inspector's remarkable friendliness towards the project may have been Mendelsohn's courtship of the city's leading architect, Paul Bonatz. Throughout his life, Mendelsohn was more comfortable with architects whom he could worship as masters or indulge as disciples than with equals of his own generation. In the teens he had paid homage to van de Velde and Olbrich, in the twenties to Wright and Poelzig. Traveling to Stuttgart in July 1926, Mendelsohn was anxious to meet Bonatz. In a letter to Hans Hildebrandt, whom he asked to arrange the meeting, Mendelsohn admitted that his interest in Bonatz stemmed partly from his conviction that the older architect's approval would help assure a speedy acceptance of the Stuttgart store design by local authorities.[55] When Bonatz escorted Mendelsohn up the tower of his famous train station, one of the city's most prominent landmarks, he branded the direction the young had taken "false."[56] Nonetheless, Mendelsohn paid another call on him the following summer and seems to have had a real regard for the man who had once been Fischer's assistant.[57]

Both patron and architect were acutely aware of the publicity value a store building could command.[58] This awareness permeated their approach to the department store in general and to the Stuttgart store in particular. Neither was content with merely dressing up the traditional store in the finery of a new style, but neither, despite Schocken's protests about its cost, intended the building to be merely functional. Instead, they created a dynamic image of functionalism to stimulate public interest in the building and the firm it housed, recognizing that the store's overall appearance was as important as the individual contributions of well-designed display windows, graphics, night lighting, and interior organization. This image, located, above all, in the bold construction of the stair tower and supplemented by the use of inexpensive brick and the lack of ornament, bespoke modernity and celebrated the consumer benefits of industrialization.

As he had done in the Herpich store, Mendelsohn manipulated the frame of the building to allow the almost complete glazing of the ground floor display windows. And once again night lighting played an important role in creating a glamorous public image for the building (Fig. 89). The balance Mendelsohn struck between light and dark, solid and void, was certainly planned as much in terms of the building's night as its daytime appearance. Although the building was not equipped with external lights, the large lettering that in Stuttgart spelled out the Schocken name across a ledge above the Eberhardsstraße display windows was illuminated from within at night. This lettering appeared even in early studies for the building. Schocken had reservations about such an immodest use of his name, but he recognized its importance to the building's design as well as its function.[59]

Mendelsohn drew upon an American department store and upon factories at home and abroad to create an appropriately efficient and industrial image for the Stuttgart store. One of the highlights of his trip to Chicago had been his discovery of Louis Sullivan's architecture. Upon his return, he read Sullivan's *Autobiography of an Idea*,

FIGURE 89

Schocken Department Store, Stuttgart, night view. (Source: Foto Marburg/Art Resource NY, Neg. 1.175.834.)

translated Wright's eulogy on Sullivan, and included a photograph of Sullivan's Schiller Building in *America*. When the American architectural historian Fiske Kimball published an article in *Wasmuths Monatshefte für Baukunst* lauding America's classical architects as the country's real modernists, Mendelsohn responded with a defense of Sullivan.[60] Sullivan's Carson, Pirie, Scott store, built between 1899 and 1906, was, like the Schocken store in Stuttgart, prominently sited on the corner of an important thoroughfare, in this case Chicago's State Street (Fig. 90). Although department store owners customarily sought such corner sites, which their architects frequently chose to accent with cylindrical volumes easily visible at a distance, Mendelsohn was undoubtedly thinking of Sullivan when he borrowed not only this treatment but also the recessed tripartite upper-story windows of the Chicago store.[61] Mendelsohn completely transformed Sullivan's composition, however, to accord with his own bolder, more technological, and more publicity-oriented goals.

FIGURE 90

Louis Sullivan, Carson, Pirie, Scott Department Store, Chicago, Illinois, 1899–1904. (Source: David Philips, Chicago Architectural Photography Co.)

Sullivan was not the only American influence upon the Stuttgart design. The store's spatial animation and the juxtaposition of its red brick and cream-colored travertine reflected its architect's admiration for the brick-infilled frames of American reinforced concrete factories.[62] In *Russia, America, Europe* Mendelsohn praised the architects of one strongly banded New York factory building for using only as much glass as their building system required and contrasted it with the more extensive glazing of what he saw as an unnecessarily decorative Soviet curtain wall (Fig. 91).[63] Mendelsohn commented in 1928 on the importance of industrial architecture as the source for the New Building:

> Industrial construction is thus leading the way to the new architecture. As industry discovered the new materials or caused their discovery, it inevitably created the necessary means and places of

FIGURE 91

"Daylight factory," New York. (Source: Mendelsohn, *Rußland-Europa-Amerika*.)

> production. . . . Industry . . . is the starting point and bearer of the development that leads from the decay of civilization to a new creative culture. This development is based on the same needs and the same intellectual attitude.[64]

Nor were Mendelsohn's sources exclusively American. The stair tower became a fitting exclamation point to the entire design when he exposed its steel frame. The tower's thick steel bands emphasized the tension between structure and transparent skin. "Naked structure compels truthfulness," he had written in *America*, where he had also praised a construction view for offering "an X-ray picture of the finished building."[65] Here, in the tower, he left the steel skeleton he had so admired in American skyscrapers unmasked by wall structure, thereby opening the interior of the building to the street. Such a decision would have been almost unthinkable without the precedent of Gropius and Meyer's model factory for the Werkbund exhibition in Cologne in which they had cantilevered a pair of cylindrical stairs out from a thick concrete core and, using the thinnest of mullions, wrapped glass around the whole (Fig. 92).[66] Its gridded glass membrane and graceful stair made Gropius and Meyer's the more elegant solution, but Mendelsohn's was far more energetic. Furthermore, the Werkbund factory stairs were attached to a static com-

FIGURE 92

Walter Gropius and Adolf Meyer, model factory, Werkbund exhibition, Cologne, 1914. (Source: Bauhaus Archiv, Berlin, Neg. 6019/3.)

position, whereas Mendelsohn's tower was well integrated into a dynamic whole.

The motif's main function, however, was to bring to the building's key corner the spatial drama buried deep in the interior of most department stores, where masterfully engineered skylit atria provided light and drew the attention of shoppers to the merchandise displayed on upper stories.[67] By moving this grid of glass and steel to the exterior, Mendelsohn created the greatest possible public interest in the building and freed its interior for more straightforward selling purposes. He commented in a lecture delivered in 1933, "A department store is an exhibition of saleable goods and not of unsaleable architecture. Out of the staircase tower [I made] a mountain of glass-rings, an advertisement which requires to be paid for only once and *works for always*."[68]

In his prewar critique of Messel's Wertheim store, Schocken had characteristically complained of its luxuriousness, epitomized by its many atria. The first of these glass-roofed courtyards, located at the center of the original building, was eventually joined, as the store expanded, by a whole series of them of which the grandest was the almost Piranesian space Messel created as part of the Leipzigerplatz addition.[69] This palatial imagery and the fantasies that accompanied it did not interest Schocken. Instead, the Stuttgart store was organized around a small, uncovered court which unglamorously served as the entrance to the loading dock. Perhaps no other combination of architect and patron in Europe would have failed to place an atrium at the center of the Stuttgart store's block-deep site. Mendelsohn merely extended the first story out into the courtyard as he had done in the Herpich store, again capping the extension with a skylight.

The abolition of the atrium dramatically symbolized Schocken's desire both to eschew unnecessary costs and to acknowledge the postwar political and economic power of the working class. After the opening in 1929 of the Schocken store in Waldenburg, the local socialist newspaper credited it with increasing the purchasing power of the town's workers.[70] Mendelsohn, too, must have realized the social implications of his design. Two months after the store's opening, he commented on the relationship between architectural change and its social and political equivalents in response to a questionnaire from the *Frankfurter Zeitung*, "There is just as logical a connection between clinging to traditional forms and looking backwards politically as between supporting the new architectural purpose of our age and its revolutionary political ideas."[71]

Although Mendelsohn's design for the building was generated by the image of a store glimpsed by the potential shopper strolling by or driving down the main thoroughfare – a glint of steel and glass expanding into insistent horizontal bands – his plan for the interior space was equally successful. The industrial imagery of the Eberhardstraße facade was reinforced inside by the simplicity of many of the interiors. The one breathtaking spatial experience available within was the dizzying climb up or down the corner stair tower. The journey could also, of course, be made by elevator, or by a less dramatic back stair that projected into the courtyard (Fig. 93). Economic considerations rather than architectural splendor determined the interior arrangement of most the store, and even the stair tower substituted drama for spaciousness.[72]

Each of the sales floors had a slightly different sequence of clearly laid out counters. On the first floor, shoppers entered and exited by cash registers near which were emblazoned slogans trumpeting the reasons for the firm's success (Fig. 94). As had been the case in his other stores, Mendelsohn carefully arranged the display of goods so that free-standing interior columns would not interrupt the aisles but would instead be wrapped with counter space. From the public re-

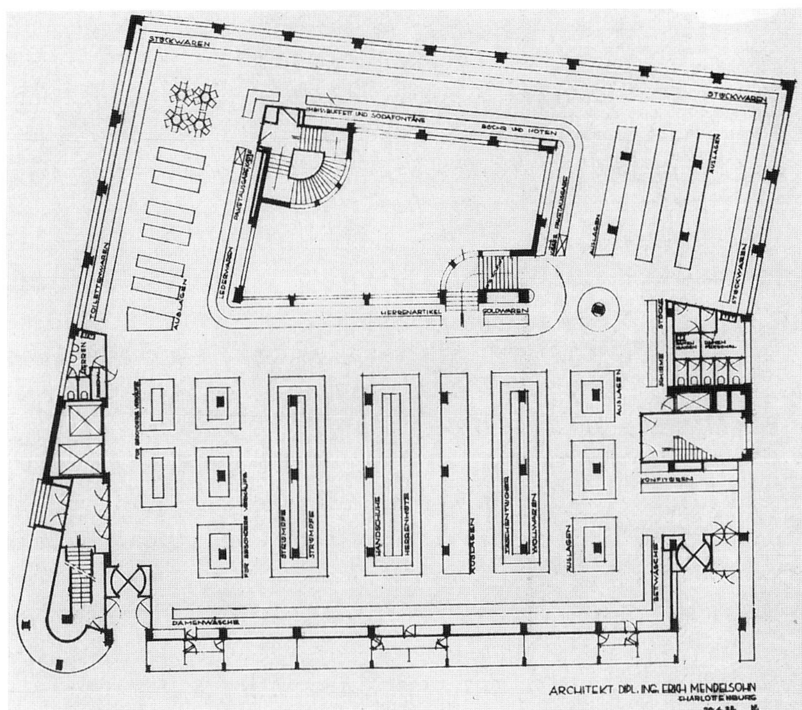

FIGURE 93

Erich Mendelsohn, Schocken Department Store, Stuttgart, ground floor plan. (Source: Staatliche Museen zu Berlin, Kunstbibliothek.)

freshment room to the director's office tucked into the top story of the Steinstraße tower, all the store's interiors were provided with simple wooden furniture, a decision that ignored the new fashion for chairs made of metal tubing.

Schocken's speech at the store's dedication touched on his sense of the building's balance of dynamic and functional components and stressed his attention to costs. He began with a tribute to dynamism and organicism that could almost have been written by Mendelsohn, a statement which was far more aesthetic in its orientation than were his surviving prewar thoughts about store buildings:

> The architect, if he is a true architect, has created a new organism from inorganic material. . . . We often see that such architectural masterpieces display a unity which seems well suited to the building, but not its interior content. . . . Here is the dynamic balance: filling it with that which is given by its content – a balance with many incalculables![73]

Such observations did not, however, prevent him from also voicing more characteristic concerns. He complained at length about the rising cost of construction, joking that if one had to ask the cost of building, one could not afford it. These high costs, he noted, made

FIGURE 94

Schocken Department Store, Stuttgart, cash register area. The built-in signage reads, "Good values on all merchandise at all times for all customers – therefore no rebates, no special promotional sales, no credit." (Source: Staatliche Museen zu Berlin, Kunstbibliothek.)

the rational planning of the interiors an absolute necessity. "This is the link between the style and the absence of luxury in our building," he noted.[74]

Finally, Schocken's speech demonstrated his familiarity with the vocabulary being used to describe the new architecture of which he was such a prominent patron. He used the terms "*Neues Bauen*" and "*Neue Sachlichkeit,*" which German critics employed most often during the twenties to describe this architecture. He included the first in a description of the dynamism inherent in new construction techniques and referred to the second while setting forth the rational plans of his stores. Of the latter he said, "In fact, we are building from the viewpoint of the *Neue Sachlichkeit*. Architecture is a purely economic affair; all technical perfections are exploited in the examination of the beauty of the whole, which results technically from the new means [of production]."[75]

There were plenty of architects in Germany and the rest of Europe ready to make such statements during the 1920s, but clients who

FIGURE 95

Erich Mendelsohn, Schocken Department Store, Chemnitz, Germany, 1928–30. (Source: Staatliche Museen zu Berlin, Kunstbibliothek.)

could hold them to this standard were rare. The evolving relationship between Schocken and his architect illustrates the importance both men also placed upon keeping abreast of architectural fashion; it also exposes the degree to which they understood and addressed the marketing functions of the department store.

CHEMNITZ

In the Schocken store in Chemnitz, begun in 1928 and completed two years later, Mendelsohn pared his arsenal of effects down to a vertical composition dominated by a single sweeping gesture (Fig. 95). Spurred in part by the increasing simplicity of Berlin's commercial architecture, he responded with a design that even more patently resembled a factory. At the same time, Mendelsohn's rivalry with Ludwig Mies van der Rohe and his reworking in the Chemnitz store of the already famous facade of the Bauhaus studio block, demonstrated his ability to remain up to date and degree to which his success was predicated upon his willingness to adjust designs rooted in issues of structure and form to reflect the more complex functional

FIGURE 96

Schocken Department Store, Chemnitz, perspective sketch, 1929. (Source: Staatliche Museen zu Berlin, Kunstbibliothek.)

requirements of the department store. Advertising – the overall image of the building within the city as well as shop windows and signage – continued to be among the most important of these requirements.

Despite their differences over the building in Stuttgart, Schocken discussed with Mendelsohn in late 1927 the possibility of a commission for a store in Chemnitz.[76] By the following fall, Mendelsohn was working on the design of its facade.[77] Schocken's site was a pie-shaped wedge facing Brückenstraße. The curved street line, as seen in a preliminary site plan, faced the junction of two minor streets with this main artery.[78] The architect initially experimented with juxtaposing a tall, curving rear block following the site line to the right of Brückenstraße against a lower, stepped facade on Brückenstraße itself.[79] Next he raised and regularized the street facade, marking the rear block with a tall "Schocken" sign (Fig. 96). In December 1929 the *Berliner Tageblatt* published a model showing a far simpler scheme.[80] In this model Mendelsohn eliminated the prominent lettering and indeed everything but the one smooth curve, capped by recessed setbacks. The completed building, dedicated on May 15, 1930, was in all but one particular built according to this model.[81] While the model showed an open terrace in the center of the ninth story, this facade was completely glazed in the final building.

This daring turn from the contrapuntal massing of his earlier stores introduced a bold unity into Mendelsohn's architecture and was part of a new emphasis on simplicity that accompanied the larger transformation of the urban streetscape at the end of the Weimar building boom. Mendelsohn's immediate inspiration seems to have been a building by the Luckhardt brothers and Alfons Anker, a firm that designed a number of Mendelsohnian projects, many of them based on Mendelsohn's Kemperplatz competition entry and the Herpich store.[82] The facade of the Telschow building by the Luckhardts and Anker of 1924–26 on Berlin's Potsdamerplatz followed the curve

FIGURE 97

Hans and Wassily Luckhardt and Alfons Anker, Telschow-Haus, Berlin, 1928. (Source: Akademie der Künste, Berlin, Neg. 16.-3.-4.7.a.)

of the street as it bent around a corner (Fig. 97).[83] In response to this new austerity – as yet unrivaled in downtown Berlin – Mendelsohn dramatically reduced the complexity of his Chemnitz design, eliminating all elements that detracted from the basic compositional volume.

More profoundly, the new design reflected Mendelsohn's awareness of a series of projects by Mies van der Rohe dating from 1928 and 1929. Five years earlier, Mies had begun De Stijl – and Constructivist-related explorations into spatial organization that, with his earlier technological visions, would by 1930 make him Germany's leading modern architect. Only a year older than Mendelsohn, he too opened his own office in 1912. In the early 1910s, Mies experimented with classicism rather than with Expressionism. He remained little known in the first years after the war, when he divided his architectural activity between suburban villas that made no major break with his prewar work and daring projects for curtain-walled office buildings. Despite his central role in the Weissenhofsiedlung, a housing exhibit held in Stuttgart in 1927, Mies was almost as reluctant as

Mendelsohn to forsake his prewar taste for monumentality in favor of the fashion for stucco (he had at first planned to build the Tugendhat house out of brick).[84] Also like Mendelsohn, Mies remained grounded in the realities of construction. Furthermore, by the middle of the decade this formidable rival had become a joiner and an organizer – an editor of the magazine *G*, a Bauhaus faculty member, and a Werkbund leader.[85] Mendelsohn, on the other hand, remained isolated by both his temperament and his religion from the innermost circles of Berlin's architectural community.

Mies's houses and the German pavilion at the International Exposition of 1929 in Barcelona demonstrated this architect's appeal to wealthy industrialists and to the German government. Strict functionalists had already labeled Mendelsohn old-fashioned, but they represented no threat to his thriving practice, as they were out of touch with his patrons' needs.[86] These encompassed advertising as well as the rational plans and elevations that were the hallmark of functionalism. Mies, on the other hand, offered an elegance that might interest, if not the pragmatic Schocken, then men who, like Herpich and Petersdorff, were interested in lavish modernity. In projects for an eight-story department store on Leipzigerstraße (the Adam Building), for a bank building in Stuttgart which also contained C. and A. Brenninkmeyer's clothing store, and for the redesign of Berlin's Alexanderplatz, and in an entry in a competition for an office building on Friedrichstraße (Fig. 98), Mies attempted to find patrons for a new urban architecture of curtain-walled slabs.[87]

Because Mendelsohn and Mies were not close personal friends who frequently discussed their work with one another and because the specific date of the Chemnitz model does not survive, no exact accounting of the relationship between these projects can be made. Nonetheless, Mies's designs were widely known through their publication in the German architectural press.[88] Furthermore, each was for a commission that Mendelsohn himself might have received; indeed, he did win the competition for the Friedrichstraße office building. Also influential was Mies's concrete office building project, which Gropius had included in the Bauhaus exhibition in 1923 and which had been widely published in the years following (Fig. 99).[89] Prompted by the monolithic quality of the Einstein Tower to find a more skeletal use for concrete, Mies drew a transparent glass skin over a stark concrete frame with bolder cantilevers than those he had used in the steel frames of the Adam Building and Friedrichstraße projects.[90] The simple volumes and glass-curtain walls of these projects in turn set the tone for the evolving refinement of Mendelsohn's

FIGURE 98

Mies van der Rohe, competition entry for the design of an office building on Friedrichstraße, photomontage, Berlin, 1929. (Source: The Mies van der Rohe Archive, The Museum of Modern Art, New York.)

design for the Chemnitz store. Here he proved that he could build a Miesian curtain wall, reinterpreted in his own more vigorous terms, while retaining the curves that in his mind were so closely attached to the theory of relativity and the character of modern life.

The finished structure of the Chemnitz Schocken store revealed the boldness of Mendelsohn's conception, even when compared to Mies's recent projects. By cantilevering the facade three and a half meters forward of this concrete frame, Mendelsohn was able to eliminate totally the piers interrupting the window bands of his earlier work, as well as of the Telschow building. This frame was clearly visible in the many night views of the building published at the time of its completion, and its architect also published construction drawings explaining its structure.[91]

The many differences between the Schocken facade and the facades of Mies's project could be justified, for the most part, on strictly functional grounds, although they also accorded with Mendelsohn's personal taste. The curve of the facade, for instance, reflected the shape of the site. Mendelsohn's decision to alternate bands of travertine cladding with the 1.8-meter-high windows resulted from Schocken's persistent demand for usable cabinetry.[92] The fully glazed stair towers flanking these windows produced a juxtaposition typical of Mendelsohn's drawings for entirely imaginary projects and provided closure. Otherwise, the bands of travertine and glass would

FIGURE 99

Mies van der Rohe, concrete office building project, 1922. Charcoal, crayon on tan paper, 54½ × 113¾". The Mies van der Rohe Archive, The Museum of Modern Art, New York, gift of the architect. (Source: © 1996 The Museum of Modern Art, New York.)

have threatened to look like, in Hegemann's words, "a stack of pancakes." In a glowing review, Hegemann noted the impracticality of fully glazed facades and compared the store favorably with the Bauhaus.[93] In both the Bauhaus and Mendelsohn's own Petersdorff store, the placement of radiators against the exterior wall had impeded other uses of the interior space immediately abutting this wall. In Chemnitz, instead of disrupting this space with steam radiators, Mendelsohn installed hot-air heating.[94] He also claimed, in an article accompanying Hegemann's review, that clerestory lighting uninterrupted by facade piers provided the best lighting for the store's deep floor area, which lacked openings in the side walls.[95]

Nor did Mendelsohn ignore advertising issues, although their expression was more muted in Chemnitz than it had been in Stuttgart. For the store's first-floor elevation, he assembled all of his accumulated knowledge about display window design, marrying the clerestory found in the two earlier Schocken stores with the protective inset he had developed for the Petersdorff store. Mendelsohn inserted four entrances into the lengthy facade but kept the displays that flanked the deep corridors leading to them quite narrow. This minimized interference with the more valuable space intended to attract potential customers, to whom he paid more attention than he gave to those already committed to entering the store.[96] He also crowned each entrance bay with letters spelling out the Schocken name. Because Schocken now believed that the large-scale interior illumination of the building at night was more effective, there were no *Lichtreklame*. Instead, advertising banners could be hung from a procession of flagpoles.[97]

Finally, Mendelsohn's arrangement of the recessed upper stories

FIGURE 100

Schocken Department Store, Chemnitz, sales floor. (Source: Staatliche Museen zu Berlin, Kunstbibliothek.)

FIGURE 101

Larkin factory R/S/T block, interior. Lockwood, Greene, and Company, Buffalo, New York, 1911. (Source: Courtesy of Jack Quinan.)

of the Chemnitz store ensured that his dramatic composition would not overwhelm its traditionally scaled five-story environs. Here, too, Mendelsohn drew upon his earlier commercial buildings, now fully exploiting the setback, in which three stories stepped progressively away from the wall plane, as a source of compositional dynamism. Although Henry-Russell Hitchcock and Philip Johnson later compared this aspect of the building to the stepped compositions of American skyscrapers, in Chemnitz it also served to stress the facade's nature as a free-floating plane, an aesthetic goal completely at odds with the monolithic quality of the American work of Mendelsohn's friend Ely Jacques Kahn, for example.[98] The setbacks did, however, simultaneously produce the same generous attitude toward urban scale achieved by the American towers and served to distinguish the public selling floors from private, recessed office space.

Even more than its Stuttgart counterpart, the Chemnitz store, particularly in its interior, reflected Mendelsohn's admiration for American daylight factories, which were organized in repetitive bays and designed to allow the maximum amount of light to penetrate their concrete frames (Fig. 100). In Chemnitz, Mendelsohn and his patron returned to the unadorned interior arrangement they had already used in Nuremberg, forsaking the more complex cabinetry and lighting effects of the Stuttgart store. Half again as large as their counterparts in Stuttgart and spread along a single facade, the sales floors of the Chemnitz store were the largest and simplest Mendelsohn had yet designed. The unadorned interior frame was almost indistinguishable from those of the factories Mendelsohn had visited in Buffalo and Detroit (Fig. 101). This rhythmic orchestration of vast spaces provided an easily perceived disposition of the spartan sales area, whose unity was enhanced by the continuous linoleum flooring which also reflected a little light into the deep interiors.[99] Seductive niches and dramatic effects were entirely absent, a tribute once again to Schocken's faith that the panoply of low-priced goods would almost sell themselves to any interested buyer. The store also included such new touches as revolving doors on the two central entrances and, inside, three escalators connecting the sales floors.

Like its predecessors, Mendelsohn's final Schocken store reflected his and his patron's understanding of the building type and its relationship to industrial prototypes. Mendelsohn and Schocken both thought it their business to be in tune with consumers' experiences of mass production upon their lives. This meant for Schocken and later for his architect the need for an even clearer expression of the relationship between the places in which goods were produced and those in which they were sold. In Chemnitz, Mendelsohn replaced the Stuttgart store's tension between the parts of a complexly articulated volume with more subtle relationships between building and street and between form and construction. Instead of focusing on the transparency of the metal frame, as he had in the Petersdorff store, he turned toward the enclosure and articulation of space, juxtaposing the solidity of the frame against the lightness of the wall. The result was a building in which he once again deftly tailored the latest architectural fashions, as well as industrial imagery, to suit a specific site and store.

7

"A SPLENDID DEMONSTRATION OF THE MODERN SPIRIT"

BETWEEN the publication of the Einstein Tower in 1921 and the opening of the Weissenhofsiedlung (housing complex) in 1927 Mendelsohn's stature as one of Europe's leading modern architects was almost universally acknowledged. He maintained this position through the rest of the decade even as the Stuttgart housing exhibition, Le Corbusier's villas, the Dessau Bauhaus, and new Soviet architecture presented images of geometric purity and almost ethereal lightness that would eventually marginalize the position within the modern movement of his own dynamic functionalism. And although it would be several more years before the Weissenhof constellation of architects – Mies, Gropius, Le Corbusier, and Oud – would be enshrined as the core of the modern movement, Mendelsohn quickly altered the character of his own work to be more in keeping with this new image. He apparently made this change, which consisted of a turn from the dynamic opposition of individual parts toward a greater synthesis of the whole and the abandonment of much of his earlier emphasis on the tactile variety of materials, for two reasons. First, doing so signified his allegiance to the precepts of the Weissenhof at exactly the time when these were most controversial within Germany, where they were condemned by the right as un-German and even Jewish, especially by the newly formed group of conservative architects who called themselves Der Bloch (the Block). The second – as detailed in the last chapter – was to protect his thriving practice from inroads by Mies van der Rohe, who had organized the Stuttgart exhibition and who probably hoped that his own increasing fame would enable him to challenge Mendelsohn's dominance of modernist commercial architecture in Germany.

FIGURE 102

Weissenhofsiedlung, Stuttgart, 1928. (Source: Landesbildstelle Württemburg, Neg. 24099.)

In 1928 Mendelsohn decisively simplified massing, signage, and night lighting in four major commissions. In addition to the Schocken store in Chemnitz, these included a pavilion he built for the Rudolf Mosse Company at the Press exhibition in Cologne, a villa for himself in the Berlin suburbs, and Columbushaus. Whereas Mendelsohn's earlier stores had the greatest impact in Germany, the Chemnitz store and Columbushaus were key to the dissemination of the modern movement in Great Britain, Scandinavia, and the United States. At the same time, however, Mendelsohn's sensitivity to the needs of the client, in one case himself and his own family, ensured that his work, while taking account of new trends, would remain distinctive.

THE WEISSENHOFSIEDLUNG AND THE BLOCK

Held in Stuttgart, the 1927 Werkbund exhibition *Die Wohnung*, or "the dwelling," was centered on the Weissenhofsiedlung, a housing complex built by seventeen of Europe's leading modern architects (Fig. 102). Within the German architectural community the exhibition touched off a furor in which many of the leaders of the previous generation of reformers disassociated themselves from the radical new buildings. Mendelsohn, who had turned down an invitation to participate in the exhibit, played no part in this debate. Only when the controversy spilled into the political arena, where it became an issue of international modernity versus parochial nationalism, did he chose the modern camp, a choice conditioned by his political loyalties to Zionism and to a united Europe.

It was ironic, in view of Mendelsohn's later sympathy for the exhibition, that he had actually refused an invitation to be among its architects. The issue for him seemed to be more his distrust of Mies than his attitude toward the reputation and direction of the modern movement as a whole. The Stuttgart city government, local architects, and representatives of the Werkbund who began to plan the exhibit at the same time that Mendelsohn was designing the local Schocken store included him on the first four lists of the architects they hoped would contribute designs.[1] When in July 1926 the city council's building committee skipped over him, his friend Richard Döcker, a local architect whom he had known since at least 1922, wrote to alert him.[2] Döcker, who eventually supervised the exhibit's construction, wanted it to include architects who had actually built, such as Mendelsohn, and not merely theorized about the new architecture, and he wondered if Mendelsohn could stir up support in Berlin for such a change in policy. Mendelsohn replied after consulting with Walter Behrendt and casually asking an evasive Mies about the exhibit. In his letter, Mendelsohn did not actually take a position vis-à-vis the exhibit or his inclusion in it but noted that he had learned from his own battles with the authorities the importance of a united front.[3] In the meantime, Mies, who declared that Mendelsohn's absence would constitute a "lacuna," successfully lobbied the Stuttgart committee to reinstate him, a fact apparently unknown to Mendelsohn.[4]

A new battle was brewing, however, over the issue of the architects' compensation. To cut costs the city refused to allow the standard Union of German Architects contract to apply, instead offering a lump sum to be divided equally among the participants. Hugo Häring, who as secretary of the Ring believed it was his responsibility to enforce professional standards, withdrew from the exhibit. Mendelsohn, suspicious of Mies and following the rumors he had heard through Döcker about the city council list, also declined to participate. He cited the volume of work he had recently taken on but also expressed his regret at the split between Häring and Mies.[5] While many of his colleagues welcomed any chance to build, even without complete compensation, Mendelsohn, who had a large number of private commissions, had no need to seek the extra work or the attendant publicity.

Mendelsohn visited the exhibit at least twice, initially while it was still under construction in early July 1927. He returned later that month for its opening. In letters to his wife, he singled out for praise the contributions of Behrens, Oud, Le Corbusier, and Josef Frank.[6] Two years later, however, he attacked the supposed practicality of Le Corbusier's contribution, calling it overly artistic and noting that it had far exceeded its allotted budget.[7] Nowhere did he express regret about his refusal to be included. Undoubtedly, he preferred his more profitable private commissions, especially as these freed him from the constraints of collaboration with colleagues.

At the exhibition, Mendelsohn saw buildings that ranged from the geometric purity of contributions by Le Corbusier and Mies to Scharoun's exuberantly curved balconies. The participants belonged to two distinct generations. Behrens and Poelzig were included because they had prepared the way for more youthful and radical participants like Oud, Le Corbusier, Mies, the Tauts, and Scharoun. Yet a uniform surface of stucco, most often painted white, tied the ensemble together and emphasized taut, thin surface planes. Much more than Gropius's exhibition at the Bauhaus in 1923, the Weissenhofsiedlung established an easily recognizable image for the work of a new generation of European modern architects, an image that would be codified in the Museum of Modern Art's exhibition in New York in 1932.

Mendelsohn's vigorously textured, multicolored, and resoundingly permanent Schocken store – under construction down the hill – was entirely different from this pristine ensemble. With its balance of the aesthetic and the pragmatic, the Stuttgart store was an aggressively forceful presence. Like its Weissenhof counterparts, it was patently unaristocratic, and it was equally unallied with bourgeois pretensions to grandeur, but it also verged on the monumental. Even the transparent stair tower was marked on the exterior by broadly projecting bands of steel, and the stairway itself was obviously wrapped around a sound interior core. Like all successful commercial architecture, it was also more obviously exciting than the staid explorations of pure form essayed by most of the Weissenhof architects.

Before the Weissenhofsiedlung, Stuttgart's fame in progressive architectural circles was based on a quarter-century of meeting modern needs through vigorous, abstracted, and often monumental forms. Mendelsohn's professor, Theodor Fischer, had taught in Stuttgart before moving to Munich. His assistant Paul Bonatz remained there. During the first three decades of the century, the students of Fischer and Bonatz, together with such figures as Hildebrandt, who translated Le Corbusier's *Vers une architecture* into German, made the city a center for architectural reform both within and beyond the

FIGURE 103

Paul Bonatz, Graf Zepplin Hotel, Stuttgart, 1929–31, with main train station in background. (Source: *Moderne Bauformen*, 1931.)

boundaries of tradition. Stuttgart's most famous new building was Bonatz's enormous train station, designed and started before the war and finally completed in 1927. Its austere evocation of the German Romanesque included, behind its great hall, a train shed as convincing in its technological modernity as the interior of Otto Wagner's Post Office Savings Bank of 1904–6 in Vienna. Later Bonatz built the Graf Zepplin Hotel across the street from the station, a building entirely lacking in historical references (Fig. 103). Its materials – pale stone cladding and metal mullions – and form – a simple rectangle ornamented with a curved, cantilevered window band – echoed Mendelsohn's Herpich store.

Until 1926 Germany's two generations of modern architects apparently worked together in relative harmony, their shared respect for Behrens and Poelzig papering over the widening stylistic and theoretical differences between them. In May 1926 this unity was shattered by attacks upon Mies's plans for the Weissenhofsiedlung written by Bonatz and his Stuttgart colleague Paul Schmitthenner. They cannot have been pleased that Mies, a relatively unknown and much younger architect living in Berlin, had been put in charge of an exhibit in the city where they were accustomed to being acknowledged as the leaders of the architectural community. Bonatz later expressed an admiration for aspects of the exhibit, but Schmitthenner remained a bitter opponent of the New Building and increasingly sought to counter the work of the younger generation with virulent nationalism. Within the architectural community battle lines were drawn only slowly and remained ambiguous. For instance, Hermann Muthesius and Werner Hegemann, liberals of the old school, both wrote attacks on the Weissenhofsiedlung in which they voiced formal rather than political objections to the complex.[8]

The founding in 1928 of the Block in opposition to the Ring made the split in the German architectural establishment that had become obvious in the controversy over the Weissenhofsiedlung a permanent one. Yet the Block's members – German Bestelmeyer, Bonatz, Emil Fahrenkamp, Wilhelm Kreis, Schmitthenner, and Paul Schultze-Naumberg – were not simply antimodernists. Several were students or former colleagues of Fischer's, and all not only admired the prewar activities of the Werkbund but believed themselves to be furthering its cause. They built office buildings, department stores, and other examples of modern urban architecture, which, if distinguishable from the New Building, especially because of a lingering emphasis on stability and weight, were not necessarily antagonistic to it. Indeed, Fahrenkamp's work on occasion was obviously indebted to Mendelsohn's example. Rather than rejecting modernity, these architects, most of whom would later support the Nazis, sought to continue the prewar balance between industry and art, a goal that they shared with others, such as Bruno Paul, Poelzig, and Heinrich Tessenow in Berlin and Fritz Höger in Hamburg, who did not join the group. Their existence pushed Mendelsohn further toward the more rationalist adherents of the New Building.[9]

Most troubling, in 1926 Bonatz had compared Mies's Weissenhof plan to that of a Jerusalem suburb. After the exhibition's construction an infamous postcard labeled it an "Arab village." Mendelsohn, as a Jewish architect whose clients were also Jewish, was vulnerable to similar attacks. Even though he had not built or designed any stucco-clad housing since 1924 (several of his projects loosely in this style were for sites in the British Mandate of Palestine), most of his buildings featured the flat roofs that were an especial target of nationalist sentiment. Furthermore, the two strands of the new architecture – capitalist and socialist, private and public, commercial and residential – were not perceived as distinct entities by either their advocates or their opponents. The occasionally very real stylistic distinctions between the redevelopment, led by Mendelsohn, of German retail architecture, and the housing settlements, intended for workers and built in the suburbs and by the midtwenties an important aspect of the new, pragmatic architecture, did not at the time obscure the essential unity of artistic goals. Although the issues surrounding retailing and workers' housing now appear quite different, in these years articles about the two appeared side by side in the Werkbund journal *Die Form* and other such publications. For a society fascinated equally by the United States and the Soviet Union, both its commercial and residential architecture could be approached through unornamented construction symbolizing rational efficiency. In both cases, this outlook eliminated sentimental vestiges of aristocratic grandeur.[10]

One of the critics who confronted the dilemma of the similarity between the new residential and commercial architecture and their overlapping patrons was the socialist Alexander Schwab. Schwab's fiercely leftist political commitment eventually led him to become the head of the *Rote Kämpfer* or "Red Army" resistance group. He died in prison in 1943.[11] In 1930 Schwab, using the pseudonym Albert Sigrist, published a book on the new architecture. In his book, *Das Buch von Bauen*, Schwab questioned the possibility of distinguishing between the capitalist and the socialist elements of the New Building. "The New Building has a Janus face," he wrote. "It is indeed both bourgeois and proletarian, high capitalistic and socialistic. One can even say autocratic and democratic. But one thing it is not – it is no longer individualistic."[12] Schwab specifically pointed out the difficulty of placing Mendelsohn definitively in either camp. He noted that Mendelsohn had worked for the capitalist Mosse Publishing Company, on the one hand, and for the Soviet government, on the other. Believing that the new, almost mass-produced architecture sprang from the economic conditions created by an expanding capitalism, he welcomed it as evidence of the emergence of the circumstances that must eventually lead to socialism.[13]

Modern architecture's perceived ties to capitalism and socialism provided ample fodder for the attacks made upon the entire younger generation of modernists by right-wing critics. These critics, typically slightly older, sought a more permanent, traditional, and nationalist architecture that would ameliorate the economic and social changes brought by the Industrial Revolution. Like workers' housing, department stores were major targets of this opposition to economic, political, and cultural – as well as architectural – modernity. The Stuttgart Schocken store appears not to have been a specific target of opposition to the New Building, as its 1928 opening was overshadowed locally and nationally by the controversy over the Weissenhofsiedlung. Yet the stylistic distinctions that separated it from the Weissenhof housing could not protect Mendelsohn from the right-wing opposition to modernism unleashed by the exhibition. As political criticism mounted, nationalists attacked the Weissenhof and the entire architectural movement for which it stood as "un-German and Bolshevik."[14] Department stores, too, aroused the hostility of these opponents, including Adolf Hitler, because of their "internationalism" and because the overwhelming majority of them were owned by Jews.[15]

In the thirties, Hitler's Nazi regime would include proponents of modern capitalism interested in expanding Germany's industrial base to serve rearmament. But although some members of the Block welcomed the opportunity to participate in the expansion of the country's downtowns, the criticism voiced in the twenties by Schultze-Naumberg, its most strident member, focused on romantic evocations of a precapitalist German communal fabric undisturbed by class dissension or by "foreign" (the term encompassed the country's Jews) influence.[16] In rhetoric that appealed in particular to the lower middle classes, Nazi critics accused department stores, which sold manufactured goods and utilized new systems of distribution, of selling at unfairly low prices and of displacing the owners of smaller, local shops. Nazis charged that by coercing manufacturers to lower prices, department store owners undercut the well-being of "good Germans." One such critic, Hans Buchner, attacked department store promotional tactics, emblematic of a highly developed capitalist economy, and complained specifically about the enticements offered by advertising and window displays. The antimodern quality of Buchner's argument was especially apparent in his complaint that department stores had replaced handmade craft wares with shoddy products made by machine.[17]

In Stuttgart, the Schocken store and the Weissenhofsiedlung, as their contemporaries on both the left and the right recognized, were the products of the same economic system and of the same cultural celebration of rational production and management. Both were the result of thirty years of close cooperation between German industrialists, merchants, architects, and designers. While only the Weissenhof exhibit was directly organized by the Werkbund, the group that most completely embodied this cooperation, the Schocken store was, if anything, a more complete expression of the group's agenda, as it responded directly to a program set by a patron who shared those

FIGURE 104

Erich Mendelsohn, Rudolf Mosse Pavilion, Press exhibition, Cologne, 1928. (Source: F. R. Yerburg, *Modern European Buildings*, New York, 1928.)

goals and not merely to theoretical principles. Spurred by the controversy over the Weissenhof, Mendelsohn soon adjusted his own style.

THE MOSSE PRESS PAVILION

In his only exhibition building, the Mosse Pavilion at the Press exhibition held in 1928 in Cologne, Mendelsohn signaled a shift in his style to an international audience (Fig. 104). His reprise of the lightweight white boxes of the Weissenhof exhibit emphasized the almost magical – and certainly ephemeral – way in which news was collected and disseminated internationally. The pavilion's fashionable lack of substantiality coincided with his patrons' regard for radio and for graphic design, for technology and style over substance, along with its character as a temporary building. That it was a container for exhibits trumpeting the Mosse firm's wide range of activities gave a slightly different political slant to architectural strategies which Mendelsohn had borrowed from an even more radical (but also more fittingly propagandistic) source than Weissenhof – Soviet Constructivism.

The Press exhibition, a celebration of the international print media, was organized under the auspices of Cologne's mayor, Konrad Adenauer, who sought to reintroduce Germany into the community of nations and to make the city a center for such fairs.[18] Although it has largely been forgotten the exhibition attracted considerable publicity at the time. Its opening was front-page news in Germany, and the details of its architecture were extensively reported.[19] The exhibition's main building, Adolf Abel's Convention Hall, provided a permanent site for future, smaller-scale fairs. Located on the east bank of the Rhine, just across the river from Cologne's famous cathedral, the exhibition was organized around Abel's semicircular International Hall, which housed the contributions of most exhibitors from abroad. The pavilions of German publishers and of a sprinkling of nations were clustered on the fairground beyond. El Lissitsky's Soviet exhibit inside the International Hall and Otto Bartning's Steel Church are the two contributions best remembered today, but at the time, the Mosse pavilion was hailed as one of the highlights of the entire fair. Paul Ferdinand Schmidt wrote in the art magazine *Der Cicerone*, "At the top is the brilliant building of the Mosse Publishers . . . a splendid demonstration of the modern spirit."[20] In this small, but deftly executed structure, Mendelsohn indicated that the new antimonumental architecture could equal the liveliness of his earlier and more permanent buildings.[21]

The Rudolf Mosse firm was one of the giants of the German media and as such was expected to build a pavilion equal to those erected by such rivals as Ullstein, its major Berlin competitor.[22] Its architecture needed to attract the attention of fairgoers both during the day and at night, of the readers of its many publications, and of the editors of architecture magazines. If these magazine editors chose to illustrate the pavilion as an example of contemporary taste, it would mean further publicity for the firm.[23] From the beginning, Mendelsohn organized his design around the radio antenna, whose height dominated all of his drawings for the building. Early drawings also document his search for the most effective location for the identifying sign, which was second only to the antenna in importance and had to be clearly visible at a distance. Ultimately, a vertical sign spelling out the firm's name braced the stiff antenna mast located at the rear of the upper story. From this sign Mendelsohn strung guide wires which led to another antenna in the rear of the building.

The exhibits inside its pavilion charted the expanding activities of the Mosse firm. In 1923 graphics on the Mossehaus facade listed an advertising agency, three newspapers, a book publisher, city directories, and a telegraphic code. Five years later the company also included a news service and printing shop.[24] Mendelsohn divided the ground-story interior of the exhibit pavilion into four dark V-shaped

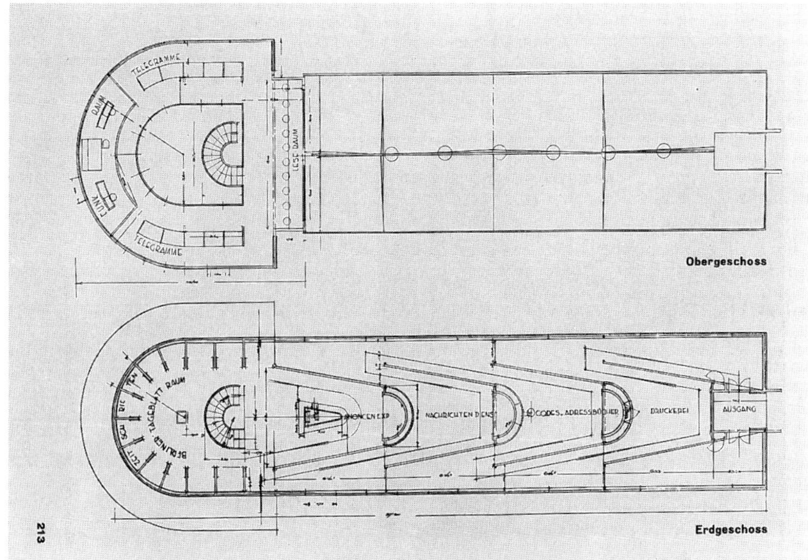

FIGURE 105

Mosse pavilion, plans. (Source: Staatliche Museen zu Berlin, Kunstbibliothek.)

display areas for illuminated transparencies describing the advertising agency, news service, telegraphic code and directories, and printing shop (Fig. 105). The advertising agency's bay doubled as a small theater where the company showed a film about the history and operation of the *Berliner Tageblatt*. An aisle wrapped around these exhibits led at the front – underneath the upper story – to a semicircular room (where the firm's newspapers and the latest teletype news were displayed) and to a semicircular stair. On the upper story, side rooms for radiograms arriving from around the world flanked a central radio installation. Outside, loudspeakers affixed to the second-story roof announced the most important news.[25]

Mendelsohn built the Mosse pavilion out of steel and glass, with thin white walls that established the continuity between it and the other publishers' pavilions at the fair and between the Press pavilions and the Weissenhofsiedlung of the previous year.[26] This broke with his well-established preference, evident even in the heavily glazed Petersdorff store, for more permanent materials. Stone and brick were patently inappropriate, however, for a building designed to stand for just a few months. Instead, Mendelsohn noted, characteristically, that the pavilion's transparency enabled him to abolish gravity.[27] This emphasis on glass rather than stucco walls, in addition to the overtly propagandistic elements of the program, not least among them the sign-carrying radio mast, distinguished Mendelsohn's building from its Weissenhof precursors and pointed to the inherently different needs of the new commercial and residential architectures. No Weissenhof precedents existed for the publicity-charged architecture required by Mendelsohn's advertising-conscious patrons. Rather, it was Soviet architecture which, despite the entirely different political content of its message, offered useful strategies for communicating with a mass audience.

Throughout the twenties, Soviet architects and artists experimented with architectural form and with lettering in search of compelling propagandistic techniques to use for two- and three-dimensional art, architecture, stage design, and political rallies. Mendelsohn's choice of illustrations from his trips to the Soviet Union to use in his book included a number of schemes in which graphics were prominent. Although he quibbled about whether their propaganda aims were suited to the temperament of the Russian people and to economic conditions in the Soviet Union, he certainly understood their potential effectiveness in more industrialized societies.

In the Mosse pavilion, Mendelsohn drew upon Soviet projects such as the Vesnin brothers' entry in the 1923 competition for a Moscow palace of labor (Fig. 106) and an otherwise unidentified design for the "Radjansko Selo" newspaper in Kiev. He was inspired by the Vesnins' propagandistic program, the graphic legibility of the Kiev project, and the technological bravado of both. Among the many functions assigned to the program for the palace of labor was the task of housing Moscow's central radio station. In a celebration of technological romanticism, the Vesnin design sported three tall antenna masts and a lattice of wires connecting them. Furthermore, two screens, not visible in the Vesnins' perspective drawing, were to broadcast to the public on the street the time of day, news headlines, and weather statistics.[28] Mendelsohn's integration of the Mosse pavilion's sign-laden antenna into his architectural composition and his highly technological program, freighted with advertising, depended upon such Soviet precedents. At the same time, the appreciative tone of Mendelsohn's description of the newspaper building for Kiev hints at the goals he set for himself in the Mosse design. "The new materials: glass, steel, concrete, yield their most extreme strength – the least mass, the most slender skeleton, the highest expression of tension," he wrote, adding, "Glass especially lends itself toward the elimination of massiveness with an increase in lightness and transparency."[29]

Refusing to renounce the dynamism intrinsic to his success as an architect of commercial buildings, Mendelsohn updated familiar themes in the Mosse Press Pavilion. Once again, his experience abroad was the key to his success. In this case it provided him with a strategy for integrating signage and other motifs that trumpeted

FIGURE 106

Aleksandr, Leonid, and Viktor Vesnin, competition entry for a palace of labor, Moscow, 1923. (Source: Mendelsohn, *Rußland-Europa-Amerika.*)

new communication technologies using forms and materials that most Germans equated with the Weissenhofsiedlung. Mendelsohn's design for his own house permitted similar experiments. Here, every bit as much as in his stores, Mendelsohn sought a kind of modern luxury: bare of ornament, enthralled with technology, and attuned to the latest developments in the other visual arts.

THE HOUSE AM RUPENHORN

In the summer of 1928, the architect completed plans for a suburban villa for his wife and himself (Fig. 107). Sheathed in pale yellow stucco, it was built of brick and steel.[30] The villa ostensibly adhered to the aesthetic pioneered by Weissenhof architects such as Mies. It was enlivened by a wealth of high-tech gadgetry, but it lacked the spatial tension of many other pioneering villas. Instead, Mendelsohn, understandably, fulfilled his desire for personal comfort. Custom-

FIGURE 107

Erich Mendelsohn, Villa am Rupenhorn, Berlin, 1928–30. (Source: Staatliche Museen zu Berlin, Kunstbibliothek.)

made built-in cabinetry cloaked the villa's machinery, paintings and sculpted reliefs hung on the walls, and enormous windows opened onto broad terraces, providing views of the lake below. In this home, Berlin's most luxurious showplace for the new architecture and one of its creator's calmest compositions, the couple entertained visitors from throughout Germany and abroad.

Since the days of their courtship, Mendelsohn had dreamed of designing a house for his wife, Luise. In 1914 he had presented her with a birthday gift of drawings for such a dwelling. In the midtwenties, as his fame and architectural practice expanded, the couple began to grow apart, and Luise Mendelsohn began to sense that she was becoming less important to her husband. The architect built the house to reassure her of his continued devotion and to provide her with a fitting backdrop against which she could lead her own life as a musician and hostess. After years of inhabiting a series of cramped apartments they would at last have a real home. The architect, accustomed to remaining at his office long into the night, also designed the house as a refuge from his work, a place in which he would finally be surrounded by a physical environment that met his high aesthetic standards.[31]

In the midtwenties, on a ramble around the Havel, the river that winds through Berlin's western outskirts, Luise Mendelsohn came upon the long, narrow lot, which ran from Am Rupenhorn – a quiet street that was already the site of an important villa by Hermann Muthesius – down to the Stoßen See, a small lake that feeds into the Havel.[32] Although the architect had originally contemplated building a combined house and studio in Babelsburg or Kladow or at a Westend site closer to public transportation, the Mendelsohns purchased the Am Rupenhorn land in 1927. In July of the following year, Mendelsohn submitted the plans for a single-family house without a studio to the building authorities; husband, wife, and daughter Esther moved in two years later.[33]

Mendelsohn proceeded with plans for the house despite having many reservations. He was certain that Germany's current economic and political stability would not last and uncomfortable with temporarily evading this reality through the construction of a sumptuous retreat. The Russian revolution's failure to produce a successful new world, epitomized by the split between Trotsky and Stalin, could, he predicted, result only in war:

> Millions are yelling for war, which will eat them as victims. And we? . . . We build a house which is so modest that it keeps us from becoming accomplices? . . .
>
> We take on burdens that are not ours . . . are in spirit against the capitalist order, but we gorge ourselves on capital. . . .
>
> From habit, from indolence, from swimming along with the stream, from greed for possessions, from self-indulgence and the desire to be able to afford everything!
>
> We tend to gloss over these vanities with beauty – wishes and fads of ideals – but reality exhausts us and diminishes our spirit.
>
> Granted, we are young and ready to give up everything at the given hour – that is easily said when the sun is shining. But where is courage on cold days?
>
> Let us consider! . . . Why . . . don't we go to the barricades which are necessary . . . when the fiasco is so clear, the future so opaque? . . .
>
> The war will come and grab us too.[34]

The exquisitely designed and decorated house, sited on the crest of the hill overlooking the lake, was surrounded by an aura of tran-

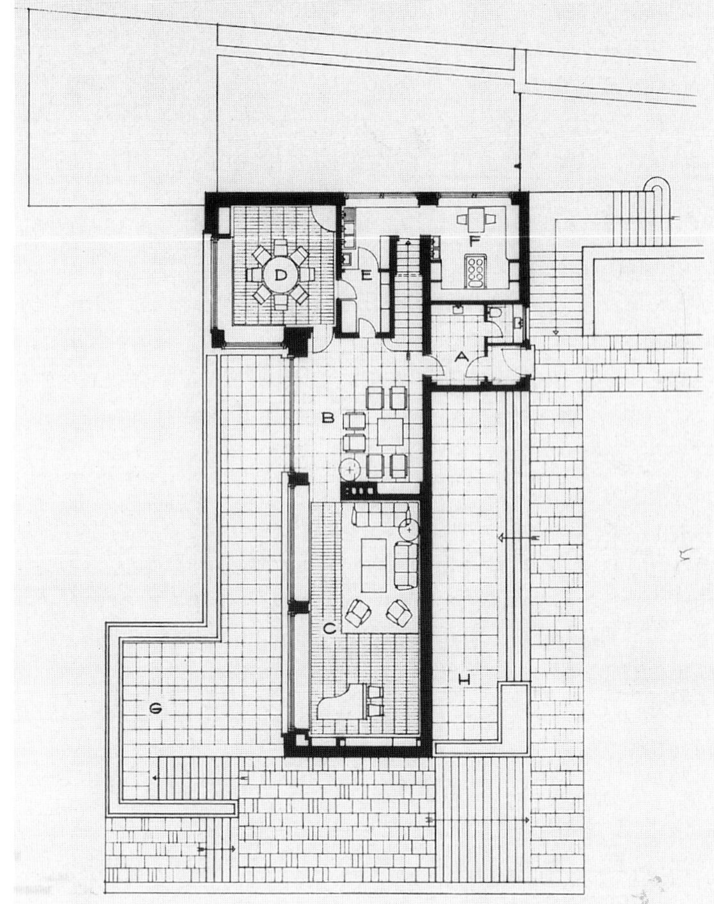

FIGURE 108

Villa am Rupenhorn, floor and site plans. (Source: Staatliche Museen zu Berlin, Kunstbibliothek.)

quility far removed from its architect's all-too-justified fears. The relationship between the house and the carefully landscaped grounds was intricate in comparison to the relatively simple plan of the T-shaped interior (Fig. 108).[35] A limestone boundary wall enclosed a rectangular lawn. A second set of walls and the windowless elevation of the ground-story street facade created a terrace for entertaining a short flight of steps above the street level. The main rooms of the house faced the lake. Here, in a deft bit of technological drama also found in Mies's Tugendhat House in Brno, Czechoslovakia, enormous picture windows could be lowered into the basement.

The villa's interior lacked the tight complexity that had characterized the small Weissenhof units (Fig. 109). Instead, partitions projecting out from the exterior walls divided generously scaled rectangular rooms from one another. The dynamic tension that characterized Mendelsohn's shopfronts was entirely absent in these serene

FIGURE 109

Villa am Rupenhorn, living room. (Source: Staatliche Museen zu Berlin, Kunstbibliothek.)

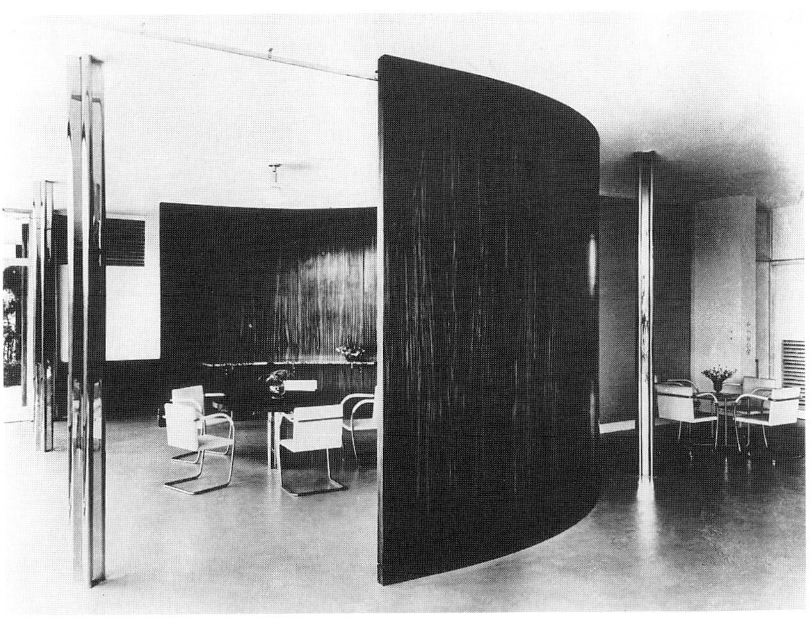

FIGURE 110

Mies van der Rohe, Villa Tugendhat, living room, Brno, Czechoslovakia, 1928–30. (Source: Alberto Sartoris, *Gli Elementi dell' Architettura Funzionale*, Milan, 1935.)

spaces. And, although the following year in an essay on the modern European factory building he wrote that the standardization growing out of the increased mechanization of the building trades led from "formless wild growth" to "elementary form," sophisticated simplicity rather than a machine aesthetic characterized most of the decoration of his villa.[36] Mendelsohn designed almost every visible detail especially for the house, for which he also bought two paintings by the French artist Amédée Ozenfant and a bronze bas-relief by Ewald Mataré.[37]

Mendelsohn's house was also a showplace for the technological innovations that defined a new standard of luxury and that allied the dwelling with the industrial appearance of his department stores and office buildings. However, Mendelsohn kept these out of sight of the main rooms.[38] He found an organic metaphor for this arrangement, comparing it to the location of the mechanical functions of the human body beneath the skin. Despite his frequent condemnation of nineteenth-century architecture, he largely adhered to standards of comfort established in that era. He also accepted the picturesque nineteenth-century conception of nature's importance for human spiritual renewal. In contrast to the small, technologically efficient apartments of those who were more interested in train and airplane travel than in establishing permanent residences, he defined his ideal home as:

> A house roomier than the insubstantial box for dwelling, but organized in such a manner that (in ten years) servants can be cut down to a minimum, in close proximity to the vegetable garden that enlarges the living space, quiet, sunny, and so healthy that trips to spas become unnecessary. Daily contact with the city is to be avoided, all normal needs should be obtainable in close proximity. House by house, garden by garden, gramophone by gramophone, man by man.[39]

Although Mendelsohn was himself temperamentally suited to the role of world traveler, this image of a delightful suburban life infused the design of his own home. Rather than offering a refuge from urban cares, however, the house quickly became a celebrated gathering place where the Mendelsohns entertained architects and public figures from around the world, including André Gide, Albert Kahn, Henry Morganthau, Lewis Mumford, J. J. P. Oud, and Chaim Weizmann. The French Embassy frequently brought visitors to see the house, and Mendelsohn enjoyed telling his diplomatic guests of his hopes for a united Europe. It was also a setting for numerous musical evenings for which Einstein, violin in hand, arrived by boat from across the lake to play beside Luise Mendelsohn.[40]

Despite the socialist mystique of the Siedlungen, in many countries – most notably France and the United States – the first flowering of the New Building was almost entirely limited to the design of substantial private houses. Only in Germany, where they were overshadowed as well by new commercial buildings, did such commissions provide only a relatively minor showcase for new architectural ideas. Although a number of these houses were built on the outskirts of major German cities, just one of the movement's principal adherants there – Mies van der Rohe – could be said (despite his efforts to attain larger, more commercial work) to specialize in the type. Not surprisingly, it was Mies's Tugendhat House in Brno, almost exactly contemporary with Mendelsohn's Am Rupenhorn house, that offered an even more complete synthesis of the New Building and haut bourgeois standards of luxury (Fig. 110). With it, Mies provided the spatial experimentation yardstick against which critics would later measure Mendelsohn and find him wanting. Whereas Mendelsohn buried structural columns in the external walls, Mies emphasized the independence of the non–load-bearing partitions of macassar and onyx from the sleek steel columns that supported the flat roof. The resulting spaces were far less conventional than Mendelsohn's routinely open rectangles.[41]

Within just a few years the differences between the two villas would be obvious to almost everyone who commented upon them; in retrospect, what is more remarkable is the degree to which Mendelsohn was able to identify himself with the mainstream of the New Building throughout the twenties. Originally, however, few distinguished between the members of the Ring; workers' housing, department stores, villas, and the Bauhaus were part of a single campaign to modernize German architecture.

AT HOME AND ABROAD: THE ARCHITECT'S GROWING REPUTATION

Throughout the decade, Mendelsohn was among the most famous of all German architects. By decade's end, his work was also widely known abroad, where it had already begun to transform the image of modernity in Britain and the United States. Never before had the publicity given the individual architect and his or, far more rarely, her work been more intrinsic to a successful practice. Not surprisingly, Mendelsohn was as attuned to the benefits of this attention for his practice as he was to the integration of advertising into his designs for stores and for the Universum Cinema. Even more astounding is the degree to which critics and editors initially echoed his own claims for his work.

In 1924 *Wasmuths Monatsheft für Baukunst*, the country's most lavish architecture journal, devoted an entire issue to Mendelsohn's work.[42] Furthermore, Hermann George Scheffauer quickly brought out an English translation, marketed as a monograph.[43] The completion of the Schocken store in Nuremberg and Herpich Furriers in Berlin resulted in another flurry of articles, but it was the exhibit of his work in 1928, mounted by Berlin's Neumann-Nierendorf Gallery, and his publication two years later of the monograph *Erich Mendelsohn: Das Gesamtschaffen des Architekten* (Erich Mendelsohn: The Complete Works) that made clear to his contemporaries the scope of his accomplishments.[44] And by that time the opening of the Schocken store in Chemnitz was generating yet more attention for him.[45]

The critical assessment was overwhelmingly positive. The articles about the Chemnitz store, which Mendelsohn considered to be his best work, were studded with praise for its simplicity and functionalism.[46] Hegemann was the most enthusiastic, lauding Mendelsohn for eliminating the bronze mullions he had used in the Herpich and Petersdorff stores, which the Chemnitz design made seem fussy.[47] Westheim also commended Schocken who was, he wrote, one of the few merchants to bring the best and most simply designed manufactured goods to the consumer at low prices.[48] The Stuttgart critic Karl Konrad Düssel described the functionalism of the Schocken stores as "poetic" in an article that praised their clean lines, unostentatious character, and light-filled interiors. He believed that this poetry, by which he meant their formal beauty and their metaphoric references to technology, resulted from Mendelsohn's substitution of an aesthetic based on good proportions for the sentimentality of historical ornament. Proclaiming that Mendelsohn had produced a new department store form, rather than a mere type, Düssel emphasized his own distrust of architectural prototypes and expressed his preference, which he shared with the architect, for the mediation of a machine aesthetic through the lens of individual creativity.[49]

Meanwhile, it became increasingly difficult to find a new store in Germany that was not influenced by Mendelsohn's example, even if the majority of imitators remained cautious, toning down the innovations that most obviously eroded the boundary between store and factory. Architects like Eisenlohr and Pfennig, Fahrenkamp, Bruno Paul, and Otto Rudolf Salvisberg used richer materials and lightly ornamental touches to temper the extreme rationalism of their prototype (Fig. 111).[50] They continued in many cases to orient their buildings around spacious atria, and their use of advertising was more sedate, although shop windows and night lighting remained critically important. In their Brueniger store in Stuttgart, for instance,

FIGURE 111

Eisenlohr and Pfennig, E. Brueniger store, Stuttgart, 1931. (Source: *Moderne Bauforme*, 1931.)

Eisenlohr and Pfennig followed a harmonic rather than contrapuntal rule, imposing symmetry on Mendelsohn's dynamic original by placing a variant of its prominent corner stair tower at each end of their main facade.[51] At the same time, they felt free to make almost exact quotations, despite the close proximity of their building to one of Mendelsohn's own. Thus they imitated the lettering and setbacks of Mendelsohn's nearby Eberhardstraße facade. They also borrowed the inset first floor from the Petersdorff store, improving on that motif by adding a band of electric lights underneath the overhanging cornice as Mendelsohn himself had done in Mossehaus.

Mendelsohn's rise to fame culminated in 1931 in his inclusion among the thirteen visual artists named to the Prussian Academy by Culture Minister Adolf Grimme. The Academy, increasingly polarized along political lines, had in 1919 elected Käthe Kollwitz, the most important socially engaged artist of her generation, and the neoclassicist architect Bruno Paul to prevent its being disbanded in the wake of the November Revolution. By 1930 it had taken a more conservative tack, awarding membership to the ultranationalist architect and critic Paul Schultze-Naumburg. The institution was also weakened by tensions among its three sections, one each for artists, musicians, and writers. In 1931 Grimme organized a reform, which included the naming of new members. They were leaders of Expressionist painting and of postwar architecture and included, in addition to Mendelsohn, the painters Emil Nolde, Karl Schmidt-Rottluff, Otto

Dix, and Ernst Ludwig Kirchner, and the architects Mies van der Rohe, Bruno Taut, and Martin Wagner. Grimme also gave musicians and writers more power in relation to the numerically dominant artists and attempted to strengthen the Academy's educational component, which had been losing ground to more innovative schools like the Bauhaus. Because these elections took place outside of normal channels and weighted the membership toward more extreme forms of modernism, they were extremely controversial.[52]

Interest in Mendelsohn and the new German architecture of which he was a part continued to increase abroad, where his work often seemed far more overtly functional than it did at home. In May 1930 Mendelsohn lectured at the Academy in Copenhagen and the Architectural Association and the Architectural Club in London.[53] His *Complete Works* was reviewed in Britain, and a variant appeared in France as a special issue of the magazine *L'Architecture Vivante*. In France, Jean Badovici labeled Mendelsohn "one of the prophets of modern architecture."[54] Reviews of *Complete Works* and the Universum Cinema by British critics demonstrated how unusual Germany's technologically infused architecture still seemed to them. The critics in Britain were largely immune to the fantastical qualities of Mendelsohn's buildings. Instead, they saw the Universum Cinema as an example of the characteristic austerity of contemporary German architecture, itself a product of the economic hardship and social changes that resulted from having lost the war.[55] J. R. Leathart, for instance, writing in 1930, noted its "functional severity" and described it as an example of "extreme Teutonic efficiency and directness of purpose." Howard Robertson and F. R. Yerbury faulted the lack of exterior monumentality of a building whose solidity far exceeded that of such contemporary edifices as, for instance, the Petersdorff store.[56] In his review of *Complete Works*, Aldous Huxley, uncomfortable with the puritanism that he, like most British observers, believed characterized the New Building, focused instead on Mendelsohn's drawings.[57]

Mendelsohn also remained among the best known of the European modernists in the United States, where his work was championed by a broad spectrum of those interested in rejecting the still pervasive influence of Beaux-Arts training.[58] His inclusion in the CONTEMPORA Exposition of Art and Industry at the Art Center in New York in 1929 prompted Frank Lloyd Wright to comment of Mendelsohn's work that it "is romantic, a powerful realization of the picturesqueness of our special machine brutalities, and one may see a fresh simplicity in his sentiment and a vigorous power of expression in nearly everything he does."[59] An exhibit brochure included a tribute in which Norman Bel Geddes set forth the reasons for Mendelsohn's continuing appeal not only to his colleagues in the architectural community but also to potential clients and to the larger public that they in turn sought to attract:

> [The contemplation of architecture] relieves the commonplaceness of everyday activity and leads toward more ultimate possibilities. Architecture in its purest form is a creation in terms of space which reaches our finest feelings. As a creative form it demands freedom of thought, freedom from dogma, freedom of history. . . . The architect is more than a builder, more than an organizer in terms of steel, stone, glass; he goes beyond the spatial mathematics of the engineer; he is an artist. In the rhythmic spacing of solids and voids he embodies strength and nobility with imagination, courage, integrity. . . . With the dramatist's instinct he adds the emotional quality that attracts and inspires humanity for all future time. . . . Erich Mendelsohn is such an Architect.[60]

The dichotomy between the reception of the Universum Cinema by the Germans, who had focused on its air of fantasy, and by the British, for whom it could almost have been a factory, highlights the degree to which German architecture was still viewed as a radical innovation by the nations that it would influence during the thirties. Whether adopted on stylistic or economic grounds or as an example of the nurturing by democracies of a way of designing and building often rejected by Germany's own fascist government after 1933, the modernist architecture built on these foreign shores owed much to Mendelsohn. One repercussion of the Depression, for instance, was the smaller budgets available to cinema architects. In Germany, cinema construction came to an almost complete halt, leaving the Universum with no immediate progeny. In America, smaller, but still ornamented, Art Deco cinemas replaced the huge fantasy palaces of the twenties; while in Britain, Odeon chain architect Harry Weedon built a number of cinemas loosely modeled on the Universum and other Mendelsohn sources (Fig. 112).[61]

During the thirties, there was an international demand for Mendelsohnian buildings. Mendelsohn himself received commissions to design department stores abroad; other architects incorporated his innovations into their own designs. In 1932 Mendelsohn designed the Bachner store in Ostrava, Czechoslovakia (completed in 1934), and, in collaboration with Rudolf Emanuel Jacobson, the Dobloug-Garden store in Oslo, Norway, which opened the following year.[62]

FIGURE 112

Harry W. Weedon, Odeon Cinema, Scarborough, England, 1936. (Source: Courtesy of Harry W. Weedon and Partners, Birmingham.)

Joseph Emberton's Simpson's Department Store in London of 1935 (Fig. 113) and George Howe and William Lescaze's Philadelphia Savings Fund Society (PSFS) skyscraper of 1929–32 (Fig. 114) were two of the most notable pioneering Mendelsohnian buildings, although Swedish examples could also be cited.[63] Emberton designed Simpson's in collaboration with Laszlo Moholy-Nagy and Felix Samuely. By this time, Samuely had already worked with Mendelsohn on the De La Warr Pavilion in Bexhill, designed in 1934, which had the first all-welded steel skeleton in Britain, a method of construction repeated for Simpson's. The London store imitated the play of solid and void, metal detailing, prominent lettering, and night illumination of Mendelsohn's Herpich store. Almost a decade after the Herpich store had changed the conventions of Berlin's commercial architecture, Simpson's introduced an unornamented aesthetic dependent on machine-age imagery and construction to Piccadilly – a site as prominent in London, the largest metropolis in Europe, as Leipzigerstraße was in Berlin.

The PSFS building represented an even more significant innovation – the application to the American skyscraper of lessons learned from Mendelsohn's commercial architecture. Even more than the German department store or cinema, the American skyscraper was recognized around the world as *the* emblem of architectural modernity. From Mendelsohn, Howe and Lescaze took the contrapuntal design of a

FIGURE 113

Joseph Emberton, Simpson's Department Store, London, 1935. (Source: *The Architectural Review*, 1936.)

rounded base (which at street level contained a clothing store) set against the cantilevered upper stories of the Market Street facade. The architects used banded windows as emblems of modernity separated from their original department store function. They extended the scale of the windows opening onto the second-story banking hall, where light bounced off not Mendelsohn's painted concrete frames, but the rich marble customary in American bank interiors of the period (even after the rejection of classical convention).[64] The prominent neon sign spelling out "PSFS" in enormous red letters perched atop the tower, while not directly attributable to Mendelsohn's influence, was also in keeping with German architectural advertising.

COLUMBUSHAUS

Nothing demonstrated Mendelsohn's ability to remain in the forefront of the modern movement more than the reception accorded his final building in Berlin – Columbushaus. Greeted with lengthy articles

FIGURE 114

George Howe and William Lescaze, Philadelphia Savings Fund Society, Philadelphia, Pennsylvania, 1929–32. (Source: *The Architectural Record*, 1931.)

in the German and British architectural press, it was heralded as the most up-to-date office building in Europe because of its exterior appearance and its interior arrangement.[65] In Columbushaus, Mendelsohn combined an astonishing variety of income-producing spaces in a plan and cross section that were by far the most complex of his German career. The tightly unified facades of Columbushaus were nonetheless fashionably free of the exaggerated tension between parts responsible for the dynamism of the Schocken store in Stuttgart. Us-

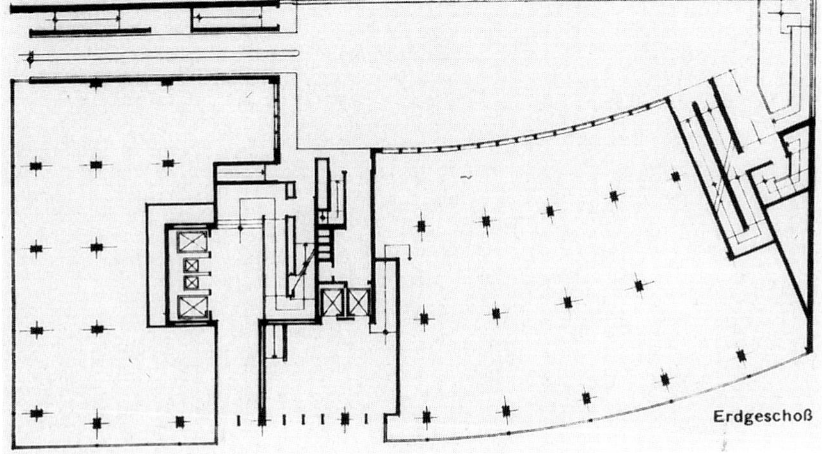

FIGURE 115

Erich Mendelsohn, Columbushaus, ground floor plan. (Source: Staatliche Museen zu Berlin, Kunstbibliothek.)

ing a narrow range of clearly mechanistic materials – glass, limestone, and steel – Mendelsohn still avoided monotous rationalization. In the two facades, one gently curved, that rose gradually above the neighboring buildings to the crescendo of the joint between them, Mendelsohn exploited function to create subtle differences within the most orderly edges of one of the city's most chaotic spaces.

The new Columbushaus program called for a beer cellar or wine bar in the uppermost of the two cellars, seventeen hundred square meters of retail space on the first floor, a café or restaurant on the second floor, seven stories of office space, and, on the terrace of the top story, yet another café or restaurant. In 1931 Mendelsohn reworked the plans he had developed for the Galeries Lafayette to accommodate this diversity of uses (Fig. 115). For instance, the shift between completely open sales floors and office spaces that, although they could be rented as open floors were to be divided by the tenants, prompted him to provide maximum access to the windows facing a reconfigured rear court. Mendelsohn made only minor changes to the exterior, however, apart from the critical issue of height. Most importantly, with the Depression, Wagner's grand transportation schemes had been put on hold; although the new building followed the same curve on Friedrich-Ebertstraße, its Bellevuestraße facade no longer sheltered a subway entrance, because construction of the accompanying station had been delayed.[66] Instead, Mendelsohn built the first floor flush with the plane of the upper stories, eliminating the recessed display windows of the Galeries Lafayette design.

The building's complexity was fully revealed to the public in a much-published cross section (Fig. 116), which showed that the arrangement of the first and second stories was radically different from

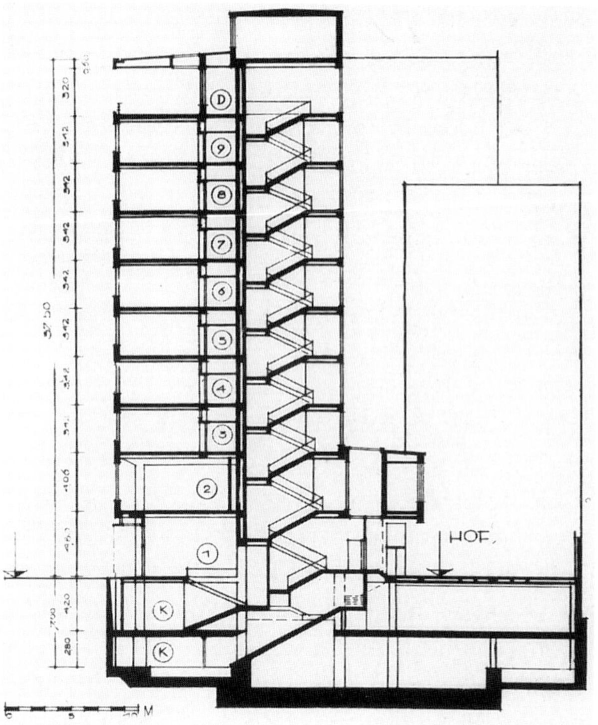

FIGURE 116

Columbushaus, cross section. (Source: Staatliche Museen zu Berlin, Kunstbibliothek.)

those of the upper eight floors, a distinction that was far less clear on the facade where the lower stories were marked only by more extensive glazing befitting their commercial purposes.[67] Only the cellars ran beneath the entire site, but the two lower floors were deeper than the office floors above them and their system of vertical supports was also distinct. On these two floors Mendelsohn located three sets of piers just behind the window wall, in the center of the building, and at the point where the exterior wall of the upper floors met the broader bulk of the lower stories, leaving clear space on the first floor for display windows and in the café above for a row of tables with uninterrupted views of the square. Upstairs, in the culmination of his many experiments with cantilevers, Mendelsohn built the floor slabs of the open office areas out from pairs of piers framing the interior corridor. These cantilevers spanned widths of up to seven-and-a-half meters, with the forward piers resting on tranverse beams running under the floor of the third story, thereby freeing the café and ground floor of disruptive piers. At the level of the open roof terrace restaurant, a volume of this same depth was defined by a long, dramatically cantilevered roof canopy.[68]

The modern image of Columbushaus was enhanced by the details of its construction and the inclusion of a number of up-to-date mechanical systems, many of them housed in the lower of the two reinforced concrete cellars. Most obviously, the building's skeleton was clearly visible in the slender but structural mullions placed at 1.3 meter intervals, which also served in the office stories as potential terminations for the modular interior dividing walls.[69] Along Bellevuestraße a metal grillwork screened enclosed fire stairs and an open ventilation flue. Ventilation was an important feature of the building and was intended to work so well that the office tenants would have no need to open their double-glazed windows, thus creating a permanent barrier against the noise and dirt of some of the city's busiest streets. The windows of the two cafés, in contrast, could slide back, making patrons feel more a part of the lively square below. The building's visual and material lightness led Mendelsohn and the authors of other early descriptions to stress the attention that the architect had in fact paid to insulation against heat, cold, and vibration.[70] And, of course, provisions were made for *Lichtreklame*. Although Mendelsohn later claimed he would have preferred to build an entirely glazed curtain wall, he inserted bands of limestone between the windows of each story to provide space for removable neon lettering. Mendelsohn arranged these bands, like the interior office spaces, to allow for maximum flexibility. This entailed the installation of small metal racks above and below the window sills to hold the changing letters and to supply electric current.[71]

Mendelsohn and his patrons sought the most modern possible architecture, not only because it would help attract tenants in an almost nonexistent market but also because of its conjunction with inexpensive building methods. As in the United States, where the Empire State Building was erected in the space of a mere sixteen months during 1930 and 1931, the completion of Columbushaus in only twelve months saved its sponsors money and generated an enormous amount of favorable publicity.[72] Construction began at the end of April 1931; exactly a year later the building was ready to receive tenants. Work on the concrete foundations and the two cellar levels took three months and was executed by Dykerhoff and Widmann, who had also worked on the Einstein Tower. A second Berlin construction firm, Boswau and Knauer, took over the work at the end of July. Sixty-eight workdays later they completed the steel frame of the building, holding a topping out ceremony on October 18, 1931. By that time, the floors of the lower stories were in place, and work had begun on the limestone and the plumbing. Exterior work was completed in November. By January 11, 1932, all windows had been installed, which allowed the heating equipment to be turned on for the benefit of the workers completing the interior finishings.[73] The speed of the work contributed greatly to the building's image as ultramodern and efficient. It also proved that Mendelsohn's fascination with American construction techniques was not an academic interest but part of his extraordinary capacity to build well-planned structures in a style which, more than that of any American skyscraper of the day, represented their inherently mechanical character.

Columbushaus was an extraordinary accomplishment of which Mendelsohn was justly proud. He transferred his own office to the building, which also housed a new partnership formed by Erich Karweik and Charles du Vinage, two of his most trusted associates (a Woolworths on the ground floor contributed an appropriate American note).[74] Ordinarily, any architect who had just completed such a building could face the future with optimism, secure that its fame would ensure further commissions, but circumstances in Germany at the end of 1932 were far from ordinary; Mendelsohn would spend only a few months in his new office.

CONCLUSION

BY 1932, a year in which Mendelsohn received only two commissions, both outside of Germany's borders, the conditions that had produced and nourished his architecture during the last dozen years had ended in Germany. As the economic crisis destabilized the never-strong Republican government, the country's political chaos was aggravated by the activities of the increasingly popular Nazis. As a Jewish supporter of the Republic and an architect whose patrons had included a socialist trade union and the Soviet government, Mendelsohn could at best regard the Nazis with contempt. Although one of Europe's most renowned architects, at forty-six Mendelsohn faced an uncertain and possibly bleak future in Germany. His reputation was also waning in the Netherlands and the United States, where he was best known for buildings that forecast rather than fulfilled the new style embodied by Columbushaus. Already in May 1931, when work on that building had just begun, Hegemann made public the story that Oud, on a visit to Berlin, had greeted Mendelsohn in a chance encounter on the street with the words, "Three days ago a colleague and countryman of yours . . . told me, 'Mendelsohn is blind and bankrupt!' And here you sit, facing me safe and sound in your Mercedes? It is as if I had seen a ghost."[1]

The account of Mendelsohn's disappearance from the center stage first of German and then of modern architecture is a poignant one in which it is difficult to separate the moral issues surrounding a prominent German Jew driven into exile by the Nazis from the exclusively architectural issue of his almost simultaneous departure from the stylistic forefront. The dynamic functionalism that had brought Mendelsohn such success in Weimar Germany often seemed inappropriate to the conditions and commissions he found abroad, especially in the British Mandate of Palestine but also in the United States. Key to the story was the rise of a new American definition of the modern movement in architecture. This definition, by Henry-Russell Hitchcock and Philip Johnson, would eventually replace the one developed in Germany, as the New Building became the International Style. Also critical was the use the Nazis made of advertising techniques pioneered during the Weimar era to serve the interests of an authoritarian state rather than to promote individual consumer products. This shift left Mendelsohn and most German intellectuals of his generation uncomfortable with their own earlier enthusiasm for mass culture. Thus although Mendelsohn was extraordinarily successful in gaining major commissions in the first few years after he left Germany, the conditions of this success coincided exactly with the grounds for his later marginalization. Before addressing these issues, however, one must first recount the circumstances that drove the architect into exile and describe the fate of the buildings he left behind.

THE FINAL YEAR IN GERMANY

Early in 1932 Mendelsohn published *Neues Haus – Neue Welt (New House – New World)*, a monograph devoted to the house into which he and his family had moved two years earlier.[2] The house had not initially been widely publicized, because it was a particularly private and personal design.[3] Now, with new construction on the decline throughout Germany, the architect craved the attention, accompanied perhaps by commissions, that a book might attract. The text, which included contributions by Amédée Ozenfant and Erwin Redslob, was published in English, French, and German to generate the widest possible audience, and it was quickly reviewed by both the French and the British architectural press.[4] Mendelsohn had every reason to believe that his book, like his house, would be a success. Yet the reviews were mixed. The house was seen not as a modern solution to the problem of the single-family villa, the type which was the locus of most of the recent experiments by Mies and Le Corbusier celebrated in the New York exhibit at the Museum of Modern Art organized by Hitchcock and Johnson in the same year, but as the symbol of the architect's own economic success and thus a flash point for professional jealousy.[5] Germany was becoming uncomfortable for Mendelsohn on intellectual grounds well as for political and economic reasons.

Ozenfant used his introduction to criticize his former colleague Le

Corbusier's declaration that the house was a machine for living.[6] This polemical position prompted only a "but of course" from sympathizers and obscured the highly mechanized features of Mendelsohn's house, such as the glass walls that slid down into the basement or its kitchen appliances, which might otherwise have won admiration from functionalists.[7] Instead, the house was attacked as an example of an outmoded type, the luxurious single-family villa. Hegemann, for instance, while admitting that the house had been designed before the beginning of the economic crisis, criticized its lavishness and noted that dwellings built at a tenth the cost were the solution to Berlin's housing problems. Finally he labeled it as an outdated example of "Wilhelminismus," the ultimate insult for the politically antimonarchist and culturally modernist Mendelsohn.[8]

Mendelsohn's difficulties with Hegemann, who professed to still admire the architect's work, were emblematic of the disintegrating support for modern architecture in Germany. During the late twenties, this influential editor, who for the most part espoused a less stylistically adventurous modernism than Mendelsohn's, had briefly defended him. As Germany's economic and political crisis deepened, Hegemann shied away from controversial buildings or statements that might further alienate support for the urban planning and housing issues that he considered most important. He found much grist for criticism in Mendelsohn's May 1932 speech at the Congress of the International Institution for Cultural Collaboration in Zurich.[9] Entitled "The Creative Sense of Crisis," it was published late in the summer by Bruno Cassirer as a pamphlet.[10] In it Mendelsohn confirmed his oft-stated view that out of the ashes of World War I had begun to rise a new world in which new achievements in art, architecture, economics, and science promised a better future. Of his own discipline, he commented:

> And so *architecture* triumphs – in the standard of building, of construction, of details of the plan and of technical details over the resistance of individualistic styles. . . .
>
> Architecture achieves the necessary harmony between interior and exterior, between function and plan, between plan and form.
>
> It rejects the preconceived pattern and appearances as ends in themselves – the misuse of structural members as decoration is alien to it.
>
> The new architecture strives towards the immediate, free and original shaping of every job; towards the optimum; towards the planned organism, towards the architectonic organism. As a consequence of this, function and aesthetic enjoyment coincide in it.

> In harmony with light, it activates the innate delight of the masses in space, and turns the building into a manifesto.
>
> Architecture once more speaks a basic language which the whole world understands.[11]

This characteristic statement presented Mendelsohn's usual balance of functional and aesthetic concerns, phrased in vaguely Expressionist language, but addressing the same issues of style, construction, and cultural viability as Hitchcock and Johnson. Hegemann, however, believed it to be completely outdated. He appended a long critique of the pamphlet to a short, but largely favorable, review of Columbushaus. Hegemann believed that Mendelsohn was naive; the utopian nature of Mendelsohn's speech alienated him because it ignored the very real crisis that had by 1932 supplanted the brief flowering of optimism after the November Revolution and again in 1925–29. Furthermore, as a patriot whose principal foreign ties were to American and English advocates of regional styles, Hegemann shrank from Mendelsohn's call for entirely new cultural universals.[12]

Mendelsohn continued to try to maintain a hopeful outlook. In September he wrote to his wife that the impending move of his office to Columbushaus on the first of October might give him "the environs in which to develop a new start."[13] Although he added in the same letter that he wanted to remain in Germany, he spent the fall making plans in concert with Ozenfant and with his old friend Wijdeveld for a European Mediterranean Academy in the South of France. Here Mendelsohn foresaw teaching architecture through a combination of basic instruction in materials, construction, representation (he cited perspectives, photography, and film), and three-dimensional planning. These concerns would, he wrote, be united with a belief in the role intuition played in creating a living work of art.[14]

Hitler became chancellor on January 30, 1933. Based on his experiences following the November Revolution, Mendelsohn, despite his allegiance to the Republic, recognized the invigorating artistic climate that political change could produce. His uneasiness about the Nazis – who despite their ties to nationalist architects like Schulze-Naumburg did not immediately make clear their largely antimodern architectural stance – was conditioned more by fears of anti-Semitism than of artistic censorship.[15] In a January 30 letter to his wife, who was vacationing in Switzerland, he wrote:

> I tried to explain the political situation to [their daughter] Esther. . . . The positive you know from my "creative" position on the

> crisis: national concept – always needed, social concept – today necessarily anti-Marxist. . . . The negative possibilities cannot be defined in such a clearcut manner.[16]

The latter centered on the discrimination the country's Jews were sure to face in the new Third Reich. Mendelsohn expected prejudice, but he could not envisage the horrors that lay ahead. Even the normally astute Schocken reassured him that although he could not expect government commissions or an appointment to the faculty of the University of Berlin, he would continue to find employment.[17]

These thin threads of optimism quickly snapped. By February Mendelsohn voiced a number of almost contradictory themes. Appalled by the Nazis and by the immediate threat they posed especially to Jews but also to German cultural achievements made since the 1918 revolution, he could be quite clearheaded about the lack of opportunity that awaited him under the new regime. His inclusion in the Trienniale International Exhibit of Architecture in Milan, where Mussolini's government did not yet discriminate against Jews, offered a glimmer of hope that there might be room for him in a fascist society.[18] Yet Mendelsohn was wounded not to be among the architects invited to compete for the new Reichsbank, from which he was undoubtedly excluded because he was Jewish rather than because he was a modernist. (Mies not only entered but was a prizewinner.)[19] As Mendelsohn had already done in portions of his Zurich lecture, he also assumed at times the highly Expressionist Nietzschean tone he had avoided in the first years after the war. He admitted on February 3 that the economic prosperity of the late twenties had drawn him too far from his original goal of a new order. Now, he increasingly sought refuge in the plans for the European Mediterranean Academy. By March he realized that he had no prospects for further commissions in Germany. With his wife he left Berlin for Amsterdam on the last day of the month. Five months later he was expelled from the newly aryanized Union of German Architects.[20] Mendelsohn never returned to Germany.

THE BUILDINGS

Mendelsohn's German buildings belong to the early days of the modern movement. For a brief while German modernists believed that a new style would rise out of a cauldron of pragmatism and symbolic effectiveness and give concrete form to a better world. As intended, Mendelsohn's designs captured the spirit of an age when technology and the city were as much the occasion for celebration as the latest movie and when war and economic crisis blurred some of the distinctions between bourgeois housing and stores and those built for the working class. Dominating Potsdamerplatz, Columbushaus demonstrated that – although not as tall as the Chrysler and Empire State Buildings – German high-rises were thoughtfully integrated into the city as a whole and that their design went further in representing the technology used to construct them. But the new architecture did not rest upon a cultural consensus. Many Germans, especially those on the right, were ambivalent about or openly hostile toward the new world evoked by it. And in the end, no architectural vision, no individual building, no example of urban planning, could prevent Hitler from being named chancellor.

By the time of Mendelsohn's death two decades after his departure from Germany an alarming amount of the physical evidence of his German career had already been erased, first by the Nazi torching of Jewish property on Kristallnacht in 1938, second by the Allied bombardments and invasion of 1944–45, and finally by postwar governments in both Germanies.[21] In Berlin, the Herpich buildings were destroyed during the war, as were a number of other nearby Mendelsohn buildings and renovations, and Mossehaus was badly damaged. Columbushaus, situated like Mossehaus on what became the border between a divided city, survived the war only to be torched in 1953. Only some of the interior structure of the Nuremberg Schocken store remains. The Cohen-Epstein store in Duisburg was also destroyed. Despite international protests, the Schocken store in Stuttgart was torn down in 1960 to be replaced with a more up-to-date windowless box on a wider street.[22]

The human toll was also enormous. The architect was joined in exile by a large number of his patrons, several of whom had been special targets of Nazi persecution. In 1932 anti-Semitic demonstrations were held in front of Mossehaus, while Freundlich battled with Hans Ludendorff, the head of the Potsdam Observatory and the brother of the famous general, over the research conducted in the Einstein Tower. Einstein settled in Princeton, New Jersey, Freundlich first in Turkey and then in Scotland. The Zionist Schockens and Cohens left for Palestine, although Salman Schocken himself, like Mendelsohn, later moved to the United States, where the anti-Zionist Lachmann-Mosses also eventually lived.[23]

Heretofore this study has focused on the relationship between Mendelsohn's architecture and the modern cultural conditions of the Weimar Republic. To fully understand the degree to which

FIGURE 117

Erich Mendelsohn, Jewish Youth Center, Essen, Germany, 1930–33 (lower foreground). (Source: Alte Synagoge, Stadt Essen.)

buildings as well as people fell victim to the Hitler regime, one must, however, turn from the main current of dynamic functionalism to the checkered history of the last and least known of Mendelsohn's German buildings, the Jewish Youth Center in Essen that he designed in 1930 for his own religious community. (Fig. 117). Throughout his German career, Mendelsohn had built for the Jewish community in his native East Prussia. His early cemetery chapel in Allenstein was joined during the twenties by one in Königsberg (today Kaliningrad, Russia) and a lodge in nearby Tilsit (today the Russian city of Sovetsk).[24] It was thus not surprising that when the Jewish community in Essen, which earlier in the century had erected Germany's largest synagogue, once again decided to build, it turned to Mendelsohn.[25]

The center, which doubled as a memorial to those of the city's Jews who had died fighting in World War I, was largely completed in 1931. Concrete piers and structural masonry built by the local offices of Dyckerhoff and Widmann supplemented the mostly steel-framed construction. The forms, as well as the construction methods and the contractors, were familiar. A broad curve faced Ruhrallee, the principal street onto which the building fronted. Only a single story high, it contained the dining hall and kitchen. Behind it a four-story tower, rendered asymmetrical by the contrapuntal vertical glazing of the stair tower versus the horizontal bands of the room to the right, contained a chapel, a music room, a library, a reading room, and meeting rooms. Perpendicular to this tower on the rear of the site rose a lower block containing the gymnasium, which doubled as an auditorium.[26] The building was amply glazed throughout but, in choices that separated all of Mendelsohn's religious structures of the Weimar era from his most daring commercial work, the glazing never dramatized the structural system and there were no cantilevers.

Overshadowed by the far larger and more prominently sited Columbushaus, the building garnered little attention.[27] In 1933, before its official opening, the Jewish Youth Center was seized by the local Nazis and returned to its owners only the following year. Here Jewish youths found temporary refuge in a busy range of activities. It would not last long. The Nazis returned again on Kristallnacht in 1938, this time burning the building. The ruins were cleared by the city government the next spring. Today the city's small postwar synagogue sits on the centrally located site, which was restored to the few Jews who settled in Essen after the Second World War.[28]

EXILE

In 1937 and 1938 respectively, Walter Gropius and Ludwig Mies van der Rohe accepted prestigious academic appointments in the United States. The work of both architects had been prominently featured in the 1932 exhibit at the Museum of Modern Art in New York, which brought them to the attention of their eventual employers.[29] Their immigration on the eve of World War II was instrumental in converting their particular pedagogies and formal predilections into the almost universal language of the architectural establishment throughout the postwar world. From the classrooms and campuses that they transformed at Harvard and the Illinois Institute of Technology, and from Mies's equally influential architecture office, the two men promulgated an approach to form and construction largely divorced, especially in the case of Mies, from Mendelsohn's explicit celebration of the dynamic dimension of modern life. And although the transition from Weimar Germany to postwar America was not always seamless, both men concluded their careers as unchallenged leaders of their profession.

Exile was not always so easy. The very different trajectory of Mendelsohn's career resulted in a diminished awareness not so much of his principal buildings by the public, for the Einstein Tower and, to a lesser degree, the Schocken stores in Stuttgart and Chemnitz remained textbook examples of the architecture of the 1920s, but of his own understanding of the relationship between architecture and the larger society, particularly a vibrant urban culture that included commerce as well as industry, and dynamism as well as function. In exile Mendelsohn settled successively in Britain, Palestine, and the United States. Only in the first was he able to translate his German formulation of dynamic functionalism successfully onto foreign shores. In Palestine his Zionism, tempered by a respect for the local Arab vernacular, led him in an altogether different direction. Here he was able to build an enormous amount, while still begrudging his rivals the commissions that got away. Only when he arrived in the United States did his diminished status become inescapably obvious.

The Mendelsohns settled in London in 1933. They remained six years, although for much of the period the architect was frequently commuting to Palestine. They were joined in Britain by a number of other German émigrés and were welcomed even by those members of the local architectural community who found Mendelsohn's work too radical.[30] The Germans transformed Britain from a conservative backwater architecturally speaking, in which Georgian classicism, occasionally tempered by the whimsy of a Lutyens or an Art Deco flourish, remained popular, to one of the rare outposts – along with Scandinavia – of the New Building.[31] Mendelsohnian models were widely adopted, especially for cinemas and department stores. Completed in 1935 and the product of a widely publicized competition, Mendelsohn's own De La Warr Pavilion in Bexhill, designed in collaboration with Serge Chermayeff, offered dramatic evidence of the lightness and openness possible with the new style, while retaining, in its spiral stair and projecting bay windows, a dynamic character appropriate to its mix of functions. These included an auditorium and restaurant with a large seaside terrace (Fig. 118).[32]

Initially Mendelsohn was among the luckiest of exiles, quickly establishing himself in Palestine even more successfully than in Britain, although he moved to Jerusalem only in 1939. The number, variety, and scale of his commissions in the British Mandate easily surpassed those awarded during these years to other adherents of modern architecture, including Le Corbusier as well as Gropius and Mies. Mendelsohn found it relatively easy to transfer the status he had won in Germany to his Palestinian practice. His continued success in winning commissions could even be attributed to some of the same patrons. Schocken, for instance, commissioned a house and library in Jerusalem and was instrumental in Mendelsohn's being asked to design the Hadassah Medical Center on Mount Scopus. And even before he

FIGURE 118

Erich Mendelsohn and Serge Chermayeff, De La Warr Pavilion, Bexhill, England, 1934–35. (Source: Staatliche Museen zu Berlin, Kunstbibliothek.)

had begun to practice among them, younger émigré architects from throughout Eastern and Central Europe regarded his German work as their principal source of inspiration, although they often found the master himself imperious and dismissive of their own considerable achievements.[33]

Mendelsohn and Schocken were part of the torrent of Zionist refugees from Central Europe who during the thirties flooded into Eretz Israel, as they called the land that would become an independent nation only in 1947. For them, Mendelsohn built houses and a bank but above all an infrastructure of medical and educational institutions: the Hadassah Hospital on Mount Scopus in Jerusalem, the Government Hospital in Haifa, buildings for an agricultural institute in Rehovat and for the Hebrew University in Jerusalem. The largely institutional nature of these commissions, Mendelsohn's deep emotional involvement with the Zionist cause, and the architect's disavowal of modern mass culture, which he now believed to have been unretrievably compromised by the Nazis' use of it, encouraged him to adapt his architectural style to these new conditions. Contributing to this shift was his belief, formulated in response to his visits to the Soviet Union in the midtwenties, that industrial imagery was suited only to technologically advanced countries, which did not yet include Palestine.[34]

In his Palestinian work, Mendelsohn reformulated the basic precepts of modern architecture to suit the local climate and society, as well as to create monuments to Zionist aspirations – hardly part of

FIGURE 119

Erich Mendelsohn, Weizmann House, Rehovot, British Mandate of Palestine (now Israel), 1934–36. (Source: Staatliche Museen zu Berlin, Kunstbibliothek.)

the brief for his more famous commercial architecture. For example, he oriented his first building in Palestine – a villa for Chaim Weizmann, later the first president of Israel, and his wife, Vera – according to the Mediterranean vernacular tradition he was learning to admire, arranging it around a central patio (and a modern swimming pool!). The result was stately rather than dynamic (Fig. 119).[35] In a sensitive response to the desert climate, Mendelsohn limited the scale of window openings in all his Palestinian commissions, eliminating the transparent glazing typical of his German commercial work. Instead, he relied upon strong shadows to animate the sober massing of facades like that of the nursing school block of the Hadassah Medical Center. Like all his commissions in Jerusalem, this complex also adhered to local building regulations stipulating stone facings, a requirement that suited the architect's new longing for buildings that, instead of responding to the transitory fashions of modern mass culture, would affirm the permanence of the Jewish resettlement of their ancient homeland.[36]

In 1941 the Mendelsohns fled Jerusalem, which Mendelsohn feared would fall to Rommel's troops, for the United States. His high-handed attitude towards his younger colleagues, his defiant championship of Arab culture and rights, and his friendship with the British High Commissioner had already damaged his reputation among younger Zionists. Now this defection, in which he was joined by Schocken, closed the door on the possibility of his ever regaining the respect he had enjoyed in Mandate Palestine during the thirties.[37] Nor would he recapture such a role in his new homeland. In the twenties, Mendelsohn had been *the* European modern architect to most Americans interested in the subject, but the situation was vastly different when he finally arrived in New York. Here he found that his German work counted for little as he once again sought to reestablished himself. Nor was his creation of a new regional architecture for Palestine particularly applicable to his American circumstances. With the American declaration of war soon after his arrival, civilian construction came to an almost complete halt. Mendelsohn waited five often bitter years to secure his first American commission, which was for a synagogue in St. Louis; he began teaching at the University of California in Berkeley only in 1948.

From first the economic and then the institutional needs of Jews in Germany and Palestine Mendelsohn now turned his attention to the spiritual needs of American Jews. The major achievement of his American years was a series of four synagogues. In designing them, beginning in 1946, he turned from the almost classical reliance on mass, light, and shadow characteristic of his Middle Eastern buildings to creating organic compositions and using building materials reminiscent of the work of Frank Lloyd Wright and reflecting the regionalism of the San Francisco Bay Area in which he eventually settled (Fig. 120).[38] He focused on issues of program and planning. Through the creation of a new synagogue type, he sought to nourish a sense of community among the members of the congregations for which he worked. He supplemented sanctuaries with classroom blocks in which children could be schooled in the traditions of their religion and integrated social halls into the design of the temples so that informal gatherings could take place in close proximity to sacred space. Indeed, the thin barrier between the two could be removed during the High Holy Days, extending the seating capacity of the sanctuary to accommodate the expected overflow of worshippers. Finally, he adapted his German experience as a pioneer in the use of indirect light to create an appropriately spiritual ambiance through the use of natural light that poured into the sanctuary from above. Mendelsohn's work for the Jewish community also included a hospital in San Francisco and an unbuilt project for a Holocaust memorial in New York City.

If Mendelsohn's last two decades were characterized by a retreat from modernist spectacle towards the spiritual life of an endangered people, he was not unique. The collapse of the global economy during the early thirties made many doubt the ability of mass production and other technological innovations to improve the quality of their

FIGURE 120

Erich Mendelsohn, B'nai Amoona Synagogue and Community Center, St. Louis, Missouri, 1946–50. (Source, Zevi, *Erich Mendelsohn: Opera Completa.*)

lives. In the early the thirties, Le Corbusier's architecture acquired a more rooted quality, as he employed stone walls and organically curved forms alongside more familiar mechanical imagery in the Swiss Pavilion. Meanwhile, Gropius and Mies were temporarily pushed from center stage by the revitalized career of Frank Lloyd Wright and the fledgling work of Aalvar Aalto, both particularly sensitive to organic texture and form. And while a rejuvenated regionalism flourished within the modern movement, beyond it the issue of monumental architecture, largely dormant in Europe during the twenties, reemerged as central in democratic as well as authoritarian states, thus producing the final phase of Gunnar Asplund's Woodland Cemetery in Stockholm as well as Albert Speer's plans for the rebuilding of central Berlin. In this context, Mendelsohn's choosing to house the secular and religious institutions of Jewish communities in Palestine and the United States in buildings that departed from dynamic functionalism is hardly surprising.

The issue of spirituality was never far from Mendelsohn's mind in his last years, although it had been almost entirely absent from his German writings, including those that dated from the flowering of Expressionist architecture just after World War I. In his book about his trip in 1924 to the United States, for instance, Mendelsohn had stressed the raw energy of the new world, especially of the city centers in which skyscrapers jostled against slums. Yet, the ornamental appliqué he observed in American downtowns marred, he believed, the potential of the steel frame to equal in monumental simplicity the power of reinforced concrete grain silos.[39] It would be Mies rather than Mendelsohn who in the United States would achieve this simplicity shorn of the messy vitality with which Mendelsohn had infused the German commercial architecture of the twenties.

Mendelsohn, like many German exiles, retreated during the thirties and forties from the enthusiasm for technology and mass culture that had been integral to dynamic functionalism. It was no longer possible to believe that these cultural forces, so inextricably intertwined with his career in Germany, would necessarily produce a more liberal and equitable society. The Weimar Republic had never been able to harness the advertising industry in its own defense; its successors were far more adept.[40] And despite the antimodern polemics of pro-Nazi architects such as Schultze-Naumburg, the new regime was also skillful in its manipulation of modern industrial symbolism.[41] The most dramatic transformation of Mendelsohn's architectural legacy was the way in which Albert Speer effectively converted the floodlights that washed across Weimar cinema buildings into the spectacular Cathedral of Light at the annual Nuremberg rallies, shattering a generation's faith in the innocence of technology.[42] Writing in 1940, Mendelsohn declared that "the machine does not follow [man], it strikes at him with his own weapons and makes him its helpless victim."[43] Nor was his reaction unusual. In the late 1930s, many began to champion modern art as an untainted alternative to mass culture. Dominating American intellectual life after the Second World War, this position made it difficult for architectural critics to understand cultural products of the twenties, among them montage and Constructivism, as well as the dynamic functionalism that had attempted to fuse the two.[44] Mendelsohn's architecture was detached from definitions of the modern movement's mainstream and relegated to the status of an organic alternative to the International Style.[45]

In architecture, as in all the visual arts, this shift was encouraged by the activities of the Museum of Modern Art in New York. Largely through the influence of Hitchcock and Johnson's book *The International Style*, published after the exhibit of that name took place, their view and appellation of recent European architecture came to dominate later American interpretations. It also eased the path in America for the architects they favored – Le Corbusier, Gropius, and Mies. Although Mendelsohn's work was included in both the exhibit and the book, and was the subject of a second exhibition at the museum in 1941, dynamic functionalism remained outside of the museum's canon. If the effect of this marginalization was straightforward, limiting Mendelsohn's prestige during his years in the United States and assessments of his career ever since, the reasons for it were varied.

The first, although apparently trivial, probably mattered to the young Philip Johnson. In 1930, when Johnson had traveled to Berlin to assist Henry-Russell Hitchcock in preparing the exhibit, Mendelsohn had hung up on the brash young man who telephoned with hackneyed questions about modern architecture.[46] The American apparently found Mies van der Rohe more hospitable, and he began to plan a monograph on him. Although Mies, like Mendelsohn, was by that time being criticized at home by extreme functionalists, his work was lionized by the museum and, for the most part, by Johnson, throughout the remainder of his career.[47]

The second set of reasons were more complex and more central to the critical ambitions of the two young curators and of Alfred Barr, the only slightly older museum director who had hired them. The three made it clear that they sought an aesthetic basis rather than a functional one for Europe's new architecture, one whose narrow stylistic and broad geographic range left little room for Mendelsohn. Although they included his Chemnitz Schocken store in their survey, their ultimate goal was not an accurate history of modern European architecture, but the dissemination of a new style across the United States. Seeking a unified image that would supplant the lingering eclecticism of most American architecture, the exhibit's organizers purposely played down the diversity within contemporary European architecture. Furthermore, not only did the dynamic half of dynamic functionalism encourage the use of flexible curvilinear forms which remained distinct from the Platonic masses favored by the largely formalistic definition of the International Style, but its functional qualities detracted from the new emphasis on aesthetics.[48]

Mendelsohn was distressed – but scarcely surprised – to see himself increasingly regarded as an outsider within a tradition he had helped to found. He had always expected, for instance, to emigrate. Envy and religious prejudice tainted contemporary appraisals of him and his work and limited his cooperation with fellow émigrés. Gropius, for instance, during his own exile in England, commented in 1934 about Mendelsohn's possible participation in a Royal Institute of British Architects exhibit:

> [Maxwell] Fry just as the RIBA deems it important that the exhibit displays the work of a pure German architect, which is not to be confused with the work of an unpatriotic Mendelsohn. Because I myself am no special friend of the Jew, I have no influence over this view. We are in agreement that we, when possible, should have the significant work of a entirely and absolutely German citizen.[49]

As Gentiles, neither Mies nor Gropius had to directly confront the horrors of a regime that they never publicly opposed during the thirties. In contrast to Mendelsohn's flexible approach to local conditions and his commitment to using architecture to sustain his religious community, Gropius made only minor accommodations to regionalism, and Mies led the way back after the war to the abstract certainties of the International Style.[50]

What were the implications of the triumph of the formalism of the International Style over the flexibility of first the commercial architecture of the Weimar era and then the regionalism of the thirties and forties? Mendelsohn was marginalized by the attention drawn to the very issues that have most interested architects of the last quarter-century, as they try to move beyond the narrow vision of modernity transposed so easily from German to American shores. Elegant as is Miesian minimalism, it cannot fully compensate for the loss of vitality as well as variety that comes from a narrow mechanistic interpretation of the modern movement. Luckily the victory was always more strongly rooted in historiography and critical interpretation than in the actual built environment, as architects from Le Corbusier to Team X quickly mounted their own challenges to the newly monolithic story of the modern movement. Yet the extent to which recent architectural discourse, from the writings of Robert Venturi, Denise Scott-Brown, and Albert Rossi through the critical regionalism espoused by Kenneth Frampton, reintroduces issues of mass culture, memory, and place making addressed in the first decades of the modern movement demonstrates the importance of more nuanced accounts of the history of twentieth-century architecture.[51]

Exile converted Gropius's pedagogy and Mies's formal investigations from radical innovations into established conventions. It provided stable institutional settings from which the two men could address large international audiences, drawn from both within and beyond the profession of architecture. At the same time, however, this shift from the particular to the general cost the reformulated modern movement much of its once lively appeal. As firmly bounded plinths replaced the transparent approachability of sidewalk display windows and the question of signage was relegated to the highway strip, the memory of the original meaning of architectural modernism – to create an architecture in the spirit of distinctively modern times – faded. Returning to the career of Erich Mendelsohn reminds us of what was lost.

Dynamic functionalism gave the New Building the flexibility to fulfill the demands of a wide assortment of patrons for whom contemporaneity was important: scientists celebrating relativity, urban planners ensuring the continued vitality of urban centers, real estate developers exploiting the German excitement about foreign modernisms, merchants trumpeting their ties to mass production, and cinema owners offering new forms of entertainment. Too often defended as the last refuge of individual artistry and an organic relationship between form and materials – both of which were certainly cherished by Mendelsohn – dynamic functionalism was most important for the way in which it tied the new architecture to the larger culture. For as long as it flourished so did the hope that the new style could encompass almost any building type or human emotion. Although not identical with the more obviously objective work of Gropius and Mies, Mendelsohn's approach to architecture remains important to anyone interesting in looking beyond the postwar emphasis on timeless monumentality to recover the original reasons for the success of a new vision of architecture which responded so specifically to the spirit of the times.

NOTES

INTRODUCTION

1. After their emigration to Great Britain, Mendelsohn and his wife adopted English spellings of their names, Eric and Louise. Because this work deals only with the years in which they lived in Germany, I will use the German spellings Erich and Luise. Similarly, all place names will be those in use during the period under discussion.
2. Hans Rudolf Morganthaler, *The Early Sketches of German Architect Erich Mendelsohn (1887–1953): No Compromise with Reality* (Lewiston: Edwin Mellen Press, 1992), and Sigrid Achenbach, *Erich Mendelsohn, 1887–1953, Ideen, Bauten, Projekte* (Berlin: Staatliche Museen Preußischer Kulturbesitz, 1987), 35–51.
3. "Ausstellung Mendelsohn," *Der Städtebau* 16 (1919): 67; W[alter] C[urt] B]ehrendt, "Kunstausstellungen: Berlin," *Kunst und Künstler* 18 (1920): 184; and K[arl] Sch[effler], "Kunstausstellungen: Berlin," *Kunst und Künstler* 18 (1920): 183.
4. Oskar Beyer, "Eine neue Monumental-Architektur," *Feuer* 2 (1920): 111–15, was the first extended notice in the German press of Mendelsohn's work. See also Oskar Beyer, "Introduction," Erich Mendelsohn, *Brief eines Architekten*, ed. Oskar Beyer (Munich: Prestel, 1961), 9. Wijdeveld devoted the entire October 1920 issue of *Wendingen* to Mendelsohn, including Beyer's "Architectuur in izjer en beton," 4–14, whereas Hermann George Scheffauer's "Dynamic Architecture: New Forms of the Future," *The Dial* 70 (1921): 323–28, introduced the architect to an American audience.
5. David De Long, *Bruce Goff: Toward Absolute Architecture* (New York: Architectural History Foundation, 1988), 14–18, and Lisa Germany, *Harwell Hamilton Harris* (Austin: University of Texas Press, 1991), 16.
6. *Erich Mendelsohn: The Complete Works* (New York: Princeton Architectural Press, 1992), 249. This is an English translation of *Erich Mendelsohn: Das Gesamtschaffen des Architekten* (Berlin: Rudolf Mosse Buchverlag, 1930).

7. Mendelsohn himself never used the term dynamic functionalism, although he did subtitle a 1923 lecture "Dynamics and Function." Erich Mendelsohn, "The International Consensus of the New Architectural Concept, or Dynamics and Function," *Complete Works*, 22–34. Norbert Huse, *"Neues Bauen," 1918 bis 1933, Moderne Architektur in der Weimarer Republik* (Munich: Moos, 1975), 33, uses the similar term "functional dynamism" to describe Mendelsohn's work. I cannot claim to have coined the term. In February 1995 I saw it used in the text of wall labels describing Mendelsohn's approach that were part of an exhibit on the architect on display in the De La Ware Pavilion in Bexhill, England (Mendelsohn designed this building in collaboration with Serge Chermayeff).
8. Terry Smith, *Making the Modern: Industry, Art, and Design in America* (Chicago: University of Chicago Press, 1993), 19, 52.
9. Jost Hermand and Frank Trommler, *Die Kultur der Weimarer Republik* (Munich: Nymphenburger, 1978); Detlev J. K. Peukert, *The Weimar Republic: The Crisis of Classical Modernity*, trans. Richard Deveson (1987, New York: Hill and Wang, 1991); and John Willett, *Art and Politics in the Weimar Republic, The New Sobriety, 1917–1933* (New York: Pantheon, 1979). I am particularly indebted to Andreas Huyssen, *After the Great Divide: Modernism, Mass Culture, and Postmodernism* (Bloomington: Indiana University Press, 1986), and Maud Lavin, *Cut with the Kitchen Knife: The Weimar Photomontages of Hannah Hoch* (New Haven: Yale University Press, 1993).
10. Susan Buck-Morss, *The Dialectics of Seeing: Walter Benjamin and the Arcades Project* (Cambridge: MIT Press, 1989), 309–11.
11. Helmut Lethen, *Neue Sachlichkeit, 1924–1932. Studien zur Literatur des "Weissen Sozialismus"* (Stuttgart: J. P. Metzler, 1975).
12. Mendelsohn was always a key figure in Zevi's thesis. See, for instance, Zevi's *Erich Mendelsohn, Opera Completa* (Milano: ETAS Kompass, 1970), and "Contro l'International Style e il postmoderno un'architettura moderna expressionista organica," *Architettura, cronache e storia* 83 (1994): 754–55. Early and recent explorations of the Expressionist – New Building divide can be found respectively in Barbara Miller Lane, *Architecture and Politics in Germany, 1918–1945* (1968; Cambridge: Harvard University Press, 1985), 41–68, and Vittorio Magnano Lampugnani and Romana Schneider, eds., *Moderne Architektur in Deutschland 1900 bis 1950: Expressionismus und Neue Sachlichkeit* (Stuttgart: G. Hatje, 1994).
13. Hans Hildebrant, "Moderne Baukunst," *Berliner Tageblatt*, April 12, 1928.
14. E. Redslob, "Erich Mendelsohn," *Berliner Tageblatt*, November 25, 1929.
15. Karl Scheffler, "Erich Mendelsohn," *Kunst und Künstler* 26 (1928): 354–56.
16. C. Belli, *Il volto del secolo. La prima cellula dell'architecttura razionalista italiana* (Bergamo, 1988), 24–26, 33, cited in translation

in Richard Etlin, *Modernism in Italian Architecture, 1890–1940* (Cambridge: MIT Press, 1991), 590.

17. Smith, *Making the Modern*, 340.
18. Cervin Robinson and Joel Herschmann, *Architecture Transformed: A History of the Photography of Buildings from 1839 to the Present* (Cambridge: MIT Press, 1987), 58, 92–97, 115.
19. Hans Rudolf Morganthaler, "The Early Drawings of Erich Mendelsohn (1887–1953)" (Ph.D. diss., Stanford University, 1988), 264, cites a discriminatory reference to Mendelsohn's Judaism made by Friedrich Perzynsky in a letter of February 5, 1919, to Walter Gropius. For the climate of the time, see also Reginald Isaacs, *Walter Gropius: Der Mensch und sein Werk* (Berlin: Gebr. Mann Verlag, 1983), 176, 224, 251.
20. Huse, *"Neues Bauen,"* 113–19; Karl Heinz Hüter, *Architektur in Berlin, 1900–1933* (Stuttgart: Kohlhammer, 1988), 326–45; and Charlotte Benton, "Mendelsohn and the City," *Erich Mendelsohn, 1887–1953* (London: Modern British Architecture, 1987), 49–57, all address this aspect of Mendelsohn's work.

CHAPTER 1

1. *Die Berliner Illustrirte Zeitung*, September 4, 1921: cover.
2. Barbara Eggers, "Der Einsteinturm – die Geschichte eines Monumentes der Wissenschaft," *Der Einsteinturm in Potsdam: Architektur und Astrophysik* (Berlin: Ars Nicolai, 1995), 89–91.
3. For its relationship to its neighbors, see Michael Bollé, "Einsteins großer Bruder: Die Observatorien auf dem Telegraphenberg," *Brandenburgerische Denkmalpflege* 2 (1993): 72–97; Barbara Eggers, "Die Geschichte des Telegrafenbergs in Potsdam bis 1900," *Einsteinturm in Postdam*, 11–25; and Peter Müller, "Die beiden Observatorien in Potsdam and Babelsberg," *Sterne und Weltraum* 30 (1991): 550–51.
4. Erich Mendelsohn, "The Work of Erich Mendelsohn," 7, typescript of a lecture delivered in Pittsburgh in 1924, Mendelsohn Archive.
5. Erwin Finlay Freundlich, letter to Erich Mendelsohn, July 2, 1918, Achenbach, *Mendelsohn*, 64, anticipated beginning construction that August.
6. Erich Mendelsohn, *Der Schöpferische Sinn der Krise* (1932; Berlin: Duttmann, 1986), 34.
7. Ronald W. Clark, *Einstein, The Life and Times* (New York: World Publishing, 1971), 86–89, and Albert Einstein, "Zur Elektrodynamik bewegter Körper," *Annalen der Physik*, 4th ser, 17 (1905): 891–921.
8. Clark, *Einstein*, 115–16, and Albert Einstein, "Über das Relativitätsprinzip und die aus demselben gezogenen Folgerungen," *Jahrbuch der Radioactivität und Elektronik* 4 (1907): 411–62, and 5 (1908): 98–99.
9. Clark, *Einstein*, 141–42, and Albert Einstein, "Über den Einfluß der

Schwerkraft auf die Ausbreitung des Lichtes," *Annalen der Physik*, 4th ser., 35 (1911): 898–908.

10. Käthe Freundlich, letter to Lewis Pynes, April 29, 1973, File 11, no. 241, Albert Einstein Archives, Hebrew University, Jerusalem, copy, Princeton University.
11. Klaus Hentschel, *Der Einstein-Turm* (Heidelberg: Spektrum Akademischer Verlag, 1992), and Klaus Hentschel, "Physik, Astronomie und Architektur – Der Einsteinturm als Resultat des Zusammenwerkes von Einstein, Freundlich und Mendelsohn," *Einsteinturm in Potsdam,* 35–40.
12. Clark, *Einstein*, 161–62, 174–76.
13. Albert Einstein, "Erklärung der Perihelbewegung des Merkur aus der allgemeinen Relativitätstheorie," *Preußische Akademie der Wissenschaften, Sitzungsberichte*, 2nd pt. (1915): 831–39, and Albert Einstein "Die Grundlage der allgemeinen Relativitätstheorie," *Annalen der Physik*, 4th ser., 49 (1916): 769–822.
14. Erwin Finlay Freundlich, *The Foundations of Einstein's Theory of Gravitation*, trans. Henry L. Brose (1916; New York: Dutton, 1920). The Einstein archive contains letters to and from Freundlich about the manuscript for this book. Additional letters from Einstein to Freundlich are in the collection of the Pierpont Morgan Library, New York.
15. Erwin Finlay Freundlich, "Über die Gravitationswirkung auf die Spektrallinien," *Astronomische Nachrichten* 202 (1915): 17–32. See Freundlich, *Foundations*, 66–67, for another description of this experiment. See also Erwin Finlay Freundlich, "Wie es dazu kam, daß ich den Einsteinturm errichtete," *Physikalische Blätter* 25 (1969): 538–41.
16. Christa Kirsten and Hans-Jürgen Treder, eds., *Albert Einstein in Berlin, 1913–1933*, 2 vols. (Berlin: Akademie, 1979), 1: 22–23. See Hentschel, *Einstein-Turm*, 51–58, on the academic politics behind Struve and von Seeliger's actions.
17. Erwin Finlay Freundlich, letter to Erich Mendelsohn, July 2, 1918, Achenbach, *Mendelsohn*, 61–2.
18. The first was enclosed in a letter of July 10, 1918, to his wife. It could have preceded Mendelsohn's receipt of Freundlich's letter. See Sigrid Achenbach, " 'Das Gesicht dem Andern eindeutig zu machen, das ist Alles.' Erich Mendelsohn's Skizzen zum Einsteinturm," *Einsteinturm in Potsdam*, 68, and Achenbach, *Mendelsohn*, 60, which includes the inscription linking it to a specific letter.
19. Clark, *Einstein*, 237–305. From March 24 to April 12, 1922, the *Berliner Tageblatt* carried frequent notices about Einstein's visit to Paris.
20. Clark, *Einstein*, 254–260, and Albert Einstein, "Meine Antwort," *Berliner Tageblatt*, August 27, 1920. In the days immediately before and after the meeting, this newspaper also reported many details of the controversy.
21. Fritz Stern, *Dreams and Delusions: The Drama of German History* (New York: Knopf, 1987), 25–50. For the relationship between the

debate and the reception of Freundlich's activities within the completed Tower, see Hentschel, *Einstein-Turm*, 127–54.

22. Freundlich estimated at that time that the building itself would cost 225,000 to 250,000 marks and that scientific equipment would bring the project's total cost to 500,000 marks. He hoped to raise additional money from industrialists and to persuade them to donate materials and equipment for the building at cost. Freundlich's fund-raising activity is documented in the Einstein Stiftung archive, in the archives of the former Akademie der Wissenschaft der Deutschen Demokratischen Republik, Berlin. See Kirsten and Treder, *Einstein in Berlin*, 1: 177–79, 2: 91–93, and Eggers, "Einsteinturm," 76–79.
23. Louise Mendelsohn, "My Life in a Changing World," 25, for Mendelsohn's enthusiasm for Nietzsche. Copies of this undated, unpublished memoir are in the collections of the Mendelsohn archive, Kunstbibliothek, Staatliche Museen Preußischer Kulturbesitz; Ita Heinze-Greenberg, Haifa; and the Department of Architecture and Design, Museum of Modern Art, New York.
24. Iain Boyd Whyte, *Bruno Taut and the Architecture of Activism* (Cambridge: Cambridge University Press, 1982).
25. Morganthaler, *Early Sketches*, 1–3, 48. For Mendelsohn's early years, see also Arnold Whittick, *Erich Mendelsohn*, 2nd ed. (London: Hill, 1956), 34–48, and L. Mendelsohn, "My Life," 19–32.
26. Winfried Nerdinger, *Theodor Fischer, Architekt und Städtebauer, 1862–1938* (Berlin: Ernst, 1988), and Gabriel Schickel, "Theodor Fischer als Lehrer der Avantgarde," in Vittorio Magnano Lampugnani and Romana Schneider, eds., *Moderne Architektur in Deutschland 1900 bis 1950: Reform und Tradition* (Stuttgart: Verlag Gerd Hatje, 1992), 55–67.
27. Zevi, *Opera Completa*, 6, and Morganthaler, "Early Drawings," 48–68.
28. Achenbach, *Mendelsohn*, 15–30; Louise Mendelsohn, "Biographical Note on Eric," *L'architettura, Cronache e storia* 9 (1963): 304; and Morganthaler, *Early Sketches*, 7–10.
29. Erich Mendelsohn, letter to Luise Maas, January 4, 1914, Oskar Beyer, *Eric Mendelsohn: Letters of an Architect*, trans. Geoffrey Strachan (London: Abelard-Schuman, 1967), 29. Although the German and English editions of Mendelsohn's letters are not identical, I will cite only the English edition, except when referring to letters or portions of letters included only in its German counterpart.
30. Morganthaler, "Early Drawings," 49.
31. Dieter Bartetzko, *Illusionen in Stein, Stimmungsarchitektur im deutschen Faschismus, Ihre Vorgeschichte in Theater- und Film-Bauten* (Reinbeck: Rohwelt, 1985), 189–206; Dieter Bartetzko, *Zwischen Zucht und Ekstase, Zur Theatralik von NS-Architektur* (Berlin: Gebr. Mann, 1985), 135–40; and Peter Jelavich, *Munich and Theatrical Modernism, Politics, Playwriting, and Performance, 1890–1914* (Cambridge: Harvard University Press, 1985), 208–17.

32. Hugo Ball, "Das Münchener Künstlertheater (Eine prinzipielle Beleuchtung)," *Phoebus* (May 1914): 68–74; Jelavich, *Munich and Theatrical Modernism*, 217; L. Mendelsohn, "Biographical Note," 34; Morganthaler, *Early Sketches*, 9; and Peg Weiss, *Kandinsky in Munich: The Formative Jugendstil Years* (Princeton: Princeton University Press, 1979), 102–3, 202–3.
33. John Elderfield, ed., *Hugo Ball, Flight Out of Time: A Dada Diary* (New York: Viking, 1974), 10. The architect also traveled to Berlin that March to ask Reinhardt for advice. Erich Mendelsohn, letter to Luise Maas, March 24, 1914, Beyer, *Letters*, 32.
34. Jelevich, *Munich and Theatrical Modernism*, 217–35; Weiss, *Kandinsky*, 92–106; and Rose-Carol Washton Long, *Kandinsky: The Development of an Abstract Style* (Oxford: Clarendon, 1980), 52–64.
35. Donald E. Gordon, *Expressionism, Art and Idea* (New Haven: Yale University Press, 1987).
36. Wassily Kandinsky, *Concerning the Spiritual in Art*, trans. M. T. H. Sadler (1912; New York: Dover, 1977).
37. Morganthaler, *Early Sketches*, provides a groundbreaking discussion of Mendelsohn's early drawings. See also Zevi, *Opera Completa*, xiii – lxxvii; Julius Posener, *Aufsätze und Vorträge*, 1931–1980 (Braunschweig/Wiesbaden: Vieweg, 1981), 175–77; and Julius Posener, "Eröffnungsrede der Mendelsohn-Ausstellung in der Akademie der Künste," *Der Mendelsohn-Bau am Lehniner Platz: Erich Mendelsohn und Berlin* (Berlin: Schaubühne am Lehniner Platz, 1981), 10.
38. Kandinsky, *Concerning*, 31, and Weiss, *Kandinsky*, 22–40.
39. Erich Mendelsohn, letter to Luise Maas, November 10, 1914, Beyer, *Letters*, 34.
40. Kathryn Bloom Hiesinger, *Art Nouveau in Munich, Masters of Jugendstil* (Philadelphia: Philadelphia Museum of Art, 1988), 152–53, and Sigfried Wuhmann, *Hermann Obrist: Wegbereiter der Moderne* (München: Stuck-Jugendstil-Verein, 1968).
41. Nerdinger, *Fischer*, 103–12, 233–38, and Spangenburg, "Zwei monumentale Hallenbauten in Eisenbeton," *Deutsche Bauzeitung, Mitteilungen über Zemet-, Eisen- und Eisenbeton* 44 (1910): 162. Morganthaler, *Early Sketches*, 59, points out that Prof. Emil Edler von Mecenseffy published *Die künstlerische Gestaltung des Eisenbetonbaus* (Berlin: Wilhelm Ernst & Sohn, 1911), a handbook on reinforced concrete while Mendelsohn was a student.
42. See Kathleen James, "An Alternative Modernism: Organic Architecture in Wroclaw," in *Body, Technology, and Design*, ed. Michael Underhill and Max Underwood (Washington: American Collegiate Schools of Architecture, 1993), 129–34.
43. Max Berg, "Die Jahrhunderthalle und das neue Ausstellungsgelände der Stadt Breslau," *Deutsche Bauzeitung* 47 (1913): 462–66, and Erich Mendelsohn, letter to Luise Maas, August 20, 1913, Beyer, *Letters*, 26. See also Mendelsohn, "International Consensus," 28–29.

44. Erich Mendelsohn, letter to Luise Maas, March 14, 1914, Beyer, *Letters*, 29–32.
45. Achenbach, *Mendelsohn*, 36; Morganthaler, "Early Drawings," 38, 43–44; and Zevi, *Opera Completa*, 10–11. The existence of three versions of this design, of which the earliest (Zevi, *Opera Completa*, 11, fig. 8) is relatively conservative, suggest that this was Mendelsohn's first project for an industrial structure. Erich Mendelsohn, letter to Luise Maas, March 14, 1914, Beyer, *Letters*, 32, on the Turbine Hall.
46. Although Morganthaler, *Early Sketches*, 40, argues that Mendelsohn intended the solid masses in the 1914 drawings to be constructed out of steel plates, rather than concrete, I believe that Mendelsohn's interest in concrete, and the use that Behrens had made of this material in his AEG Turbine Factory, enable one to interpret these pylons as concrete forms.
47. Reyner Banham, *A Concrete Atlantis* (Cambridge: MIT Press, 1986), 181–94, and Karin Wilhelm, *Walter Gropius: Industriearchitekt* (Braunschweig/Wiesbaden: Vieweg, 1983), 41–59.
48. Stanford Anderson, "Modern Architecture and Industry: Peter Behrens and the Cultural Politics of Historical Determinism," *Oppositions* 11 (1977): 52–71; Joan Campbell, *The German Werkbund: The Politics of Reform in the Applied Arts* (Princeton: Princeton University Press, 1978); and Francesco Dal Co, *Figures of Architecture and Thought, German Architecture Culture*, 1880– 1920 (New York: Rizzoli, 1990), 171–261.
49. Erich Mendelsohn, letter to Luise Maas, September 14, 1914, Beyer, *Letters*, 33. Fischer introduced the Mendelsohns to van de Velde in 1915, and Mendelsohn resumed the acquaintance when he himself became famous after World War I. See Erich Mendelsohn, "Henri Van de Velde, dem verehrten Meister," and "Zwei Begegnungen mit Henri van de Velde zum 70. Geburtstag des Meisters," *La Cité* 11 (1933): 92–93. Mendelsohn's final tribute to van de Velde appears in A. M. Hammacher, *Le Monde de Henry van de Velde* (Anvers: Edition fonds Marcator, 1967), 302.
50. Campbell, *German Werkbund*, 58–69, and Muthesius/Van de Velde, "Werkbund theses and antitheses," in *Programs and Manifestoes of Twentieth-Century Architecture*, ed. Ulrich Conrads, trans. Michael Bullock (1964; Cambridge: MIT Press, 1971), 28–31.
51. Erich Mendelsohn, letter to Luise Maas, April 4, 1915, Beyer, *Letters*, 36.
52. Erich Mendelsohn, letter to Luise Maas, June 20, 1915, Mendelsohn, *Briefe*, 36–67. Initially rejected for the army because of his poor eyesight, Mendelsohn enlisted in the engineering corps in 1915 to avoid being drafted into the infantry. He remained in Berlin for his training.
53. L. Mendelsohn, "My Life," 32; Erich Mendelsohn, letter to Luise Mendelsohn, June 29, 1917, copy, Heinze-Greenberg collection, and Erich Mendelsohn, letters to Erwin Finlay Freundlich, August

31 and October 29–30 1917, copies, Heinze-Greenberg collection. Beyer, *Letters*, 43, includes excerpts from the October letter. After her husband's death in 1953, Luise Maas Mendelsohn made typescript copies of his letters to her and of a few other letters he had written. These typescripts form the basis of the two published collections of the letters. Luise Mendelsohn gave a copy of these typescripts to Ita Heinze-Greenberg, who kindly allowed me access to them. The Getty Center for the History of Art and the Humanities, Santa Monica, California, owns the original typescripts.

54. Erich Mendelsohn, letter to Luise Mendelsohn, June 18, 1915, copy, Heinze-Greenberg collection.
55. Beyer, *Letters*, 37–42; Mendelsohn, *Briefe*, 38–43; and Morganthaler, "Early Drawings," 90.
56. Achenbach, "Gesicht dem Andern," 55–63; Hentschel, "Physik, Astronomie und Architektur," 42–43; Morgenthaler, "Early Drawings," 183–88; and Zevi, *Opera Completa*, 32–33.
57. Erich Mendelsohn, letter to Luise Mendelsohn, June 17, 1917, Heinze-Greenberg collection: "Der Bewegungsausgleich – in Masse und Licht – Masse braucht Licht, Licht bewegt die Masse – ist gegenseitig, parallel, sich ergänzend. Die Masse ist klar aufgebaut, wenn das Licht sie ausgleichend bewegt. Rückschluß auf die Kontur! Das Licht ist richtig verteilt, wenn es die bewegte Masse ausgleicht. Rückschluß auf die Darstellung! Das ist allgemeines Gesetz der Ausdruckskunst."
58. Erich Mendelsohn, "Personal Data and Total Work of Erich Mendelsohn," typescript, Getty Center for the History of Art and the Humanities, Santa Monica.
59. Erich Mendelsohn, letter to Luise Maas, August 1, 1914, Mendelsohn, *Briefe*, 28.
60. Mendelsohn, *Briefe*, 28–52.
61. The only architect at the group's original meeting, he was apparently invited because of his friendship with Max Pechstein, for whom his wife had posed. For the Novembergruppe, see Helga Kliemann, *Die Novembergruppe* (Berlin: Gebr. Mann, 1967); L. Mendelsohn, "My Life," 28; and Joan Weinstein, *The End of Expressionism* (Chicago: University of Chicago Press, 1990), 23–106. For the Arbeitsrat, see also Morganthaler, "Early Drawings," 262–64; Whyte, *Taut*, 96–97; and Iain Boyd Whyte, *Crystal Chain. Arbeitsrat für Kunst, Berlin, 1918–1921: Ausstellung mit Dokumentation* (Berlin: Akademie der Künste, 1980), 145, which notes that Mendelsohn was an active member. No evidence of his participation, beyond his 1920 lecture described below, is given, however, in this or any of the other standard sources on the group, nor do such references appear in his letters.
62. Isaacs, *Gropius*, 202, 1127, is in error when he claims that Mendelsohn was included in this exhibit.
63. Erich Mendelsohn, letters to Luise Mendelsohn, June 7 and 17, 1920, copies, Heinze-Greenberg collection. Finsterlin's letters to Mendelsohn are in the Mendelsohn archive. See also Susan King,

The Drawings of Eric Mendelsohn (Berkeley: University of California, 1969), 36; Posener, "Eröffnungsrede," 11; and Whyte, *Taut*, 134–37.

64. Achenbach, *Mendelsohn*, 16. Here he met Gustav Hermann. See L. Mendelsohn, "Biographical Note," 311.
65. Morganthaler, "Early Drawings," 269; and "Das Problem einer neuen Baukunst," *Berliner Tageblatt*, January 29, 1920, confirm that the lecture was written for the Cassirer exhibit and only repeated for the Arbeitsrat early the following year. The text appears in Mendelsohn, *Complete Works*, 7–21.
66. Rosemarie Haag Bletter, "The Interpretation of the Glass Dream – Expressionist Architecture and the History of the Crystal Metaphor," *Journal of the Society of Architectural Historians* 40 (1981): 32–43; Campbell, *German Werkbund*, 82–111; Huse, *"Neues Bauen,"* 26; Morganthaler, "Early Drawings," 111–12; and Whyte, *Taut*, 156–63.
67. Mendelsohn was reacting not only to the ideas and writings of Bruno Taut but also possibly to a prewar text, Josef Capek, "Moderne Architektur," *Der Sturm* 5 (1914): 18. Karl Scheffler, *Die Architektur der Großstadt* (Berlin: Bruno Cassirer Verlag, 1913), 65, also anticipates aspects of Mendelsohn's argument.
68. The large number of drawings for the factory that survive includes several ground plans, rare among the wartime sketches, while a large plaster model of it probably featured prominently in the exhibit at the Paul Cassirer Gallery. See Zevi, *Opera Completa*, 42, for the drawings, and Oskar Beyer, "Architectuur," 8–9, for the model. See also Morganthaler, "Early Drawings," 240–42.
69. Mendelsohn, "Problem," 18–19.
70. Posener, "Eröffnungsrede," 10–11.
71. For somewhat contradictory accounts of the design process, which began in 1918, see Achenbach, "Das Gesicht dem Andern," 53–65; Kathleen James, "Expressionism, Relativity, and the Einstein Tower," *Journal of the Society of Architectural Historians* 53 (1994): 392– 413; and Eggers, "Einsteinturm," 82–84. Following the extensive evidence she presents in "Das Gesicht dem Andern," I now agree with Achenbach's dating of her fig. 61 to 1918 rather than 1917, but not with her belief that figs. 59 and 60 were drawn in 1919 rather than 1920, a supposition which would also seem to be supported by the new evidence offered by Egger's account. Erich Mendelsohn's letters to Luise Mendelsohn, June 7, 21, 24, 26, and 28, 1920, copies, Heinze-Greenberg collection, document Kaprowski's contribution, mostly as the executor of working drawings. See also Posener, *Aufsätze und Vorträge*, 96.
72. It may have been then that Mendelsohn learned that the tower shaft would have to be wider than Freundlich had indicated in his 1918 description of the building's program, for immediately afterwards he wrote his wife that he was thickening its diameter. Erich Mendelsohn, letter to Luise Mendelsohn, May 12, 1920, Mendelsohn, *Briefe*, 53–54, and Erich Mendelsohn, letter to Luise Mendelsohn,

May 13, 1920, copy, Heinze-Greenberg collection. See also Joachim Krausse, "Gebaute Weltbilder von Boullée bis Buckminster Fuller," *Arch+* 116 (1993): 36–37, and idem, "Vom Einsteinturm zum Wunder von Jena," in *Albert Einstein*, ed. Thomas Neumann (Berlin: Elefanten, 1989), 62–64, for possible relationship between the Tower's optical equipment and that of U-boats, with which Zeiss had experience.

73. Erich Mendelsohn's letters to Luise Mendelsohn, May 27, 1917, July 8 and 31, 1918, and August 9, 1918, copies, Heinze-Greenberg collection, document his consultations with an engineer named Salomonsen, who later collaborated with him on the Red Flag factory in Leningrad (Mendelsohn, *Complete Works*, 118). Salomonsen worked for Rothbert and Company, a firm of construction contractors. Erwin Findlay Freundlich, *Das Turmteleskop der Einstein Stiftung* (Berlin: Springer, 1927), 6, writes that two engineers from Carl Zeiss named Meyer and Villiger and a third, from the Siemens and Halske Company, named Böttcher, collaborated with Mendelsohn in the Tower's design.

74. The case of the Einstein Tower repeats that of the celebrated AEG Turbine Hall in Berlin, where Behrens had designed a building casing whose construction referred metaphorically to the activities housed within. Anderson, "Modern Architecture and Industry," 60–61, and Tilmann Buddensieg, *Industriekultur: Peter Behrens and the AEG, 1907–1914*, trans. Iain Boyd Whyte (Cambridge: MIT Press), 59–66. See also Banham, *Concrete Atlantis*, 186, and Wilhelm, *Industriearchitekt*, 41–49, for the extent to which Gropius and Meyer's Fagus factory represented a collaboration with Eduard Werner, the architect originally awarded the commission.

75. Freundlich, *Turmteleskop*, 4. For the telescopes themselves, see *Mount Wilson Solar Observatory of the Carnegie Institution of Washington, Annual Report of the Director* (1907): 139, 149, and pl. 8,(1909): 178–9, (1910): 175–76 and pl. 2, (1912): 177–78; Helen Wilson, Joan Warnow, and Charles Weiner, eds., *The Legacy of George Ellery Hale* (Cambridge, MA, 1972), 21, 42–45, 75, 239; and Rolf Riekher, *Fernrohre und ihre Meister* (Berlin, 1990), 256–59. Hale's contribution to the development of the type of spectograph later used in the Einstein Tower is set forth in Donald E. Osterbrook, "Failure and Success: Two Early Experiments with Concave Gratings in Stellar Observatories," *Journal of Astronomical History* 17 (1986): 119–29. Wilson et al., *Hale*, 67–69, prints the full text of a 1913 exchange of letters between Einstein and Hale about Freundlich's experiments. See also Hentschel, *Einstein-Turm*, 63–66 and 89, and Krausse, "Gebaute Weltbilder," 32–33, for the general importance of Mt. Wilson, although they err in several of the details of its history and, in Hentschel's case, confuse the Snow telescope with the Yerkes Observatory.

76. Apparently only two autograph plan drawings survive from the entire design process. See Achenbach, "Das Gesicht dem Andern," 66.

77. Achenbach, *Mendelsohn*, 70, fig. 63. She also notes (63) that three preliminary drawings for this design accompanied Erich Mendelsohn, letter to Luise Mendelsohn, June 18, 1920, copy, Heinze-Greenberg collection.
78. Erich Mendelsohn, letter to Luise Mendelsohn, May 7, 1920, copy, Heinze-Greenburg collection. Yet only a few days later he turned down the opportunity to be included in an exhibit organized by the Arbeitsrat because "one cannot build a new world with words and pictures." Erich Mendelsohn, letter to Luise Mendelsohn, May 13, 1920, Beyer, *Letters*, 51.
79. Erich Mendelsohn, letters to Luise Mendelsohn, June 2, 18, and 20, 1918, copies, Heinze-Greenberg collection. Zevi, *Opera Completa*, 62, fig. 15, for a photograph of one of the models, perhaps the one documented in the June 2 and 18, 1920, letters, as Mendelsohn planned to send a photograph of this one to his wife. Oskar Beyer, "Architectuur," 10, and Heinrich Klotz, *Twentieth-Century Architecture: Drawings, Models, Furniture from the Exhibition of the Deutschen Architektur Museum, Frankfurt am Main* (New York: Rizzoli, 1989), 42–43, for the final model.
80. Erich Mendelsohn, letter to Luise Mendelsohn, May 14, 1920, copy, Heinze-Greenberg collection.
81. Erich Mendelsohn, letters to Luise Mendelsohn, June 9 and 18, 1920, copies, Heinze-Greenberg collection.
82. Erich Mendelsohn, letter to Luise Mendelsohn, June 28, 1920, copy, Heinze-Greenberg collection: "Linie muß sterben, muß Massenumriß werden. . . . Architektur ist Massenherrschaft."
83. In conversations with the author, Daniel Shay Friedman compared the exterior form of the tower's shaft to a human spine. Almost all the drawings published in Zevi, *Opera Completa*, are now in the Mendelsohn archive. Fig. 11 is not. Kirsten and Treder, *Einstein in Berlin*, 1: opp. 184, state that the original of this drawing and of a perspective sketch showing the Tower as built are in the collection of the Zentral Institut für Astrophysik der Akademie der Wissenschaft der Deutschen Demokratischen Republik. Jeffrey Meikle, *The Twentieth Century Limited, Industrial Design in America, 1925–1939* (Philadelphia: Temple University Press, 1979), 30, reports that Mendelsohn, in 1924, gave the second of these drawings to Norman Bel Geddes and that it is now in the Bel Geddes archive at the University of Texas in Austin. This author did not find either drawing in the first collection and believes the Texas sheet to be a printed copy.
84. Mendelsohn first experimented with moving the above-ground work spaces from the front to the rear in 1919, a year in which he worked only intermittently on the design. See Mendelsohn, *Complete Works*, 55.
85. Erich Mendelsohn, letters to Luise Mendelsohn, June 18 and 28, 1920, copies, Heinze-Greenberg collection.
86. Mendelsohn, *Complete Works*, 45, and Zevi, *Opera Completa*, 62, figs. 6, 7, and 10, and 65, fig. 2, for studies for the final elevation.

87. Erich Mendelsohn, letters to Luise Mendelsohn, June 29 and July 2, 1920, copies, Heinze-Greenberg collection.
88. Erich Mendelsohn, letter to Luise Mendelsohn, June 30, 1920, copy, Heinze-Greenberg collection.
89. Erich Mendelsohn, letters to Luise Mendelsohn, June 24 and July 3, 1920, copies, Heinze-Greenberg collection.
90. Erich Mendelsohn, letters to Luise Mendelsohn, June 21 and 26, 1920, copies, Heinze-Greenberg collection.
91. Erich Mendelsohn, letter to Luise Mendelsohn, June 14 and 21, 1920, Beyer, *Letters*, 53–54.
92. Erich Mendelsohn, letter to Luise Mendelsohn, June 26, 1920, copy, Heinze-Greenberg collection. The new estimate rose from an old figure of 300,000 (suggesting that Freundlich's perennial optimism had affected his judgment in May when he mentioned a much lower figure) to 500,000 marks. Two days later the impact of donated materials brought the figure down.
93. "Bautennachweise," *Bauwelt* 11 (1920): 392, reported the granting of the building permit on July 15.
94. Freundlich, *Turmteleskop*, 6. The latter were among Germany's leading experts in reinforced concrete construction and had built Fischer's Garrison Church and Berg's Centennial Hall. Gustav Adolf Platz, *Die Baukunst der Neue Zeit* (1972; Berlin: Propylaen, 1930), pls. 204 and 254. The extent of their experience and of prewar concrete construction in Germany generally strongly suggests that they could have built the Tower out of concrete had the materials been available.
95. L. Mendelsohn, "Biographical Note," 306.
96. Mendelsohn, "Beschreibung des Baues für den Turmspektographen auf dem Gelände des Astrophysikalischen Observatoriums," Geheimes Staatsarchiv Preußischer Kulturbesitz Merseburg, Ministerium für Wissenschaft, Kunst und Volksbildung, Rep. 76 V c Sekt. 1 Tit. 11 Teil II Nr. 6 i Bd. 1, Bl. 7: Die architektonische Gestaltung entspricht dem inneren Bedürfnis und hält sich an die formalen Bedingungen der Eisenbetonkonstruktionen.
97. Mendelsohn, "Work," Mendelsohn Archive, 8, and Julius Posener, "Eröffnungsrede," 11.
98. Miles David Samson, "German-American Dialogues and the Modern Movement before the 'Design Migration,' 1910–1933" (Ph.D. diss. Harvard University, 1988), 120, cites Karl Bernhard, "Hochhäuser oder Skelett," *Zentralblatt der Bauverwaltung* 41 (1921): 44, who declared that the price of steel was twenty-five times higher than its prewar cost and that of concrete fifteen times higher. See also *Bauwelt* 11 (1920) for reports on the cost and availability of materials.
99. Hochbauamt Potsdam, Report to the Prussian Kultusministerium, October 28, 1920, Geheimes Staatsarchiv Preußischer Kulturbesitz, Merseburg, Ministerium für Wissenschaft, Kunst und Volksbildung, Rep. 76 V c Sekt. 1 Tit. 11 Teil II Nr. 6 i Bd. 1, Bl. 28: "Die Anbauten des Turmes am Erdgeschoß sollen nach Angabe des Ar-

chitekten in Eisenbeton ausgeführt werden. . . . Nach Angabe des Architekten erklären sich die für Ziegelmauerwerk wenig geeigneten Formen daraus, daß die Ausführung ursprünglich in Eisenbeton gedacht war, dann aber aus Ersparnisrücksichten in Backstein erfolgte. Um entsprechende Änderungen vorzunehmen, ist die Bauausführung schon zu weit vorgeschritten." See also L. Mendelsohn, "Biographical Note," 306, and Erich Mendelsohn, letter to Arnold Whittick, March 20, 1950, Mendelsohn archive, in which he denied that he had had trouble with the building's shuttering and blamed the compromise completely on the unavailability of concrete. For a construction photograph, see Zevi, *Opera Completa*, 65, fig. 20. Kenji Sugimoto, *Albert Einstein: A Photographic Biography*, trans. Barbara Harshav (New York: Schocken Books, 1989), 95, illustrates a photograph taken after the Tower was damaged in World War II, which again shows the brick structure exposed by damage to the stucco cladding. The substitution is also discussed in Eggers, "Einsteinturm," 83–85.

100. For the details of these amendments to the original design, see Eggers, "Einsteinturm," 91–96.
101. Eric Mendelsohn, "Background to Design," *Architectural Forum* 98 (1953): 106.
102. Erich Mendelsohn, letter to Luise Mendelsohn, June 15, 1920, Beyer, *Letters*, 53. The letter to Whittick cited in note 99 above mentions redesign work, but the resemblance of the finished structure to the drawings published in Beyer, "Architectuur," 12–13, calls the extent of Mendelsohn's later claim into question.
103. The archive of the Einstein Stiftung contains the July 1920 figure and the final figure, dated December 19, 1922.
104. Freundlich, *Turmteleskop*, 6.
105. Richard Neutra, letter to Dione Niedermann, December 1921, Dione Neutra, *Richard Neutra: Promise and Fulfillment, 1919–1932, Selections from the Letters and Diaries of Richard and Dione Neutra* (Carbondale: Southern Illinois University Press, 1986), 54. A photograph of the completed workroom appeared in the *Berliner illustrirte Zeitung*, July 30, 1922: 586.
106. A photograph published in 1924 ("Erich Mendelsohn, Bauten und Skizzen," *Wasmuths Monatshefte für Baukunst* 8 [1924]: 10) of the low-ceilinged overnight room where astronomers could take a break from stargazing shows three more of these chairs and a matching table.
107. He can also certainly share credit for the fact that the building's suitability for its scientific purposes has never been challenged. For the history of the experiments and observations conducted in the tower, see Hentschel, *Einstein-Turm*, 107–26; Friedrich Wilhelm Jäger, "Der Einsteinturm und die Relativitätstheorie," *Einsteinturm in Potsdam*, 31–33; Jürgen Staude, "Sonnenforschung am Sonnenobservatorium des Einsteinturms der Astrophysikalischen Instituts Potsdam," *Einsteinturm in Potsdam*, 100–4; and Jürgen Staude, "Das Sonnenobservatorium Einsteinturm in Potsdam: Er-

forschung solarer Magnetfelder und der Physik von Sonnenflecken," *Sterne und Weltraum* 30 (1991): 505–9.

108. Freundlich, *Foundations*, 66–67.
109. Freundlich, *Turmteleskop*, 11–19, and Richard Neutra, letter to Dione Niedermann, December 1921, Neutra, *Promise and Fulfillment*, 54.
110. Freundlich, *Turmteleskop*, 19–27.
111. Ibid., 27–33.
112. Richard Neutra, letter to Dione Niedermann, December 1921, Neutra, *Promise and Fulfillment*, 54.
113. Paul Forman, "Weimar Culture, Causality, and Quantum Theory, 1918–1927: Adaptation by German Physicists and Mathematicians to a Hostile Intellectual Environment," *Historical Studies in the Physical Sciences* 3 (1971): 1–115.
114. Erich Mendelsohn, letter to Luise Mendelsohn, June 16, 1919, copy, Heinze-Greenberg collection: "Disput zwischen uns Dreien über ungeahnte Zusammenhänge und Kongruenzen von Energie und Materie, die nach Einstein keine getrennten Begriffe sind sondern die gleiche, nur unter anderem Druck stehende Lebensquelle, daraus Folgerung der Kongruenz von Geist und Animalischem im Gegensatz zur überlieferten Trennung der Begriffe. Daraus die Wahrscheinlichkeit der Energielösung durch Einwirkungen von aussen – also durch Erlebnisse – und nicht morphologisch durch Vererbung und Alleinherrschaft der Blutpotenz."
115. Stanford Anderson, "The Legacy of German Neoclassicism and Biedermeier: Behrens, Tessenow, Loos and Mies," *Assemblage* 15 (1991): 63–87; Fritz Neumeyer, "Nexus of the Modern," in *Berlin, 1900–1933, Architecture and Design*, ed. Tilmann Buddensieg (New York: Cooper-Hewitt Museum, 1987), 34–45; and Julius Posener, *Berlin auf dem Wege zu einer neuen Architektur, Das Zeitalter Wilhelms II* (München: Prestel, 1979), 369–81.
116. Wolfgang Pehnt, *Expressionist Architecture*, trans. J. S. Underwood and Edith Kästner (New York: Praeger, 1973), 49–50; Bartetzko, *Illusionen in Stein*, 24–92; and Bartetzko, *Zwischen Zucht und Ekstase*, 59–133. Mendelsohn, too, flirted with a revived classicism in the early years of the decade, as demonstrated by Erich Mendelsohn, letters to Luise Maas, September 6 and October 3, 1911, Beyer, *Letters*, 24–25. Morganthaler, "Early Drawings," 100–12, draws attention to Egyptian motifs in a group of 1914 drawings. Although he turned to industrial architecture later that year, the prominent bases that he gave his factory projects reminded Beyer, "Monumental-Architektur," 112–14, of Egyptian mastabas.
117. Bartetzko, *Illusionen in Stein*, 75–77, 82; Peter Hutter, *Die feinste Barbarei: Das Völkerschlagdenkmal bei Leipzig* (Mainz am Rhein: Philipp von Saubern, 1990); Posener, *Berlin auf dem Wege*, 91–104; Rud. Wolle, "Das Völkerschlachtdenkmal bei Leipzig," *Deutsche Bauzeitung, Mitteilung über Zement, Beton-und Eisen-*

beton 41 (1907): 33, 37–39; and Dimitri Tselos, "Richardson's Influence on European Architecture," *Journal of the Society of Architectural Historians* 29 (1970): 156–62. Mendelsohn stopped in Leipzig on his 1913 trip to see Berg's Centennial Hall. He stayed long enough to see Taut's Steel Pavilion, and it is almost inconceivable that he did not also visit the new monument, which stood near the exhibit ground. Erich Mendelsohn, letter to Luise Maas, August 23, 1913, copy, Heinze-Greenberg collection. L. Mendelsohn, "My Life," 7– 8, describes Schmitz's work admiringly, but she does not mention the Leipzig monument. Posener, *Berlin auf dem Wege*, 62, notes the probable connection between the Einstein Tower and the Battle of the Nations Monument.

118. King, *Drawings*, 14. See also Reyner Banham, "Mendelsohn," *Architectural Review* 116 (1954): 89; Bill Chaitkin, "Einstein and Architecture," in *Einstein, The First Hundred Years*, ed. Maurice Goldsmith (Oxford: Pergamon), 131–44, for discussion of the Tower's Futurist qualities. Boccioni's sculpture had been exhibited in Paris in 1913 and published by the artist himself the following year. It was well known in Berlin's Expressionist circles, where the artist had been championed by Herwath Walden, the influential editor of *Der Sturm*. See M. Calvesi and E. Coen, *Boccioni: L'Opera Completa* (Milano: Electra, 1983), 466. Erich Mendelsohn, letter to Luise Mendelsohn, October 31, 1912, copy, Heinze-Greenberg collection, refers to Futurist art.

119. Umberto Boccioni, *Pittura, scultura futuriste: Dinamismo plastico* (Milano: Edizione Futuriste "Poesia," 1914), and Esther Coen, *Umberto Boccioni* (New York: Metropolitan Museum of Art, 1988), 227–61.

120. Mendelsohn, "International Consensus," 24.

121. Huse, *"Neues Bauen,"* 132, note 58, cites F. Schumacher, "Mechanisierungen," *Kulturpolitik, Neue Streifzüge eines Architekten* (Jena, 1920), 145–72, as a source for this analogy. Erich Mendelsohn, letter to Luise Mendelsohn, July 14, 1917, copy, Heinze-Greenberg collection, refers to Olbrist as its source. See also Erich Mendelsohn, "The Three Dimensions of Architecture – Their Symbolic Significance," a 1952 lecture cited in L. Mendelsohn, "Biographical Notes," 302.

122. In addition to its publication in *Die Berliner illustrirte Zeitung*, it was featured in "Der neue Einstein-Turm auf dem Telegraphenberg in Potsdam," *Berliner Tageblatt, Der Welt-Spiegel*, September 4, 1921: 3, the Sunday supplement of the capital's most prestigious paper. See also "Der Potsdamer Astronomentag," *Berliner Tageblatt*, August 26, 1921. Pictures of it could also be found in many of Berlin's cigar stores according to Richard Neutra, letter to Dione Niedermann, October 1921, Neutra, *Promise and Fulfillment*, 49.

123. Erich Mendelsohn, "My Own Contribution to the Development of Contemporary Architecture," University of California–Los An-

geles School of Architecture, March 17, 1948, Beyer, *Letters*, 166, provides one of the first documented instances of this famous story, which both Erich and Luise Mendelsohn often recounted.

124. Gerhard Peters, "Die neue Baukunst in Deutschland," *Deutsche Monatshefte* 3 (1926): 168.
125. J. F. Staal "Naar Anleidung van Erich Mendelsohn's Ontwerpen," *Wendingen* 3, 10 (1920): 3.
126. Jean Badovici, "Entretiens sur l'architecture vivante: Erich Mendelsohn" *L'architecture Vivante* 3 (1925): 16, "Bauten und Skizzen," 5–11; Adolf Behne, *Der Moderner Zweckbau* (München: Masken, 1926), 38–39; Sheldon Cheney, *The New World Architecture* (London: Green, 1930), 319; Walter Müller-Wulckow, *Architektur der Zwanziger Jahre in Deutschland* (1929–32, vol. 1, p. 1; Konigstein: Langewiesche, 1975), pl. 58; Platz, *Baukunst*, 70; Herman George Scheffauer, "Erich Mendelsohn," *Architectural Review* 53 (1923): 156–59; and J. G. Wattjes, *Moderne Architectuur* (Amsterdam: Kosmos, 1927), pl. 124.
127. T. P. Bennett, *Architectural Design in Concrete* (London, 1927), 11, LXII, LXIII; Francis S. Onderdonk, *The Ferro-Concrete Style* (New York: Architectural Book Press, 1928), 239–41; and Julius Vischer and Ludwig Hilberseimer, *Beton als Gestalter* (Stuttgart: Hoffmann, 1928), 17.
128. Behne, *Der Moderne Zweckbau*, 38; Platz, *Baukunst*, 70; and E. M. Hajos, "Berliner Architektur und Architektur von Heute," *Die Kunstwanderer* (1929): 493–97.
129. Scheffauer, "Mendelsohn," 158. Badovici, "Entretiens," 16, also refers to the occult.
130. Staal, "Naar Anleidung," 3.
131. "Peter Behrens," *Berliner Tageblatt*, November 5, 1924.
132. Karl Weidle, *Goethehaus und Einsteinturm. Zwei Pole heutiger Baukunst* (Stuttgart: Zaugg, 1929).
133. Paul Ferd Schmidt, "Erich Mendelsohn," *Der Cicerone* 12 (1930): 220.
134. Arthur Segal, letter to Erich Mendelsohn, April 24–25, 1924, Mendelsohn Archive.
135. Müller-Wülckow, *Architektur der Zwanziger Jahre*, 1:8.
136. This remark is especially interesting because Hellwag's article "Der Einsteinturm," *Dekorative Kunst* 29 (1926): 157–60, is based on his visit to the Tower, through which he was probably guided by Freundlich.
137. Paul Westheim, "Mendelsohn," *Das Kunstblatt* 4 (1923): 307. Einstein was also accused of seeking publicity rather than scientific truths. See Max Born, letter to Albert Einstein, October 13, 1920, Max Born, ed., *The Born-Einstein Letters*, trans. Irene Born (New York: Walker and Company, 1971), 39. The tone of Westheim's comments was echoed in Peter Meyer, *Moderne Architektur und Tradition* (Zurich: Girsberger, 1928), 8. See also Behne, *Der Moderne Zweckbau*, 45.
138. Erich Mendelsohn, "International Consensus," 33.

CHAPTER 2

1. Julius Posener in his two meetings with the author in September 1988 and April 1989 told her of letters he had seen, now in an Israeli collection, in which Mendelsohn expressed the wish to settle in Palestine with Wijdeveld and de Klerk. See also L. Mendelsohn, "Biographical Note," 348. For his interest in the United States, see Erich Mendelsohn, letter to Lewis Mumford, January 8, 1925, Beyer, *Letters*, 75. L. Mendelsohn, "My Life," 76, notes that in 1926 the Soviets also invited him to remain in Russia.
2. For his trip to Palestine, see Ita Heinze-Mühleib, *Erich Mendelsohn, Bauten und Projekte in Palästina (1934–1941)* (München: Scaneg, 1986), 66–84, and Gilbert Herbert and Silvina Sosnovsky, *Bauhaus on the Carmel and the Crossroads of Empire: Architecture and Planning in Haifa during the British Mandate* (Jerusalem: Yad Izhak Ben-zvi, 1993), 98–121.
3. Wim de Wit, ed., *The Amsterdam School, Dutch Expressionist Architecture, 1915–1930* (New York: Cooper-Hewitt Museum, 1983), and Suzanne S. Frank, *Michel de Klerk, 1884–1923, An Architect of the Amsterdam School* (Ann Arbor: UMI Research Press, 1984).
4. Nancy Troy, *The De Stijl Environment* (Cambridge: MIT Press, 1982).
5. Staal, "Naar Anleidung," 2–3.
6. In later life Mendelsohn claimed to have taken the trip in 1919. See Erich Mendelsohn, "Own Contribution," Beyer, *Letters*, 166. Whittick, *Mendelsohn*, 75, was the first to date it to 1919, and later scholars have followed his example. An exception, Achenbach, *Mendelsohn*, 18, gives it as 1920, repeating the date given in Erich Mendelsohn, letter to J. J. P. Oud, August 25, 1923, Nederlands Documentatiecentrum voor de Bouwkunst (hereafter NDB), Amsterdam, and implied by Mendelsohn, "International Consensus," 22. Erich Mendelsohn, letters to H. C. Wijdeveld, March 7 and April 2, 1921, NDB, fix the lecture date as March 26, 1921, as does Erich Mendelsohn, "Gedanken zur neuen Architektur," *De nieuwe Kronick*, March 26, 1921, cited in Behne, *Der Moderne Zweckbau*, 78.
7. Erich Mendelsohn, letter to Henricus Wijdeveld, June 3, 1922, NDB.
8. Erich Mendelsohn, "International Consensus," 22–34.
9. Erich Mendelsohn, "International Consensus," 29, and Walter Gropius, "The Theory and Organization of the Bauhaus," reprinted in translation in Tim Benton and Charlotte Benton, eds., with Dennis Sharp, *Form and Function: A Source Book for the History of Architecture and Design, 1890–1939* (London: Crosby Lockwood Staples, 1975), 125.
10. Claudine Humblet, *Le Bauhaus* (Lausanne: Edition L'Age de Homme, 1980), 110, and Isaacs, *Gropius*, 299.
11. Mendelsohn, "International Consensus," 31.

12. Beyer, *Letters*, 184, places this lecture in Stuttgart, but Erich Mendelsohn, letter to J. J. P. Oud, August 25, 1923, NDB, refers to Oud's Weimar lecture, documented in Herbert Bayer, Walter Gropius, and Ise Gropius, eds., *Bauhaus, 1919–1928* (Boston: Bradford, 1959), 80.
13. Günther Stamm, *J. J. P. Oud: Bauten und Projekte 1906 bis 1963* (Mainz: Kupferberg, 1984).
14. Erich Mendelsohn, letter to Luise Mendelsohn, August 19, 1923, Beyer, *Letters*, 59–60.
15. Erich Mendelsohn, letter to J. J. P Oud, August 25, 1923, NDB.
16. Erich Mendelsohn, letter to J. J. P. Oud, September 16, 1923, Beyer, *Letters*, 61–63 (Beyer mistakenly dated this letter to November, which would place it after Mendelsohn's 1923 Dutch lecture tour; the correct date comes from the original in the NDB), and J. J. P. Oud, letters to Erich Mendelsohn, August 31 and October 11, 1923, Mendelsohn Archive.
17. Erich Mendelsohn, "Zur neuen Architektur," *Berliner Tageblatt*, December 13, 1923, and excerpted in "Bauten und Skizzen," 4. The text was also published in *Architectura, Weekblad van het Genvotschap, Architectura et Amicita* 28.4 (1928), and in 1930 in Mendelsohn, *Complete Works*.
18. Gropius, "Bauhaus," Benton et al., *Form and Function*, 119.
19. Mendelsohn, "International Consensus," 24.
20. Mendelsohn, "International Consensus," 34.
21. Hugo Häring, "Approaches to Form," Benton et al., *Form and Function*, 103–5, and Behne, *Der Moderne Zweckbau*, esp. 42, 46. Behne quotes a key passage from Mendelsohn's 1923 lecture near the conclusion of his essay (68).
22. Peter Berg, *Deutschland und Amerika, 1918–1929, Über das deutsche Amerikabild der zwanziger Jahre* (Lübeck: Matthiesen, 1963), 132–44; Frank Costigliola, *Awkward Dominion: American Political, Economic, and Cultural Relations with Europe, 1919–1930* (Ithaca, NY: Cornell University Press, 1984), 167–83; Hermand and Trommler, *Kultur*, 49–58; Lethen, *Neue Sachlichkeit*, 25–51; Beeke Sell Tower with an essay by John Czaplicka, *Envisioning America: Prints, Drawings, and Photography by George Grosz and His Contemporaries, 1925–1933* (Cambridge, MA: Busch Riesinger Museum, 1990); and Willett, *New Sobriety*.
23. Costigliola, *Awkward Dominion*, 111–26.
24. Ibid., 14–66; Berg, *Deutschland*, 96–120; Lethen, *Neue Sachlichkeit*, 20–25; and Samson, "German-American Dialogues," who offers the most thorough assessment of the architectural implications of *Amerikanismus*.
25. Mark Twain, "The German Chicago," *The Complete Essays of Mark Twain*, ed. Charles Nieder (Garden City, NY: Doubleday, 1963), 87–98; Arnold Lewis, "A European Profile of American Architecture," *Journal of the Society of Architectural Historians* 37 (1978): 265–82; and Rainer Hans Tolzmann, "Objective Architecture: American Influences in the Development of Modern

German Architecture" (Ph.d. diss., University of Michigan, 1975), 153–204.

26. Anthony Alofsin, *Frank Lloyd Wright: The Lost Years* (Chicago: University of Chicago Press, 1993), 72–78, and Walter Gropius, *Deutscher Werkbund Jahrbuch* (1913): following 17.
27. Banham, *Concrete Atlantis*; Samson, "German-American Dialogues"; and Tower and Czaplicka, *Envisioning America*. See also "Postface," Jean-Louis Cohen, *Erich Mendelsohn Amerika: Livre d'Images d'un Architecte* (Paris: Les Éditions du Demi-Cercle, 1992), 225–41.
28. *Der Schrei nach dem Turmhaus, Der Ideenwettbewerb Hochhaus am Bahnhof Friedrichstraße, Berlin 1921/22* (Berlin: Argon, 1988), 215–26, and Samson, "German-American Dialogues," esp. 118–38.
29. Erich Mendelsohn, "New York," *Berliner Tageblatt*, January 3, 1925, and "Frank Lloyd Wright," *Berliner Tageblatt*, January 22, 1925. Excerpts from Erich Mendelsohn, *Amerika: Bilderbuch eines Architekten* (Berlin: Rudolf Mosse, 1926), also appeared as "Mendelsohn," *Die Böttcherstrasse* 1 (1928): 18–19. For an English-language edition, see *Erich Mendelsohn's "Amerika"* (New York: Dover, 1993), from which all translations in this text are taken. For another account of the trip and analysis of the book it spawned, see Samson, "German-American Dialogues," 196–218.
30. L. Mendelsohn, "Biographical Note," 317.
31. Winfried Nerdinger, *Walter Gropius* (Berlin: Gebr. Mann, 1985), 9–28, and Tolzmann, "Objective America," 205–49.
32. Erich Mendelsohn, "Das Schiff," *Berliner Tageblatt*, December 4, 1924, reprinted in *Baukunst* 2 (1926): 92, and Beyer, *Letters*, 65–66.
33. Erich Mendelsohn, letter to Luise Mendelsohn, October 9, 1924, Mendelsohn, *Briefe*, 59.
34. Erich Mendelsohn, letter to Luise Mendelsohn, October 11, 1924, Mendelsohn, *Briefe*, 59–60.
35. Erich Mendelsohn, letter to Luise Mendelsohn, October 16, 1924, Beyer, *Letters, 67.*
36. L. Mendelsohn, "My Life," 37.
37. Mendelsohn, *Amerika*, 5–86.
38. Erich Mendelsohn, letter to Luise Mendelsohn, October 19, 1924, Mendelsohn, *Briefe*, 63–65, and October 22, 1924, excerpted, Beyer, *Letters*, 68–69, complete text, copy, Heinze-Greenberg collection.
39. Erich Mendelsohn, letter to Luise Mendelsohn, October 22, 1922, copy, Heinze-Greenberg collection. In the original German interspersed with Mendelsohn's newly acquired English the passage reads: "Schlagrythmus with Cream. . . . Rhythmus der Motoren und das Speed of life, das sie mitmachen, ohne es zu verstehen, das sie verstehen, ohne es analysieren zu können, das sie analysieren, ohne es zusammenreissen zu können. . . . Feuer unter die Sohlen, in die Hände, Kapitäle zertrümmernd, Säulenbasis der Wolkenkratzer. Wollt Ihr Häute, schöne, mit Luft aufpumpen oder wollt Ihr erst

Gerüst bauen, aus Stahl, sichtbar, lieber nackt und kräftig als behängt mit Perlketten, Stück für Stück ein Dollar."

40. Erich Mendelsohn, letters to Luise Mendelsohn, October 24 and 29, 1924, Beyer, *Letters*, 69–71.
41. Erich Mendelsohn, letter to Luise Mendelsohn, October 29, 1924, Beyer, *Letters, 70.*
42. Karl Lönberg-Holm, letter to Oud, October 21, 1924, NDB.
43. Erich Mendelsohn, letter to Luise Mendelsohn, November 8, 1924, Beyer, *Letters*, 74, and L. Mendelsohn, "My Life," 65.
44. Erich Mendelsohn, letter to Henricus Wijdeveld, February 18, 1925, NDB. The following year, after Sullivan's death, Mendelsohn translated Wright's eulogy (Frank Lloyd Wright, "Louis Sullivan," *Berliner Tageblatt*, March 28, 1925).
45. Erich Mendelsohn, letter to Luise Mendelsohn, November 5, 1924, Beyer, *Letters*, 71–74.
46. Erich Mendelsohn, letters to Henricus Wijdeveld, November 5 and 11, 1924, NDB, and Erich Mendelsohn, "Frank Lloyd Wright," in *The Work of Frank Lloyd Wright*, ed. Henricus T. Wijdeveld (Santpoort: Mees, 1925), 96–100, reprinted in *Wendingen* 7 (1926): 96– 100, and *Wasmuths Monatshefte für Baukunst* 10 (1926): 244–46. See also Erich Mendelsohn "Frank Lloyd Wright," *Berliner Tageblatt*, January 22, 1926, reprinted as "Besuch bei Wright," *Baukunst* 2 (1926): 56, and the address he delivered at the opening in 1929 of the Wright exhibition at the Berlin Academy of Arts, published as Erich Mendelsohn, "Frank Lloyd Wright," *Berliner Tageblatt*, June 17, 1931, and in translation in Beyer, *Letters*, 108–9. The same year he also lauded Wright in Erich Mendelsohn, "Frank Lloyd Wright und seine historische Bedeutung," *Das neue Berlin* 1 (1929): 180–81. See also Anthony Alofsin, "Frank Lloyd Wright and Modernism," in *Frank Lloyd Wright Architect*, ed. Terrance Riley with Peter Reed (New York: Museum of Modern Art, 1994), 32–57, although Alofsin is wrong in claiming that Mendelsohn knew of Wright only through Neutra, as the Austrian began working in Mendelsohn's office only after the lecture of 1919 in which Mendelsohn had discussed Wright's work.
47. In a conversation in September 1989 with the author, Mrs. Neutra reminisced about how difficult it had been not to laugh and thus expose the extent of the distortion caused by her husband's tactfulness.
48. Lewis Mumford, *Sticks and Stones, A Study of American Architecture and Civilisation* (New York: Boni and Liveright, 1924). Mumford would have heard of Mendelsohn from Scheffauer, "Dynamic Architecture," 323–28. See also Robert Wojtowicz, "The Lewis Mumford Decades: Studies in architectural History, Criticism, and Urbanism, 1922–1962" (Ph. diss., University of Pennsylvania, 1990).
49. Mendelsohn, letter to Lewis Mumford, January 8, 1925, Beyer, *Letters*, 75. Wojtowicz, "Mumford," 289, notes that it was published

with the assistance of Walter Curt Behrendt as *Vom Blockhaus zum Wolkenkratzer* (Berlin: Bruno Cassirer, 1926).

50. Erich Mendelsohn, letter to Henricus Wijdeveld, February 18, 1925, NDB. See also Erich Mendelsohn, letter to Walter Gropius, March (?) 1928, Beyer, *Letters*, 99.
51. Erich Mendelsohn, letter to Lewis Mumford, December 24, 1925, Beyer, *Letters*, 88–89; Lewis Mumford, *The Brown Decades, A Study of the Arts in America, 1865–1895* (New York: Harcourt, Brace, 1931); and Lewis Mumford, *Sketches from Life: The Autobiography of Lewis Mumford, The Early Years* (New York: Dial, 1982), 429.
52. Mumford, *Sketches from Life*, 429. See also Wojtowicz, "Mumford."
53. Werner Hegemann, *Amerikanische Architektur und Stadtbaukunst, ein Überblick über den heutigen Stand der amerikanischen Baukunst in ihrer Beziehung zum Städtebau* (Berlin: Wasmuth, 1925), and Adolf Rading, rev. of *Amerika: Bilderbuch eines Architekten*, by Erich Mendelsohn, *Die Form* 1 (1926): 132. For another comparison of these two books, see Dietrich Neumann, *"Die Wolkenkratzer kommen!" Deutsche Hochhäuser der Zwanziger Jahre: Debatten, Projekte, Bauten* (Braunschweig/Wiesbaden: Vieweg, 1995), 76–77.
54. Mendelsohn, *Amerika*, 40.
55. Mendelsohn, "New York"; Mendelsohn, "Frank Lloyd Wright"; first advertisement for *Amerika: Bilderbuch eines Architekten, Berliner Tageblatt*, November 5, 1925; "Im Rudolf Mosse Buchverlags," *Der Welt-Spiegel, Berliner Tageblatt*, December 13, 1925: 3; "Wie Amerika Baut: Ein Buch mit Bildern des Architekten Erich Mendelsohn," *Berliner Tageblatt*, January 7, 1926; Edgar Widell, "Wie Amerika jetzt baut," *Berliner Tageblatt*, December 13, 1927; and "Im Spiegel der Architektur," *Der Welt-Spiegel, Berliner Tageblatt*, April 22, 1928: 2.
56. According to the photography credits in the second (1928) edition, Mendelsohn took only half of the illustrations in the book. See also Robinson and Herschmann, *Architecture Transformed*, 97 and Christopher Phillips, "Resurrecting Vision: European Photography Between the Two World Wars," in Maria Morris Hambourg and Christopher Phillips, *The New Vision: Photography Between the World Wars* (New York: Metropolitan Museum of Art, 1989), 287. It is possible that even some of the most famous photographs of Chicago's grain elevators are not Mendelsohn's work. For instance, in Vischer and Hilberseimer, *Beton*, 104, fig. 224, and 106, fig. 227, are credited to a Dr. Stödtner. For a discussion of the book's place in the history of photography, see also Christopher Phillips, "Twenties Photography: Mastering Urban Space," in *The 1920s: Age of the Metropolis*, ed. Jean Clair (Montreal: Montreal Museum of Fine Arts, 1991), 218–25.
57. Erich Mendelsohn, letter to Luise Mendelsohn, July 11, 1927, Beyer, *Letters*, 96.

58. Phillips, "Resurrecting Vision," 277, documents the particular popularity of Lang's photograph.
59. Patty Lee Parmalee, *Brecht's America* (Oxford, OH: Miami University Press, 1981), 69–76.
60. El Lissitzky, letter to Erich Mendelsohn, December 1, 1926, Mendelsohn Archive.
61. El Lissitzky, "Glaz Arkhitektora," *Stoitelnaya promyshlennost* 2 (1926), reprinted in translation in *Photography in the Modern Era*, ed. Christopher Phillips (New York: Metropolitan Museum of Art, 1989), 221–26.
62. Maria Morris Hambourg, "From 291 to the Museum of Modern Art: Photography in New York, 1910–1937," in Hambourg and Phillips, *New Vision*, 3–64.
63. Herman Scheffauer, "The Skyscraper Has Found No Favor in European Cities" *New York Times Magazine*, August 22, 1926: 11, 22.
64. Norman Bel Geddes, letter to Henricus Wijdeveld, December 5, 1924, NDB.
65. Werner Hegemann, "Norman Bel Geddes' Entwurf eines Schauspielhaus mit versenkbarer Bühne," *Wasmuths Monatshefte für Baukunst* 8 (1924): 125–30.
66. In this respect they followed the example of Behren's earlier AEG designs and Mendelsohn's own department stores; the glazed staircase of the Schocken store in Stuttgart reveals a staircase, after all, rather than an elevator.
67. Le Corbusier, *Towards a New Architecture*, trans. Frederick Etchells (1927; New York: Dover, 1986), 146, and Mendelsohn, "International Consensus," 28.
68. Meikle, *Twentieth-Century Limited*, 48–55, 135–50; Smith, *Making in the Modern*, 353–84; and Richard Guy Wilson, Diane H. Pilgrim, and Dickran Tashjian, *The Machine Age in America, 1918–1941* (New York: Brooklyn Museum, 1986), 55–57.
69. Mendelsohn, *Amerika, xi.*
70. Hermand and Trommler, *Kultur*, esp. 353–437, and Willett, *New Sobriety*.
71. Costigliola, *Awkward Dominion*, 154–64, 168, 178–80.
72. Erich Mendelsohn, *Rußland – Amerika – Europa: ein architektonischer Querschnitt* (1929; Basel: Birkhäuser, 1989).
73. Anatole Kopp, *Constructivist Architecture in the USSR* (London: Academy Editions, 1985) and Selim O. Kahn-Magomedov, *Pioneers of Soviet Architecture, The Search for New Solutions in the 1920s and 1930s* (New York: Rizzoli, 1987).
74. Erich Mendelsohn, letter to Luise Mendelsohn, August 19, 1923, Beyer, *Letters*, 60.
75. Erich Mendelsohn, letters to Luise Mendelsohn, August 7, 11, 15, 19, and 25, 1925, Beyer, *Letters*, 86–88. Mendelsohn was also invited to compete for the commission to design the Palace of Soviets. See Zevi, *Opera Completa*, 185, and Alberto Samona, *Il Palazzo del Soviet, 1931–33* (Rome: Officina, 1976).

76. Erich Mendelsohn, letter to Luise Mendelsohn, July 31, 1925, Beyer, *Letters*, 92, and Mendelsohn, *Complete Works*, 118–26, where he shared credit with Erich Laaser and with Salomonsen. Leonie Pilawski, "Neue Bauaufgaben in der Sowjet-Union," *Die Form* 5 (1930): 234, published a photograph of the powerhouse. See also Peter Knoch, "Nieder mit dem Eklektizmus! Industriearchitektur in Leningrad, 1917–1939," *Bauwelt* 83 (1992): 106–15.
77. Mendelsohn, *Complete Works*, 251, and L. Mendelsohn, "Biographical Note," 322.
78. "B. Taut, E. Mendel'son v. Moskve," *Izvestia*, May 29, 1926, cited in Mario de Michelis and Ernesto Pasini, *La citta sovietica, 1925–1937* (Venice: Marsilio, 1976), 30.
79. Erich Mendelsohn, letters to Luise Mendelsohn, July 31, August 1 and 4, 1926, Beyer, *Letters*, 92–93.
80. El Lissitzky, letter to his mother, undated, Sophie Lissitzky-Küppers, *El Lissitzky: Life, Letters, Texts*, trans. Helene Aldwinckle and Mary Whittall (London: Thames and Hudson, 1980), 71; L. Mendelsohn, "My Life," 79; and S. Frederick Starr, *Melnikov: Solo Architect in a Mass Society* (Princeton: Princeton University Press, 1978), 135–36.
81. Erich Mendelsohn, letter to Luise Mendelsohn, August 4, 1926, Beyer, *Letters*, 93.
82. Erich Mendelsohn, letters to Luise Mendelsohn, July 11, 14, and 21, 1927, Beyer, *Letters*, 96–97.
83. A. D., "Die Architektur Russlands und Amerikas, Ein Vortrag EM," *Berliner Tageblatt*, February 21, 1928. Erich Mendelsohn, letter to Luise Mendelsohn, July 22, 1928, copy, Heinze-Greenberg collection, wrote that he was writing the book's introduction and that the book followed the lecture quite closely.
84. They won, however, warm praise in Lewis Mumford, "Steel Chimneys and Beet-top Cupolas," *Creative Art* 4 (1928): xliv.
85. Erich Mendelsohn, letter to Luise Mendelsohn, July 14, 1927, Beyer, *Letters*, 97.
86. Mendelsohn, *Rußland*, 5, 214, 217, and K. Michael Hays, *Modernism and the Posthumanist Subject: The Architecture of Hannes Meyer and Ludwig Hilbersheimer* (Cambridge: MIT Press, 1992).
87. Mendelsohn, *Rußland*, 16, 171, 185, 217.
88. Erich Mendelsohn, letter to Luise Mendelsohn, August 26, 1923, Beyer, *Letters*, 60. See also Edward Said, *Orientalism* (New York: Pantheon, 1978).
89. Mendelsohn, *Rußland*, 37–112.
90. Pehnt, *Expressionist Architecture*, 52–53, and Gordon, *Expressionism*.
91. Gropius, "Bauhaus," in Benton et al., *Form and Function*, 119, and Fritz Neumeyer, "Mies as Self-Educator," in *Mies van der Rohe: Architect as Educator*, ed. Rolf Achilles, Kevin Harrington, and Charlotte Myhrum (Chicago: Mies van der Rohe Centennial Project, Illinois Institute of Technology, 1986), 27–36.

92. Hannes Meyer, "The New World," in Benton et al., *Form and Function*, 106–9.
93. Erich Mendelsohn, letter to Luise Mendelsohn, August 1, 1926, copy, Heinze-Greenberg collection: "Rußland, früher der Koloß auf tönernen Füssen, lebt heute, da ihm die "Füsse" abgehackt sind, die es sich lieber selbst verkrüppelt hat, als weiter zu vegetieren, lebt von seinem Herzen." L. Mendelsohn, "My Life," 73, remembers that on their first trip they were appalled by the shortages of food and by the censorship.
94. Mendelsohn, *Rußland*, 115, 117. Theo van Doesburg, *On European Architecture: Complete Essays from Het Bouwbedrijf, 1924–1931*, trans. Charlotte I. Loeb and Arthur L. Loeb (Basel: Birkhäuser Verlag, 1990), 183–209, for a similar critique, published originally in 1928 and 1929.
95. Erich Mendelsohn, letter to Luise Mendelsohn, August 1, 1926, Beyer, *Letters*, 92.
96. Mendelsohn, *Rußland*, 138, 152, 158.
97. Mendelsohn, *Rußland*, 112ff. Many of the photographs are identified in the 1989 edition of *Rußland*.
98. Mendelsohn, *Russland*, 140.
99. Mendelsohn, *Rußland*, 142–212.

CHAPTER 3

1. Mendelsohn, *Complete Works*, 73–75, 90–103.
2. Iain Boyd Whyte, *The Crystal Chain Letters* (Cambridge: MIT Press, 1985), 146–49, 154–57, for Taut's longing to build.
3. Achenbach, *Mendelsohn*, 9, 18, for the housing, which still stands; Mendelsohn, *Complete Works*, 40–41, for the factory; and Zevi, *Opera Completa*, 52, for the garden pavilion.
4. Hermann also donated 20,000 marks to the construction of the Einstein Tower according to the subscription list, Einstein Stiftung archive.
5. Alfred Lappe, *Luckenwalde* (Berlin-Halensee: Dari, 1930), 68.
6. Mendelsohn, *Complete Works*, 63. Achenbach, *Mendelsohn*, 64, dates most of the drawings for the factory to 1920 based on references to Luckenwalde in Mendelsohn's letters. These probably refer, however, to his first factory for Hermann. Erich Mendelsohn, letters to the Luckenwalde Stadtbauamt, November 29, 1921, and August 31, 1922, collection of Wälzlagerwerk, Luckenwalde, document the submission of his drawings for first the factory sheds and then the powerhouse. Surviving dated blueprints in the same collection, which confirm that the sheds were built according to the November 1921 design, are illustrated in Karin Carmen Jung and Dietrich Worbs, "Funktionelle Dynamik: Die Hutfabrik Steinberg-Hermann and Co. in Luckenwalde von Erich Mendelsohn," *Bauwelt* 83 (1992): 116–21. A review of Julius Vischer and Ludwig Hilbeseimer, *Beton als Gestalter*, in *Moderne Bauformen* 31 (1932): 116, names Rothart and Company as the contractors.

7. Onderdonk, *Ferro-Concrete*, 186–87, figs. 272–73.
8. Mendelsohn, "Work," 10.
9. H. J. Krauss, "Eisenbetonkonstruktion für eine Tuchweberei in M.-Gladbach," *Deutsche Bauzeitung, Mitteilungen über Zement, Beton- und Eisenkonstruktion,*" 20 (1923): 81. See also Vischer and Hilberseimer, *Beton*, 21–47.
10. John Berlowitz, "Die Lösung des Entnebelungsproblem," *Berliner Tageblatt, Technische Rundschau*, July 2, 1924: 155. The load-bearing frame of the structure was concrete; its walls were brick and concrete, as were those of the manufacturing sheds. For the roof Mendelsohn used vertically laid planks covered with a rubberoid surface which did not mask their distinctive pattern. Mendelsohn, *Complete Works*, 63. Erich Mendelsohn, letter to Luise Mendelsohn, July 4, 1922, copy, Heinze-Greenberg collection, wrote that the dyeworks and manufacturing sheds totaled 9,000 square meters and cost 5 million marks, and that the 1,000 square meter power station cost 7 million marks – an indication of the pace of inflation.
11. The drawing is inscribed with the date June 3, 1922. See also Zevi, *Opera Completa*, 76, fig. 4, which he dates to 1921. Ironically, Mendelsohn believed (see "Problem," *Complete Works*, 13) that he was translating Olbrich's plasticity into a material the Austrian had not had access to, although in fact Olbrich's neoclassical Tietz store in Darmstadt had a concrete frame. See Börner, "Der Eisenbeton-Konstruktion des Warenhauses Tietz in Düsseldorf," *Deutsche Bauzeitung, Mitteilungen über Zement-, Beton- und Eisenbeton* 43 (1909): 57–60.
12. Erich Mendelsohn, letter to Luise Mendelsohn, June 19, 1922, Beyer, *Letters*, 55.
13. Marco Biraghi, *Hans Poelzig: Architectura, Ars Magna, 1869–1936* (Venezia: Arsenale Editrice, 1992), 20; Julius Posener, *Hans Poelzig: Reflections on His Life and Work* (New York: Architectural History Foundation, 1992), 15, 70–72; and Matthias Schirren, "Sachliche Monumentalität. Hans Poelzigs Werk in den Jahren 1900–1914," in Lampugnani and Schneider, *Reform und Tradition*, 96–97.
14. In 1929, upon the occasion of Poelzig's sixtieth birthday, Mendelsohn wrote "Hans Poelzig," *Berliner Tageblatt,* April 27, 1929, reprinted in translation in Beyer, *Letters*, 105–7.
15. Volker Rolf Bergham, *Modern Germany: Society, Economy and Politics in the Twentieth Century* (Cambridge: Cambridge University Press, 1982), 69, 72.
16. Schmidt, "Mendelsohn," 220.
17. While the Einstein Tower was widely recognized as the symbol of the years immediately after the war, the Steinberg, Hermann factory was presented into the middle thirties as an example of distinguished contemporary industrial architecture. Adolf Behne, a leader of the Arbeitsrat, was the factory's first champion. He featured it in an article he wrote in 1924 ("Die moderne Fabrik," *Berliner Illustrierte Zeitung*, February 17, 1924: 131) and in *Der Moderne Zweckbau.* In the latter (40), he praised Mendelsohn's organization of the pro-

duction process, which served, he wrote, as an arm of the machinery. The factory was also included in C. G. Holme, ed., *Industrial Architecture* (London: The Studio: 1935), 81, a survey of the most modern industrial architecture in Europe.

18. Richard Neutra, letter to Lily Müller Niedermann, April 1922, Neutra, *Promise and Fulfillment*, 62; Fritz Stahl, "Das neue Rudolf Mosse-Haus," *Berliner Tageblatt*, 5, 1923; "Bauten und Skizzen," 33–39; and Erich Mendelsohn, *Complete Works*, 82.
19. Posener, *Aufsätze und Vorträge*, 175.
20. Werner E. Mosse, "Rudolf Mosse and the House of Mosse, 1867–1920," *Leo Baeck Institute Yearbook* 4 (1959): 239–40, and Modris Eksteins, *The Limits of Reason: The German Democratic Press and the Collapse of Weimar Democracy* (Oxford: Oxford University Press, 1975), 12–19, 32–34. For a parallel interpretation of the rival Ullstein Verlag, see Lavin, *Cut with the Kitchen Knife*, 51–53.
21. Paul W. Massang, *Rehearsal for Destruction, A Study of Political Anti-Semitism in Imperial Germany* (New York: Harper, 1949); W. E. Mosse, *Jews in the German Economy, The German-Jewish Economic Elite, 1820–1935* (Oxford: Clarendon, 1987); Sanford Ragnis, *Jewish Response to Anti-Semitism in Germany, 1870–1914, A Study in the History of Ideas* (Cincinnati: Hebrew Union College Press, 1980); and Irene Runge and Uwe Stelbrink, *George Mosse: "Ich bleibe Emigrant,"* (Berlin: Dietz Verlag, 1991), 6–25.
22. Donald L. Niewyk, *The Jews in Weimar Germany* (Baton Rouge: Louisiana State University Press, 1980), 96–129, and Bruce B. Frye, "The German Democratic Party and the 'Jewish Problem,' " *Leo Baeck Institute Yearbook* 21 (1976): 152. For Erich and Luise Mendelsohn's reaction to Rathenau's assassination, see Erich Mendelsohn, letter to Luise Mendelsohn, June 25, 1922, Mendelsohn, *Briefe*, 55–56, and L. Mendelsohn, "My Life," 56.
23. Max Osborn, Adolph Dinath, Franz M. Feldhaus, *Berlins Aufstieg zur Weltstadt* (Berlin: 1929), 140.
24. "Das Gutenberghaus," *Blätter für Architektur und Kunsthandwerk* 17 (1904): 91 and pl. 120, and "Geschäftshaus Rudolf Mosse," *Berliner Architekturwelt* 7 (1905): 95–96 and figs. 140–43.
25. Mosse, "Mosse," 251, and Theodor Wolff, *Through Two Decades*, trans. E. W. Dickes (London: William Heinemann, 1936), 147–56.
26. Eksteins, *Limits of Reason*, 169.
27. Campbell, *German Werkbund*, 10, 110; Eksteins, *Limits of Reason*, 31–69; Mosse, "Mosse," 243–47; and Gotthartes Schwartz, *Theodor Wolff und das "Berliner Tageblatt"; eine liberale Stimme in der deutschen Politik, 1906–33* (Tübingen: Mohr, 1968).
28. Eksteins, *Limits of Reason*, 105–9.
29. Wolf van Eckardt, *Eric Mendelsohn* (New York: Braziller, 1960), 18, was not aware, and L. Mendelsohn, "Biographical Notes," 311, had forgotten, that Lachmann-Mosse's own *Berliner Tageblatt* had also published photographs of the Einstein Tower. Both credit the photograph on the cover of the *Berliner illustrirte Zeitung*, pub-

lished by the rival Ullstein Press, with gaining Mendelsohn the commission.

30. Richard Neutra, *Life and Shape* (New York: Appleton-Century-Crofts, 1962), 155, and Zevi, *Opera Completa*, 72.
31. Early schematic sketches show a band of new construction atop the existing building. See Achenbach, *Mendelsohn*, 66, cat. 177. Mendelsohn, *Complete Works*, 81, dates Mossehaus 1921 to 1923, but according to Richard Neutra, letter to Lily Müller Niedermann, March 1922, Neutra, *Promise and Fulfillment*, 59, he received the commission only in March 1922. Neutra, *Life and Shape*, 154, later described beginning work on the design immediately after he went to work with Mendelsohn in November 1921.
32. *Der Schrei nach dem Turmhaus*, 280–83.
33. Ludwig Hilberseimer, *Großstadt Architektur* (Stuttgart: Hoffman, 1928), 59–60; Schirren, "Sachliche Monumentalität," 98–99; and Matthias Schirren, *Hans Poelzig: Die Pläne und Zeichnungen aus dem ehemaligen Verkehrs- und Baumuseum in Berlin* (Berlin: Ernst und Sohn, 1989), 62–63.
34. "Die Wirkungsfeld des Architekten im Industriebau," *Bauwelt* 2.120 (1911): 35–37, and Max Osborn, "Ein neuer Typus," 25–28.
35. Karl Ludwig Spengmann, "Form folgt Bewegung," *Bauwelt* 79 (1988): 364–70.
36. Mendelsohn, "International Consensus," 23–24.
37. Ibid., translation from Conrads, *Programs*, 72.
38. Mendelsohn, "Work," 12. See also Erich Mendelsohn, "Das Schiff," *Berliner Tageblatt*, December 4, 1924.
39. Mendelsohn, "Work," 12.
40. Dione Niedermann, letter to Lily Müller Niedermann, April 1922, trans. Dione Niedermann Neutra, Dione Niedermann Neutra collection, Los Angeles. For an alternative view of Lachmann-Mosse as a friend of all that was modern, from Hindemuth to the Soviet Union, see Runge and Stelbrink, *Mosse*, 19.
41. Richard Neutra, letters to Lily Müller Niedermann, April 1922, Neutra, *Promise and Fulfillment*, 62, and Erich Mendelsohn, letter to Luise Mendelsohn, June 22, 1922, Beyer, *Letters*, 56.
42. Erich Mendelsohn, letter to Luise Mendelsohn, August 6, 1922, Beyer, *Letters*, 58.
43. Andrea Bärnreuther, *Paul Rudolf Henning – der Verlust der Utopie in der modernen Architektur* (Berlin: Staatlichen Museen Preußischer Kulturbesitz, 1991), 4–6.
44. Rudolf Paul Henning, "Keramik und Baukunst," *Die Form* 1 (1926): 76–78. For another way of gauging the innovativeness of Mossehaus's tilework compare it with the other illustrations of contemporary buildings published in Karl Matthies, *Moderne Gross-Ziegelbauten* (Berlin: Tonindustrie-Zeitung, 1926). A photograph of the Mossehaus entrance appears as plate 29.
45. Erich Mendelsohn, letter to Luise Mendelsohn, June 22, 1922, Beyer, *Letters*, 56.
46. Erich Mendelsohn, letter to Luise Mendelsohn, June 17, 1920, copy,

Heinze-Greenberg collection. The most complete account of the office is Regina Stephan, *Studien zu Waren- und Geschäftshäusern Erich Mendelsohns in Deutschland* (München: Tudev, 1992), 39–41.

47. Richard Neutra, letter to Lily Müller Niedermann, November 1, 1921, trans. Dione Neidermann Neutra, Neutra collection, lists the names of those who worked with him: "Kosina, a Viennese, Pilzing, Rembein from Berlin, Brieggemann came from Frankfurt . . . Pezold, whom I knew from Luckenwalde." In the notes which accompany her translation Dione Niedermann Neutra writes that Korn and Biel also worked for Mendelsohn in 1922. Kosina came to Berlin after the war and left Mendelsohn's employ in 1923. See Otto Brattskoven, *Heinrich Kosina* (Berlin: Deutsche Architektur-Bücherei, 1929), viii.
48. Eckardt, *Limits of Reason*, 15.
49. Thomas Hines, *Richard Neutra and the Search for Modern Architecture: A Biography and History* (New York: Oxford University Press, 1982), 9–31.
50. Neutra knew Mendelsohn's work not only from German publications but also from Scheffauer's article in the American publication *The Dial.* Richard Neutra, letter to Dione Niedermann, October 1921, Neutra, *Promise and Fulfillment*, 49.
51. Richard Neutra, letters to Lily Müller Niedermann, November 1, 1921, trans. Dione Niedermann Neutra, Neutra collection. See also Rudolf Schindler, letter to Richard Neutra, March 12, 1921, and Richard Neutra, letter to Rudolf Schindler, April 25, 1921, Esther McCoy, *Vienna to Los Anegles: Two Journeys, Letters between R. M. Schindler and Richard Neutra, Letters of Louis Sullivan to R. M. Schindler* (Santa Monica, CA: Art + Architecture Press, 1979), 131, 133.
52. Richard Neutra, letter to Lily Müller Niedermann, January 1922, Neutra, *Promise and Fulfillment*, 57, and McCoy, *Vienna to Los Angeles*, 28.
53. Neutra, *Life and Shape*, 154, and Richard Neutra, letter to Lily Müller Niedermann, December 1921, Neutra, *Promise and Fulfillment*, 54.
54. Richard Neutra, letter to Lily Müller Niedermann, April 1922, Neutra, *Promise and Fulfillment*, 62. See also Posener, *Aufsätze und Vorträge*, 97.
55. Richard Neutra, letters to Dione Neutra, July and August 1922, Neutra, *Promise and Fulfillment*, 70–71; Erich Mendelsohn, letters to Luise Mendelsohn, August 4, 8, 9, 11, and 27, 1922, copies, Heinze-Greenberg collection; McCoy, *Vienna to Los Angeles*, 28–29; Mendelsohn, *Complete Works*, 250; and "Erinnerungen an Erich Mendelsohn," *Bauwelt* 39.3 (1968): 56–58. In conversations with the author in September 1988 and April 1989 Julius Posener described Du Vinage as Mendelsohn's most trusted assistant, more because of his criticism and ideas than his actual work.
56. Richard Neutra, letter to Dione Niedermann, August 1922, Neutra, *Promise and Fulfillment*, 71.

57. See Max Taut and Franz Hoffmann's Allgemeine Deutsche Gewerkschaftbund administration building of 1922–23, located only a few blocks to the east of Mossehaus and illustrated in Hans Joachim Stark, "Bürohäuser der Privatwirtschaft," in *Industriebauten, Bürohäuser* (Ernst: Berlin, 1971), 193–94, vol. 9 of *Berlin und seine Bauten*, and Max Taut, "Das Bürohaus des Allgemeinen Deutschen Gewerkschaftsbundes Berlin," in *Frühlicht: Eine Folge für die Verwirklichung des neuen Baugedankens*, ed. Bruno Taut (1922; Berlin: Ullstein, 1963), 194–97. Mendelsohn's use of forms associated with Bruno Taut did not, however, signal any new sympathy for Expressionist architectural theory. Instead, he reiterated his objections to Taut in a letter written while he was designing Mossehaus, declaring, "Our era will not be formed from art and mysticism." Erich Mendelsohn, letter to Luise Mendelsohn, June 10, 1922, copy, Heinze-Greenberg collection: "Mit Kunst und Mystik ist unsere Zeit nicht zu gestalten."
58. Hines, *Neutra*, 33–34. Neutra's drawings for the project are now in the collection of the University of California, Los Angeles. They consist primarily of studies for the faceted window surrounds and for Lachmann-Mosse's office, as well as Neutra's alternative scheme for the project. The Mossehaus window surrounds demonstrate the Mendelsohn office's interest in prewar Czech experiments with Cubist architecture, despite Mendelsohn's criticism of a Czech Werkbund installation in Mendelsohn, "Problem," 10. See Morganthaler, "Early Drawings," 256; Ivan Margolius, *Cubism in Architecture and the Applied Arts, Bohemia and France, 1910–1914* (Newton Abbot: David and Charles, 1979); Vladimir Slepeta, "Cubism in Prague," *Daidalos* 39 (1991): 64–71; and Jaroslav Vokoun, "Bohemian Cubism," in *The Anti-Rationalists*, ed. J. M. Richards and Nikolaus Pevsner (Toronto: University of Toronto Press, 1973), 106–10. The admiration seems to have been mutual. Slepeta (70) quotes Novotny's article "L'architecture et l'art décoratif moderne in Tchéchoslovaquie" in *L'amour de l'art*, which echoes Mendelsohn's description in "International Consensus" of the effect of relativity upon architecture.
59. Mendelsohn, *Collected Works*, 82. The most detailed description of the building is Stephan, *Studien*, 67–69.
60. Especially when compared to the furnishings for the double villa on Berlin's Karolingerplatz shown in Mendelsohn, *Complete Works*, 74.
61. Reyner Banham, *Theory and Design in the First Machine Age* (London: Architectural Press, 1960), 139–47.
62. Erich Mendelsohn, letter to Luise Mendelsohn, October 30, 1917, copy, Heinze-Greenberg collection; and Mendelsohn, "Problem," *Complete Works*, 17.
63. Richard Neutra, letter to Dione Niedermann, undated, Neutra collection, described preparing twenty-five plasticine models for the Kemperplatz competition entry, a description which reinforces this interpretation of the importance of volume to Mendelsohn. See also

E. A. Karweik, letter, January 28, 1967, "Erinnerungen an Erich Mendelsohn," 56, on the importance of the model to Mendelsohn's design process.

64. Behne, *Der Moderne Zweckbau*, 21, 34, for a contemporary description of the importance of movement in Wright's compositions.
65. Erich Mendelsohn, letter to Luise Mendelsohn, July 8, 1922, copy, Heinze-Greenberg collection.
66. Neutra, *Life and Shape*, 156–57; "Schweres Einsturzunglück in unserem Verlagshaus" and "Das Bauunglück in unserem Verlagshaus," *Berliner Tageblatt*, January 24, 1923; "Das Einsturzunglück in unserem Verlagshaus," *Berliner Tageblatt*, January 25, 1923. See also Fischer, "Der Deckeneinsturz im Mossehaus," *Bauwelt* 15 (1924): 487–88, and P. Gräf, O. Kübler, and A. Brauer, "Sachverständige zu einem Deckeneinsturz," *Die Bauwelt* 15 (1924): 1080–81.
67. "Sparsame Bauweisen," *Technische Rundschau, Berliner Tageblatt*, July 4, 1923: 103, and Helen Searing, "Betondorp: Amsterdam's Concrete Garden Suburb," *Assemblage* 3 (1987): 116, 140.
68. Stahl, "Mosse-Haus," in *Probleme der neuen Stadt Berlin*, ed. Hans Brennert and Erwin Stein, vol. 18 of *Monographien deutscher Städte* (Berlin-Friedenau: Deutscher Kommunal, 1926), 198; Mario von Bucovich, *Berlin* (Berlin: Albertus, 1928), 112; E. M. Hajos and L. Zahn, *Berlin Architektur der Nachkriegszeit* (Berlin: Albertus, 1928), ix and pl. 3; Max Osborn, *Berlin* (Leipzig, 1926), 270; and Sasha Stone and Adolf Behne, *Berlin in Bildern* (Wien: Epstein, 1929), 57.
69. Platz, *Baukunst*, 86; Müller-Wulckow, *Architektur*, 1:9–10 and pl. 93; and Maurice Casteels, *The New Style: Architecture and Decorative Arts* (London: Batsford, 1931), pl. 23.
70. "Kl. R.," "Eisen, Beton und Eisenbeton," *Die Rote Fahne*, June 26, 1924. I thank Sherwin Simmons for this reference.
71. For instance, a calendar for 1924 topped with a drawing of Mossehaus was inserted into the December 8, 1923, edition of the newspaper. In 1924 the building also appeared, logolike, in advertisements for the newspaper's weekly overseas edition and in advertisements for the *Berliner Morgen Zeitung*, as illustrated in Wilhelm Lotz, "Die deutsche Presse und die neue Gestaltung," *Die Form* 3 (1928): 135. The building also appeared in news articles. See Willy Lesser, "Technik und Architektur bei der Aufstockung von Gebäuden," *Technische Rundschau, Berliner Tageblatt*, October 8, 1924: 225.
72. Mendelsohn gave Neutra full credit for four houses in the Zehlendorf section of Berlin (Hines, *Neutra*, 36–37). Richard Neutra, letter to Lily Müller Niedermann, November 1, 1921, Neutra collection, described supervising the construction of the double house on Berlin's Karolingerplatz. In a second letter, dated January 9, 1923, in the same collection, he was working on two projects in Haifa, the Rutenberg power station and Carmel Garden City.
73. For more detailed accounts, see Leszek Jodlinkski, *Dom Tekstylny*

Weichmanna w Gliwicach Nieznane dzielo Ericha Mendelsohna (Gliwice: Muzeum w Gliwicach, 1994) and Stephan, *Studien*, 53–62.

74. Richard Neutra, letter to Lily Müller Niedermann, March 1922, Neutra, *Promise and Fulfillment*, 59. Neutra, *Life and Shape*, 157, claims complete credit for the design.
75. Erich Mendelsohn, letter to Luise Mendelsohn, June 22, 1922, copy, Heinze-Greenberg collection: "Korn brütet über Gleiwitz."
76. Erich Mendelsohn, letters to Luise Mendelsohn, June 22 and August 15/16, 1922, copies, Heinze-Greenberg collection: "beschwindigt."
77. Hermann Schildberger, "Das Seidenhaus Weichmann," in *Gleiwitz*, vol. 12 of *Monographien Deutscher Städte*, ed. Karl Schabik (Berlin: Berlin-Friedenau: Deutscher Kommunal, 1925), 259. This article also contains photographs of the interior.
78. Richard Neutra, letter to Lily Müller Niedermann, March 1922, Neutra, *Promise and Fulfillment*, 59.
79. Schildberger, "Seidenhaus Weichmann," 259.
80. Hermann Sörgel, "Ein internationaler Entwicklungsquerschnitt," *Baukunst* 2 (1926): 43–53.
81. Mendelsohn, "Work," 12.
82. Jean Badovici, "La Maison d'Aujourd'hui," *Cahiers d'Art* 1 (1926): 13. Badovici mistakenly identified it as a private house.
83. L. Mendelsohn, "My Life," 165, 211, demurred, describing what she saw as Wright's egotism and anti-Semitism.

CHAPTER 4

1. Clair, *The 1920s*, demonstrates that the view was not unusual.
2. Scheffler, *Großstadt*, 14, for such a use of "City," also commonplace in the pages of the *Berliner Tageblatt* during the twenties.
3. Georg Simmel, "The Metropolis and Modern Life," in *Classic Essays on the Culture of Cities*, ed. Richard Sennett (New York: Appleton-Century-Crofts, 1969), 47–60. See also Timothy O. Benson, "Fantasy and Functionality: The Fate of Utopia," 12–55, and David Frisby, "Social Theory, the Metropolis, and Expressionism," 88–111, in *Expressionist Utopias: Paradise, Metropolis, Architectural Fantasy*, ed. Timothy O. Benson (Los Angeles: Los Angeles County Museum of Art, 1993).
4. For the importance of traffic to the architect, see Erich Mendelsohn, "Das neuzeitliche Geschäftshaus," an undated manuscript in the Mendelsohn Archives quoted in Stephan, *Studien*, 199–201.
5. Scheffler, *Großstadt*, 68.
6. Franz Hessel, *Ein Flaneur in Berlin* (1929 as *Spazieren in Berlin* Berlin: Das Arsenal, 1984), 146.
7. Francesco Passanti, "Wolkenkratzer für Le Corbusier," in *L'Esprit Noveau: Le Corbusier und die Industrie, 1920–1925*, ed. Stanislaus von Moos (Berlin: Ernst, 1987), 64, for Mendelsohn's admiration

of *L'Esprit Nouveau*, but Mendelsohn, "International Consensus," 34, for his early criticism of Le Corbusier's design for The City of Three Million.

8. This approach has been too often ignored by accounts which focus on the development of Siedlungen on the outer fringe of the city or on the proposals of Hilberseimer and other radicals, none of which were actually built at this time. See Ludovica Scarpa, *Martin Wagner e Berlin, Case e citta nella repubblica de Weimar, 1919–1933* (Rome: Officina, 1983), and Fritz Neumeyer, "Metropolis or the Dissolution of the City? The Struggle of the 1920s Against the Big City," in Clair, *The 1920s*, 300–19.
9. Horst Matzerath, "Berlin, 1890–1940," in *Metropolis, 1890–1940*, ed. Anthony Sutcliffe (London: Mausell, 1984); and Berghahn, *Modern German Society*, 272.
10. His other urban planning projects in the capital city included the German Metal Workers' Union on Alte Jakobstraβe of 1929–30 and the competition entry of 1929 for an office complex for the German Nitrogen Syndicate on Hoffman-von-Fallerslebenplatz. Zevi, *Opera Completa*, 178–84, and Achenbach, "Buildings and Projects," unpaginated.
11. Helga Behn, "Die Architektur des deutschen Warenhauses von ihren Anfängen bis 1933" (diss. University of Köln, 1984), 91–98; Behne, *Der Moderne Zweckbau*, 17–19; Tilmann Buddensieg, "From Academy to Avant-Garde," *Berlin*, 125–31; Posener, *Auf dem Wege*, 369–85, 475–81; Peter Stürzebecher, "Warenhäuser," in *Handel und Gewerbe*, Part A, *Handel*, vol. 4 of *Berlin und Seine Bauten* (Berlin: Ernst, 1975), 1–28, 12–18, and Klaus Konrad Weber, Klaus Konrad, and Peter Gürttler, "Die Architektur der Warenhäuser," in *Handel und Gewerbe*, Part A, 28–39.
12. Behne, *Der Moderne Zweckbau*, 19–21, for a critique of the store.
13. See also Zevi, *Opera Completa*, 116, figs. 2 and 5, which also have inscriptions that mention Hoffmann.
14. Hans J. Reichhardt and Wolfgang Schäche, *Ludwig Hoffmann in Berlin, Die Wiederentdeckung eines Architekten* (Berlin: Transit, 1986).
15. Erich Mendelsohn, letters to Luise Mendelsohn, April 27 and 29, 1924, copies, Heinze-Greenberg collection. For a second account of the entire controversy, see Stephan, *Studien*, 74–78.
16. Werner Hegemann, "Berliner Neubauten und Ludwig Hoffmann," *Wasmuths Monatshefte für Baukunst* 11 (1927): 185, 194, and Erich Mendelsohn, letter to Luise Mendelsohn, May 1, 1924, Beyer, *Letters*, 63–64. See also Neumann, *Wolkenkratzer*, 31.
17. Erich Mendelsohn, letter to Luise Mendelsohn, May 2, 1924, Beyer, *Letters*, 64. See also Fritz Stahl, "Berliner Baupolizei und Bauwesen," *Berliner Tageblatt*, May 8, 1924.
18. Fritz Stahl, "Der Hilferuf der Architekten," *Berliner Tageblatt*, May 15, 1924, and Bund Deutscher Architekten, letter to the minister of social welfare, May 13, 1924, Beyer, *Letters*, 64–65.
19. Erich Mendelsohn, letters to Luise Mendelsohn, May 15 and July

14, 1924, copies, Heinze-Greenberg collection; Hegemann, "Hoffmann," 193; and Schirren, *Poelzig*, 103–5.

20. Paul Westheim, "Bemerkungen," *Das Kunstblatt* 8 (1924): 60, who admitted being motivated by principle alone, as he had not yet seen Mendelsohn's design. Mendelsohn's unpublished letters and the Westheim article both refer to a second project for which Mendelsohn also sought approval. A store in the Hackescher Markt, it was never built.
21. Erich Mendelsohn, letter to Luise Mendelsohn, January 16, 1925, copy, Heinze-Greenberg collection (names Rothbart as the contractor and adds that the steelwork would be done by Breest), and February 10, 1925, Beyer, *Letters*, 76.
22. Erich Mendelsohn, letter to Luise Mendelsohn, February 10, 1925, Beyer, *Letters*, 76.
23. Werner Hegemann, "Eine wichtige Berliner Stadtbauanfrage," *Städtebau* 20 (1925): 156, and Erich Mendelsohn, letters to Luise Mendelsohn, July 8 and 17, August 5 and 25, 1925, Beyer, *Letters*, 85–88, for partial texts, and copies, Heinze-Greenberg collection, for complete texts, also the source for additional letters of July 9 and August 7 and 19.
24. Erich Mendelsohn, letter to Luise Mendelsohn, August 25, 1925, Beyer, *Letters*, 88.
25. Erich Mendelsohn, letter to Luise Mendelsohn, August 21, 1925, copy, Heinze-Greenberg collection, and Hegemann, "Berliner Stadtbauanfrage," 156.
26. Werner Hegemann, *Das steinerne Berlin* (Lugano: Hegner, 1930), 480.
27. King, *Drawings*, 57, in which Luise Mendelsohn claimed that the Ring was her husband's idea. See also F. Borsi and G. K. König, *Architettura dell'Espressionismo* (Genova: Vitale e Ghianda, 1967), xlii; Karin Kirsch, *The Weissenhofsiedlung, Experimental Housing Built for the Deutscher Werkbund, Stuttgart, 1927*, trans. David Britt (New York: Rizzoli, 1989), 16; Richard Pommer, "Mies van der Rohe and the Political Ideology of the Modern Movement," in *Mies van der Rohe, Critical Essays*, ed. Franz Schulze (Cambridge, MIT Press, 1990), 104, 136; and Franz Schulze, *Mies van der Rohe, A Critical Biography* (Chicago: University of Chicago Press, 1985), 118–19. The opposition to his own designs made Mendelsohn sympathetic to the difficulties confronted by colleagues. When in the spring of 1925 Walter Gropius expressed fear that a hostile article in the architectural periodical *Baugilde* might endanger support for the Bauhaus in Dessau, Mendelsohn sent a telegram, on behalf of the Ring, which defended the school. Thanking him for his quick and friendly help, Gropius wrote that the telegram had "knocked out" the opposition (Walter Gropius, letter to Erich Mendelsohn, March 28, 1928, Bauhaus archive, Berlin). Mendelsohn acted despite his private misgivings about the direction in which Gropius was leading the institution, believing that it was more important to create a united front against the most damaging attacks than to

publicly air their more minor differences of opinion (Erich Mendelsohn, letter to Lyonel Feininger, February 3, 1925, and letter to Laslo Moholy-Nagy, March 23, 1925, Bauhaus archive).

28. Mosse, "Mosse," 249, and *Der Mendelsohn-Bau am Lehniner Platz*, 41. Much of the information in the latter publication comes from Helge Pitz and Winfried Brenne's unpublished 1980 "Dokumentation der 50 jähriger Geschichte des Universum-Kinos, 1928–1978."
29. *Der Mendelsohn-Bau am Lehniner Platz*, 40, and Karl-Heinz Metzger and Ulrich Dunker, *Der Kurfürstendamm; Leben und Mythos des Boulevards in 100 Jahren deutscher Geschichte* (Berlin: Konopka, 1986), 74–76.
30. Metzger and Dunker, *Kurfürstendamm*, 17–100.
31. Ibid., 101–56.
32. Erich Mendelsohn, letters to Luise Mendelsohn, June 28 and July 2, 1925, copies, Heinze-Greenberg collection, and Eksteins, *Limits of Reason*, 105–9, 224–31, 259, 301–2.
33. Erich Mendelsohn, letter to Luise Mendelsohn, July 2, 1925, copy, Heinze-Greenberg collection: "praktischer, geschäftsmässiger Bau."
34. Erich Mendelsohn, letter to Luise Mendelsohn, July 2, 1925, copy, Heinze-Greenberg collection: "Ich verwies ihn, daß nicht der Zweck, sondern die Möglichkeit, die in dem Zweck liegt, das allein Massgebende sei, das befruchtet, ansporni und mitreißt. Stadtbau ist immer Zweckbau wie jede Aufgabe und seine Möglichkeiten erst gäben die eigentlichen Aufgaben unserer Zeit."
35. Mendelsohn, *Complete Works*, 216, and *Der Mendelsohn-Bau am Lehniner Platz*, 41.
36. Erich Mendelsohn, letter to Luise Mendelsohn, July 11, 1925, copy, Heinze-Greenberg collection. An article of November 1926 in the *Berliner Tageblatt* announced that Bachmann's apartments would be completed the following year and that their construction was being financed by a $1.5 million American loan. "300 neue Wohnungen im Westen," *Berliner Tageblatt*, November 25, 1926, reprinted in *Der Mendelsohn-Bau am Lehniner Platz*, 48.
37. Mendelsohn, *Complete Works*, 96–101.
38. Erich Mendelsohn, letter to Luise Mendelsohn, July 2, 1925, copy, Heinze-Greenberg collection.
39. Erich Mendelsohn, letter to Luise Mendelsohn, June 28, 1925, copy, Heinze-Greenberg collection.
40. Mendelsohn, *Complete Works*, 216, for details of the program. Achenbach, *Mendelsohn*, 77–78, dates the first two schemes to 1925 and identifies the drawings that accompany each of the three. Mendelsohn, *Complete Works*, 217, published a photograph of a model for the central section of the third scheme, excluding both of Bachmann and Mendelsohn's housing blocks. "300 neue Wohnungen," 48, fixes the date of this scheme.
41. *Der Mendelsohn-Bau am Lehniner Platz*, 42.
42. Mendelsohn, *Complete Works*, 216, number 3, for details of the final program, and 218, for a photograph of an early model of this

version. Achenbach, *Mendelsohn*, 77, dates the substitution of the apartment hotel to the end of 1927 or the beginning of 1928. Erich Mendelsohn, letters to Luise Mendelsohn, July 20 and 22, 1928, Beyer, *Letters*, 100–1, discuss winning permission to build the hotel.

43. *Der Mendelsohn-Bau am Lehniner Platz*, 53–54.
44. George R. Collins and Christiane Crasemann Collins, *Camillo Sitte: The Birth of Modern City Planning* (New York: Rizzoli, 1986).
45. Collins and Collins, *Sitte*, 93, and Nerdinger, *Fischer*, 23–35, 99.
46. Metzger and Dunker, *Kurfürstendamm*, 26–38, and Ernst Heinrich, "Mehrgeschossiger privater Mietshausbau auf Einzelgrundstücken von 1896 bis 1933," *Wohnungsbau*, Part B, 39–74.
47. Adolf Dornath, "Das neue Kabarett der Komiker, Architektur und Stadtbild," *Berliner Tageblatt*, September 21, 1928, reprinted in *Der Mendelsohn-Bau am Lehniner Platz*, 68.
48. The product of the city's phenomenal nineteenth-century growth and the real estate speculation which accompanied it, the rental barracks were already notorious before World War I. See Johann Friedrich Geist and Klaus Küvers, *Das Berliner Mietshaus, 1865–1945* (Munich: Prestel, 1984).
49. Manfredo Tafuri, *The Sphere and the Labyrinth* (Cambridge: MIT Press, 1987), 226, writes that by 1930 Wagner would rather have located workers' housing in the city core, but the high cost of real estate there forced him to build only on the outskirts.
50. Norbert Huse, ed., *Vier berliner Siedlungen der Weimarer Republik: Britz, Onkel Toms Hütte, Siemensstadt, Weisse Stadt* (Berlin: Publica, 1984).
51. "Berlin," *Schöpferische Sinn*, 16–17.
52. Erich Mendelsohn, "Berlin-Paris-Midi," *Berliner Tageblatt*, November 30, 1932, Beyer, *Letters*, 123–24.
53. *Der Mendelsohn-Bau am Lehniner Platz*, 26, for the complete mix of apartment sizes, which included four- and-a-half-, four-, three-, and two-and-a-half-room layouts. For details of the four- and two-and-a-half-room plans, see Hans-Henning Joeres with Barbara Schulz, "Liste der Mehrfamilienhäuser, 1918–1945," in *Wohnungsbau*, Part B, *Die Wohngebäude – Einfamilienhäuser*, vol. 4 of *Berlin und seine Bauten* (Berlin: Ernst, 1975), 369–548, who date the block to 1926–28, following the dating given for the whole complex in Mendelsohn, *Complete Works*, 216. The Cicerostraße housing was first published, however, only in 1929, when a photograph of the balconies appeared in "Neue berliner Perspektive," *Der Welt-Spiegel, Berliner Tageblatt*, May 12, 1929: 2. The apartment-hotel appeared in "Apartmenthaus am Lehniner Platz in Berlin," *Bauwelt* 22.46 (1931): 21–28, and Heinz Johannes, *Neues Bauen in Berlin* (Berlin: Deutscher Kunst, 1931), 27. See Joeres and Schulz, "Liste," 510, for the details of Wagner's and Taut's housing.
54. And while Mendelsohn's brick street-front balconies provided a characteristically lively note, they were considerably more subdued than those Hugo Häring built in Siemenstadt in 1929. It is possible that Hans Scharoun's Am Parkring apartment houses in Insterburg

of 1924, illustrated in Christine Hoh-Slodczyk, Norbert Huse, Günther Kühne, and Andreas Tönnesmann, *Hans Scharoun – Architekt in Deutschland, 1893–1972* (München: Verlag C. H. Beck, 1992), 22, fig. 8, were a source for the Cicerostraße balconies.

55. Metzger and Dunker, *Kurfürstendamm*, 136. One was a Rudolf Mosse travel agency. Mosse travel bureau advertisement, *Berliner Tageblatt*, April 17, 1929.
56. L. Mendelsohn, "My Life," 98, refers to an English company's project for developing the hotel, which, as built, was scaled down from the plan illustrated in *Der Mendelsohn-Bau am Lehniner Platz*, 47.
57. "Eine neue Fassade Berlins," *Der Welt-Spiegel, Berliner Tageblatt*, March 24, 1929: 3. *Der Mendelsohn-Bau am Lehniner Platz*, 26, 45, and Mendelsohn, *Complete Works*, 222–23. See also Ditta Ahmadi, "Liste der Passagen, Ladenzeilen und Einkaufszentrum," *Bauten für Handel und Gewerbe*, 287.
58. Martin Wagner, "Das Formproblem eines Weltstadtplatzes," *Das neue Berlin* 1 (1929): 37.
59. Achim Wendschuh, "Brüder Luckhardt und Alfons Anker, Gemeinsame und einsame Werk-Jahre – eine Chronologie," *Brüder Luckhardt und Alfons Anker*, 154; Francesco Fresa, "Brüder Luckhardt und Alfons Anker: Werkverzeichnis und Bibliographie," *Brüder Luckhardt und Alfons Anker, Schriftenreihe der Akademie der Künste Berlin*, vol. 21 (Berlin: Akademie der Künste, 1991), 222–23; Wagner, "Das Formprobleme eines Weltstadtplatzes," 33–38; and Ludwig Hilberseimer's defense of Mies's losing entry, *Das neue Berlin* 1 (1929): 39–41. See also Huse, *"Neues Bauen,"* 109–12, and Scarpa, *Wagner*, 103–22.
60. *Der Schrei nach dem Turmhaus*, 167–85, and Neumann, *Wolkenkratzer*, 31. See also Werner Hegemann, "Das Hochhaus am Bahnhof Friedrichstraße," *Wasmuths Monatshefte für Baukunst* 14 (1930): 125–28, 191–95, especially Charles du Vinage, "Hochhaus Friedrichstraße," 191–92, a description of Mendelsohn's entry.
61. Hermann G. Pundt, *Schinkel's Berlin: A Study in Environmental Planning* (Cambridge: Harvard University Press, 1972), 63–67.
62. Janos Frecot and Helmut Geisert, eds., *Berlin im Abriss* (Berlin: Medusa, 1981), 73, and Horst Mauer, Lásló F. Föld'nyi, Ulrich Pfeiffer, and Alfred Kerndil, *Der Potsdamer Platz: Eine Geschichte in Wort und Bild* (Berlin: Nishen, 1991).
63. *Das neue Berlin* 1 (1929): 87; Hüter, *Berlin*, 353–54; and Scarpa, *Wagner*, 122–28. That the basic scheme, if not the published model, dated back to at least 1928 is confirmed by the description in "Am Potsdamer Platz wird gebaut: 'Galeries Lafayette,' " *Berliner Tageblatt*, May 5, 1928.
64. Harold Roos, "Berlins Fern-und Nahverkehr," *Das neue Berlin* 1 (1929): 142–43.
65. Frecot and Geisert, *Berlin*, 72.
66. "Das neue Gesicht des Potsdamer Platzes," *Berliner Tageblatt*, January 5, 1928.
67. "Gründung der Galeries Lafayette Akt.-Ges. in Berlin –15 Mil. M.

Kapital" and "Am Potsdamer Platz." See also "Neuer Krach um die Bellevue-Ecke," *Berliner Tageblatt*, February 24, 1928; "Um Galeries Lafayette" *Berliner Tageblatt*, November 16, 1928; and "Das neue Gesicht des Potsdamer Platzes."

68. "Am Potsdamer Platz" and "Die Warenhausecke am Potsdamer Platz," *Berliner Tageblatt*, July 21, 1928. Max Deubner, "Das Columbushaus," *Deutsches Bauwesen* 7.6 (1932): 43, for the figure of 500 square meters. Ernst Sagebiel, "Die Konstruktion des Columbus-Hauses, *Zentralblatt der Bauverwaltung* 52 (1932): 543, gives it as 550 square meters.
69. "Die Entwicklung zum Hochhaus," *Berliner Tageblatt*, May 24, 1931.
70. Norma Evenson, *Paris: A Century of Change, 1878–1978* (New Haven: Yale University Press, 1979), 150–52.
71. *Der Schrei nach dem Turmhaus*, 186–214, and Hüter, *Berlin*, 298–300. See Zevi, *Opera Completa*, 110, for Mendelsohn's imaginary skyscraper projects from the early twenties.
72. Stark, "Burohäuser," 183–204.
73. "Die Entwicklung zum Hochhaus" and "Hochhäuser in Berlin," *Zentralblatt der Bauverwaltung* 52 (1932): 542. See also Rainer Stommer, *Hochhaus: Der Beginn in Deutschland* (Marburg: Jonas, 1990), 15–16, 24–44, 159–65.
74. Mendelsohn, *Complete Works*, 236, and Erich Mendelsohn, "Das Columbushaus in Berlin in 29 Bildern," *Wasmuths Monatshefte für Baukunst* 27 (1933): 85. "The New Mendelsohn Building," *Architectural Review* 73 (1933): 57–63, is based upon this text.
75. "Das neue Gesicht des Potsdamer Platzes," *Der Welt-Spiegel, Berliner Tageblatt*, December 2, 1928: 10, and Mendelsohn, "Columbushaus," 82, where it was noted that it stood for two years. That the advertisements changed over time can be seen in two photographs published in Frecot and Geisert, *Berlin*, 74, 95.
76. Mendelsohn, *Complete Works*, 235.
77. Mendelsohn, "Columbushaus," 82.
78. Erich Mendelsohn, Martin Wagner, and Martin Kressling "Werden Wolkenkratzer," *Berliner Tageblatt*, September 25, 1928, and "Keine Galeries Lafayette," *Berliner Tageblatt*, February 5, 1929. See also Sagebiel, "Konstruktion," 543, who refers to a second refusal in 1930.
79. "Lafayette Hochhaus?" *Berliner Tageblatt*, June 13, 1929. See "Bellevue Strasse 2," *Berliner Tageblatt*, May 17, 1930, for the assertion by a right-wing city councilor that the Galeries Lafayette organizers had bribed four members of the council to gain their support for the project.
80. "Lafayette im Westen," *Berliner Tageblatt*, August 13, 1929. The French firm intended to hire Philip Schaefer to design their Westend store. Schaefer's recent Karstadt store had been the first major department store in this part of Berlin and the only significant Weimar-era store in the city designed completely independently of Mendelsohn's influence.

81. "Kolumbushaus [sic]," *Berliner Tageblatt*, March 29, 1931; Erich Mendelsohn, "Das Hochhaus am Potsdamer Platz," *Bauwelt* 22 (1931): 447; and Bellevue-Immobilien A. G. advertisement, *Technische Rundschau, Berliner Tageblatt*, February 3, 1932: 8. "Das Hochhaus am Potsdamer Platz," was reprinted in *Technische Rundschau, Berliner Tageblatt*, February 3, 1932: 1, and in Werner Hegemann, "Luckhardts und Erich Mendelsohn's Neubauten am Potsdamer Platz," *Wasmuths Monatshefte für Baukunst* 15 (1931): 232.
82. Hrant Pasdermadjian, *The Department Store* (1956; New York Times, 1976), 45.
83. Stark, "Bürohäuser der Privatwirtschaft," 157–59; Hegemann, "Neubauten am Potsdamer Platz," 226–32; Wendschuh, *Brüder Luckhardt*, 154–55; and Fresa, *Brüder Luckhardt*, 230.
84. Mendelsohn, "Columbushaus," 60.
85. Mendelsohn, "Columbushaus," 81–85.
86. Sagebiel, "Konstruktion," 543.

CHAPTER 5

1. Hermand and Trommler, *Kultur*, esp. 56, 404–5; Samson, "German-American Dialogues," 239–46; and Klaus Popitz, *Plakate der Zwanziger Jahre aus der Kunstbibliothek Berlin* (Berlin: Staatliche Museen Preußischer Kulturbesitz, 1987). Mendelsohn's imitation of the language of advertising also appeared in Alfred Döblin's novel *Berlin Alexanderplatz*. Döblin even wrote an article on advertising and literature, "Reklame und Literatur," *Reklame und Publikum, Berliner Tageblatt*, August 10, 1929.
2. Alain Weill, "Advertising Art," 226–35, and Victoria de Grazia, "The American Challenge to the European Art of Advertising," 236–48, both in Clair, *The 1920s*; Stuart Ewan, *Captains of Consciousness: Advertising and the Social Roots of the Consumer Culture* (New York: McGraw-Hill, 1977), 41–109; and Roland Marchand, *Advertising the American Dream* (Berkeley: University of California Press, 1985).
3. Mendelsohn, *Amerika*, 54, 52.
4. The pun comes from Robert Venturi, "A Bill-Ding Board Involving Movies, Relics, and Space," *Architectural Forum* 128.4 (1968): 74.
5. Hays, *Modernism*, 23–147.
6. C. A. Herpich Söhne advertisements, *Berliner Tageblatt*, June 29 and July 2, 1927.
7. Osborn et al., *Berlins Aufstieg, 67.* Carl August's sons also had founded separate stores in Leipzig, the traditional center of the German fur trade, and in New York. The Berlin store also had branches in London and Paris until the war forced their abandonment.
8. C. A. Herpich Söhne advertisement, *Berliner Tageblatt*, January 5, 1919, mentions skirts and blouses; additional advertisements, *Ber-*

liner Tageblatt, June 29 and July 3, 1927, draw attention to the firm's carpet business.

9. Henrik Schnedler, "Kaufhäuser," *Handel und Gewerbe*, Part A, 136.
10. C. A. Herpich Söhne advertisement, *Berliner Tageblatt*, January 5, 1919, gives only these addresses. The resemblance of the first sketches to the bays of the original numbers 9 and 11 buildings suggests that Herpich did not yet own number 13. Werner Hegemann, "Eine wichtige Berliner Stadtbauanfrage," *Städtebau* 20 1925): 156, illustrates the original buildings.
11. Mendelsohn, *Complete Works*, 104, illustrates the first phase of the completed building. See also Hegemann, "Berliner Neubauten," 194–97, figs. 18–21.
12. Werner Hegemann, "Neue Baukunst und Wohnungspolitik," *Wasmuths Monatshefte für Baukunst* 13 (1929): 1, first published a photograph of the entire building in January.
13. Werner Hegemann, "Die Strasse als Einheit," *Städtebau* 20 (1925): 106, and Paul Schaefer, "Vermischtes: Ein interessantes berliner Fassadengerüst," *Deutsche Bauzeitung* 59 (1925): 191–92.
14. Fresa, "Brüder Luckhardt und Alfons Anker," 91, and Taut, *Frühlicht,* 77, 117, 214, 222–23.
15. Deutsche Travertine und Marmorwerke Ladensatze Karl Teich advertisement, *Wasmuths Monatshefte für Baukunst* 11.10 (1927): i, identifies the stone as "Kelheimer Auerkalkstein." Schultz and Holdefluß advertisement, *Architektur und Schaufenster* 24.6 (1927): unpaginated, takes credit for the bronze. Hugo Häring, "Probleme in der Lichtreklame," *Bauhaus: Zeitschrift für Gestaltung* 2 (1928): 7, commented in 1928 that new displays erased the boundary between the store and the street.
16. For instance, Zevi, *Opera Completa*, 113, fig. 1. These bays, originally rectangular, in later drawings became cylinders with windows etched into one side. See p. 112, fig. 2.
17. K. Werner Schulze, "Geschäfts- und Warenhäuser," *Der Industriebau* 20 (1929): 218, and Stürzebecher, "Warenhäuser," 9–10.
18. Quoted in Hays, *Modernism*, 165. See also Winfried van der Will, "The Body and the Body Politic as Symptom and Metaphor in the Transition of German Culture to National Socialism," in *The Nazification of Art: Art, Design, Music, Architecture and Film in the Third Reich*, ed. Brandon Taylor and Winfried van der Will (Winchester: Winchester Press, 1990), 29–43.
19. W. Kreis, "Das neue Bauschaffen," *Deutsches Bauwesen* 6 (1930): 74, 77, fig. 10. See also "Heilige Sonne: ewiges Licht," *Der Welt-Spiegel, Berliner Tageblatt*, October 14, 1928: 46, which illustrates Mendelsohn's Petersdorff store.
20. Werner Hegemann, *Facades of Buildings* (London: Benn, 1929), 27. See also Platz, *Baukunst*, 86–87, and Alphens Schneegans, "Vom Schaufenster zur Schauhalle," *Deutsche Bauzeitung* 63 (1929): 820.
21. Karl-Ernst Osthaus, "Das Schaufenster," *Jahrbuch des Deutschen Werkbundes* (1913): 59–69, and Klaus Strohmeyer, *Warenhäuser,*

Geschichte, Blüte, und Untergang im Warenmeer (Berlin: Wagenbach, 1980), 143–50. See also Jürgen Krause, "Reklame-Kultur," in *1910 Halbzeit der Moderne: van de Velde, Behrens, Hoffmann und die Anderen*, ed. Klaus-Jürgen Sembach (Stuttgart: Hatje, 1992), 185–202, and Sherwin Simmons *"Kitsch oder Kunst?* Kokoschka's *Der Sturm* and Commerce in Art," *The Print Collector's Newsletter* 23 (1992): 162–63.

22. Johannes Molzahn, "Economics of the Advertising Mechanism," in Benton et al., *Form and Function*, 226; *Architektur und Schaufenster* 24–25 (1927–28), originally a supplement of *Die Konfektion*, the German textile industry trade journal; and Geno Ohlischlaeger, "Schaufensterdekorationen: Die künstlerische Ausgestaltung der Schaufenster," *Berliner Tageblatt*, December 30, 1924. See also Jean-Paul Bouillon, "The Shop Window," in Clair, *The 1920s*, 162–81, who identifies the roots of this development in the Wiener Werkstätte.
23. For the prewar roots of this point of view, see Buddensieg, *Industriekultur*, 14–15, while its postwar Soviet corollary is examined in John E. Bowlt, "A Brazen Can-Can in the Temple of Art: The Russian Avant-garde and Popular Culture," *Modern Art and Popular Culture, Readings in High and Low*, ed. Kirk Varnadoe and Adam Gopnik (New York: Museum of Modern Art, 1990), 134–58. The persuasive communicative strategies of the Berlin Dada circle, which manipulated American advertising techniques and other aspects of mass culture to advance radical political as well as commercial goals are seen by Tower, *Envisioning America*, 63–80, but not Lavin, *Cut with the Kitchen Knife*, as an exception. So, according to Hays, *Modernism*, was Hannes Meyer.
24. For a discussion of the larger cultural implications of this shift, see Samson, "German-American Dialogues," esp. 93–155.
25. Ernst Reinhardt, "Gestaltung der Lichtreklame," *Die Form* 4 (1929): 74, and Wilhelm Schnarrenberger, "Reklamearchitektur bildend," *Die Form* 3 (1928): 268–72.
26. Adolf Behne, "Kultur, Kunst und Reklame," *Neues Bauen, neues Gestalten: Das neue Frankfurt; Die neue Stadt: eine Zeitschrift zwischen 1926 und 1933*, Heinz Hirdina, ed. (Dresden: VEB Verlag der Kunste, 1984), 229–32; Adolf Behne, "Kunstausstellung Berlin," *Das neue Berlin* 1 (1929): 150–52; Walter Dexel, "Reklame in Stadtbild," *Das neue Frankfurt* 1 (1926): 45–49; Häring, "Probleme," 7; Ludwig Hilberseimer, "Die neue Geschäftstraße," in Hirdina, *Neues Bauen*, 235–40; and Ernst May, "Städtebau und Lichtreklame," in *Licht und Beleuchtung*, ed. Wilhelm Lotz (Berlin: Reckendorf, 1928), 45 (a Werkbund publication), republished in translation as "Town Planning and Illuminated Advertisements," Benton et al., *Form and Function*, 238–40. Even Siegfried Kracauer, among the most critical of left-wing intellectuals, recognized the artistic possibilities inherent in mass culture and preferred their expression to historicist escapism, arguing in his essay "The Mass Ornament" that "the pleasure gained from the mass ornament is

legitimate. . . . No matter how low one rates the value of mass ornament, its level of reality is still above that of artistic production which cultivates absolute noble sentiments in withered forms." Siegfried Kracauer, "The Mass Ornament," trans. Barbara Correll and Jack Zipes, *New German Critique* 5 (1975): 70. This appreciation of advertising as a form of modern art was not shared by architects based in countries where commercial architecture continued to be dominated by those whose skills were primarily decorative. See Theo van Doesburg, "Paris 1925: Exposition internationale des arts décoratifs et industriels modernes" and "New Accommodation Standards," in *On European Architecture*, 41–44, 98–103.

27. Behne, "Kunstausstellung Berlin," 150–52. His view echoed that of Frantz Jourdain's turn-of-the-century appreciation of French advertising posters. See Meredith Clausen, *Frantz Jourdain and the Samaritaine: Art Nouveau Theory and Criticism* (Leiden: E. J. Brill, 1987), 114–18.
28. One of his articles on the subject was illustrated in part with images from Mendelsohn's book, as was the more critical Dexel, "Reklame," 45, fig. 1.
29. This typical German romanticizing of America contrasts with the situation described by Weill and de Grazia.
30. Behne, "Kultur, Kunst und Reklame," 229. Mendelsohn had been far less optimistic about the content of these illustrations.
31. Taut, *Frühlicht*, 77, 117, 214, 222–23. For his interest in new dramatic forms, including his plans for a Kandinsky-like pageant, see Benson, *Expressionist Utopias*, 294–98.
32. Bayer et al., *Bauhaus*, 20–21, 146–50, and Christoph Mohr and Michael Müller, *Functionalität und Moderne: Das neue Frankfurt und seine Bauten, 1925–1933* (Köln: Edition Fricke im Rudolf Miller Verlag, 1984), 177–85. Kurt Schwitters and Laszlo Moholy-Nagy ran their own advertising agencies, and John Heartfield and Hannah Hoch made montages for commercial as well as for political purposes. See the Bronx Museum of Art, *Moholy-Nagy: Fotoplastikers: The Bauhaus Years* (New York: Bronx Museum of Art, 1983), 21; Maud Lavin, "Advertising Utopia: Schwitters as Commercial Designer," *Art in America* 73.10 (1985): 134–39; Matthew Teitelbaum, ed., *Montage and Modern Life, 1919–1942* (Cambridge: MIT Press, 1992), esp. Maud Lavin, "Photomontage, Mass Culture, and Modernity: Utopianism in the Circle of New Advertising Designers," 36–59; Lavin, *Cut with the Kitchen Knife*, esp. 47–68; and Hans Wingler, *The Bauhaus: Weimar, Dessau, Berlin, Chicago*, trans. Wolfgang Jabs and Basil Gilbert (Cambridge: MIT Press, 1969), 480–83, 515.
33. Adolf Schmidt-Volker, "Die Reklameabteilung in einem modernen Geschäftsbetrieb," *Das Geschäft* 1 (1924): 50.
34. Pasdermadjian, *Department Store*, 45.
35. Paul Mazur, *Principles of Organization Applied to Modern Retailing* (New York: Harper, 1927), published in German as *Modern*

Warenhaus-Organisation (Berlin, 1928). According to his son Gabriel, Mendelsohn's patron Epstein traveled to America in the mid-twenties to study New York's department stores. See also H. G. Reissner, "The Histories of 'Kaufhaus N. Israel' and of Wilfried Israel," *Leo Baeck Institute Yearbook* 3 (1958): 241, for a study trip made in 1927–28 by a member of this department store family.

36. Joseph Siry, *Carson, Pirie Scott, Louis Sullivan and the Chicago Department Store* (Chicago: University of Chicago Press, 1988), 128–39.
37. Mendelsohn, *Complete Works*, 105, 108.
38. Adolf Schuhmacher, *Ladenbau* (Stuttgart: Hoffmann, 1934), 75, figs. 5–7, on the importance of this lighting scheme to the impact of the facade's graphics. For its replacement in 1930 with blue neon lights that followed the curves of the two side wings, see *Baumeister* 21 (1930): 9.
39. August Endell, *Die Schönheit der großen Stadt* (Stuttgart: Verlag von Strecker and Schröder, 1908), 61.
40. The pages of *Die Berliner illustrirte Zeitung* and of *Der Welt-Spiegel*, the illustrated Sunday supplement of the *Berliner Tageblatt*, are full of *Lichtreklame*, and trace the path from an interest in foreign, especially American, examples, to the birth of homegrown ones.
41. "Statistik der Lichtreklame," *Berliner Tageblatt*, April 3, 1928.
42. Hermann Muthesius, "Architektur und Lichtreklame," *Berliner Tageblatt*, January 8, 1925, introduced the position on *Lichtreklame*, which then became a staple of articles in the Werkbund monthly *Die Form*. See also Werner Oechslin, "Lichtarchitektur," in *Architektur – licht – architektur*, ed. Ingeborg Flagge (Stuttgart: Karl Krämer Verlag, 1991), 101–18, and idem, "Lichtarchitektur," Lampugnani and Schneider, *Expressionismus und Neue Sachlichkeit*, 117–31.
43. "Umbau Herpich, Berlin," *Architektur und Schaufenster* 24.3 (1927): 9; "Neue berliner Architektur," *Der Welt-Spiegel, Berliner Tageblatt*, April 10, 1927: 2; and Max Landsbert, "Lichtreklame und Fassadenarchitektur," *Deutsche Bauzeitung* 61 (1927): 678, figs. 9, 10.
44. May, "Städtebau und Lichtreklame," 239–40.
45. Lotz, *Licht und Beleuchtung*, 62. See also Wilhelm Lotz, "Berlin im Licht," *Die Form* 3 (1928): 358–59.
46. Reinhardt, "Gestaltung," 73–84.
47. Bärbel Schrader and Jürgen Schebera, *Kunstmetropole Berlin, 1918–1933, Die Kunststadt in der Novemberrevolution; Die "Goldenenr" Zwanziger; Die Kunststadt in der Krise* (Berlin: Aufbau, 1987), 136–40.
48. Hüter, *Berlin*, 335. Berlin blackouts were reported in the *Berliner Tageblatt* on January 22, 1919, March 26, 1920, and November 6, 1920. Krausse, "Gebaute Weltbilder," 35, cites, without giving a source, as a more personal possible source for Mendelsohn's interest in lighting his wartime experience with searchlights.

49. Arthur Korn, *Glass in Modern Architecture* (1929; London: Barie and Rockeff, 1967), unpaginated.
50. "Der Neubau Petersdorff, Breslau," *Architektur und Schaufenster* 25.5 (1928): unpaginated, and Georg Grimm, *Kauf-und Warenhäuser* (Berlin: Schottländer, 1928), 324.
51. "Der Neubau Petersdorff, Breslau," 1928, unpaginated, includes a photograph of the earlier buildings on the site.
52. Mendelsohn, *Complete Works*, 201.
53. The caption to an illustration in *Die Baugilde* 10 (1928): 1130, notes that the steelwork was done by Breest and Company of Breslau.
54. Walter Curt Behrendt, *Der Sieg des neuen Baustils* (Stuttgart: Wedekind, 1927), 33, describes the Wilhelmstraße facade of the Weichmann silk store as a precedent for this cantilever.
55. "Der Neubau Petersdorff, Breslau," 1928, unpaginated.
56. Meeting notes, June 13, 1927, Salman Schocken archive, Schocken Institute for Jewish Research of the Jewish Theological Seminary of America, Jerusalem.
57. Deutsches Kupfer Institut advertisement, *Moderne Bauformen* 28 (1929): 2. It was constructed by Schultz and Holdefleiss of Berlin, who installed windows supplied by R. Blume, also of Berlin, the only firms from outside Breslau, besides Mendelsohn's own office, whose work on the building is recorded. Werner Hegemann, "Mendelsohn und Hoetger ist nicht 'fast ganz die Selbe," *Wasmuths Monatshefte für Baukunst* 12 (1928): 419, and "Firmenregister," *Architektur und Schaufenster* 25.5 (1928): unpaginated.
58. Deutsche Kupfer Institut 3.
59. Emil Lange, "Ein Geschäftshaus von Erich Mendelsohn," *Schlesische Monatshefte* 5 (1928): 199.
60. Hegemann, "Mendelsohn und Hoetger," 419, and Hilberseimer, "Die neue Geschäftstraße," 238.
61. Mendelsohn, "Own Work," 7.
62. "Der Neubau Petersdorff, Breslau," 1928, unpaginated. The night view of the building appeared in "Was gibt es Neues in Breslau," *Berliner illustrirte Zeitung*, November 17, 1929: 2084. "Firmenregister" unpaginated, credits the Breslau firm of George Frey and Company with installing the lighting.
63. Lotz, *Licht und Beleuchtung*, 62. See also W. Kreis, "Das neue Bauschaffen," *Deutsches Bauwesen* 6 (1930): 74, 77, fig. 10.
64. Erich Mendelsohn, "Die moderne Industriebau auf dem Kontinent," *Europaische Revue* 5 (1929): 478.
65. Mendelsohn, *Complete Works*, 141.
66. Stephan, *Studien*, 96–107, for the best discussion of this building.
67. "Leiser-Filiale Schonhauser Allee 80, Berlin Nord, Architekt Dipl.-Ing. Erich Mendelsohn," *Bauwelt* 21 (1930): 15–16, and "Leiser-Schuh-Filiale," *Die Form* 6 (1931): 371–78.
68. Stuart Ewen and Elizabeth Ewen, *Channels of Desire: Mass Images and the Shaping of American Consciousness* (Minneapolis: University of Minnesota Press, 1992): 141.

69. Ludwig Hiberseimer, "Internationale neue Baukunst," *Moderne Bauformen* 9 (1927): 332, paired the Herpich store with the Bauhaus.
70. Anne Friedberg, *Window Shopping: Cinema and the Postmodern* (Berkeley: University of California Press, 1993) on the relationship between department stores and cinemas.
71. Ewen and Ewen, *Channels of Desire*, 18–20.
72. Bartetzko, *Illusionen in Stein*, 224–74; Bartetzko, *Zucht und Ekstase*, 133–65; Michael Esser, "Spaces in Motion: Remarks on Set Design in the German Silent Film," in Buddensieg, *Berlin*, 169–83; Hermand and Trommler, *Kultur*, 151–58; Anton Kaes, "Mass Culture and Modernity: Notes Toward a Social History of Early American and German Cinema," in *The Relationship in the Twentieth Century*, vol. 2 of *America and the Germans; An Assessment of a Three-Hundred-Year History*, ed. Frank Trommler and Joseph McVeigh (Philadelphia: University of Pennsylvania Press, 1985), 317–31; and Siegfried Kracauer, *From Calgari to Hitler, A Psychological History of the German Film* (Princeton: Princeton University Press, 1947).
73. P. Morton Shand, *Modern Theater and Cinema Architecture* (London, 1930), 15, 20, and 24, and 27. As noted in D. St., "Ausseneffekte an den Kinos," *Berliner Tageblatt*, January 29, 1925, the night lighting of cinemas was originally introduced from America. However, it was first used in Germany in conjunction with an emerging modern architectural style. See also Ditta Ahmadei, "Lichtspieltheater," and "Liste der Lichtspieltheater" *Bauwerke für Kunst, Erziehung und Wissenschaft*, Part A, *Bauten für Kunst*, vol. 5 of *Berlin und seine Bauten* (Berlin: Ernst, 1983, 162–206; Rolf-Peter Baacke, *Lichtspielhausarchitektur in Deutschland von der Schaubühne bis zum Kinopalast* (Berlin: Frölich und Kaufmann, 1982); Peter Boeger, *Architektur der Lichtspieltheater in Berlin: Bauten und Projekte, 1919–1930* (Berlin: Verlag Willmuth Arenhövel, 1993); Klaus Kreimeier, *Die Ufa-Story: Geschichte eines Filmkonzerns* (München: Carl Hanser Verlag, 1992), esp. 133–46; Francis Lacloche, *Architecture de Cinemas* (Paris: Moniteur, 1981); Thomas J. Saunders, *Hollywood in Berlin: American Cinema and Weimar Germany* (Berkeley: University of California Press, 1994); and Dennis Sharp, *The Picture Palace and other Buildings for the Movies* (London: Praeger, 1969).
74. Sabine Röder, "Traumspiele mit Kulissen," *Der dramatische Raum: Hans Poelzig, Malerei Theater Film* (Krefeld: Krefeld Kunstmuseen, 1986), 8. Erich Mendelsohn, letter to Luise Mendelsohn, June 17, 1920, Beyer, *Letters*, 54, describes the tour Poelzig had just given him through this building. Posener, *Poelzig*, 122, notes Marlene Moeschke Poelzig's contribution to the design of the lobby columns.
75. Ahmadi, "Lichtspieltheater," *Bauwerke für Kunst, Erziehung und Wissenschaft*, Part A, *Bauten für die Kunst*, vol. 5 of *Berlin und Seine Bauten*, 169–171; Ahmadi, "Liste der Lichtspieltheater," *Bauwerke für Kunst*, 192; Baacke, *Lichtspielhausarchitektur*, 34–35;

and Boeger, *Lichtspieltheater*, 59–68; Posener, *Poelzig*, 165–70, 196–97.

76. Siegfried Kracauer, "Ansichtspostkarte," originally published in the *Frankfurter Zeitung* on May 26, 1930, reprinted in *Straßen in Berlin und anderswo* (Berlin: Das Arsenal, 1987), 37.
77. Siegfried Kracauer, "Cult of Distraction: On Berlin's Picture Palaces," trans. Thomas Y. Levin, *New German Critique* 40 (1987): 91–92.
78. Ahmadi, "Lichtspieltheater," 172–74; Ahmadi, "Liste der Lichtspieltheater," 194–95; Baacke, *Lichtspielhausarchitektur*, 45–46; and Boeger, *Lichtspieltheater*, 97–102.
79. David Naylor, *American Picture Palaces: The Architecture of Fantasy* (New York: Prentice Hall, 1981), and Maggie Valentine, *The Show Starts on the Sidewalk: An Architectural History of the Movie Theater, Starring S. Charles Lee* (New Haven: Yale University Press, 1994).
80. Garth Jowett, *Film: The Democratic Art* (Boston: Little, Brown and Company, 1976), and Ewen and Ewen, *Channels of Desire*, 71–72.
81. Erich Mendelsohn, "Zur Eröffnung des 'Universum,' " *Der Montag*, September 17, 1928, republished in *Der Mendelsohn-Bau am Lehniner Platz*, 49, and in translation in Dennis Sharp, *Modern Architecture and Expressionism* (New York: Braziller, 1966), 126.
82. "Ein Lichtspieltheater," *Die Form* 4 (1929): 85–87.
83. Zevi, *Opera Completa*, 155–63.
84. This device appeared in 1925 in the power station of his Leningrad factory and again in 1927 in his project for an exhibition hall near the Berlin Zoo. The exhibition hall project, published in Mendelsohn, *Complete Works*, 168–69, provided the precedent for the specific advertising function of the tower and influenced the location and design of the shops.
85. Early views of the building show the sign advertising itself and the neighboring shops and apartments. The rental office for all three was located in one of the cinema building's shops.
86. Günther Herkt, "Das UFA-Lichtspielhaus 'Universum' in Berlin," *Deutsche Bauzeitung* 63 (1929): 176.
87. Theodor Böll, quoted in *Die Metropole: Industriekultur in Berlin am Anfang des 20. Jahrhunderts*, ed. Jochen Boberg, Tilmann Fichter, and Eckhardt Gillen (München: Beck, 1986), 100. For the earlier design, see *Der Mendelsohn-Bau am Lehniner Platz*, 52.
88. "Ein Lichtspieltheater," 85–87; H. Bauer, "Erich Mendelsohn: Lichtspielhaus 'Universum,' " *Das Kunstblatt* 14 (1930): 106–8; A. D., "Erich Mendelsohns Architektur," *Berliner Tageblatt*, September 17, 1928, reprinted in *Der Mendelsohn-Bau am Lehniner Platz*, 67; and Günter Herkt, "Probleme des Tonfilm Theaters," *Wasmuths Monatshefte für Baukunst* 13 (1929): 429–34. See also *Der Mendelsohn-Bau am Lehniner Platz*, 53–54, for Mendelsohn's account of the building, focusing on the safety of its escape routes, which accompanied his April 28, 1928, application for a building permit.

89. Mendelsohn, *Complete Works*, 231, and "The Universum Cinema, Berlin, Erich Mendelsohn Architect," *Architect's Journal* 75 (1932): supplement.
90. These are illustrated and described in A. Wedemeyer, "Die Moderne Künstliche Beleuchtung," *Deutsche Bauzeitung* 65 (1931): 80. Wedemeyer, "Beleuchtung," 83, also illustrates a display window designed by Mendelsohn for an otherwise unidentified Herpich store in which rows of similar light troughs frame the space.
91. Reyner Banham, *The Architecture of the Well-Tempered Environment* (Chicago: University of Chicago Press, 1984), 201–3, on the lighting of the the two Herpich stores and their relationship to the Universum auditorium. Banham conflates the exterior of 9–13 Leipzigerstraße of 1924 with the Herpich shop of 1927 at 123a.
92. Mendelsohn, "Zur Eröffnung," 49. For a direct view from the projection booth towards the screen, see *Baumeister* 21 (1930): 10.
93. Mendelsohn, *Complete Works*, 232, and Mendelsohn, "Zur Eröffnung," 49. David Atwell, *Cathedrals of the Movies* (London: Architectural Press, 1980), 62, cites the influence throughout Europe of the Universum's aisleless auditorium.
94. A. D., "Erich Mendelsohns Architektur," 67.
95. Howard Robertson and F. R. Yerbury, "The Architecture of Tension," *The Architect and Builders' News* 122 (1929): 707.

CHAPTER 6

1. Stephen, *Studien*, fig. 30.
2. Paul Westheim, "Zeitlupe," *Das Kunstblatt* 14 (1930): 219, for Schocken's reading of Loos. Salman Schocken, speech delivered in Jerusalem on the occasion of Erich Mendelsohn's fiftieth birthday, March 15, 1937, typescript, Schocken archive, claimed that the stores were the least expensive erected in Weimar Germany. See also Siegfried Moses, "Salman Schocken: His Economic and Zionist Activities," *Leo Baeck Institute Yearbook* 5 (1960): 79. According to his son Gabriel's conversation with the author in March 1989, Henry Epstein, a part-owner of the Cohen-Epstein store in Duisburg for which Mendelsohn built an addition in 1926, was a friend of Schocken's and a fellow Zionist.
3. Mendelsohn, *Rußland*, 185, and Erich Mendelsohn, letter to Luise Mendelsohn, August 15, 1925, Beyer, *Letters*, 87.
4. Moses, "Schocken." 73–104, and Konrad Fuchs, *Ein Konzern aus Sachsen: Das Kaufhaus Schocken als Spiegelbild deutscher Wirtschaft und Politik, 1900 bis 1953* (Stuttgart: Deutsche Verlags-Anstalt, 1992).
5. Rainer Stommer, "Vom Traumpalast zum Warencontainer. Die Warenhausarchitektur der zwanziger Jahre," *Deutsche Bauzeitung* 124. 10 (1990): 142, identifies the former Schocken store in Crimmitschau, built in 1928, as a Mendelsohn building. Stephan, *Studien*, 30, demonstrates that it was actually the work of Bernhard Sturtzkopf. The Schocken archive includes albums devoted to each

store. Each gives basic information about the building and includes exterior photographs and some plans. Mendelsohn is the only architect Schocken employed named in the albums.

6. Moses, "Schocken," 76–81. See also Susan Porter Benson, *Counter Cultures: Saleswomen, Managers, and Customers in American Department Stores, 1890–1940* (Urbana: University of Illinois Press, 1986), 64–66 for a description of "scientific" retailing, a similar merchandising strategy pioneered by American department store owner Edward Filene, and Salman Schocken's "Zur Eröffnung des Kaufhauses Schocken in Nürnberg," October 11, 1926, lecture, printed text, Schocken archive.
7. Pasdermadjian, *Department Store*, and Julius Hirsch, "Die Warenhäuser wachsen," *Berliner Tageblatt*, August 26, 1926.
8. Salman Schocken, *Die Entwicklung der Warenhäuser in Deutschland* (Leipzig, n.d.). See also Salman Schocken, "Warenhausbauten," *Der Kaufmann und das Leben* (1913) 1–6, 33–39.
9. Ilustrated in Fuchs, *Konzern aus Sachsen*, 23.
10. Schocken, March 15, 1937, speech, Schocken archive.
11. Kurt Blumenfeld, *Im Kampf um den Zionismus, Briefe aus fünf Jahrzehnten*, ed. Miriam Sambursky and Jochanan Ginat (Stuttgart: Deutsche, 1976), 86. Blumenfeld had also introduced Mendelsohn to Pinkas Rutenberg, whose offer of a commission to design a power plant in Haifa, never built, took Mendelsohn to Palestine in 1923.
12. Schocken, March 15, 1937, speech.
13. *Neue Baukunst* 5.8 (1929): 4–5. This is not the building illustrated in Fuchs, *Konzern aus Sachsen*, 102.
14. Berlin office album, Schocken archive, includes a plan bearing Mendelsohn's initials. He may have had a hand, as well, in an addition made in 1927 to the Zwickau store. Schocken, March 15, 1937, speech, refers to Mendelsohn's "Stuttgart, Zwickau, and Chemnitz" stores. The Zwickau album, Schocken archive, includes minimal documentation of the 1927 facade, which resembles Mendelsohn's Deukon Haus, built the same year in Berlin.
15. Stephen M. Poppel, "Salman Schocken and the Schocken Verlag," *Leo Baeck Institute Yearbook* 17 (1972): 93–113.
16. Else Lasker Schüler, *"Was soll ich hier tun?": Exilbriefe an Salman Schocken: dokumentarische Erstausgabe mit vier Briefen Schockens im Anhang* (Heidelberg: Schneider, 1986). See also Gershom Scholem, ed., *The Correspondence of Walter Benjamin and Gerschom Scholem, 1932–1940*, trans. Gary Smith and Andre Lefevre (New York: Schocken, 1989).
17. Moses, "Schocken," 86–88.
18. Meredith Clausen, "The Department Store – Development of the Type," *Journal of Architectural Education* 39:1 (1985): 20–29; John Williams Ferry, *A History of the Department Store* (New York: Macmillan, 1960); Robert Hendrickson, *The Grand Emporiums: The Illustrated History of America's Great Department Stores* (New York: Stern and Day, 1979); Michael B. Miller, *The Bon Marché: Bourgeois Culture and the Department Store, 1869–*

1920 (Princeton: Princeton University Press, 1981), 165–69; Pasdermadjian, *Department Store*; and Rosalind Williams, *Dream Worlds: Mass Consumption in Late Nineteenth-Century France* (Berkeley: University of California Press, 1982), 1–15.

19. Neil Harris, "Shopping – Chicago Style," in *Chicago Architecture, 1872–1922: Birthplace of a Metropolis*, ed. John Zukowsky (Munich: Prestel-Verlag, 1987), 137–55, and Siry, *Carson, Pirie, Scott.*
20. Benson, *Counter Cultures*, and Miller, *Bon Marché*, 165–69.
21. Behn, "Warenhauses"; Strohmeyer, *Warenhäuser*; and Stürzebecher, "Warenhäuser," 1–28.
22. Hilberseimer, *Großstadt*, 57, compared the "material romanticism" of Mies van der Rohe's fully glazed skyscraper projects to Mendelsohn's pragmatic approach in Nuremberg.
23. As demonstrated by the frequency with which it was published. In addition to the sources cited below, see "Eine neuer Warenhaustyp," *Der Welt-Spiegel, Berliner Tageblatt*, December 25, 1926: 2; Grimm, *Kauf- und Warenhäuser*, 63–64; Müller-Wulckow, *Architektur*, vol. 1, pl. 97; and Hilberseimer, *Großstadt*, 57–58.
24. Salman Schocken and Overberg (Mendelsohn's project manager for the commission), telephone conversation transcript, May 28, 1926, Schocken archive, and Schocken, March 15, 1937, speech. For a more detailed account of the store and its design, see Stephan, *Studien*, 83–95.
25. Salman Schocken, letter to Erich Mendelsohn, June 15, 1926, copy, Schocken archive.
26. Salman Schocken and Overberg, telephone conversation transcript, May 28, 1926, Schocken archive.
27. His work required no continuity with the third facade, which was separated by a corner building from the rest of the store. "Um die neue Gestaltung," *Das neue Frankfurt* 2 (1928): 171, and Nuremberg album, Schocken archive, which contain unpublished photographs of the building and documents minor alterations in 1928, 1929, and 1931. See Centrum Industriekultur Nürnberg, *Architektur in Nürnberg, 1900–1980* (Stuttgart; Gerd Hatje, 1981), 67, for a photograph that gives a glimpse of the existing structure.
28. Entrance to the store entailed walking past additional displays. An 80-centimeter deep extension of the show windows screened the Aufseßplatz facade from the entrance vestibule. "Das neue Kaufhaus Schocken in Nürnberg," *Architektur und Schaufenster* 24.1 (1927): 3.
29. "Kaufhaus Schocken," 3, for the basic interior layout of the Nuremberg store. For the Herpich interior, see Mendelsohn, *Complete Works*, 105; for Petersdorff, Otto Zucker, "Konstruktion und Architektur," *Wasmuths Monatshefte für Baukunst* 14 (1930): 477–78; Heinrich Klette, "Der neue architektonische Stil des Geschäftshauses," *Der Welt-Speigel, Berliner Tageblatt*, May 20, 1928: 2, who notes that Heinrich Tischler, a local architect, designed the cabinetry and selected the furnishings; "Ladenmöbel,"

Die Form 4 (1929): 434; and "Firmenregister," *Architektur und Schaufenster* 25.5 (1928): unpaginated.

30. Salman Schocken, letter to Erich Mendelsohn, September 24, 1926, Schocken archive, stressed the importance of the store's opening to his architect, asking Mendelsohn to arrive two weeks early to work on such final details as the interior colors.
31. Schocken, "Zur Eröffnung": "Es wird jetzt viel über Typisierung und Normierung gesprochen; mehr gesprochen, als getan."
32. Schocken, "Zur Eröffnung": Die Kunst eines Meisters zeigt sich in der Fähigkeit der Auslese, der Reduktion, in der Fähigkeit, vom Unwesentlichen abzusehen, das Stoffliche zu beschränken, die tragenden Säulen zu erkennen, mit wenigen Hauptlinien das Notwendige zu gestalten."
33. Erich Mendelsohn, speech delivered at the opening of the Nuremberg Schocken store, October 11, 1926, Beyer, *Letters*, 93–94, excerpted in *Literarische Welt* 4.10 (1928): 1, and as Erich Mendelsohn, "Gestalte deine Zeit!" *Innen Dekoration* 37 (1927): 47.
34. Erich Mendelsohn, October 11, 1926, speech, Beyer, *Letters*, 94.
35. Erich Mendelsohn, October 11, 1926, speech, Beyer, *Letters*, 95.
36. The design and construction of the Schocken store in Stuttgart offer one of the best-documented opportunities to study Mendelsohn at work. Schocken kept copies of the letters between the offices of patron and architect; with the same passion for detail that often exasperated his architect, he also made typewritten transcripts of telephone conversations. An unusual number of surviving autograph drawings supplement this written record; there are also a few construction photographs. The entire written archive is in the Schocken archive. The drawings are in the Mendelsohn archive.
37. Salman Schocken, letter to Erich Mendelsohn, April 26, 1927, Schocken archive, quotes from Erich Mendelsohn, letter to Salman Schocken, January 10, 1926.
38. Erich Mendelsohn, letter to Luise Mendelsohn, July 11, 1926, Beyer, *Letters*, 89.
39. Erich Mendelsohn, letter to Dr. Plant, December 1927, Beyer, *Letters*, 98–99.
40. L. Mendelsohn, "Biographical Note," 302–3; Neutra, *Life and Shape*, 156; and Charles Du Vinage, "Erich Mendelsohn's Skizzen," *Wasmuths Monatshefte für Baukunst* 14 (1930): 352.
41. Achenbach, *Mendelsohn*, 56–67.
42. Erich Mendelsohn, "Harmonische und kontrapunktische Führung in der Architektur," *Baukunst* 1 (1925): 179.
43. Erich Mendelsohn, letter to Luise Mendelsohn, July 11, 1926, Beyer, *Letters*, 89.
44. Salman Schocken, letter to Erich Mendelsohn, September 17, 1926, Schocken archive.
45. Meeting notes, June 13, 1927, Schocken archive. The extra story of the stair tower, detectable in photographs, is not shown on the elevation published in Mendelsohn, *Complete Works*, 159.

46. Erich Mendelsohn, letter to Salman Schocken, June 22, 1927, Schocken archive.
47. Salman Schocken, letter to Erich Mendelsohn, September 21, 1926, Schocken archive.
48 Salman Schocken, letter to Erich Mendelsohn, September 30, 1926; and Salman Schocken, internal memo, November 1, 1926, Schocken archive. The contractor's name was Heinze; Julius Schneider supplied the steel frame.
49. Böhning (representing Schocken) and Overberg, telephone transcript, December 3, 1926, Schocken archive.
50. Salman Schocken, letter to Erich Mendelsohn, December 28, 1926, Schocken archive.
51. Overberg, letter to Salman Schocken, December 30, 1926, Schocken archive.
52. Salman Schocken, letter to Erich Mendelsohn, April 26, 1927, and Salman Schocken and Overberg, telephone transcript, May 27, 1927, Schocken archive.
53. Meeting notes, June 13, 1927, Schocken archive. Undated contract filed between Erich Mendelsohn, letter to Adolf Lauster and Company, July 4, 1927, and Adolf Lauster and Company, letter to Erich Mendelsohn, July 5, 1927, Schocken archive.
54. Erich Mendelsohn, letter to Luise Mendelsohn, July 6, 1927, Beyer, *Letters*, 96.
55. Erich Mendelsohn, letter to Hans Hildebrandt, June 6, 1926, Getty Center for the Visual Arts and the Humanities, Santa Monica. Mendelsohn also appointed Heibeck, the member of his office who had supervised the construction of the Nuremberg store, to the same task in Stuttgart, in part because Heibeck's wife was related to the city building inspector. See Overberg, letter to Salman Schocken, December 1, 1926, Schocken archive.
56. Erich Mendelsohn, letter to Luise Mendelsohn, July 16, 1926, copy, Heinze-Greenberg collection.
57. Erich Mendelsohn, letters to Luise Mendelsohn, July 21, 1926, copy, Heinze-Greenberg collection, and July 6, 1927, Beyer, *Letters*, 96.
58. The printed material for the opening of the Stuttgart store won acclaim for the quality of its graphics and for publicizing Schocken's espousal of rational production. See "Werbedrucksache," *Die Form* 3 (1928): 372–73. Schoken's correspondence with Mendelsohn is laced with references to strategies for incorporating images of the new stores into posters and other advertising. The two men consulted, for instance, about which graphic artists to hire (Salman Schocken, letter to Erich Mendelsohn, August 19, 1926; and Erich Mendelsohn, letter to Salman Schocken, August 25, 1926, Schocken archive). Mendelsohn also made drawings to be used especially for advertising purposes. Even construction played a publicity role. Mendelsohn kept a photographic record of the Stuttgart building's progress and suggested to Schocken that a construction photograph of the corner stair tower would make a particularly effective adver-

tisement (Erich Mendelsohn, letter to Salman Schocken, June 13, 1928, Schocken archive). See also Stephan, *Studien*, 27–29.

59. Salman Schocken, dedication speech for the October 4, 1928, opening of the Stuttgart store, untitled typescript, 3, Schocken archive.
60. Mendelsohn, "Frank Lloyd Wright," *Wasmuths Monatshefte für Baukunst*, 244, cites Fiske Kimball, "Sieg des jungen Klassizismus über den 'Funktionalismus der 90er Jahre,'" *Wasmuths Monatshefte für Baukunst* 9.6 (1925).
61. Juan Pablo Bonta, *Architecture and Its Interpretation, A Study of Expressive Systems in Architecture* (New York: Rizzoli, 1979), 105–9, 122–25; Clausen, *Jourdain*, 197–203; and Clausen, "Department Store," 20–29.
62. Banham, *Concrete Atlantis*, 23–107.
63. Mendelsohn, *Rußland*, 180.
64. Mendelsohn, "Industriebau," 479.
65. Mendelsohn, *Amerika*, 75, and as translated by Neumeyer, "Nexus of the Modern," 67.
66. Posener, *Aufsätze und Vorträge*, 181. Banham, "Mendelsohn," 91, cites a design by Arthur Korn for a store in Haifa, entered in the competition which Mendelsohn and Neutra had won in 1923. King, *Mendelsohn*, 15, 25, compares these stairs to chambered nautilus shells owned by Mendelsohn.
67. Schmidt, "Mendelsohn," 225. See also Huse, *"Neues Bauen"*, 113–14.
68. Mendelsohn, "Own Work," 7.
69. Posener, *Auf dem Wege*, 453–64.
70. Moses, "Schocken," 79.
71. Erich Mendelsohn, response to a questionnaire in the *Frankfurter Zeitung*, December 1928, Beyer, *Letters* 102. See Samson, "German-American Dialogues," 178, for an analysis of the way in which Neue Sachlichkeit could play such a revolutionary role even within a highly capitalist context.
72. Details of the interior plan were being worked on in October 1927 and were completed the following April. See Salman Schocken, letter to Erich Mendelsohn, October 13, 1927, Schocken archive, and Karl Konrad Düssel, "Drei Kaufhäuser Schocken in Nürnberg, Stuttgart und Chemnitz von Erich Mendelsohn," *Moderne Bauformen* 11 (1930): 480–82. Louis Parnes, *Bauten des Einzelhandels* (Zurich: Orell Füsseli, 1935), 144–45, published charts of the amount and percentage of space in leading department stores devoted to a variety of functions. The 10,000-square-meter Stuttgart store, one-tenth the size of Messel's Wertheim store, had one of the lowest percentages of space given over to bathrooms, entrances, stairs, and elevators, and one of the highest of usable furnished space.
73. Schocken, October 4, 1928, speech, 2: "Dann hat der Baumeister aus dem unorganischen Material, wenn er ein echter Baumeister ist, einen neuen Organismus geschaffen. . . . Wir sehen oft, daß solche architektonischen Meisterstücke eine Einheit zeigen, die für das Ge-

bäude wohl geeignet erscheint, nicht aber für das, was das Gebäude nachher füllt . . . Hier aber steht die dynamische Rechnung: das Füllen mit dem, was von innen gegeben ist, – eine Rechnung mit viel Unwägbarem!"

74. Schocken, October 4, 1928, speech, 5–6: "Damit hängt der Stil und der nicht vorhandene Luxus unseres Hauses zusammen."
75. Schocken, October 4, 1928, speech, 2, 7: "Tatsächlich bauen wir unter dem Gesichtspunkt der neuen Sachlichkeit, Architektur ist eine reine wirtschaftliche Angelegenheit; alle technischen Vollkommenheiten werden ausgenutzt; Untersuchungen des Ganzen nach Schönheit, die aus den neuen Mitteln heraus sich technisch ergibt."
76. Erich Mendelsohn, letter to Salman Schocken, December 7, 1927, Schocken archive. Scarcely any documentation from after the October 1928 opening of the Stuttgart store exists in this archive. Achenbach, *Mendelsohn*, 81, refers to a drawing still in the archive of the firm's Zwickau offices, and, although this author was unable to locate them, it is possible that other documentation of the Chemnitz construction also remained in Germany when the bulk of the files were transferred to Jerusalem.
77. Erich Mendelsohn, letter to Salman Schocken, September 14, 1928, Schocken archive.
78. Mendelsohn, *Complete Works*, 244. Düssel, "Kaufhäuser," 483, for a later plan with four, rather than three, entrances. A copy of the final plan corresponding to the rear facade as built and as visible in Zevi, *Opera Completa*, 176, fig. 327, exists in the Schocken archive album for the store.
79. Zevi, *Opera Completa*, 144, fig. 3, identifies this drawing as being for the Stuttgart store. He publishes it correctly as color plate III. He makes the same mistake with two more drawings for the Chemnitz store published as 144, fig. 2, and 145, fig. 13.
80. "Ein Baumeister unserer Zeit," December 8, 1929, *Der Welt-Spiegel, Berliner Tageblatt*: 2. See also W. G., "Kaufhaus Schocken, Chemnitz," *Kunstblatt* 14 (1930): 95.
81. Moses, "Schocken," 76.
82. Fresa, "Brüder Luckhardt und Alfons Anker," 193, for their entry in the Chicago Tribune Competition, which grafted a vertical version of the Mossehaus canopy onto the facade of Mendelsohn's Kemperplatz competition entry. Page 202, for their Hirsch store in Berlin of 1925–27, lit in a similar fashion to the Herpich store.
83. Fresa, "Brüder Luckhardt und Alfons Anker," 206–7. Its publication as "Der Neue Fassadenstil in den berliner Straßen," *Der Welt-Spiegel, Berliner Tageblatt*, April 15, 1928: 2, indicates that it was largely complete by the time Mendelsohn was designing the Chemnitz store.
84. Wolf Tegethoff, *Mies van der Rohe: The Villas and Country Houses* (New York: Museum of Modern Art, 1985), 90–91.
85. Schulze, *Critical Biography*, 83–143.
86. Westheim, "Mendelsohn," 305–9, and Meyer, *Moderne Architektur*, pls. 7, 11.

87. Schulze, *Critical Biography*, 146–51, and Arthur Drexler, *An Illustrated Catalogue of the Mies van der Rohe Drawings in the Museum of Modern Art, Part 1* (New York: Garland, 1986), ii, 540.
88. "Entwurf," *Bauwelt* 20 (1929): 3, "Geschäftshaustyp," *Baumeister* 27 (1929): 362; and Korn, *Glass*, 11, 12.
89. Julius Posener, "Betrachtung über Erich Mendelsohn," *Bauwelt* 79 (1988): 375–76, Neumann, *Wolkenkratzer*, 98–99, and K. Werner Schulze, "Geschäfts- und Warenhäuser," *Industriebau* 20 (1929): 220, where it appeared in an article whose focus was Mendelsohn's Stuttgart Schocken store.
90. Fritz Neumeyer, *The Artless Word: Mies van der Rohe on the Building Art*, trans. Mark Jarzombek (1986; Cambridge: MIT Press, 1991), 198. See also Posener, *Aufsätze und Vorträge*, 82.
91. Erich Mendelsohn, "Baubeschreibung des Architekten," *Wasmuths Monatshefte für Baukunst* 14 (1930): 354.
92. Mendelsohn, "Baubeschreibung," 355.
93. Werner Hegemann, "Erich Mendelsohn's Kaufhaus Schocken-Chemnitz," *Wasmuths Monatshefte für Baukunst* 14 (1930): 345–47. See also C. Kerster, "Eisenbetonskelettbauten," *Neues Bauen in Eisenbeton*, ed. Deutscher Beton-Verein (Berlin-Charlottenburg: Zement, 1937), 143.
94. W. H., "Konstruktion und Architektur und Kaufhaus Schocken," *Wasmuths Monatshefte für Baukunst* 14 (1930): 460.
95. Mendelsohn, "Baubeschreibung," 355.
96. Parnes, *Bauten*, 76.
97. Salman Schocken, "Zwischen Produktion und Konsum," *Vier Vorträge über den gegenwärtigen Stand und die Aufgaben des Grosseinhandels* (Berlin, 1931), 47, the text of a November 12, 1931, lecture Schocken delivered to a general meeting of the Verband Deutscher Waren- und Kaufhäuser EV, a trade organization.
98. Henry-Russell Hitchcock and Philip Johnson, *The International Style* (1932; New York: Norton, 1967), 177.
99. Mendelsohn, "Baubeschreibung," 356.

CHAPTER 7

1. Richard Pommer and Christian Otto, *Weissenhof 1927 and the Modern Movement in Architecture* (Chicago: University of Chicago Press, 1991), 173–74.
2. Richard Döcker, letter to Mendelsohn, August 11, 1926, Mendelsohn archive, and Erich Mendelsohn, letter to Luise Mendelsohn, August 6, 1922, copy, Heinze-Greenberg collection.
3. Erich Mendelsohn, letter to Richard Döcker, August 22, 1926, Mendelsohn archive.
4. Ludwig Mies van der Rohe, meeting notes, September 14, 1926, Pommer and Otto, *Weissenhof*, 176–77.
5. Kirsch, *Weissenhof*, 56–57, and Pommer and Otto, *Weissenhof*, 52–54.
6. Erich Mendelsohn, letters to Luise Mendelsohn, July 6, 1927, Beyer,

Letters, 96, and July 21, 1927, copy, Heinze-Greenberg collection. See also Frank Krause, "Weissenhof-Bauleiter-Erinnerungen," *Die zwanziger Jahre des Deutschen Werkbunds*, ed. Deutscher Werkbund und der Werkbund Archiv (Giessen: Anabas, 1982), 113.

7. Mendelsohn, *Rußland*, 186.
8. Kirsch, *Weissenhof*, 13–14, 36–39, 199–200, and Pommer and Otto, *Weissenhof*, 47–52.
9. Lane, *Architecture and Politics*, 125–67; Winfried Nerdinger, ed., *Süddeutsche Bautradition im 20. Jahrhundert: Architekten der Bayerischen Akademie der Schönen Kunst* (Munich: Kastner and Callwey, 1985); Christian Otto, "Modern Environment and Historical Continuity: The Heimatschutz Discourse on Germany," *Art Journal* 43 (1983): 148–57; and Richard Pommer, "The Flat Roof: A Modernist Controversy in Germany," *Art Journal* 43 (1983): 158–69.
10. Schulze, "Geschäfts- und Warenhäuser," 214, for the replacement of aesthetics with technology and economics as the primary factors in department store architecture.
11. Albert Sigrist [Alexander Schwab], *Das Buch von Bauen* (Berlin: Bücherkreis, 1930). For Schwab's true identity and biography, see Hüter, *Berlin*, 325.
12. Sigrist, *Buch*, 65.
13. Ibid., 72, 12–13, 211.
14. Lane, *Architecture and Politics*, 125–45.
15. Hans Buchner, *Warenhauspolitik und Nationalsozialismus*, Nationalsozialistische Bibliothek 13 (Munich: Eber, 1931), and Strohmeyer, *Warenhäuser*, 153–58.
16. Jeffrey Herf, *Reactionary Modernism* (Cambridge: Cambridge University Press, 1984), and Lane, *Architecture and Politics*, 133–34, 137–40.
17. Buchner, *Warenhauspolitik*, 4–5.
18. Jeremy Anysley, "Pressa Cologne, 1928: Exhibitions and Publication Design in the Weimar Period," *Design Issues* 10.3 (1994): 53–76; Wolfram Hagspiel, "Bauwerke und Ausstellungsgestaltung internationale Kölner Ausstellungen," in *Frühe Kölner Kunstausstellungen*, ed. Wulf Herzogenrath (Cologne: Wienand, 1981), 76; and H. C. Adenauer, "Zur Eröffnung der Pressa," *Berliner Tageblatt*, May 12, 1928.
19. Walter Riezler, "Gespräch vor den Pressabauten," *Die Form* 3 (1928): 197–211; Walter Riezler, "Die Sonderbauten der Pressa," *Die Form* 3 (1928): 257–61; Paul Ferdinand Schmidt, "Die Kunst auf der Pressa," *Der Cicerone* 20 (1928): 589–92; L. S. E., "Bildende Kunst auf der Pressa," *Die Kunst* 60 (1929): 50–55; and Walter Bourke, "Rund um die Kölner Pressabauten," *Stadtbaukunst* 9 (1928): 49–54.
20. Schmidt, "Pressa," 591.
21. *Internationale Presse-Ausstellung: Amtlicher Katalog* (Cologne: 1928); *Pressa: Kulturschau am Rhein* (Berlin: Schröder, 1928); and Hagspiel, "Bauwerke."
22. After the completion of Mossehaus, Mendelsohn received a succes-

sion of minor commissions from the company. These included an unbuilt 1924 booking office for the interior of Mossehaus, a 1924 booth for the Berlin automobile exhibition, and a 1927 powerhouse for Mossehaus. Zevi, *Opera Completa*, 114, 140.

23. The pavilion was illustrated or discussed in the *Berliner Tageblatt* alone in: A.D., "Erich Mendelsohn Ausstellung," March 27, 1928; "Eine Erich Mendelsohn Ausstellung in der Galerie Neumann and Nierendorf in Berlin, *Der Welt-Spiegel*, April 15, 1928: 3 (photograph of model); "Bilder von der 'Pressa' in Köln," *Der Welt-Spiegel*, June 3, 1928: 2 (photograph of building at night); Fritz Engel, "Pressa," June 7, 1928; and "Pressa-Marche," *Jede Woche Musik*, June 16, 1928 (photograph of building).
24. Richard Hamburger, *Das Zeitungs- und Anzeigenwesen, Zeitungsverlag und Annoncen Expedition Rudolf Mosse* (Berlin: Organisations Verlagsgesellschaft, 1928), vol. 3 of *Meisterbetriebe deutscher Wirtschaft*.
25. *Internationale Pressa-Ausstellung*, 264, which many articles quoted almost verbatim. See also Engel, "Pressa," and Mendelsohn, *Complete Works*, 209–15.
26. *Internationale Pressa-Ausstellung*, 264, states that it was constructed by the Berlin firm of Georg O. Richer and Schädel.
27. Mendelsohn, *Complete Works*, 209.
28. K. Paul Zygas, "Cubo-Futurism and the Vesnins' Palace of Labor," *The Avant Garde in Russia, 1910–1930: New Perspectives*, ed. Stephanie Barron and Maurice Tuchman (Los Angeles: Los Angeles County Museum of Art, 1980), 112.
29. Mendelsohn, *Rußland*, 176.
30. Burkhard Bergius and Julius Posener with the assistance of Dirk Föster and Dieter Renschler, "Die Liste der Individuell geplanten Einfamilienhäuser, 1896–1968," *Wohungungsbau*, Part C, *Die Wohnungsgebäude – Einfamilienhäuser* (Berlin: Ernst, 1975), 188–89, vol. 4 of *Berlin und seine Bauten*.
31. Erich Mendelsohn, letter to Luise Mendelsohn, July 11, 1926, copy, Heinze-Greenberg collection, and L. Mendelsohn, "My Life," 45–80. Their last apartment consisted of three rooms in a Westend building designed by August Endell.
32. For Muthesius's Tieteur House, see Harwig Beseler and Niels Gutschow, *Kriegsschicksale deutscher Architektur, Verluste – Schäden – Wiederaufbau, Eine Dokumentation für das Gebiet der Bundesrepublik Deutschland* (Neumünster: Wachholtz, 1988), i, x.
33. Erich Mendelsohn, letters to Luise Mendelsohn, July 10, 1926, and July 6, 1927, copies, Heinze-Greenberg collection; July 20 and 22, 1928, Beyer, *Letters*, 100–1; and July 28, 1928, copy, Heinze-Greenberg collection; L. Mendelsohn, "Biographical Note," 342; and L. Mendelsohn, "My Life," 80–86.
34. Erich Mendelsohn, letter to Luise Mendelsohn, December 16, 1928, Mendelsohn, *Briefe*, 84–85. L. Mendelsohn, "My Life," 56, 84, for her own suspicions that political activity was more important than architecture.

35. The landscaping was the work of Heinrich Friedrich Wiepking-Jürgensmann. Achenbach, *Mendelsohn*, 82.
36. Mendelsohn, "Industriebau," 478.
37. Achenbach, *Mendelsohn*, 82, and Erich Mendelsohn, *Neues Haus – Neue Welt* (Berlin: Mosse, 1932), unpaginated.
38. Samson, "German-American Dialogues," 486, for an account by Catharine Bauer of Mendelsohn's pride in one of these rational touches, the Murphy bed in his study.
39. Erich Mendelsohn, "Gruppe Nr. 1 – Gruppe Nr. 2," *Haus, Hof, Garten, Berliner Tageblatt*, May 16, 1931.
40. L. Mendelsohn, "My Life," 94–101.
41. Maxwell Fry, *Art in the Machine Age: A Critique of Contemporary Life through the Medium of Architecture* (London: Methuen, 1969), 111, compared the beauty of the Tugendhat House to that of Luise Mendelsohn.
42. "Bauten und Skizzen," 1–66.
43. *Erich Mendelsohn, Structures and Sketches*, trans. Hermann George Scheffauer (London: Benn, 1924).
44. The exhibit opened in March and later traveled to Darmstadt, Mannheim, and Stuttgart. See Mendelsohn, *Complete Works*, 249.
45. It appeared on the cover of *Wasmuths Monatshefte für Baukunst* and was the subject of three articles inside (Hegemann, "Kaufhaus Schocken-Chemnitz," 345–47; du Vinage, "Skizzen," 350–53; and Mendelsohn, "Baubeschreibung," 354–56). One of these, Mendelsohn's own description of the building, was reprinted in *Die Baugilde* ("Kaufhaus Schocken, Chemnitz: Architekt BDA Dipl.-Ing. Erich Mendelsohn, Berlin," *Die Baugilde* 12 [1930]: 1597–1601) and summarized in *Bauwelt* ("Kaufhaus Schocken, Chemnitz: Architekt BDA Dipl.-Ing. Erich Mendelsohn, Berlin," *Baugilde* 12 [1930]: 1597–1601). *Das Kunstblatt* published the model in March 1930 (W. G., "Kaufhaus Schocken, Chemnitz," *Das Kunstblatt* 14 [1930]: 95), and a second article focusing on Schocken himself followed after the store's opening (Westheim, "Zeitlupe," 218–19). Finally, *Moderne Bauformen* published an article on all three Schocken stores (Düssel, "Drei Kaufhäuser," 461–84), and a photo appeared in "Die neue Architektur," *Der Welt-Spiegel, Berliner Tageblatt*, June 6, 1930: 2. Nor was its popularity confined to critics. Architects and department store owners flocked to Chemnitz even after the Nazis came to power. As early as July 1928, three months after the opening of the Schocken store in Stuttgart, the Dutch architect Jan Frederik Staal wrote Mendelsohn to request plans of the stores, which Staal wished to consult before completing a design for the De Bikenkorf store in Rotterdam (J. F. Staal, letter to Erich Mendelsohn, July 13, 1928, Mendelsohn archive). As late as 1937, representatives of a Vienna store visited the Chemnitz store to study its interior arrangements (Warenhaus A. G., letter to the Chemnitz Schocken store, May 8, 1937, in the Schocken archive). The same year, Selfridges in London requested photographs; Elanto M. B. T. of Helsinki sent Ilmori Voionmaa and H. Leisten, the ar-

chitects of their new store, to visit; and W. J. R. Dreesmann of F. Vroom and Freesmann in Amsterdam wrote of his desire to see the building (Selfridges manager, letter to the Chemnitz Schocken store, October 18, 1937; Voionmaa and H. Leister, letter to the Chemnitz Schocken store, August 27, 1937; and W. J. R. Dreesmann, letter to the Chemnitz Schocken store, October 18, 1937, all Schocken archive).

46. "Mr. Mendelsohn," *Manchester Guardian*, November 18, 1933. A clipping of this article and a German translation survive in the Schocken archive.
47. Except for the bronze mullions on the first floor, all of the Chemnitz window details were crafted of wood, probably because of Schocken's close attention to cost. See Mendelsohn, "Baubeschreibung," 356.
48. Westheim, "Zeitlupe," 219.
49. Düssel, "Drei Kaufhäuser," 461–62.
50. For example, Fahrenkamp's Michel store in Wuppertal, published in P. J. Kramers, "E. Fahrenkamp und G. Schäfer, Dusseldorf, 'Kaufhaus Michel' Wuppertal," *Moderne Bauformen* 29 (1930): 449; Paul's Sinn Department Store in Gelsenkirchen, which appears in Korn, *Glass*, 55; and Salvisberg's model for a Berlin branch of the Wertheim store in "Neue Fassadensysteme," *Baumeister* 27 (1929): 363–64.
51. Klotz, *Twentieth-Century Architecture*, 104–5, publishes Rettig's unrealized 1930 design for the Atlantik Cinema in Berlin, which does copy the Petersdorff corner motif. See also Joeres, "Mehrfamilienhäuser," 415, for the Petersdorff-like balconies of Hans Scharoun and Georg Jakobowitz's 1929–30 Hohenzollerndamm 35-36 apartments in Berlin.
52. "Der Akademie der Künste wird reformiert," *Berliner Tageblatt*, August 11, 1931, and "Die reformierte Akademie," *Berliner Tageblatt*, September 24, 1931.
53. Erich Vogler, "Erich Mendelsohn: Seine Vorträge in der Kopenhagener Akademie," *Berliner Tageblatt*, May 10, 1930, and "Erich Mendelsohn in London," *Berliner Tageblatt*, May 27, 1930.
54. Jean Badovici, "Erich Mendelsohn," *L'Architecture Vivante* 10 (Winter 1932): 33.
55. W. Gaunt, "A New Utopia? Berlin – The New Germany – The Modern Movement," *The Studio* 98 (1929): 859–65.
56. J. R. Leathart, "Modern Cinema Design," *Journal of the Royal Institute of British Architects* 38. 3 (1930): 68, and Robertson and Yerbury, "Architecture of Tension," 708. Interestingly, Theo van Doesburg, a critic far more familiar with architectural experimentation on the continent, condemned Mendelsohn for what he perceived as an excess of monumentality. See Doesburg, "The Significance of Glass," Doesburg, *European Architecture*, 68.
57. Aldous Huxley, "Puritanism in Art," *The Studio* 99 (1930): 200–2. Howard Robertson, on the other hand, in "Erich Mendelsohn," *Architect and Builders' News* 123 (1930): 629–31, commended

what he saw as Mendelsohn's balance of function and lively new form.

58. See, for instance, Mumford's "Steel Chimneys and Beet-top Cupolas," xliv, and the comments made by Sheldon Cheney in his *Primer of Modern Art* (New York: Boni and Liveright, 1924) and *New World Architecture.* Also Meredith L. Clausen, *Pietro Belluschi: Modern American Architect* (Cambridge: MIT Press, 1994), 33, 48.
59. "Frank Lloyd Wright and Hugh Ferriss Discuss This Modern Architecture," *Architectural Forum* 53 (1930): 536. See also Paul Lester Wiener, "Creative Architecture of Erich Mendelsohn," *Architectural Forum* 53 (1930): 611–12, and *Creative Art* 4 (1929): xvi – xvii.
60. Norman Bel Geddes, "Erich Mendelsohn – Contempora Exposition – 1929," brochure, Mendelsohn archive, Getty Center for the History of Art and the Humanities.
61. Sharp, *Picture Palaces*, 126–46.
62. Erich Mendelsohn, letter to Luise Mendelsohn, March 12, 1932, copy, Heinze-Greenberg collection, and Stephan, *Studien*, 194–98.
63. "Current Architecture, Three London Shops," *Architectural Review* 79 (1936): 270–71, and "Store for Mssrs. Simpson, Piccadilly, London," *Architectural Record* 80 (1936): 120–29. Adolf Dornath, "Functionalism," *Berliner Tageblatt*, June 30, 1930, noted in his review of the Stockholm exhibition of 1930 that its architecture depended on the example set by Le Corbusier and Mendelsohn.
64. William Jordy, *The Impact of European Modernism in the Mid-Twentieth Century*, vol. 4 of *American Buildings and Their Architects* (Garden City, NY: Doubleday, 1976), 140–43, 434, and Lorraine Welling Lanman, *William Lescaze, Architect* (Philadelphia: Art Alliance Press, 1987), 55–56
65. "Kolumbushaus," Mendelsohn "Hochhaus," 447, and "Aufzüge im Columbushaus"; "Leuchtröhren für Lichtreklame"; Berlowitz, "Lüftung und Heizung"; Otto Biechschmidt, "Elektrizität im Columbushaus"; and E. A. Karweik, "Arbeit am Columbushaus"; all *Technische Rundschau, Berliner Tageblatt*, February 3, 1932: 1–8.
66. Deubner, "Columbushaus," 43.
67. Deubner, "Columbushaus," 44; Sagebiel, "Konstruktion," 544; and Mendelsohn, "Columbushaus," 84.
68. Sagebiel, "Konstruktion," 543–44.
69. Jürgen Joedecke, *Office Buildings*, trans. C. V. Amerongen (London: Crosby, Lockwood, 1962), 16.
70. "Kolumbushaus wächst," *Berliner Tageblatt*, October 10, 1931; Deubner, "Columbushaus," 43–45; Karweik, "Arbeit," 2; Mendelsohn, "Columbushaus," 83–84; and Sagebiel, "Konstruktion," 543–48.
71. "Kolumbushaus," "Leuchtröhren"; Erich Mendelsohn, "My Own Contribution," Beyer, *Letters*, 169; Mendelsohn, "Columbushaus," 81–88; and Mendelsohn, "Hochhaus," 447.
72. Theodore James, *The Empire State Building* (New York: Harper and Row, 1975), 61, 90.

73. Advertisements, *Technische Rundschau, Berliner Tageblatt*, February 3, 1932: 4–8; "Kolumbushaus [*sic*] wäschst"; Deubner, "Columbushaus," 43–45; Karweik, "Arbeit," 2; Mendelsohn, "Columbushaus," 83–84; and Sagebiel, "Konstruktion," 543–48. See "Haus des Deutschen Metallarbeitersverbundes," *Bauwelt* 1931 (1930): 1320, for the speedy erection of another Mendelsohn building.
74. Karweik, "Erinnerungen an Erich Mendelsohn," 56, and Erich Mendelsohn, letter to Luise Mendelsohn, July 6, 1927, Beyer, *Letters*, 96.

CONCLUSION

1. Hegemann, "Neubauten am Potsdamer Platz," 226.
2. Mendelsohn, *Neues Haus*, and A. D., "Neues Haus – Neue Welt," *Berliner Tageblatt*, January 21, 1932.
3. "Architekt Dipl.-Ing. Erich Mendelsohn, Berlin," *Bauwelt* 22.46 (1931): 17–20, is an exception.
4. Badovici, "Mendelsohn," and Howard Robertson, "Erich Mendelsohn at Home," *Architect and Building News* 130 (1932): 240–42.
5. Posener, "Zur Eröffnung," 10.
6. Amédée Ozenfant, "For Erich Mendelsohn," Mendelsohn, *Neues Haus – Neue Welt*, unpaginated.
7. P., "Mendelsohns eigenes Haus," *Bauwelt* 23 (1932): 301.
8. Werner Hegemann, "Mendelsohn-Haus und Goethe-Haus," *Wasmuths Monatshefte für Baukunst* 16 (1932): 221–42.
9. Werner Hegemann, "Der Schöpferische Sinn," *Wasmuths Monatshefte für Baukunst* 16 (1932): 548.
10. Mendelsohn, *Schöpferische Sinn*, 29–47.
11. Mendelsohn, *Schöpferische Sinn*, published in translation in Beyer, *Letters*, 122–23.
12. Hegemann, "Schöpferische Sinn," 548.
13. Erich Mendelsohn, letter to Luise Mendelsohn, September 20, 1932, copy, Heinze-Greenberg collection: "der neuen Umgebung für einen neuen Start entwickeln."
14. Erich Mendelsohn, "Architectuur," *Académie Européenne "Méditerranée,"* ed. Henricus Theodorus Wijdeveld, Amédee Ozenfant, and Erich Mendelsohn (Amsterdam, 1933), unpaginated, and Erich Mendelsohn, "Il bacino Mediterraneo e la nuova architettura," *Architettura* 11 (1932): 647–48.
15. Lane, *Architecture and Politics*, 169–216; Winfried Nerdinger, ed., *Bauhaus-Moderne im Nationalsozialismus: Zwischen Anbiederung und Verfolgung* (München: Prestel, 1993); and Pommer, "Mies van der Rohe," 117–34.
16. Erich Mendelsohn, letter to Luise Mendelsohn, January 30, 1933, copy, Heinze-Greenberg collection: "Versuchte Esther die politische Situation zu erklären, die Möglichkeiten, die in ihr beschlossen sind. Die positiven kennst Du aus meiner 'schöpferischen' Stelle zur Krise: Nationaler Begriff – immer notwendig, sozialer Begriff – antimarx-

istisch heute notwendig. . . . Die negativen Möglichkeiten sind nicht so eindeutig bestimmbar."

17. Ita Heinze-Greenberg, "Erich Mendelsohn," *Baumeister, Architekten, Stadtplaner, Biographien zur baulichen Entwicklung Berlins*, ed. Wolfgang Ribbe and Wolfgang Schäche (Berlin: Stapp, 1987), 504.
18. Erich Mendelsohn, letters to Luise Mendelsohn, February 3, 7, 8, 11, 14, and 23, 1933, partially published in Beyer, *Letters*, 125–26, copies of the complete texts, Heinze-Greenberg collection. For an unsubstantiated account of Mendelsohn's consideration of exile in Italy, see Giovanni K. Koenig, "Behrens and Thereabouts," *Casabella* 347 (1969): 2–3. 19. Pommer, "Mies van der Rohe," 118–22.
19. Pommer, "Mies van der Rohe," 188–22.
20. L. Mendelsohn, "My Life," 106.
21. Achenbach, *Mendelsohn*, 16–20, and *Der Mendelsohn-Bau am Lehniner Platz*, 16–36, for a complete accounting of the fates of Mendelsohn's Berlin buildings. For Columbushaus, see also Stephan, *Studien*, 248–51, and for the Nuremburg Schocken store, see also Beseler and Gutschow, *Kriegsschicksale*, 1455. For more recent accounts of the condition and restoration of Mendelsohn buildings still standing in Germany, see Peter Blacke, "Versatile Theater in a Restored Erich Mendelsohn Building," *Architecture* 73.9 (1984): 160–65; Jung and Worbs, "Funktionelle Dynamik," 118; Julius Posener, "Erich Mendelsohns Einsteinturm" *Einsteinturm*, 138–50; and Rolf R. Lantenschlägen, "Der Potsdamer Einsteinturm," *Deutsche Bauzeitung* 125.2 (1991): 115.
22. "Modern Monument Destroyed," *Architectural Review* 129 (1961): 293–94. See also Ignaz F. Hollay, "Schocken . . . Merkur . . . Horten: die 60 Jahre eines Stuttgarter Kaufhauses," *Deutsche Bauzeitung* 122.9 (1988): 102–12, and Stephan, *Studien*, 235–47.
23. Fuchs, *Konzern aus Sachsen*, 189–257; Hentschel, *Einstein-Turm*, 127–42; and Runge and Stelbrink, *Mosse*, 27.
24. Achenbach, *Mendelsohn*, 14–19, and Zevi, *Opera Completa*, 122–23, 128–29.
25. Edna Brocke and Michael Zimmermann, *Stationen jüdischen Lebens: Von der Emanzipation bis zur Gegenwart* (Bonn: Verlay J. H. W. Dietz, 1990), 41–49, 165–73.
26. Ibid., 165–73, and Fr. Ferse, "Verschiedenes: Das Heim der Jüdischen Jugend in Essen," *Der Stahlbau* (1932): 56, copy in the archives of the Alte Synagoge in Essen.
27. Ferse, "Verschiedenes," appears to be the only contemporary publication of the building in the national architectural press. In the only reference in the Mendelsohn literature, Achenbach, *Mendelsohn*, 19, lists it without illustrating or describing it.
28. Brocke and Zimmerman, *Stationen jüdischen Lebens*, 165–73.
29. Terence Riley, *The International Style: Exhibition 14 and the Museum of Modern Art* (New York: Rizzoli, 1992); Isaacs, *Gropius*, 810–24; and Schulze, *Critical Biography*, 205–17.

30. Reginald Blomfield, *Modernismus* (London, 1934).
31. John Allen, *Berthold Lubetkin: Architecture and the Tradition of Progress* (London: RIBA Press, 1992), and Gavin Stamp, ed., *Britain in the Thirties, Architectural Design Profile* 24 (1980).
32. Russell Stevens and Peter Willis, "Earl De La Warr and the Completion of the Bexhill Pavilion," *Architectural History* 33 (1990): 135–66, and Zevi, *Opera Completa*, 218–25. For the building's recent restoration, see Kenneth Powell and Tim Schollar, "Restoring a Milestone of Modernism," *The Architects' Journal* 199.7 (1994): 35–44.
33. Heinze-Mühleib, *Mendelsohn*, is the definitive source on Mendelsohn's years in Palestine. See also Achenbach, *Mendelsohn*, 20–22; Herbert and Sosnovsky, *Bauhaus on the Carmel*, esp. 151–55; Michael Levin, *White City: International Style Architecture in Israel, A Portrait of an Era* (Tel Aviv: Tel Aviv Museum, 1984), 36–45; and Zevi, *Opera Completa*, 239–75.
34. Mendelsohn, *Rußland*, 138, 152, 158.
35. Erich Mendelsohn, letter to Julius Posener, March 30, 1937, Beyer, *Letters*, 148–49.
36. Heinze-Mühleib, *Mendelsohn*, 139.
37. For his friendship with the British High Commissioner, see Beyer, *Letters*, 138–47.
38. See especially Walter Leedy, "Eric Mendelsohn's Park Synagogue: Vision Informs Reality," *Cleveland Sacred Landmark: A Special Issue of the Gamut* (Cleveland: Cleveland State University Press, 1989). For further information on his American work, see also Achenbach, *Mendelsohn*, 23–24, and Zevi, *Opera Completa*, 276–407. Two buildings not published by Zevi, the Radiochemistry Building for the University of California Radiation Laboratory at Berkeley and the Varian Associate building in Palo Alto, are the respective subjects of "Laboratory for Radioactive Research," *Architectural Record* 121 (June 1957): 224–26, and "For Electronic Research and Development," *Architectural Record* 116 (July 1954): 156–61.
39. Mendelsohn, *Amerika*.
40. Ute Brüning, "Bauhäusler zwischen Propaganda and Wirtschaftswerbung," in Nerdinger, *Bauhaus-Moderne*, 24–47, and Uwe Westphal, "Architecture and Advertising in Third Reich Germany," *Rassegna* 49 (1992): 58–69.
41. Herf, *Reactionary Modernism*; Lane, *Architecture and Politics*, 185–216; and Nerdinger, *Bauhaus-Moderne*, esp. Sabine Weißler, "Bauhaus-Gestaltung in NS-Propaganda-Ausstellungen," 48–63, and Nerdinger, "Bauhaus-Architekten im 'Dritten Reich,' " 153–78.
42. Bartezko, *Illusionen in Stein*; and Bartezko, *Zwischen Zucht und Ekstase*. Wilhelm Lotz, who during the twenties had praised Mendelsohn's lighting effects, was even more effusive in his enthusiastic review of Speer's work. See, for instance, his "Die Bauten des Zeppelinfeldes in Nürnberg," *Zentralblatt der Bauverwaltung* 59 (1939): 927–36.
43. Erich Mendelsohn, "Palestine and the World of Tomorrow," 9, reprinted in Heinze-Mühleib, *Mendelsohn*, 371.

44. Clement Greenberg in the United States and Theodor Adorno, who spent the war years in America before returning to Germany, were particularly instrumental in this shift. See Benjamin H. D. Buchloh, Serge Guilbaut, and David Solkin, eds., *Modernism and Modernity: The Vancouver Conference Papers* (Halifax: The Press of the Nova Scotia College of Art and Design, 1983); Huyssen, *After the Great Divide*, esp. 16–43; Martin Jay, *Permanent Exiles: Essays on the Intellectual Migration from Germany to America* (New York: Columbia University Press, 1985), 47–54, and Teitelbaum, *Montage*, esp. 36–59.
45. Siegfried Giedeon, *Space Time and Architecture* (1941; Cambridge: Harvard University Press, 1963), 394, for a dismissal of Mendelsohn.
46. Philip Johnson, letter to J. J. P. Oud, undated, NDB.
47. W. Riezler, "Kann man im Haus Tugendhat wohnen?" *Die Form* 6 (1931): 392–94.
48. See Riley, *International Style*, and Smith, *Making the Modern*, 353–404, as well as Hitchcock and Johnson, *International Style*, esp. Alfred Barr, "Preface," 12. Hitchcock and Johnson's intent is also discussed in the remainder of Johnson's correspondence with Oud in the NDB and in Robert Wojtowicz's paper "Organic' vs. 'International': Lewis Mumford and the Question of Style in 1932," delivered in March 1990 at the annual meeting of the Society of Architectural Historians in Boston. The term in its narrow sense was apparently first used in the United States by Frederick Kiesler, *Contemporary Art Applied to the Store and Its Display* (New York: Brentano's, 1930), 39. For its German antecedents, see Pommer and Otto, *Weissenhof*, 158–66.
49. Isaacs, *Gropius*, 674.
50. For the politics of the two architects, see Nerdinger, "Bauhaus-Architekten," 153–65, and Pommer, "Mies van der Rohe," 96–145.
51. Kenneth Frampton, "Prospects for a Critical Regionalism," *Perspecta* 20 (1983): 147ff.; Aldo Rossi, *The Architecture of the City*, trans. Diane Ghirardo and Joan Ockman (1966; Cambridge: MIT Press, 1982), and Robert Venturi, Denise Scott Brown, and Steven Izenour, *Learning from Las Vegas* (Cambridge: MIT Press, 1977).

SELECT BIBLIOGRAPHY

A. UNPUBLISHED SOURCES

Bauhaus. Archives. Bauhaus-Archiv, Berlin.

Einstein, Albert. Archives. Hebrew University, Jerusalem.

Einstein Stiftung. Archives. Akademie der Wissenschaft der Deutschen Demokratischen Republik, Berlin.

Hildebrandt, Hans. Archives. Getty Center for the History of Art and the Humanities, Santa Monica.

Mendelsohn, Erich. Archives. Kunstbibliothek, Staatliche Museen Preußischer Kulturbesitz, Berlin. Includes originals of letters to and from Mendelsohn, his drawings, his writings, and photographs of his buildings and projects.

Mendelsohn, Erich. Letters to Luise Mendelsohn and others. Copies, Getty Center for the History of Art and the Humanities, Santa Monica, and Ita Heinze-Greenberg collection, Haifa.

Mendelsohn, Erich. "Personal Data and Total Work of Erich Mendelsohn." Typescript, Getty Center for the History of Art and the Humanities, Santa Monica.

Mendelsohn, Louise. "My Life in a Changing World." Copies, Ita Heinze-Greenberg collection, Haifa; Department of Architecture and Design, Museum of Modern Art, New York; Mendelsohn Archive, Kunstbibliothek, Staatliche Museen Preußischer Kulturbesitz, Berlin.

Ministerium für Wissenschaft, Kunst and Volksbindung. Papers. Geheimes Staatsarchiv Preußischer Kulturbesitz, Merseburg.

Neutra, Richard. Drawings. Special collections, University of California, Los Angeles.

Neutra, Richard, and Dione Niedermann Neutra. Archives. Formerly Dione Neutra collection, Los Angeles.

Oud, J. J. P. Archives. Nederlands Documentatiecentrum voor de Bouwkunst, Amsterdam.

Schocken, Salman. Archives. Schocken Institute for Jewish Research of the Jewish Theological Seminary of America, Jerusalem.

Wälzlagerwerk, Luckenwalde. The current inhabitants of the Steinberg, Hermann Hat Factory possess original blueprints for the building and the relevant papers of the Luckenwalde Stadtbauamt.
Wijdeveld, Henricus. Archives. Nederlands Documentatiecentrum voor de Bouwkunst, Amsterdam.

B. NEWSPAPERS AND PERIODICALS

Architektur und Schaufenster, 1927–28.
Die Baugilde, 1921–33.
Baukunst, 1925–29.
Baumeister, 1921–33.
Bauwelt, 1920–33.
Berliner illustrirte [sic] Zeitung, 1921–33.
Berliner Tageblatt, 1919–33
Deutsche Bauzeitung, 1921–33.
Deutsches Bauwesen, 1930–32.
Form, 1925–33.
Kunstblatt, 1921–33.
Moderne Bauformen, 1921–33.
Das neue Berlin, 1929.
Städtebau, 1919–29.
Wasmuths Monatshefte für Baukunst, 1919–33.

C. ARTICLES, BOOKS, AND DISSERTATIONS

Achenbach, Sigrid. *Erich Mendelsohn, 1887–1953, Ideen, Bauten, Projekte*. Berlin: Staatliche Museen Preußischer Kulturbesitz, 1987.
Baacke, Rolf-Peter. *Lichtspielhausarchitektur in Deutschland von der Schaubuhne bis zum Kinopalast*. Berlin: Fröhlich und Kaufmann, 1982.
Badovici, Jean. "Entretiens sur l'architecture vivante: Erich Mendelsohn." *L'Architecture Vivante* 3 (1925): 16.
"Erich Mendelsohn." *L'Architecture Vivante* 10 (1932): 33–46.
Banham, Reyner. *A Concrete Atlantis*. Cambridge: MIT Press, 1986.
"Mendelsohn." *Architectural Review* 116 (1954): 84–93.
Bartetzko, Dieter. *Illusionen in Stein, Stimmungsarchitektur im deutschen Faschismus, Ihre Vorgeschichte in Theater-und Film-Bauten*. Reinbeck: Rohwohlt, 1985.
Zwischen Zucht und Ekstase, Zur Theatralik von NS-Architektur. Berlin: Gebr. Mann, 1985.
Bayer, Herbert, Walter Gropius, and Ise Gropius, eds. *Bauhaus, 1919–1928*. 1938. Boston: Bradford, 1959.
Behne, Adolf. *Der Moderne Zweckbau*. München: Masken, 1926.
Benson, Susan Porter. *Counter Cultures: Saleswomen, Managers, and Customers in American Department Stores, 1890–1940*. Urbana: University of Illinois Press, 1986.
Benson, Timothy O., ed. *Expressionist Utopias: Paradise, Metropolis,*

Architectural Fantasy. Los Angeles: Los Angeles County Museum of Art, 1993.

Benton, Tim, and Charlotte Benton, eds., with Dennis Sharp. *Form and Function: A Source Book for the History of Architecture and Design, 1890–1939*. London: Crosby Lockwood Staples, 1975.

Berg, Peter. *Deutschland und Amerika, 1918–1929, Über das deutsche Amerikabild der zwanziger Jahre*. Lübeck: Mattiesen, 1963.

Berlin und Seine Bauten. Vols. 3–11. Berlin: Ernst, 1971–87.

Beseler, Hartwig, and Nils Gutschow. *Kriegschicksal, Deutscher Architektur, Verluste – Schäden – Wiederaufbau, ein Dokumentation für das Gebiet der Bundesrepublik Deutschland*. 2 vols. Neumünster: Wachholtz, 1988.

Beyer, Oskar. "Architectuur in izjer en beton." *Wendingen* 3.10 (1920): 4–14.

"Eine neue Monumental-Architektur." *Feuer* 2 (1920): 111–15.

ed. *Erich Mendelsohn: Letters of an Architect*. Trans. Geoffrey Strachan. London: Abelard-Schuman, 1967.

Boeger, Peter. *Architekture der Lichtspieltheater in Berlin: Bauten und Projekte, 1919–1930*. Berlin: Verlag Willmuth Arenhövel, 1993.

Brocke, Edna, and Michael Zimmermann. *Stationen Jüdischen Lebens: Von der Emanzipation bis zur Gegenwart*. Bonn: Verlay J. W. H. Dietz, 1990.

Brüder Luckhardt und Alfons Anker. Schriftenreihe der Akademie der Kunst. Vol. 21. Berlin: Akademie der Kunst, 1981.

Buchner, Hans. *Warenhauspolitik und Nationalsozialismus*. Nationalsozialismus Bibliothek 13. Munich: Eher, 1931.

Buddensieg, Tilmann, ed. *Berlin, 1900–1933, Architecture and Design*. New York: Cooper-Hewitt Museum, 1987.

Campbell, Joan. *The German Werkbund: The politics of Reform in the Applied Arts*. Princeton: Princeton University Press, 1978.

Clair, Jean, ed. *The 1920s: Age of the Metropolis*. Montreal: Montreal Museum of Fine Arts, 1991.

Clark, Ronald. *Einstein, The Life and Times*. New York: World Publishing, 1971.

Clausen, Meredith. "The Department Store – Development of the Type." *Journal of Architectural Education* 39:1 (1985): 20–29.

Frantz Jourdain and the Samaritaine: Art Nouveau Theory and Criticism. Leiden: E. J. Brill, 1987.

Collins, George R., and Christiane Crasemann Collins. *Camillo Sitte: The Birth of Modern City Planning*. New York: Rizzoli, 1986.

Conrads, Ulrich, ed. *Programs and Manifestos in Twentieth-Century Architecture*. Trans. Michael Bullock. Cambridge: MIT Press, 1970.

Costigliola, Frank. *Awkward Dominion: American Political, Economic, and Cultural Relations with Europe, 1919–1930*. Ithaca, NY: Cornell University Press, 1984.

Doesburg, Theo van. *On European Architecture: Complete Essays from Het Bouwbedrijf, 1924–1931*. Trans. Charlotte I. Loeb and Arthur L. Loeb. Basel: Birkhäuser Verlag, 1990.

Der Einsteinturm in Potsdam: Architektur und Astrophysik. Berlin: Ars Nicolai, 1995.

Eksteins, Modris. *The Limits of Reason: The German Democratic Press and the Collapse of Weimar Democracy*. Oxford: Oxford University Press, 1975.

Erich Mendelsohn: The Complete Works. Trans. Antje Frisch. 1930. New York: Princeton Architectural Press, 1992.

Erich Mendelsohn's "Amerika." 1926. New York: Dover, 1993.

"Erinnerungen an Erich Mendelsohn." *Bauwelt* 39.3 (1968): 56–58.

Ewen, Stuart, and Elizabeth Ewen. *Channels of Desire: Mass Images and the Shaping of American Consciousness*. Minneapolis; University of Minnesota Press, 1992.

Frecot, Janos, and Helmut Geisert, eds. *Berlin im Abriß*. Berlin: Medusa, 1981.

Freundlich, Erwin Findlay. *The Foundations of Einstein's Theory of Gravitation*. Trans. Henry L. Brose. 1916. New York: Dutton, 1920.

Das Turmteleskop der Einstein Stiftung. Berlin: Springer, 1927.

Fuchs, Konrad. *Ein Konzern aus Sachsen: Das Kaufhaus Schocken als Spiegelbild deutscher Wirtschaft und Politik, 1900 bis 1953*. Stuttgart: Deutsche Verlags-Anstalt, 1992.

Gordon, Donald. *Expressionism, Art and Idea*. New Haven: Yale University Press, 1987.

Grimm, Georg. *Kauf- und Warenhäuser*. Berlin: Schottländer, 1928.

Hagspiel, Wolfram. "Bauwerke und Ausstellungsgestaltung internationale Kölner Ausstellungen." *Frühe Kölner Kunstausstellungen*. Ed. Wulf Herzogenrath, 21–146. Cologne: Wienand, 1981.

Hambourg, Maria Morris, and Christopher Phillips. *The New Vision: Photography Between the World Wars*. New York: Metropolitan Museum of Art, 1989.

Hays, K. Michael. *Modernism and the Posthumanist Subject: The Architecture of Hannes Meyer and Ludwig Hilberseimer*. Cambridge: MIT Press, 1992.

Heinze-Mühleib, Ita. *Erich Mendelsohn, Bauten und Projekte in Palästina (1934–1941)*. Beitrage zur Kunstwissenschaft 7. Munich: Scaneg, 1986.

Hentschel, Klaus. *Der Einstein-Turm*. Heidelberg: Spektrum Akademischer Verlag, 1992.

Herbert, Gilbert, and Silvina Sosnovsky. *Bauhaus on the Carmel and the Crossroads of Empire: Architecture and Planning in Haifa during the British Mandate*. Jerusalem: Yad Izhak Ben-zvi, 1993.

Herf, Jeffrey. *Reactionary Modernism*. Cambridge: Cambridge University Press, 1984.

Hermand, Jost, and Frank Trommler. *Die Kultur der Weimarer Republik*. München: Nymphenburger, 1978.

Hilberseimer, Ludwig. *Großstadt Architektur*. Stuttgart: Hoffmann, 1928.

Hines, Thomas. *Richard Neutra and the Search for Modern Architecture: A Biography and History*. New York: Oxford University Press, 1982.

Hirdina, Heinz, ed. *Neues Bauen, neues Gestalten: Das neue Frankfurt; Die neue Stadt: eine Zeitschrift zwischen 1926 und 1933*. Dresden: VEB Verlag der Kunste, 1984.

Hitchcock, Henry-Russell, and Philip Johnson. *The International Style*. 1932. New York: Norton, 1967.

Huse, Norbert. *"Neues Bauen," 1918 bis 1933, Moderne Architektur in der Weimarer Republik*. Munich: Moos, 1975.

Hüter, Karl Heinz. *Architektur in Berlin, 1900–1933*. Stuttgart: Kohlhammer, 1988.

Huyssen, Andreas. *After the Great Divide: Modernism, Mass Culture, and Postmodernism*. Bloomington: Indiana University Press, 1986.

Internationale Presse-Ausstellung: Amtlicher Katalog. Cologne, 1928.

Isaacs, Reginald R. *Walter Gropius: Der Mensch und sein Werk*. 2 vols. Berlin: Gebr. Mann, 1983.

Jelavich, Peter. *Munich and Theatrical Modernism, Politics, Playwriting, and Performance, 1890–1914*. Cambridge: Harvard University Press, 1985.

Jung, Karin Carmen, and Dietrich Worbs. "Funktionelle Dynamik: Die Hatfabrik Steinberg-Hermann and Co. in Luckenwalde von Erich Mendelsohn." *Bauwelt* 83 (1992): 116–21.

Kandinsky, Wassily. *Concerning the Spiritual in Art*. 1912. Trans. M. T. H. Sadler. New York: Dover, 1977.

King, Susan. *The Drawings of Eric Mendelsohn*. Berkeley: University of California, 1969.

Kirsch, Karin. *The Weissenhofsiedlung, Experimental Housing Built for the Deutscher Werkbund, Stuttgart, 1927*. Trans. David Britt. New York: Rizzoli, 1989.

Kirsten, Christa, and Hans-Jürgen Treder, eds. *Albert Einstein in Berlin, 1913–1933*. 2 vols. Berlin: Akademie, 1979.

Klotz, Heinrich. *Twentieth-Century Architecture: Drawings, Models, Furniture from the Exhibition of the Deutschen Architektur Museum, Frankfurt am Main*. New York: Rizzoli, 1989.

Korn, Arthur. *Glass in Modern Architecture*. 1929. London: Barie and Rockiff, 1967.

Krausse, Joachim. "Gebaute Weltbilder von Boullée bis Buckminster Fuller," *Arch +* 116 (1993): 20–84.

Lampugnani, Vittorio Magnano, and Romana Schneider, eds. *Moderne Architektur in Deutschland 1900 bis 1950: Expressionismus und Neue Sachlichkeit*. Stuttgart: Verlag Gerd Hatje, 1994.

Moderne Architektur in Deutschland 1900 bis 1950: Reform und Tradition. Stuttgart: Verlag Gerd Hatje, 1992.

Lane, Barbara Miller. *Architecture and Politics in Germany, 1914–1945*. 1968. Cambridge: Harvard University Press, 1985.

Lavin, Maud. *Cut with the Kitchen Knife: The Weimar Photomontages of Hannah Hoch*. New Haven: Yale University Press, 1993.

Lethen, Helmut. *Neue Sachlichkeit, 1924–1932. Studien zur Literatur des "Weissen Sozialismus."* Stuttgart: Metzler, 1975.

Lotz, Wilhelm, ed. *Licht und Beleuchtung*. Berlin: Reckendorf, 1928.

McCoy, Esther. *Vienna to Los Angeles: Two Journeys, Letters between R. M. Schindler and Richard Neutra, Letters of Louis Sullivan to R. M. Schindler.* Santa Monica, CA: Art + Architecture Press, 1979.

Meikle, Jeffrey. *The Twentieth Century Limited, Industrial Design in America, 1925–1939.* Philadelphia: Temple University Press, 1979.

Mendelsohn, Erich. *Briefe eines Architekten.* Ed. Oskar Beyer. München: Prestel, 1961.

"Die Moderne Industriebau auf dem Kontinent." *Europaische Revue* 5 (1929): 473–79.

Neues Haus – Neue Welt. Berlin: Mosse, 1932.

Rußland – Amerika – Europa: ein architektonsicher Querschnitt. 1929. Basel: Birkhäuser, 1989.

Der Schöpferische Sinn der Krise. 1932. Berlin: Duttmann, 1986.

Mendelsohn, Louise. "Biographical Note on Eric." *L'architettura, Cronache e storia* 9 (1963): 295–422.

Der Mendelsohn-Bau am Lehniner Platz: Erich Mendelsohn und Berlin. Berlin: Schaubühne am Lehniner Platz, 1981.

Metzger, Karl-Heinz, and Ulrich Dunker. *Der Kurfürstendamm: Leben und Mythos des Boulevards in 100 Jahren deutscher Geschichte.* Berlin: Konopka, 1986.

Meyer, Peter. *Moderne Architektur und Tradition.* Zurich: Girsberger, 1928.

Miller, Michael B. *The Bon Marché: Bourgeois Culture and the Department Store, 1869–1920.* Princeton: Princeton University Press, 1981.

Morganthaler, Hans Rudolf. "The Early Drawings of Erich Mendelsohn (1887–1953)." Ph.D. diss., Stanford University, 1988.

The Early Sketches of German Architect Erich Mendelsohn (1887–1953): No Compromise with Reality. Lewiston, NY: Edwin Mellen Press, 1992.

Erich Mendelsohn, 1887–1953: An Annotated Bibliography. Monticello, IL: Vance, 1987.

Moses, Siegfried. "Salman Schocken: His Economic and Zionist Activities." *Leo Baeck Institute Yearbook* 5 (1960): 73–104.

Mosse, Werner E. "Rudolf Mosse and the House of Mosse, 1867–1920." *Leo Baeck Institute Yearbook* 4 (1959): 237–57.

Müller-Wulckow, Walter. *Architektur der Zwanziger Jahre Deutschland.* 4 vols., 1929–1932. Konigstein: Langewiesche, 1975.

Mumford, Lewis. "Steel Chimneys and Beet-top Cupolas." *Creative Art* 4 (1928): xliv.

Sticks and Stones, A Study of American Architecture and Civilisation. New York: Boni and Liveright, 1924.

Nerdinger, Winfried. *Theodor Fischer, Architekt und Städtbauer, 1862–1938.* Berlin: Ernst, 1988.

ed. *Bauhaus-Moderne im Nationalsozialismus: Zwischen Anbeiderung und Verfolgung.* München: Prestel, 1993.

Neumann, Dietrich. *"Die Wolkenkratzer kommen!" Deutsche Hoch-*

häuser der Zwanziger Jahre: Debatten, Projekte, Bauten. Braunschweig/Wiesbaden: Vieweg, 1995.

Neutra, Dione. *Richard Neutra: Promise and Fulfillment, 1919–1932, Selections from the Letters and Diaries of Richard Neutra*. Carbondale: Southern Illinois University Press, 1986.

Neutra, Richard. *Life and Shape*. New York: Appleton-Century-Crofts, 1962.

Osborn, Max, Adolf Dinath, and Franz M. Feldhaus. *Berlins Aufsteig zur Weltstadt*. Berlin, 1929.

Osthaus, Karl-Ernst. "Das Schaufenster." *Jahrbuch des Deutschen Werkbundes* (1913): 59–69.

Parnes, Louis. *Bauten des Einzelhandels*. Zurich: Orell Füsseli, 1935.

Pasdermadjian, Hrant. *The Department Store*. 1956. New York: New York Times, 1976.

Pehnt, Wolfgang. *Expressionist Architecture*. Trans. J. S. Underwood and Edith Kästner. New York: Praeger, 1973.

Platz, Gustav Adolf. *Die Baukunst der Neue Zeit*. 1927. Berlin: Propylaen, 1930.

Pommer, Richard, and Christian Otto. *Weissenhof 1927 and the Modern Movement in Architecture*. Chicago: University of Chicago Press, 1991.

Posener, Julius. *Aufsätze und Vorträge, 1931–1980*. Braunsweig/Wiesbaden: Vieweg, 1981.

Berlin auf dem Wege zu einer neuen Architektur, Das Zeitalter Wilhelms II. München: Prestel, 1979.

Hans Poelzig: Reflections on His Life and Work. New York: Architectural History Foundation, 1992.

Pressa: Kulturschau am Rhein. Berlin: Schröder, 1928.

Riley, Terence. *The International Style: Exhibition 14 and the Museum of Modern Art*. New York: Rizzoli, 1992.

Robertson, Howard, and F. R. Yerbury. "The Architecture of Tension." *Architect and Builders' News* 122 (1929): 702–17.

Robinson, Cervin, and Joel Herschmann. *Architecture Transformed: A History of the Photography of Buildings from 1839 to the Present*. Cambridge: MIT Press, 1987.

Runge, Irene, and Uwe Stelbrink. *George Mosse: "Ich bleibe Emigrant."* Berlin: Dietz Verlag, 1991.

Sagebiel, Ernst. "Das Konstruktion des Columbus-Hauses." *Zentralblatt der Bauverwaltung* 52 (1932): 543.

Samson, Miles David. "German-American Dialogues and the Modern Movement before the 'Design Migration,' 1910–1933." Ph.D. diss, Harvard University, 1988.

Scarpa, Ludovica. *Martin Wagner e Berlin, Case e citta nella repubblica de Weimar, 1919–1933*. Rome: Officina, 1983.

Scheffauer, Hermann George. "Dynamic Architecture: New Forms of the Future." *The Dial* 70 (1921): 323–28.

"Erich Mendelsohn." *Architectural Review* 53 (1923): 156–59.

Scheffler, Karl. *Die Architektur der Großstadt*. Berlin: Bruno Cassirer Verlag, 1913.

Schildberger, Hermann. "Das Seidenhaus Weichmann." *Gleiwitz*. Ed. Karl Schabik. Monographien Deutscher Stadt. 12. Berlin-Friedenau: Deutscher Kommunal, 1925.

Schirren, Matthias. *Hans Poelzig: Die Pläne und Zeichnungen aus dem ehemaligen Verkehrs-und Baumuseum in Berlin*. Berlin: Ernst und Sohn, 1989.

Schmidt, Paul Fred. "Die Kunst auf der Pressa," *Der Cicerone* 20 (1928): 589–92.

Schmidt-Volker, Adolf. "Die Reklameabteilung in einem modernen Geschäftsbetreib." *Das Geschäft* (1924): 50–51.

Der Schrei nach dem Turmhaus, Der Ideenwettbewerb Hochhaus am Bahnhof Friedrichstraße, Berlin 1921/22. Berlin: Argon, 1988.

Schulze, Franz. *Mies van der Rohe: A Critical Biography*. Chicago: University of Chicago Press, 1985.

ed. *Mies van der Rohe: Critical Essays*. Cambridge: MIT Press, 1990.

Schulze, K. Werner. "Geschäfts-und Warnenhäuser." *Industriebau* 20 (1929): 214–23.

Sharp, Dennis. *The Picture Palace and Other Buildings for the Movies*. London: Praeger, 1969.

Sigrist, Albert [Alexander Schwab]. *Das Buch von Bauen*. Berlin: Bücherkreis, 1930.

Siry, Joseph. *Carson, Pirie Scott, Louis Sullivan and the Chicago Department Store*. Chicago: University of Chicago Press, 1988.

Smith, Terry. *Making the Modern: Industry, Art and Design in America*. Chicago: University of Chicago Press, 1993.

Staal, J. F. "Naar Anleidung van Erich Mendelsohn's Ontwerpen." *Wendigen* 3. 10 (1920): 2–3.

Stephan, Regina. *Studien zu Waren-und Geschäftshäusern Erich Mendelsohns in Deutschland*. München: Tudev, 1992.

Strohmeyer, Klaus. *Warenhäuser, Geschichte, Blüte und Untergang im Warenmeer*. Berlin: Wagenbach, 1980.

Taut, Bruno, ed. *Frühlicht, 1920–22, Eine Folge für die Verwicklung des neuen Baugedankens*. 1920–22. Berlin: Ullstein, 1963.

Tolzmann, Hans. "Objective Architecture: American Influences in the Development of Modern German Architecture." Ph.D. diss., University of Michigan, 1975.

Tower, Beeke Sell, with an essay by John Czaplicka. *Envisioning America: Prints, Drawings, and Photographs by George Grosz and His Contemporaries, 1925–1933*. Cambridge, MA: Busch Reisinger Museum, 1990.

Vischer, Julius, and Ludwig Hilberseimer. *Beton als Gestalter*. Stuttgart: Hoffmann, 1928.

Weiss, Peg. *Kandinsky in Munich: The Formative Jugendstil Years*. Princeton: Princeton University Press, 1979.

Wendschuh, Achim. "Brüder Luckhardt und Alfons Anker: Gemeinsame und einsame Werk-Jahre – eine Chronologie." *Brüder Luckhardt und Alfons Anker, Schriftenreihe der Akademie der Künste Berlin*. Vol. 21, 143–73. Berlin: Akademie der Künste, 1991.

Whittick, Arnold. *Erich Mendelsohn*. 2nd ed. London: Leonard Hill, 1956.

Whyte, Iain Boyd. *Bruno Taut and the Architecture of Activism*. Cambridge: Cambridge University Press, 1982.

Wilhelm, Karin. *Walter Gropius: Industriearchitekt*. Braunschweig/Wiesbaden: Vieweg, 1983.

Willett, John. *Art and Politics in the Weimar Republic, The New Sobriety, 1917–1933*. New York: Pantheon, 1979.

Wojtowicz, Robert. "The Lewis Mumford Decades: Studies in Architectural History, Criticism, and Urbanism, 1922–1962." Ph.D. diss., University of Pennsylvania, 1990.

Zevi, Bruno. *Erich Mendelsohn, Opera Completa*. Milano: ETAS Kompass, 1970.

INDEX